Baltimore County Maryland
Marriage Licenses
1777-1798

Dawn Beitler Smith

HERITAGE BOOKS
2007

HERITAGE BOOKS
AN IMPRINT OF HERITAGE BOOKS, INC.

Books, CDs, and more—Worldwide

For our listing of thousands of titles see our website
at
www.HeritageBooks.com

Published 2007 by
HERITAGE BOOKS, INC.
Publishing Division
65 East Main Street
Westminster, Maryland 21157-5026

Copyright © 1989 Dawn Beitler Smith

Other books by the author:
Index to the 1850 Map of Baltimore City and County [Maryland]

All rights reserved. No part of this book may be reproduced or transmitted in any form or by any means, electronic or mechanical, including photocopying, recording or by any information storage and retrieval system without written permission from the author, except for the inclusion of brief quotations in a review.

International Standard Book Number: 978-1-58549-143-8

PREFACE

The following marriage license records were copied from the record books at the Maryland State Archives in Annapolis. Each record contained three or four entries: date that the license was issued, name of the groom, name of the bride and name of the officiating minister when he reported that marriage took place. In this book the first three entries are shown with an asterisk (*) to indicate that the marriage was reported by the minster. The following marriage records are missing: 1778: December; 1779: January, February and December; 1780: January through October (10 months); 1786: November and December; 1787: January through October (10 months).

Readers should note that until Carroll County was established in 1837, the eastern part of that county belonged to Baltimore County. Also note that the marriage records of Baltimore City and Baltimore County remained as one integral set of records until 1851.

I would like to express my thanks to those who made this book possible. - To my husband, Greg, for his enthusiasm and hours of typing - to Bob Miller, for his semingly endless computer knowledge and patience to teach - and special thanks to Russ Ridgely, for making the impossible possible and giving me the confidence to forge ahead. I am grateful to you all.

Any corrections or questions are welcomed.

Dawn Beitler Smith

No person within this State shall be joined in marriage until a license shall have been obtained from the Clerk of the Circuit Court for the County in which the marriage is to be performed, or if in Baltimore City, from the Clerk of the Court of Common Pleas, OR UNLESS THE NAMES OF THE PARTIES INTENDING TO MARRY SHALL BE THRICE PUBLISHED IN SOME CHURCH OR HOUSE OF RELIGIOUS WORSHIP IN THE COUNTY WHERE THE WOMAN RESIDES ON THREE SEVERAL SUNDAYS BY SOME MINISTER RESIDING IN SAID COUNTY; PROVIDED NEVERTHELESS, THAT NAY PERSON WITHIN THIS STATE MAY MARRY ACCORDING TO THE CEREMONY USED BY THE SOCIETY OF PEOPLE CALLED QUAKERS, THE CONTRACTING PARTIES SIGNING A CERTIFICATE TO THE EFFECT THAT THEY HAVE AGREED TO TAKE EACH OTHER FOR HUSBAND AND WIFE, AND SAID CERTIFICATE BEING ATTESTED BY AT LEAST TWELVE WITNESSES; AND PROVIDED FURTHER, THAT THE SAID CERTIFICATE SHALL, WITHIN SIXTY DAYS, BE RECORDED EITHER AMONG THE RECORDS OF THE SOCIETY TO WHICH EITHER OF THE CONTRACTING PARTIES MAY BELONG, OR IN SOME COURT OF RECORD IN THE CITY OR COUNTY IN WHICH THE SAID MARRIAGE MAY BE ACCOMPLISHED.

Annotated Code of Maryland, Vol. 2, Page 1448-1449

```
Jun 11 1796    Abbet, Sarah to Disney, Benjamin*
Jul 11 1798    Abbitt, John to Little, Ann*
Apr 24 1779    Abbott, Ann to Mitchell, Joshua
Dec 16 1790    Abbott, John to Barthy, Jane
May 20 1779    Abercramby, Clementine to Naylor, William
Dec 17 1794    Abraham, Daniel to Linwell, Susannah*
Nov 11 1785    Abraham, John to Rennals, Monacha
Dec  3 1794    Abrahams, Monarchy to Carr, Isaac*
Jul  2 1785    Achenbaugh, Nancy to Crocker, Casper
Jan  8 1795    Acken, Mary to Towers, George*
Jan 12 1798    Acres, Thomas to Beny, Elizabeth*
May 20 1779    Acton, Richard to Tipton, Jemimah*
Aug 27 1796    Adair, Abraham to Edwards, Polly*
Feb 23 1798    Adair, Philip to Tuder, Elizabeth*
Apr 14 1795    Adams, Alexander to McLure, Elizabeth*
Apr 12 1796    Adams, Ann Carey to Fowler, Samuel*
Nov 11 1797    Adams, Ann to Hill, Richard*
Jun 12 1784    Adams, Anna to Berridge, William*
May 23 1783    Adams, Elizabeth to Comryngham, Robert*
Dec 25 1780    Adams, Elizabeth to Thompson, Thomas*
Jun  7 1790    Adams, Elizabeth to Young, Gideon
Jul  6 1796    Adams, Isaac to Taylor, Hetty*
Mar 10 1794    Adams, Jane to Riddell, James*
May 19 1795    Adams, Martha to Rowes, Thomas*
May 15 1794    Adams, Mary to Asher, Anthony*
Jan 31 1789    Adams, Mary to Burrell, Thomas*
Apr 25 1785    Adams, Mary to Loubies, Philipe
Jul 10 1783    Adams, Rachel to Largeau, George James*
May 26 1789    Adams, Samuel to Thompson, Agnes*
Mar 26 1796    Adams, William to Hallan, Hannah*
Jul 24 1798    Adams, William to Stewart, Patty*
May 25 1786    Adamson, John to Shepherd, Mary*
Apr  8 1790    Addison, Jemima to Clark, Edward
Oct  5 1792    Addison, John to Leech, Sally*
Oct 14 1784    Ager, Jane to Garoin, William
Jun 22 1779    Agnew, Jane to Wood, Abraham
May 27 1794    Agnew, Nancy to Deal, Michael*
Mar 18 1790    Aiels, Susannah to Osburn, Samuel*
Sep  1 1786    Aires, Hannah to Nicholson, James*
Oct 25 1797    Aires, Margaret to Hickey, Peter*
Jul  8 1797    Aisquith, Elizabeth to Watts, Edward*
Oct 27 1784    Aisquith, Lester to Bosley, Elizabeth
Jun 15 1795    Aithenson, Francis to Todd, Nancy*
Mar 23 1779    Aitherton, James to Dawson, Rebecca*
Jan  3 1798    Albers, Luider to Diffendirffer, Eve*
Jul  9 1798    Albright, Andrew to Cobenhufer, Elizabeth*
May 23 1798    Alburger, Samuel to Garrettson, Rebecca*
May 23 1794    Alcock, Joseph to Rook, Sarah*
Oct 21 1790    Alder, Frederick to Moore, Polly*
Oct 23 1781    Alder, Hannah to Sindall, William
Jul 26 1790    Alder, Robert to Nice, Mary*
Dec 29 1785    Alder, Susannah to Mackenheimer, Nicholas
Nov 14 1778    Alderson, Thomas to Smitson, Sarah*
Dec  3 1795    Aldridge, Abraham to Haley, Mary*
Feb 12 1786    Aldridge, Ann to Carson, William
Oct 13 1786    Aldridge, John to Hoskins, Dolley
```

May 1 1792	Aldridge, John to Limes, Margaret*
Dec 12 1781	Aldridge, Mary to Bedd, Absalom
Mar 9 1797	Aldridge, Mary to Ready, Samuel*
Aug 23 1798	Aldridge, Thomas H. to Myers, Catharine*
Aug 20 1791	Aleach, William to Tearson, Bridget*
Nov 24 1796	Alexander, Araminta to Betts, Solomon*
Oct 20 1795	Alexander, John to Bagford, Elizabeth*
Jun 3 1783	Alexander, Mary Estus to Lockerr, George Andrew*
Apr 10 1797	Alexander, Mary to Wallace, John*
Apr 25 1795	Alexander, William to Thornton, Rachel*
Feb 13 1797	Alexandria, Flora to James, William*
Aug 11 1797	Alexandria, Mary Ann to John, James*
Jun 4 1778	Alguire, Sarah to Jervis, Philip*
Oct 5 1790	Alken, Mary Ashberry to Gilder, Reuben*
Nov 7 1778	All, Benjamin to Pitts, Sarah*
Jan 13 1784	All, Edward to Sutton, Mary*
Dec 13 1798	All, Martha to Young, John*
Oct 21 1796	Allain, Louis to Boisson, Anne*
Apr 11 1795	Allbright, Nancy to Oldham, John*
Nov 6 1784	Allen, Ann to Dilworth, Joseph
Jan 7 1778	Allen, Bartholomew to Thomas, Sarah*
Jun 25 1797	Allen, Darcas to Nicole, David*
Oct 3 1792	Allen, Darcus to Sanders, Jasie*
Mar 7 1798	Allen, James to Holland, Sarah*
Jul 25 1792	Allen, James to Sanks, Mary*
Oct 13 1796	Allen, Jesse to Cox, Catharine*
Oct 12 1791	Allen, John to Grover, Mary*
Apr 7 1785	Allen, John to Lee, Elizabeth
May 9 1778	Allen, John to Merrikin, Sarah
Mar 23 1790	Allen, John to Penny, Lucreta Christiana*
Apr 4 1797	Allen, Lucas to Emmert, Catharine
Jul 2 1795	Allen, Margaret to Orndorff, Peter*
Sep 12 1793	Allen, Mary to Craigh, Stephen*
Oct 11 1786	Allen, Mary to Reid, John G.
Mar 17 1785	Allen, Polly to Chaplain, William
Dec 30 1795	Allen, Reubin to Wingate, Ann*
Feb 19 1778	Allen, Richard to Proctor, Catherine*
May 20 1779	Allen, Robert to Picket, Mary
Jun 12 1793	Allen, Sinah to Coleman, William*
Jul 5 1792	Allen, Susannah to Fanning, James*
Mar 7 1791	Allen, William to Dean, Sarah
Mar 2 1785	Allen, William Towson to Gott, Achsah Green*
Aug 3 1786	Allender, Averilla to Moore, John Gay
Jul 6 1789	Allender, Deborah to Stillwell, John*
Feb 2 1796	Allender, Elizabeth to Jackson, Thomas*
Aug 7 1790	Allender, John Day to Barnaby, Martha*
Jul 20 1789	Allender, John to Jervis, Hannah*
Aug 2 1778	Allender, Margaret to Holland, George*
Nov 9 1791	Allender, Sarah to Moore, William*
Sep 17 1783	Allender, Sarah to Sollers, John*
Nov 19 1788	Allender, William to Sollers, Ann*
May 23 1794	Alley, Elizabeth to McCoy, John*
Jan 22 1798	Allison, Ann Job to Gross, Simon
Jun 17 1794	Allison, Grace to McGurdy, Hugh*
Sep 7 1797	Allison, Jane to Kiersted, Luke*
Jul 2 1790	Allmon, David to Traverse, Elizabeth*

```
Jul  9 1795    Allwine, John to Wegnemyer, Catharine*
Dec 24 1788    Almark, Mary to Holler, Philip*
Oct 18 1798    Alorafts, Martha to Kingan, John*
Mar  9 1798    Alter, Adam to Arnst, Elizabeth*
May 13 1796    Alter, Christian to Wooden, Nancy*
Dec 19 1795    Alter, John to Giles, Susannah*
Aug 15 1795    Amay, Francis to Telour, Nancy*
Oct 19 1793    Ambrose, James to Ford, Charity*
Jan 28 1793    Amergist, Christian to Day, Anne*
Dec 14 1795    Amey, Catharine to Verley, John*
Jun 20 1797    Amie, Jean B. Jos. A. to Dupeiy, Helene F.J.*
Jul  6 1793    Amkerum, Elizabeth to White, Benoni
Nov 26 1782    Ammery, William to Delahon, Margaret
Jul  6 1793    Ammett, William to Rolles, Rebecca*
Oct 31 1795    Amos, Nancy to Sheppard, Thomas*
Dec 10 1791    Amos, Polly to Anderson, Joshua*
Oct 13 1778    Amos, Susannah to Smith, John*
Oct  8 1783    Amos, Thomas to Travis, Ann*
Mar 11 1784    Amoss, Elizabeth to Street, Daniel*
Dec 19 1792    Amy, Mary to Faurice, Jacob*
Aug 24 1784    Anchors, Elizabeth to Dorsey, Charles
Nov 28 1781    Anckers, Ann to Pearce, Daniel
Aug 25 1798    Anderson, Abraham to Cannon, Jane*
May  1 1788    Anderson, Abraham to McComas, Elizabeth*
Feb 13 1796    Anderson, Andrew to Dungan, Elizabeth*
Nov  4 1778    Anderson, Ann to Howard, Denoon*
May 31 1779    Anderson, Benjamin to McComas, Sarah
Feb  7 1782    Anderson, Elizabeth to Bosley, William*
Mar  4 1795    Anderson, Elizabeth to Hammond, John*
May 27 1797    Anderson, Elizabeth to Shaw, William*
Aug 10 1797    Anderson, Elizabeth to Thompson, William*
Mar 24 1781    Anderson, George to Presbury, Martha Goldsmith*
Jan  2 1796    Anderson, Jabez to Gahogan, Elizabeth*
Jan 30 1796    Anderson, James to Johnson, Sophia*
May 26 1783    Anderson, John to Brown, Susan*
Dec 10 1791    Anderson, Joshua to Amos, Polly*
Dec 10 1782    Anderson, Margaret to Smithson, Daniel*
Jul 28 1795    Anderson, Mary to Bunker, Job*
Aug 21 1797    Anderson, Mary to Graves, Ebenezer*
Jun  9 1785    Anderson, Mary to Hermon, John
Dec 11 1782    Anderson, Mary to Knight, Jacob*
Jan 17 1793    Anderson, Mary to Morgan, William*
Jan 28 1794    Anderson, Mary to Smith, Arthur*
Mar 15 1782    Anderson, Nathan to Swann, Rachel*
Nov 24 1796    Anderson, Rebecca to Deny, Neal*
Nov 25 1789    Anderson, Robert to Cole, Sarah*
Dec 30 1797    Anderson, Robert to Hick, Elizabeth*
Sep 19 1793    Anderson, Sarah to Chandless, John Hurle*
Jan 31 1793    Anderson, Sarah to Knight, Joshua*
Jun 22 1798    Anderson, Sarah to Merryman, Nicholas*
Oct  5 1785    Anderson, Susannah to Corbin, Nathan
Jun  8 1782    Anderson, William to McComus, Cordelia*
Feb  1 1793    Anderson, William to McDonald, Mary*
Jun 25 1790    Anderson, William to Patterson, Kitty
Jun 22 1778    Anderson, William to Sulivan, Mary*
Jul  2 1795    Andreas, Rebecca to Benzen, Peter*
```

```
Feb 12 1794    Andrew, Casandra to Lavigne, Augustine*
Mar  1 1792    Andrew, Maddox to Kell, Pamela*
Jan  5 1795    Andrew, Robert to Toby, Eleanor*
Feb 11 1794    Andrew, William Holland to Galloway, Mary*
Jun 21 1783    Andrews, Aberilla to Stinchcomb, George
Mar 23 1796    Andrews, Edmomd Burns to Dwier, Eleanor*
Jun 21 1784    Andrews, Mary to Garretson, Shadrick*
May  1 1783    Andrews, Moses to Brown, Catherine*
Feb 11 1782    Andrews, Ruth to Sonders, James
Apr 13 1779    Andrewson, Dickenson to Belcher, Ann
Dec 23 1788    Angell, James to Barney, Mary*
Dec 24 1798    Anna, Alec to Gallaher, John*
Dec 16 1797    Annan, Mary to White, Robert*
Jul 13 1788    Annes, Ruth to Jube--free negroes
Sep  3 1794    Annopotis, Belinda to Laybor, James*
Oct 30 1798    Anthony, Joseph to Dashield, Margaret*
May 27 1779    Apple, Christian to Bevins, Rebeccah
Jan  3 1792    Apple, Christian to Kerns, Margaret
Sep 30 1795    Apple, Christian to Wilson, Sarah*
Jul 23 1793    Appleby, Charles to Wood, Ruth*
Sep 26 1796    Appleby, John to Jacob, Ellinor Fair*
Dec  5 1795    Appleby, Urath to Mooshaw, David*
Aug  3 1796    Appleby, William to Shadders, Ruth
Jul 13 1791    Applegarth, James to Cullerson, Margaret*
Sep 11 1798    Apples, Christian to Fosoler, Ann*
Nov 21 1797    Archer, John to Kettleman, Elizabeth*
Sep  6 1790    Archibold, James to Kannady, Ann*
Dec 30 1784    Archman, Henry to Hanley, Sarah
Feb 22 1796    Argentel, Clare Theresa P. to Binillant, Stephan*
Jan 23 1793    Armacoste, Michael to Osborn, Ruth*
Jul 24 1784    Armagost, Margaret to Storm, George*
May  7 1785    Armagost, Mary to Osborne, John Jr.*
Jun  7 1794    Armand, Peggey to Dean, Thomas*
Apr 15 1797    Armistead, Judith Carter to Moale, Richard H.*
Dec 15 1777    Armitage, John to Fullhart, Mary*
Jul  2 1785    Armitage, John to Linton, Sarah
Mar 27 1784    Armitage, William to Bonfield, Elizabeth*
Jun 30 1784    Armor, William to Puntney, Rachel*
Sep  5 1792    Armorgost, Peter to Doyle, Elizabeth*
May 14 1793    Armour, David to Hillen, Mary
Apr 15 1795    Armstead, Isaac to Turner, Barbara*
Aug 25 1778    Armstrong, James to Deisdel, Peggy*
Oct 28 1779    Armstrong, James to Wells, Susannah*
Apr 12 1783    Armstrong, Jane to Crohan, Matthew*
Jul 11 1795    Armstrong, Joshua to White, Nancy*
May  1 1797    Armstrong, Rachel to Rindley, John*
Dec  6 1792    Armstrong, Solomon to Griffin, Margaret*
Feb 20 1796    Armstrong, William to Dungan, Easter*
Oct  2 1788    Armur, Samuel to Swan, Susannah*
Dec  2 1795    Arnel, Peter to Gregory, Elizabeth*
Jan  6 1784    Arnest, Caleb to Helm, Ann*
Nov 20 1798    Arnest, Margaret to Thompson, Alexander*
Oct 10 1793    Arnoh, Joseph to Connally, Ann*
Jan  5 1796    Arnold, Joseph to McKinzie, Mary*
Jul 27 1796    Arnold, Joshua to Woods, Mary*
Apr 16 1794    Arnold, Nancy to Jewell, William*
```

```
Dec 23 1797    Arnold, Peter to Holbrooks, Sarah*
Feb 21 1793    Arnold, Peter to Kettleman, Elizabeth*
Oct 24 1789    Arnold, Rebecca to Chilcoat, Joshua*
Mar  9 1784    Arnold, Richard to White, Mary
Feb 26 1781    Arnold, Ruth to Thomas, Evin
Sep 28 1789    Arnold, Sarah to Smith, John*
May 19 1798    Arnolde, John to Holbrook, Ann*
Mar  9 1798    Arnst, Elizabeth to Alter, Adam*
Nov 20 1778    Arry, James to Connelly, Elizabeth*
Aug 18 1792    Arters, Rachel to Kelley, Thomas
Feb  2 1790    Ash, James to Cromwell, Elizabeth*
Nov 14 1792    Ashbaw, John to Gray, Nancy*
Jul 13 1798    Ashburner, Mary to Keighler, Daniel
May 15 1794    Asher, Anthony to Adams, Mary*
Jul 29 1793    Ashley, Benjamin to Bibby, Catherine*
Feb 17 1781    Ashman, Eleanor to Colegate, John*
Oct 23 1781    Ashman, Mary to Pindle, Philip*
Jul 18 1781    Ashman, Rebeccah to Bird, Benjamin*
Jul  2 1796    Ashman, Thomas to Leathorn, Margaret*
Dec 27 1792    Ashman, William to Boyce, Rebecca*
Dec 25 1777    Ashmead, Joseph to Johnson, Ann*
Jul 14 1794    Ashmore, Nancy to Rew, James*
Jul 30 1786    Ashton, Ann to Mackie, Ebenezer
Dec 22 1792    Ashwell, Barnet to Forrest, Sarah*
Dec 20 1794    Askew, Catharine to Thompson, Robert*
Oct 23 1779    Askew, Elinor to Chenwoith, Richard*
Feb 16 1786    Askew, Elizabeth to Rutter, John*
Dec 10 1793    Askew, Jonathan to Porter, Mary*
Sep 22 1784    Askew, Joshua to Williamson, Elizabeth*
Jun 29 1798    Askew, Margaret to Robertson, John*
Mar 18 1784    Askew, Mary to Berry, Richard*
May 16 1795    Askew, Mary to Bouldin, John*
Jun 30 1795    Askew, Mary to O'Brian, Daniel*
Dec 21 1782    Askew, Sarah to Mullen, Patrick
Dec  9 1795    Askew, William to Calwell, Sally*
Mar 27 1779    Askew, William to Leavely, Catharine*
Aug 23 1797    Askins, Eleanor to Johnson, William*
Jul 16 1785    Aspin, Hannah to Holliwell, James
Jun 22 1798    Assailly, Constance A. to Baeonais, Lewis F.M.*
Jan 10 1795    Astermon, Catharine to Stearns, William*
Jul  5 1778    Aston, Jane to Chatterback, William*
Oct  3 1785    Aston, Villey to Maloney, Peter
Feb 19 1791    Atherton, Elinor to Carter, Henry*
Sep 13 1784    Atherton, Rebecca to Presston, John Diamond*
Oct 21 1784    Atherton, Rebecca to Smith, Jeremiah*
Apr 10 1792    Atherton, William to Bowen, Temperance*
Nov 24 1792    Atkinson, Amelia Elizabeth to Conway, James*
Jul 31 1788    Atkinson, Margaret to Stigar, Jacob*
Aug 25 1792    Atkinson, Sarah to Conway, William*
Jun  5 1779    Atkison, Rebecca to Bailey, James
May 22 1793    Atler, Mary to Crook, Walter*
Sep 15 1794    Auckerman, Catherine to Hahn, John Adam*
Aug 31 1790    Aukerman, George to Bose, Margaret*
Jun  2 1794    Aukerman, Philip to Fisher, Catharine*
May  2 1793    Aul, Thomas to Baulderson, Mary
Jul 24 1793    Auld, Hugh to Wilson, Zeperah*
```

```
Nov 23 1792    Austin, Jane to Eccleston, Abraham*
Mar 11 1793    Avelin, Louisa to Peot, Peter*
May 24 1794    Avery, Robert to MacBride, Mary*
Nov  8 1788    Aylworth, John to Wilson, Elizabeth*
Aug  7 1789    Ayres, Ruth to Hart, Henry*
Jun  6 1778    Babbs, Elizabeth to White, Charles*
Feb 24 1778    Babbs, James to Porter, Delila*
Feb 23 1796    Babcock, Clark to Flinn, Margaret*
Dec  5 1794    Back, John to Miller, Hannah*
May 29 1797    Backer, Tounis Helmig to Van Noemer, Susannah J.G.*
Jul 28 1789    Bacon, John to Joyce, Sarah*
Dec 16 1783    Bacon, Lemuel to Stacker, Mary*
Feb  2 1793    Bacon, Mary to Holmes, Gabriel*
May 22 1794    Badet, John Baptiste to Capela, Jeanne Francoise*
Oct 24 1796    Badger, Bela to Thompson, Catharine*
Jun 22 1798    Baeonais, Lewis F.M. to Assailly, Constance A.*
Oct 20 1795    Bagford, Elizabeth to Alexander, John*
May  4 1789    Bagford, Rachael to Kelly, Joseph
Nov 16 1796    Bagford, William to Creigh, Ann*
Jun 21 1798    Bagnell, Michael to Cromwell, Ann*
May  8 1793    Bagwell, Thomas to Bryan, Margaret*
May 22 1788    Bahm, Hannah to Kapolt, Lewis
Mar  4 1784    Bahn, Jacob to Slagel, Christiana*
Oct 10 1796    Bail, Robert P. to Davies, Mary Ann*
Feb  9 1796    Bailey, Amos to Rhearns, Ann*
Jun 30 1798    Bailey, Ann to Shield, Zachariah*
Jul 21 1778    Bailey, Catharine to Brannan, William*
Jun 10 1796    Bailey, Catharine to Hamilton, James
Mar 28 1798    Bailey, Evan to Irvin, Mary*
Jun  5 1779    Bailey, James to Atkison, Rebecca
Sep 24 1794    Bailey, John to Bell, Rebecca*
Jan 26 1795    Bailey, Levin to Lawder, Margaret*
Jan  5 1778    Bailey, Philip to Morgan, Mary*
Jan 10 1784    Bailey, Rachel to Cook, James
Dec 16 1795    Bailey, Ruth to Gott, Richard*
Dec 23 1790    Bailey, Sarah to Collins, George*
Sep 21 1791    Bailey, Sarah to Howard, Charles*
Jan 27 1791    Bailey, Thomas to Smith, Catherine*
Aug  2 1783    Bain, William to Howland, Mary
Dec 23 1790    Baise, Ann to Scott, John*
Oct 12 1797    Baker, Allen to Pennington, Susannah*
Jan 27 1791    Baker, Ann to Constable, Charles*
Jun 16 1783    Baker, Ann to Fallon, James*
Jul  7 1796    Baker, Barbara to Grunnor, John*
Dec 12 1796    Baker, Cary to Carrick, George*
Jun 11 1783    Baker, Christiana to Barichman, Anthony*
Aug 17 1782    Baker, Elam to Baker, Ketturah*
Feb 12 1793    Baker, Elizabeth to Duvall, Richard
Jan  4 1786    Baker, Elizabeth to Hamilton, Samuel
Mar 31 1796    Baker, Ephraim to Reemey, Tacy*
Dec 20 1791    Baker, Hannah to Fisher, Robert*
Nov 26 1791    Baker, Hellin to Jones, Joshua Merrican
Feb 28 1786    Baker, John Frederick to White, Elizabeth
Jan 22 1783    Baker, John to Doyel, Mary*
Jun 26 1794    Baker, John to Dungan, Mary*
Aug 17 1782    Baker, Ketturah to Baker, Elam*
```

Apr 14 1795	Baker, Keturah to Hill, William*
Nov 16 1796	Baker, Keturah to Morgan, William*
Sep 13 1796	Baker, Manning to Clair, Rebecca*
Apr 25 1793	Baker, Milky to Baulderson, Johnson*
Aug 14 1798	Baker, Morris to Gladman, Rachel
Jul 16 1796	Baker, Nancy to Peacock, William*
Mar 16 1791	Baker, Nathan to Bosley, Belinda*
Aug 19 1784	Baker, Providence to Luten, King
Apr 2 1785	Baker, Samuel to Oadle, Sarah
Apr 27 1782	Baker, Sarah to Ousler, John
Jun 11 1784	Baker, Thomas to Taylor, Mary*
Apr 25 1798	Bakerven, Peter to Hulk, Catharine
May 3 1798	Balden, John to Jones, Elizabeth*
Jun 25 1789	Baldry, William to Green, Mary*
May 26 1798	Baldwin, Abraham to Jenny, Sarah*
Oct 5 1796	Ball, Elizabeth to Masters, Thomas*
Jul 16 1798	Ball, Mary to Bremire, John Ferman*
Jan 10 1795	Ball, Mary to Burns, Adam*
Nov 18 1795	Ball, Mary to Tull, William*
Jun 27 1794	Ball, Samuel to Veal, Elizabeth*
Aug 24 1793	Ball, Stephen to Satch, Hannah*
Oct 21 1790	Ball, William to Dukehart, Elizabeth*
Feb 11 1797	Ball, William to Green, Ann Pamelia*
Sep 4 1794	Balspack, Barbary to Rusk, Robert*
Jun 2 1785	Bancks, Rachael to Creamer, Valuntine*
Feb 19 1781	Bangham, Urith to Pye, James*
Sep 2 1797	Bankards, Polly to Tesh, Peter*
May 19 1798	Banke, Thomas to Ferguson, Eleanor*
Feb 6 1794	Bankerd, Easter to Wyeman, Jacob*
Feb 4 1795	Banks, Andrew to Bowers, Catharine*
Jan 9 1782	Banks, David to Miller, ELizabeth*
Oct 4 1794	Banks, Eleanor to Jones, Isaac*
Apr 14 1781	Banks, Elizabeth to Conoway, John
Feb 12 1791	Banks, Mary to Barrett, Edward*
Jan 2 1783	Banks, Milly to Cowan, Lewis*
Jan 31 1798	Banks, Prudence to Porter, Shadrack*
Sep 11 1788	Banks, William to Connoway, Susannah*
Nov 5 1783	Bankson, James to Hull, Susan*
May 16 1778	Bannan, Thomas to Sheppard, Mary*
Dec 20 1780	Bantulau, Paul to Keeports, Catharine*
Feb 28 1795	Bantz, Catharine to Bantz, John*
Feb 28 1795	Bantz, John to Bantz, Catharine*
Dec 6 1794	Barbann, Louis to Corbet, Marie*
Sep 22 1797	Barbarin, Louis to Moore, Elizabeth*
Sep 12 1797	Barbary, Mary to Rye, John*
Apr 3 1795	Barber, Daniel to Norris, Alice*
Jan 12 1791	Barber, Hannah to Coe, William*
Jun 2 1797	Barbine, Margaret to Richards, Joseph*
Jan 25 1786	Barbini, Charles to Hartman, Mary*
Oct 2 1793	Barbini, Mary to Rogers, John*
Feb 9 1798	Barbon, Delila to Mobberly, John*
Oct 13 1779	Barcalow, Volentine to Iams, Elizabeth*
May 10 1778	Bard, James to Griffis, Martha*
Oct 12 1795	Bardon, Victoire to Beaupre, Louis Nau*
Sep 29 1794	Barger, Barbary to Evans, Waller*
Jun 11 1783	Barichman, Anthony to Baker, Christiana*

```
Apr 12 1797    Barils, Henry to Law, Catharine*
Dec 20 1783    Bark, Capus to Night, Shedrick*
Feb 11 1795    Barker, John to Rider, Elizabeth*
Jun 12 1781    Barker, Joseph to Quilland, Milly*
Mar 25 1778    Barkever, Mary to Gordon, James*
May 22 1778    Barkhouse, Catharine to Jeffrey, Thomas*
Mar 27 1789    Barkley, Isabella to Pest, Daniel*
Sep  7 1793    Barkman, Anthony to Hendericks, Ann
Aug 13 1796    Barkman, Elizabeth to Pelts, Jacob*
Oct 31 1798    Barktie, Thomas to McCormick, Jane*
May 12 1798    Barley, George to Hogan, Kitty*
Dec 24 1783    Barloro, Mary to Fellows, Richard*
Dec 29 1792    Barlow, Bashby to Black, William*
Dec 17 1787    Barlow, Elizabeth to Black, Christ*
Apr 15 1798    Barlow, Elizabeth to Caton, Matthew*
Nov 25 1795    Barlow, John to Randell, Milcah*
Oct 15 1796    Barlow, Joseph to Frog, Susanna
Mar  8 1788    Barnaby, Elias to Riffett, Rachel
Dec 13 1785    Barnaby, Elizabeth to Shope, William
Aug  7 1790    Barnaby, Martha to Allender, John Day*
Sep  4 1783    Barnes, Ann to King, Thomas
Aug 23 1797    Barnes, Anna to Barnes, Peter*
Jun 13 1796    Barnes, Betsey to Whitefoot, Thomas*
Feb 11 1778    Barnes, Elizabeth to Bevin, Samuel*
Aug 22 1793    Barnes, Elizabeth to Burke, John*
Apr  1 1797    Barnes, Elizabeth to Philips, James
Feb 21 1778    Barnes, Ellis to Dorsey, Ely*
Sep  7 1792    Barnes, Essenah to Barnes, Rezin*
Dec 23 1790    Barnes, Hannah to Shipley, George Ogg*
Nov  8 1797    Barnes, James to Dorsen, Mable*
Apr 25 1795    Barnes, Leaven to Sholl, Mary*
Nov 16 1797    Barnes, Margaret to Lewis, Charles
Aug 23 1797    Barnes, Peter to Barnes, Anna*
Feb 24 1783    Barnes, Philemon to Penn, Ruth*
Sep  7 1792    Barnes, Rezin to Barnes, Essenah*
Aug 16 1797    Barnes, Susanna to Williams, Abraham*
Oct 11 1781    Barnes, Tabitha to Sacklow, Aaron
Dec 12 1795    Barnes, Ursely to Kendal, Vachel*
Jun 19 1788    Barneston, Eleanor to Kent, Emanuel*
Oct 18 1785    Barneston, Elizabeth to Eichelberger, Jacob*
Jun 30 1795    Barnet, George to Smith, Rebecca*
Jul  1 1796    Barnet, James to Fitzgerald, Polly*
May  3 1794    Barneth, Susannah to Murray, Nicholas*
Apr 13 1796    Barnett, Catharine to Lindsay, Joshua*
Apr 22 1797    Barnett, Elizabeth to Hurtzot, William*
Feb  9 1788    Barnett, Jacob to Hissey, Catharine
Jan  4 1790    Barnett, Peter to Owings, Mary*
May 26 1792    Barnett, Ursula to Gow, John Hammond*
Jul 19 1782    Barney, Ann to Bond, Benjamin
Feb 25 1794    Barney, Elizabeth to Trippe, Edward*
Mar  9 1786    Barney, Hannah to Shepherd, Nathaniel
Aug  3 1784    Barney, John to Stiles, Chanty*
Feb  2 1788    Barney, Joseph Bosley to Picket, Rebecca*
Oct 30 1781    Barney, Leah to Gill, John
Dec 23 1788    Barney, Mary to Angell, James*
Oct 18 1789    Barney, Mary to Belloe, Francis
```

Dec 21 1782	Barney, Sarah to German, John
Jun 21 1793	Barneyfish, Gilbert to Redstone, Ann
Feb 1 1794	Barnor, Alexander Peter to Lashrow, Margaret*
Aug 1 1792	Barnover, Mary to Getie, Henry*
Apr 26 1781	Barns, Abel to Barns, Mary
Aug 2 1784	Barns, Adam to S_____ley, Ruth*
May 2 1782	Barns, Ann to Porter, James*
Aug 23 1781	Barns, Aquila to Gibbons, Jane
Aug 10 1784	Barns, Elijah to Shipley, Katharine
Sep 4 1783	Barns, Eliven to Slack, Hannah*
Apr 6 1789	Barns, John to Barns, Ruth*
Apr 26 1781	Barns, Mary to Barns, Abel
Apr 6 1789	Barns, Ruth to Barns, John*
Sep 27 1788	Barns, Sarah to Parlett, Martin
May 25 1798	Barny, Michael to Vaughan, Elizabeth*
Nov 3 1793	Baron, Marie L.V. to Desize, Jean Baptiste A.M.*
Jul 25 1798	Barrenea, Richard to Rowson, Ann*
Oct 2 1786	Barret, Edward to Kitten, Catharine
Oct 26 1779	Barret, William to Brett, Elizabeth*
Jan 4 1783	Barrett, Ann to Limes, Harman*
Feb 12 1791	Barrett, Edward to Banks, Mary*
Oct 3 1796	Barrett, John to Hagerty, Mary*
Dec 28 1790	Barrett, Mary to Stewart, John Cowden*
Dec 7 1797	Barry, Abigail to Hamilton, Pliney*
Nov 3 1791	Barry, Abigail to Skipper, Thomas*
Mar 27 1781	Barry, Ann to Green, Thomas
Aug 31 1779	Barry, Catherine to Eames, Luke*
Feb 4 1797	Barry, Elinor to Sollers, William*
Mar 6 1790	Barry, John to Deffidaffer, Elizabeth*
Oct 4 1778	Barry, Labourn to Watts, Ann*
Mar 13 1795	Barry, Lavallin to Stansbury, Jemimah*
Aug 8 1778	Barry, Mary to Ruff, William*
May 15 1797	Barry, Sarah to Houregan, Patrick*
Oct 11 1788	Barry, Standish to Thompson, Nancy*
Dec 16 1790	Barthy, Jane to Abbott, John
Jun 22 1798	Bartleson, Rachel to Bosley, Charles*
Jul 23 1795	Bartlet, Samuel to Freeman, Dorcus*
Dec 20 1791	Barton, Asael to Milliken, Susannah*
Jul 27 1797	Barton, Charles to Gale, Susanna*
Jun 1 1795	Barton, Charlotte to Ruth, John*
Nov 5 1785	Barton, Dorothy to Foos, Philip*
Aug 6 1795	Barton, Fanny to Ford, William*
Dec 23 1797	Barton, James to Smith, Rachel*
May 31 1783	Barton, John to Nice, Dorothy
Jun 11 1794	Barton, Lettisha to Pierce, Israel*
Mar 30 1798	Barton, Margaret to Hawkins, George*
Jun 18 1792	Barton, Mary to Lynch, Anthony*
Feb 18 1792	Barton, Nancy to Galloway, Acquila*
Dec 28 1790	Barton, Prescilla to Hopkins, William*
Oct 1 1796	Barton, Rachel to Beamer, Philip*
Oct 10 1793	Barton, Sarah to Fowler, Thomas*
Dec 16 1790	Barton, Seth to Maxwell, Sarah*
Feb 13 1790	Barton, Thomas to Holebrooks, Elinder Roon*
Jun 24 1785	Barton, Thomas to Pearce, Mary*
Nov 8 1798	Barton, Thomas to Stiner, Nancy*
Mar 28 1798	Barton, William to Riddle, Ann*

```
Mar 25 1791    Baseman, Sarah to Ogg, James*
Oct  3 1781    Bashier, Benedict to Sheriff, Martha*
Oct 18 1788    Basman, Arice to Cook, Greenbury*
Jul 23 1789    Bassage, Hannah to Joyce, Nathan*
Oct 21 1784    Bassow, Louise to DalZincount, Peter Antony Balne
Aug  4 1796    Bateman, Benjamin to Hatton, Anne*
Dec 23 1781    Bateman, Elinor to Scott, George
May 31 1782    Bateman, Henry to Linthicum, Milkey*
Mar 23 1797    Bateman, Mary to Gutthrey, William*
Aug 29 1785    Bateman, Sarah to Smith, William*
Sep 12 1797    Baterman, John to Galloway, Martha*
Aug  1 1794    Batery, Charles to Lee, Frances*
Jan 15 1795    Bates, Elizabeth to Smith, George*
May 23 1778    Bates, Rowland to Woolen, Margaret*
Nov 13 1790    Batlee, Dinah to Bowen, John*
Jun  8 1791    Batline, Joseph to Elcon, Eve*
Apr  2 1779    Batson, Henry to Smith, Margaret
Dec 22 1781    Batter, William to Myers, Elizabeth
May 28 1781    Battle, John to Jones, Sarah
Jan 12 1795    Batton, Rene Guillaume to Matthews, Jane*
Feb 24 1778    Batty, Elizabeth to Dorsey, Vachel*
Aug  6 1792    Baughman, Elizabeth to Hoopman, Christian*
Mar 26 1796    Baughman, George to Fisher, Barbary*
Aug 19 1795    Baughman, Susannah to Porter, Archibald*
Dec  4 1777    Baughon, Stephen to Shaffner, Barbara*
Sep  3 1779    Bauk, Ann to Dumont, John
Apr 25 1793    Baulderson, Johnson to Baker, Milky*
May  2 1793    Baulderson, Mary to Aul, Thomas
Jan 25 2794    Baum, Barbara to McDonnell, John*
Feb  3 1785    Baum, Catharine to Myer, Christian*
Dec 24 1798    Baum, Susanna to Woodworth, Isaac*
Dec 28 1793    Bauzel, Elizabeth to Holbrooke, Jacob*
Apr 13 1791    Bavin, Sarah to Stansbury, Richardson*
Feb 27 1797    Baxley, Catharine to Rothnick, Jacob*
Sep  4 1793    Baxley, George to Merryman, Mary*
Jul 16 1793    Baxley, John Jr. to Stevenson, Mary*
Sep  1 1792    Baxley, John of William to Tyson, Susannah Maria*
Nov 25 1797    Baxley, Nicholas to Pearce, Mary
Dec  1 1784    Baxley, Samuel to Sharmiller, Catherine
May 16 1795    Baxley, Sarah to Carney, Thomas*
Jul  9 1796    Baxley, Thomas to Cole, Elizabeth*
Sep  3 1783    Baxter, Barnett to Haile, Ruth
Dec 15 1792    Baxter, Delia to Heddington, Nicholas*
Nov 25 1791    Baxter, Elizabeth to Chenowith, Arthur*
Dec 31 1791    Baxter, Elizabeth to Linham, John*
Nov 26 1798    Baxter, Hester to Goalin, Thomas*
Oct 15 1783    Baxter, Margaret to Thomas, William
Feb  1 1792    Baxter, Nicholas to Perigo, Sarah*
Aug 21 1779    Baxter, Samuel to Chenowith, Sarah*
Jul 28 1791    Bayler, Andrew to Hodge, Martha*
Dec  4 1785    Bayless, Augustin to Brown, Elizabeth
Mar 27 1798    Bayley, Thomas to Godman, Elizabeth
Feb 17 1794    Bayzana, William to Moore, Susannah Aisquith*
Dec 31 1788    Beach, John to Wolf, Catherine
Mar 24 1794    Beach, Susannah to Cooper, John*
Dec 16 1794    Beach, William to Rider, Mary*
```

```
Sep 19 1793    Beachgood, Sarah to Landin, Alexander*
Aug 15 1795    Beaman, James to Johnson, Amelia*
Jan 19 1782    Beame, George to McCullister, Sarah*
Aug  5 1794    Beamer, Frederick to Lynehart, Elizabeth*
Oct  1 1796    Beamer, Philip to Barton, Rachel*
Apr  4 1795    Beamer, Susannah to Denton, John*
Dec  6 1780    Beanman, John to Owings, Mary*
Jan 28 1783    Bear, Mary to Bosey, Charles
Jul 24 1790    Beard, Alexander to Bride, Mary*
Jun 13 1782    Beard, Lindy to Lyndon, John*
Jul 22 1783    Beard, Mary to Sharper, Enoch
Oct 11 1791    Beard, William to Homan, Mary*
Jan  4 1792    Beaseman, Elizabeth to Shipley, Brice*
Aug  3 1779    Beasings, James to Hipitey, Patience
Nov 13 1790    Beasman, George to Glover, Sally*
Apr  7 1798    Beasman, Joshua to Elder, Elizabeth*
Jun 17 1789    Beasman, Ruth to Sater, Charles
Oct  2 1798    Beat, Elizabeth to Madran, Francis*
Feb 20 1794    Beatle, Henry to Welsh, Rachel*
Nov  5 1795    Beatly, Thomas Johnson to Holliday, Achsah Chamier*
Dec 22 1798    Beatty, Eleanor to Davis, John
Feb 12 1795    Beaty, Mary to Lavinder, Levin*
Aug  1 1796    Beaudu, William to Hubon, Marie Anne*
Mar 26 1796    Beaufire, Elizabeth to Rey, Charles*
Mar 17 1796    Beaumez, Bon Albert Briois to Flueker, Sarah Lyons*
Oct 12 1795    Beaupre, Louis Nau to Bardon, Victoire*
May 11 1793    Beavan, Elizabeth to Lowe, Cornelius*
Oct 15 1778    Beavin, Elizabeth to Ford, John*
Sep 18 1784    Beays, Jane to Travers, Matthew
May 29 1795    Beazoe, Richard to Fulhart, Elizabeth*
Dec 24 1783    Beckem, John to Sticker, Elizabeth*
Nov 11 1797    Beckley, James to Campbell, Ann*
Oct 10 1783    Beckley, John to Rister, Mary*
Jan 18 1791    Becknell, Thomas to Gaither, Elinor*
Dec 12 1781    Bedd, Absalom to Aldridge, Mary
Jun 19 1793    Bedner, Mary to Wooler, Philip*
Apr 18 1795    Bedry, Elizabeth to Palmer, Horace*
Aug  8 1795    Bedson, Elizabeth to Macklefish, William*
Nov 27 1794    Beech, Ebenezer to Smoot, Eleanor*
Jul 16 1781    Beech, Margaret to O'Bryan, James*
Sep 17 1798    Behn, John H. to Briden, Violet*
Mar  5 1796    Beicher, John Lambert to Chaddrick, Frances*
Sep 23 1796    Bela, John Baptiste to Brady, Wine*
Apr 16 1796    Belanger, Mary to Vibert, Francis*
Apr 13 1779    Belcher, Ann to Andrewson, Dickenson
Oct 16 1779    Belhisle, Anastize to Simon, Andrew*
Mar 22 1794    Belk, James to Isaac, Rachel*
Nov  1 1783    Bell, Henry to Parks, Priscilla*
Nov 14 1787    Bell, John Sprigg to Griffith, Rachel*
Apr 30 1785    Bell, Lloyd to Jones, Elizabeth
Jun 28 1788    Bell, Lucy to Maloney, John*
Oct 21 1795    Bell, Mariah to Cashman, Timothy*
Apr 23 1793    Bell, Mary to Petticoat, James*
Sep 24 1794    Bell, Rebecca to Bailey, John*
Jun 18 1793    Bell, Rebecca to Miles, Zachariah*
May  6 1778    Bell, Rebecca to Tipton, Aquila*
```

```
Aug  7 1794    Bell, Russell to Stauvern, Maria*
Feb 23 1789    Bell, Ruth to Hardisty, Joshua
Feb  8 1790    Bell, Sarah to Chinowith, Richard*
Nov 16 1779    Bell, Sarah to Ingram, John*
Feb  6 1798    Bell, Sarah to Young, Michael*
Dec  7 1791    Bell, Thomas Clarke to Smith, Frances*
Mar 29 1794    Bellinger, Jean Phillipes E. to Gardner, Polly*
Oct 18 1789    Belloe, Francis to Barney, Mary
Jul 23 1783    Belt, Horatio Sharp to Dulany, Kitty
Nov 18 1797    Belt, James to Moore, Eleanor
Sep 30 1793    Belt, Joseph to Randall, Ellin*
Dec 13 1794    Belt, Merryman to Randall, Sarah*
Dec 15 1784    Belt, Rachael to Hooker, Samuel*
May 24 1790    Belt, Susannah to Griffin, York
Aug 15 1795    Beltson, Catharine to Fremaine, William*
Aug  3 1782    Bemon, Lewis to Celiston, Mary
Aug  5 1779    Benbo, Mary to Clarke, Richard*
Feb 28 1778    Bencil, Balcer to Krider, Sophia*
Dec 15 1794    Bender, Jacob to Stoner, Catharine*
Mar 26 1778    Bender, Sarah to Markell, John*
Dec 19 1781    Benfield, Hannah to Carter, Josias*
Dec 23 1783    Benfield, John to Stansbury, Cassandra*
Nov 15 1794    Bennet, John to Jackson, Sally*
Nov 24 1794    Bennet, Rachel to Powers, Barnet*
Jul 30 1798    Bennet, Richard to Curtis, Urith
Nov  5 1785    Bennett, Caleb to Wilson, Catherine*
Feb  6 1778    Bennett, Elinor to Stocksdale, Edward*
Jan 13 1791    Bennett, Elisha to Warfield, Mary*
Jan  5 1782    Bennett, George to Phillips, Mary*
Jun  2 1783    Bennett, Hannah to Foster, Comfort
Dec 30 1783    Bennett, Jane to Lindsay, Adam
Aug  6 1778    Bennett, Joel to Geoghen, Mary*
May 16 1778    Bennett, Johanna to Cahoe, John*
Feb 17 1794    Bennett, John to Ireland, Catherine*
Jun 11 1798    Bennett, Joseph to Lindon, Elizabeth*
Jan  3 1797    Bennett, Loyd to Bennett, Peggy*
Apr  3 1790    Bennett, Lydia to Johnson, Rezin
Jul  5 1779    Bennett, Mary to Lambath, Daniel*
May 21 1782    Bennett, Mary to Shelock, William
Nov  2 1796    Bennett, Milly to Davis, Francis*
Jan  3 1797    Bennett, Peggy to Bennett, Loyd*
Dec  1 1791    Bennett, Stephen to O'Neill, Catharine*
Oct 29 1798    Bennett, Thomas to King, Comfort*
Feb 23 1797    Bennix, Rachel to Maidwell, James*
Nov 25 1783    Benno, Matthew to Duloy, Nancy*
May  5 1785    Bennurman, John to Pritchard, Jane*
Sep 12 1797    Benson, Alice to Graves, Nero*
Oct  6 1792    Benson, Benjamin to Sullivan, Allender*
Oct  3 1778    Benson, James to Taylor, Mary*
Oct 17 1793    Benson, Richard to Smith, Catharine*
Aug 12 1796    Bentley, Harriot to Butler, Benjamin*
Nov  1 1797    Bentley, Mary to Close, David*
Oct  8 1796    Bentley, Michael to Caton, Eleanor*
Apr  4 1798    Benton, Elizabeth to Grover, George*
Jan 12 1798    Beny, Elizabeth to Acres, Thomas*
Jul  2 1795    Benzen, Peter to Andreas, Rebecca*
```

Jun 28 1791	Berbine, Elizabeth to Donaldson, James*
May 25 1786	Berbine, Magdaline to Thombury, Robert*
Jul 16 1795	Bermanham, William to Trumbs, Elizabeth*
May 3 1784	Bermingham, James to McClung, Rebecca*
Dec 27 1785	Bermingham, Rebecca to Christie, James
Dec 4 1784	Bernard, Charles to White, Mary*
Aug 30 1791	Bernard, Marie to Heuiler, Maximillien*
Nov 7 1780	Berneston, Thomas to ELkins, Ellen*
Nov 30 1793	Bernett, Jacob to Thompson, Mary*
Feb 9 1784	Berrage, Edward to Lyne, Mary*
Jun 12 1784	Berridge, William to Adams, Anna*
Nov 14 1793	Berru, Jacob Michael to Deagle, Mary*
Mar 17 1797	Berry, Andrew to Gilberthorp, Mary*
Oct 20 1796	Berry, Elizabeth to Peale, William*
Apr 4 1779	Berry, Lawrence to Jones, Sarah
Sep 29 1794	Berry, Lucy to Keeble, Humphrey*
Oct 26 1778	Berry, Margaret to Clark, Richard*
Dec 16 1783	Berry, Mary to McDaniel, John*
Dec 9 1796	Berry, Mary to Wisebaugh, John*
Dec 24 1793	Berry, Polly to Peale, William*
Dec 27 1790	Berry, Redmond to Hennesy, Johanna*
Mar 18 1784	Berry, Richard to Askew, Mary*
Jun 4 1798	Berry, Sarah to Carter, Charles S.*
Oct 26 1793	Berry, Sarah to Krebs, Michael*
Mar 25 1797	Berry, Sarah to Young, Henry*
Dec 2 1790	Berryman, William to Bowers, Elizabeth*
Feb 9 1795	Bertrand, John Peter to Valend, Amanda Victoire S.*
Dec 20 1792	Beset, Susannah to Green, William*
Apr 13 1784	Besse, Clodius to Mealey, Margaret
Apr 10 1784	Bethune, Louis to Smithers, Ann*
Nov 24 1796	Betts, Solomon to Alexander, Araminta*
Apr 11 1786	Betz, Conrad to Strayer, Mary
Jan 16 1778	Beucard, Sarah to Hart, Daniel*
Sep 24 1791	Bevan, Mary to Smith, Richard*
Dec 29 1795	Bevan, Richard to Guffey, Ann*
Jan 10 1793	Bevans, James to Rusk, Mary*
Jul 14 1788	Bevans, Polly to Forbes, Mattew*
Feb 11 1778	Bevin, Samuel to Barnes, Elizabeth*
Oct 5 1785	Bevin, Zana to German, Thomas
Nov 10 1785	Bevins, Joshua to Willson, Eleanor
May 27 1779	Bevins, Rebeccah to Apple, Christian
Jun 8 1784	Bias, James to Jackson, Sarah
Jun 12 1788	Biays, Elizabeth to Denny, William*
May 12 1796	Biays, James to Trimble, Sarah*
Jul 29 1793	Bibby, Catherine to Ashley, Benjamin*
Jan 14 1784	Bibby, John to Stoller, Catharine*
Nov 10 1792	Biddel, Augustine to Rutledge, Joshua*
Jun 21 1784	Biddinger, Mary to Harman, Henry*
Nov 4 1783	Biddison, Daniel to Rawlins, Elizabeth*
Nov 12 1785	Biddison, Jeremiah to Bond, Elizabeth
Mar 8 1791	Biddison, Mary to Sidden, William*
Nov 18 1784	Biddison, Mashack to Pocock, Kasenhappuck
May 4 1785	Biddison, Rebecca to Pocok, James
Oct 8 1794	Biddison, Sarah to Coal, George*
Dec 10 1785	Biddle, Abagal to Falls, Moor
Jun 10 1796	Biddle, Augustine to Forse, John*

```
Mar 26 1788    Bidot, John Peter to Tonerey, Peggy
May  7 1791    Bigger, Gilbert to Rice, Sarah
Mar 21 1792    Billmaker, William to James, Lydia*
Jun 21 1785    Billmyer, Leonard to Fletcher, Ann*
May 14 1792    Bind, Rachel to Coleby, Charles*
Feb 22 1796    Binillant, Stephan to Argentel, Clare Theresa P.*
Jul 18 1781    Bird, Benjamin to Ashman, Rebeccah*
May 18 1797    Birmingham, Mary Ann to Clarke, James*
Jun 10 1789    Birmingham, William to Herring, Elizabeth*
Nov 20 1788    Bishop, Elizabeth to Hipsler, Benjamin*
Oct 26 1797    Bishop, John to Johnson, Susannah*
Apr 29 1797    Bishop, Mary to Smith, William*
Apr  1 1796    Bishop, Mary to Thomas, Edward*
Aug 14 1797    Bishop, Nancy to Jones, John*
Jan  3 1794    Bishop, Nancy to Smith, Patrick*
Oct  8 1796    Bishop, Richard to Young, Elizabeth*
Jun  2 1794    Bishop, William to Hilton, Patience*
Dec 12 1794    Bishs, Nicholas to Turine, Nancy*
Sep 21 1796    Bitlers, John to Donavan, Elizabeth*
Jun 29 1798    Bitton, Thomas S. to Rapp, Ann Catharine*
Nov  6 1787    Bivans, Joseph to Griffin, Ann*
Feb 23 1782    Biven, Aberilla to Hanson, James*
Aug 11 1784    Bivens, John to Wilson, Mary
Aug 21 1794    Bizourd, Joseph to Paterson, Margaret*
Dec 11 1781    Black, Barbara to Bowd, Joseph
Dec 17 1787    Black, Christ to Barlow, Elizabeth*
Mar  6 1786    Black, Elizabeth to Cook, John
Oct 11 1798    Black, Elizabeth to Cunningham, Andrew*
Oct  2 1783    Black, Hannah to Brown, John
Oct 30 1798    Black, Henry to Buckley, Rachel*
Jun  5 1795    Black, James to Carroll, Mary*
Sep  5 1786    Black, Jane to Thompson, Hugh
Dec 29 1792    Black, William to Barlow, Bashby*
Oct  1 1796    Blackford, Elizabeth to Sweny, Edward*
Mar 23 1779    Blackford, Isaac to Hart, Ann*
Sep 24 1796    Blair, John to Cronan, Catharine*
Oct 10 1793    Blake, Catharine to Farrell, Timothy*
Nov 15 1798    Blake, Ebenezer to Headington, Ruth*
Sep 10 1779    Blake, Francis to Teisel, Ann*
Oct 14 1779    Blake, Mary to Burly, John*
Jun 14 1782    Blake, William Hopper to Hutchins, Martha*
Nov  4 1796    Blaking, John to Regan, Lydia*
Sep 24 1796    Blaney, Jane to Dawney, John*
Jul 30 1785    Bleany, Nathaniel to Tate, Elizabeth
Nov 18 1785    Blieze, Mary to Delisle, John
Nov 14 1796    Bliss, James to Watkins, Elizabeth
Aug 14 1790    Block, Catherine to Eberhart, Jacob*
Sep 21 1798    Block, Sophia to Grub, Conrad*
Jan 28 1797    Blood, Rachel to Newbay, Godfrey*
Feb  2 1778    Bloom, Clorcy to Dearfield, Godfrey*
Jan  6 1781    Blossom, Mary to Butler, Joseph*
Jan 29 1791    Blossom, Peter to LaBlonig, Mary Magdalen*
May 19 1786    Blossom, Rose to Nerovil, Peter*
May 23 1797    Blot, Francis to Myer, Patty*
Mar  1 1791    Blottenberger, George to Young, Mary*
Feb 24 1797    Blyth, Catharine to Ninde, James*
```

```
Jan 31 1784    Board, Ann to Griffin, Luke*
Aug 10 1785    Boas, Benjamin to Herrin, Judah*
Feb 22 1796    Bobbin, Charlotte to Clark, John*
Mar 26 1795    Bockins, Peter to Kreps, Sarah*
Sep  1 1779    Bocklob, Charles to Guth, Rebecca*
Aug 31 1779    Bocklob, Charles to Guth, Rebecca*
Aug 16 1794    Bodmim, John to Smith, Elizabeth*
Jun 21 1788    Boering, Elizabeth to Green, Henry*
Aug 30 1794    Boice, Joseph to Lockaman, Peggy*
Aug 30 1794    Boice, Joseph to Lockaman, Peggy*
Nov 20 1781    Boil, Amey to Speass, Thomas
Sep 16 1796    Boislandry, Robt. Chas. L. to Budeaille, Louise F.*
Oct 21 1796    Boisson, Anne to Allain, Louis*
Apr 23 1794    Boiven, Elizabeth to Coale, William*
Mar  2 1795    Bolahouse, Margaret to Crawford, Richard*
Apr 29 1795    Bolehouse, Magdalina to Smith, Christian*
Jan 21 1778    Bolton, Richard to Gorman, Mary*
Aug  4 1778    Bolton, Tamer to Woodward, James*
Aug 31 1790    Bolton, William to Smith, Margaret*
Jan 10 1798    Bombarger, Margaret to Clarke, John
Mar 22 1794    Bombarger, Mary to Stammer, Ulerick Barnhart*
May 10 1786    Bombarger, William to Matts, Christina*
Oct 28 1783    Bomer, Peter to Shock, Catharine*
Jun 19 1783    Bond, Alisana to Williams, John*
Jun  6 1782    Bond, Ann to Dodd, John
Nov  5 1794    Bond, Ann to Hughes, Hugh*
Jan 12 1790    Bond, Barnet to Hughes, Ruth*
Dec 19 1785    Bond, Barnett to Harryman, Sarah*
Jul 19 1782    Bond, Benjamin to Barney, Ann
Jun 27 1788    Bond, Cassandra to Hamilton, James*
Sep  7 1784    Bond, Catherine to Ford, Edmund
Dec 13 1787    Bond, Christopher to Pindell, Sarah*
Feb  3 1778    Bond, Edward to Pindell, Catharina*
Nov 12 1785    Bond, Elizabeth to Biddison, Jeremiah
Feb 25 1778    Bond, Elizabeth to Bosley, Zebulin*
Nov 15 1796    Bond, Elizabeth to Dimmet, Henry*
May 27 1795    Bond, Elizabeth to Head, John*
Jul 28 1790    Bond, Elizabeth to Reese, Daniel*
Feb 21 1778    Bond, Henry to Gorsuch, Elizabeth*
Nov 15 1797    Bond, John Pitts to Davis, Polly*
Oct 31 1795    Bond, Joseph to Hall, Ann*
Feb 26 1793    Bond, Keturah to Peddicoat, Morris*
Apr 27 1796    Bond, Leah to Price, Hezekiah*
Jun  7 1794    Bond, Leah to Wooden, Richard*
Dec 13 1791    Bond, Mary to Gott, Edward*
Oct  3 1796    Bond, Mordecai to Hughes, Hannah*
Aug 29 1789    Bond, Nicodemus to Stevenson, Mary*
Mar 20 1794    Bond, Peter to Morris, Elizabeth*
Nov 22 1796    Bond, Philip to Hemling, Magdaline*
Feb  8 1788    Bond, Rachel to Harryman, George
Aug  1 1782    Bond, Richard to Stevenson, Rachel
May  5 1796    Bond, Sarah to Gregory, James*
Mar 13 1778    Bond, Susanna to Hammond, Isaac*
Apr 21 1786    Bond, Susannah to Carr, Aquila*
Aug  4 1797    Bond, Thomas to Harryman, Elizabeth*
Jul 24 1783    Bond, Thomas to Jordan, Sarah*
```

```
Dec 20 1791    Bond, Thomas to Talbott, Ann*
Jan 22 1781    Bond, Thomas to Wright, Hannah*
Jan 12 1792    Bond, Thomas to Yates, Sarah*
Nov  3 1796    Bond, William to Cromwell, Susannah*
Aug 12 1796    Boner, Hugh to Silk, Mary*
Mar 27 1784    Bonfield, Elizabeth to Armitage, William*
Apr 21 1783    Bonhorn, Blathwaite to Myers, Ann*
Nov 11 1796    Bonnet, Joseph to Ferraud, Marian*
Jun  2 1795    Bonsal, Jesse to Stapleton, Mary*
Feb 13 1794    Bonsal, Robert to Fonerden, Martha*
Apr 30 1778    Book, John to Millering, Ann*
Jun 16 1791    Boon, John Cockey Robert Bailey to Hale, Elizabeth*
Feb 14 1784    Boon, Mary to Stevenson, William*
Feb 13 1784    Boon, Mary to Steward, Ezekiel*
Mar 26 1790    Boon, Robert to Griffith, Achsah*
Jul 29 1797    Boon, Robert to Hancock, Nancy*
Nov  7 1792    Boone, John to Griffen, Sarah*
Mar 13 1791    Boone, Susannah to Hook, Jacob
Sep 25 1797    Booth, Michael to Fitzgerald, Susannah*
Jul 14 1792    Booth, William to Kogt, Jane*
Jun 16 1795    Bordan, Mary to Davis, John*
Aug  1 1798    Bordely, John to Stark, Catharine
Jul  9 1798    Bordely, William C. to Keener, Margaret*
Jan  4 1794    Borderie, Bernard to Bulger, Elizabeth*
Mar 26 1785    Bordley, Sarah to Rule, Peter
Mar 14 1796    Bords, Adam to Hollow, Mary*
Aug 11 1786    Borein, John to Slider, Sarah*
Jun  1 1796    Boreing, Absalom to Gray, Arabella*
Aug 30 1797    Boreing, Isaac to Brown, Ann*
Aug  1 1795    Boreing, Joshua to Tipton, Elizabeth*
Jun  2 1795    Borkelt, John to Knight, Basha*
Aug 31 1790    Bose, Margaret to Aukerman, George*
Dec  5 1798    Bosen, Thomas to Wann, Ruth*
Jan 28 1783    Bosey, Charles to Bear, Mary
Sep 16 1784    Boshockney, Thomas to McDonald, Biddey*
Mar 26 1796    Bosler, John to Flanagan, Mary*
Aug 26 1789    Bosley, Ann to Parks, Archibald*
Apr 29 1793    Bosley, Bazel to Chamberlin, Rebecca*
Mar 16 1791    Bosley, Belinda to Baker, Nathan*
Feb  5 1793    Bosley, Benedict to Bosley, Elizabeth*
Mar 24 1784    Bosley, Cassandra to Chenowith, Arthur*
Jun 22 1798    Bosley, Charles to Bartleson, Rachel*
Oct  1 1798    Bosley, Eleanor to Corbin, Abraham*
Oct 27 1784    Bosley, Elizabeth to Aisquith, Lester
Feb  5 1793    Bosley, Elizabeth to Bosley, Benedict*
Jun 12 1790    Bosley, Elizabeth to Perdue, Walter
Sep 16 1779    Bosley, Ellen to Wheeler, Benjamin*
Feb 15 1793    Bosley, Isaac to Hutchins, Elizabeth
Sep  9 1782    Bosley, John to Cole, Nancy
Jul 27 1785    Bosley, John to Price, Susannah
Nov 12 1779    Bosley, Joshua to Gott, Ann
Mar  2 1797    Bosley, Keziah to Lettig, Philip*
Dec 10 1782    Bosley, Mary to Davis, John*
Jan  6 1790    Bosley, Mary to McComeskey, Moses*
Oct 22 1784    Bosley, Mary to Norris, William*
Jan 15 1791    Bosley, Nancy to Marsh, David
```

Feb 16 1781	Bosley, Rachel to Elliot, William*
Oct 10 1796	Bosley, Rachel to Littig, George*
Oct 20 1786	Bosley, Rachel to Wheeler, Richard
Jan 13 1790	Bosley, Rebecca to Cole, Thomas*
Oct 31 1789	Bosley, Sarah to Grover, William*
Dec 11 1781	Bosley, Sarah to Heddington, Zebulon
Sep 17 1783	Bosley, Susanah to Cox, William*
Feb 7 1782	Bosley, William to Anderson, Elizabeth*
Aug 4 1783	Bosley, William to Knight, Hannah*
Feb 25 1778	Bosley, Zebulin to Bond, Elizabeth*
Dec 11 1781	Bosman, Risdon to Waters, Elinor
Jan 28 1795	Bosman, Rosanna to Smith, William*
Dec 31 1784	Bosman, Sarah to Francis, William*
May 8 1797	Boss, Hays to Perrigo, Elinor*
May 26 1779	Bossel, James to Johnson, Elizabeth
Jul 30 1779	Bossen, William to Makaney, Margery*
Jun 20 1796	Bostich, Achsah to White, James*
Dec 14 1793	Boswell, Joseph to Jones, Elizabeth*
Oct 10 1793	Both, Rachel to Earnest, George*
Jan 3 1786	Botram, Catharine to Sly, John
Nov 11 1784	Botten, Robert to Ross, Ann
Jun 11 1795	Botton, Mary to Pagges, John*
Jul 30 1785	Botts, Elizabeth to Richardson, Thomas
Nov 21 1793	Botts, Jemima to Garvey, George*
Aug 11 1785	Botts, Jemima to Weary, Peterr
Jun 22 1786	Botts, Mary to Mitchell, Michael*
May 23 1795	Boucher, Frances to Douglass, George*
Nov 2 1784	Bouden, Jane to Simmons, John*
Jun 21 1792	Bouer, Ann to Dexter, James*
May 5 1796	Boulay, Sophia to Phillipe, Joseph*
May 16 1795	Bouldin, John to Askew, Mary*
Nov 23 1795	Boulin, John to Hobbs, Ally
Apr 4 1794	Bourgeois, A. Chapol to Parce, Anna Savon*
Oct 17 1797	Bourm, Sylvanus to Haslet, Rebecca Mercer*
Oct 30 1792	Bouser, Nell to Landerkin, John*
Jul 2 1796	Bouti, John to Guersois, Louisa*
Dec 11 1781	Bowd, Joseph to Black, Barbara
Dec 28 1792	Bowen, Ann to Gray, James
Dec 14 1796	Bowen, Benjamin to Evans, Jemimah*
Apr 12 1792	Bowen, Benjamin to Merryman, Elizabeth*
Oct 29 1783	Bowen, Catherine to Bowen, Joshua
Nov 24 1792	Bowen, Edward to Stansbury, Rebecca*
Dec 21 1782	Bowen, James to Robinson, Margaret*
Nov 13 1790	Bowen, John to Batlee, Dinah*
Oct 29 1783	Bowen, Joshua to Bowen, Catherine
Dec 23 1791	Bowen, Josias Jr. to Stansbury, Sarah*
May 18 1797	Bowen, Josias to Stansbury, Prudence*
Sep 3 1783	Bowen, Lydia to Watts, Thomas
Feb 25 1795	Bowen, Nancy to Wheelin, Thomas*
Jan 26 1784	Bowen, Nathan to Wilmott, Ruth*
Dec 15 1778	Bowen, Ruth to Tipton, Samuel*
Jan 4 1792	Bowen, Sabrel to Humphrey, Elizabeth*
Aug 10 1778	Bowen, Sarah to Stevenson, Mordecai*
Jun 20 1786	Bowen, Solomon to Merryman, Jemima*
Apr 10 1792	Bowen, Temperance to Atherton, William*
Jul 21 1789	Bowen, William to Hethrington, Elizabeth*

```
Sep 22 1785    Bower, Conrad to Pian, Catharine
Feb 17 1778    Bower, John to Ryleyson, Ula*
Feb  4 1795    Bowers, Catharine to Banks, Andrew*
Dec  2 1790    Bowers, Elizabeth to Berryman, William*
Jun  2 1785    Bowers, George to Weaver, Elizabeth*
Apr  4 1791    Bowers, Sarah to Spicer, Valentine*
May 26 1797    Bowles, Jane to Holton, William*
Feb 17 1784    Bowles, John to Strabble, Mary*
Mar 27 1798    Bowly, Ann Lux to Thornton, Henry*
Jun 10 1795    Bowny, Mary to Stewart, John*
Jun 25 1784    Bows, Anne to Patton, Gaskwell*
Jun  2 1796    Bowser, Isaac to Leggett, Violett*
Mar 30 1792    Boyce, Benjamin to Gudgeon, Elizabeth*
Jan 17 1786    Boyce, John to Rogers, Eleanor Addison
Dec 27 1792    Boyce, Rebecca to Ashman, William*
Apr 26 1797    Boyce, Sarah to Forney, John*
Sep 12 1796    Boyd, Adam to Boyd, Violet*
Apr 23 1778    Boyd, Francis to Tevis, Ruth*
Jan  1 1783    Boyd, James to Hanson, Eleanor*
Apr 19 1788    Boyd, Jane to Towson, Jacob T.*
Oct 30 1783    Boyd, Mary to Shead, John
Aug  6 1795    Boyd, Ruth to Starr, Obediah*
Sep 12 1796    Boyd, Violet to Boyd, Adam*
Aug 27 1794    Boye, Anthony to Brown, Sarah*
Jun  6 1795    Boyer, Elizabeth to Stevens, James*
Jul 19 1779    Boyer, Hannah to McClane, Adam
Aug 26 1785    Boyer, John to Boyes, Agness
Jan 21 1785    Boyer, Lewis to Hildebrand, Polly*
Nov 27 1794    Boyer, Nicholas to Ireland, Margaret*
Aug 28 1786    Boyer, Nicholas to Stevens, Rachel
Aug 26 1785    Boyes, Agness to Boyer, John
Oct 12 1797    Boyes, Hugh to Mooney, Eleanor*
Sep 30 1789    Boyle, John to Boyle, Margaret*
Sep 30 1789    Boyle, Margaret to Boyle, John*
Oct  4 1794    Boyle, Thomas to Gross, Polly*
Dec  6 1792    Boyle, William to Evans, Mary*
Jun 11 1792    Boyreau, John Joseph to Marzial, Marie*
Apr 19 1779    Bozimin, Edward to Shields, Mary
Jan 20 1781    Bracket, Mary Magdaline to Brooks, William*
Nov 24 1797    Brackett, Mary to Moody, William*
Feb 26 1795    Bradburn, Alexander to Taylor, Sarah*
Mar 22 1798    Bradburn, Mary to Gray, Peter*
Oct  5 1798    Bradbury, Stephen to Colgar, Margaret*
Apr  9 1791    Bradey, John to Long, Elizabeth*
Jan 23 1782    Bradfield, James to Wheeler, Ruth
Aug  5 1786    Bradford, William to Snider, Sarah*
Mar 13 1790    Bradhunt, Benjamin to Young, Delila*
May  9 1797    Bradis, Caroline to Miller, Henry*
Nov 10 1790    Bradley, Ruth to Turner, Francis*
Feb 15 1798    Bradshaw, Catharine to Thomas, William*
Oct 29 1796    Bradshaw, Nancy to Patterson, John*
May 23 1795    Bradshaw, William to Mathew, Catherine*
Apr 17 1778    Brady, Catharine to Coil, Samuel*
Nov  3 1783    Brady, John to Cunningham, Judith*
Aug 24 1793    Brady, John to McFee, Mary*
Aug 25 1784    Brady, Nancy to Nicholson, Thomas*
```

Sep	23	1796	Brady, Wine to Bela, John Baptiste*
Nov	19	1793	Bramont, John to Francoisi, Elizabeth*
Oct	23	1790	Branagan, Mary to Farker, John*
Feb	29	1788	Branch, John to Strawble, Rebecca*
Dec	14	1785	Brand, George to Norwood, Pleasance
Apr	12	1779	Brand, Mary to Flaharty, James
Dec	26	1787	Brand, Peggy to McFarlin, Michael*
Jul	21	1778	Brannan, William to Bailey, Catharine*
May	30	1778	Brannigan, Ann to Dowlan, Charles*
Mar	2	1785	Brannon, Rachel to Parks, Elisha*
Jan	4	1797	Branson, Balset to Freport, Mary*
Jan	1	1791	Branson, William to Smith, Margaret
Apr	19	1784	Brant, Elizabeth to Stevenson, William*
Dec	18	1790	Brant, Louisa to Marshall, Willaim
Apr	23	1795	Brat, Juiny to Hagerthy, Matthew*
Oct	21	1779	Brawton, Elizabeth to Gibbs, Joseph*
Dec	7	1796	Bray, James to Maloney, Margaret*
Mar	25	1797	Brays, Joseph to May, Elizabeth*
Dec	13	1792	Breard, Michael Augustus to Delord, Sophia Francois
Mar	27	1794	Breidenbach, Catherine to Trisler, George*
Nov	3	1798	Breidenbaugh, John to Morin, Nancy*
Jul	15	1796	Breidner, Eliza to Stafford, Nicholas*
Jul	16	1798	Bremire, John Ferman to Ball, Mary*
Jan	11	1790	Bremner, George to Roberts, Elizabeth*
Mar	31	1798	Brentinger, John C. to Shertain, Maria D.*
Nov	4	1789	Brereton, Sarah to Ross, Richard*
Feb	26	1781	Brereton, Thomas to Marshall, Sarah*
Nov	19	1796	Brest, Clement to Collins, Patsy*
Oct	26	1779	Brett, Elizabeth to Barret, William*
Aug	3	1784	Brett, Rachael to Heckholt, Henry*
Nov	26	1798	Breuitt, Joseph to Woodland, Cassndra Webster*
May	4	1784	Brevitt, John to Swope, Mary*
Nov	21	1781	Brewer, Elizabeth to Gray, Richard
Apr	24	1788	Brewer, John to Williams, Mary*
Oct	22	1798	Brian, Abigail to Hayes, Edward*
Oct	16	1786	Brian, Daniel to Craton, Deborah
Mar	20	1795	Brian, Mary Ann to Mack, John*
Nov	24	1797	Brian, Michael to Miller, Mary*
Dec	13	1783	Brian, Scisley to Galloway, William*
Sep	23	1782	Brice, John to Robinson, Mary Ann*
Aug	5	1797	Brick, Lydia to Trimble, John*
Jul	24	1790	Bride, Mary to Beard, Alexander*
Sep	19	1795	Bride, Nancy to Bunbury Monsier Simmons*
Sep	17	1798	Briden, Violet to Behn, John H.*
Oct	18	1798	Bridenbaugh, Elizabeth to Leypold, Frederick*
Aug	28	1778	Bridenhart, Dorrity to Laypole, John*
Jun	3	1784	Bridenhart, Mary to Hossleboch, John*
Mar	19	1788	Bridges, Daniel to Lowry, Sarah*
Sep	15	1798	Brien, Susannah to Dancer, William*
Dec	4	1797	Brigg, James to Ensor, Temperance*
Sep	19	1795	Briggs, Ann to Greenwood, Benjamin*
Sep	5	1782	Brigs, John to Reno, Mary*
Dec	15	1784	Brill, Frederick to Rihn, Elizabeth*
May	8	1797	Brillain, Mary to Hartnet, James*
May	28	1790	Brimmer, Moses to Chargo, Susannah
Jan	21	1795	Britt, Elizabeth to Davis, Henry Ferguson*

```
Jul 22 1795    Britt, Humphrey to Dunderson, Allie*
Aug 10 1793    Britt, Margaret to Stewart, James*
Aug 30 1794    Britt, Mary to Cramer, Edward*
Mar 25 1782    Brittain, Richard to Talbott, Temperence
Nov 27 1795    Brittingham, Joseph to Roches, Catharine*
Jun 19 1784    Britton, Joseph to Jones, Margaret*
May 28 1798    Broadburn, Eleanor to Moorehead, Thomas*
Feb 27 1781    Brodbech, Loys to Hohn, Peter
Jun 22 1778    Broderick, Mary to Shipton, Henry*
Nov 24 1797    Brook, Basil to Patrick, Mary
Aug  7 1790    Brooke, Deborah to Pleasants, James*
Dec 18 1787    Brooks, Barthia to Ensor, Abraham Jr.
Apr  3 1790    Brooks, Eleanor to Shipley, Rezin*
Apr  7 1785    Brooks, Elizabeth to de la Mark, John F. C. B.
Aug 23 1783    Brooks, George to Christison, Ann*
Oct 29 1785    Brooks, Hannah to Welsh, Thomas
Nov 24 1781    Brooks, James to Gardner, Martha
Aug 28 1786    Brooks, Joseph to Gardiner, Priscila*
Sep 12 1781    Brooks, Mary to Jarvis, Edward*
Jan  1 1788    Brooks, Mary to Turner, Samuel
Feb  8 1791    Brooks, Sarah to Smith, Thomas*
Jul 16 1792    Brooks, Sarah to Wright, John*
Jan 12 1781    Brooks, Tasey to Rutter, Richard
Oct 13 1779    Brooks, Thomas to Gosnell, Elizabeth*
Jan 20 1781    Brooks, William to Bracket, Mary Magdaline*
Aug 18 1796    Brooks, William to Gardner, Hannah*
Jan 23 1792    Brooks, William to Jennings, Elizabeth*
Nov 29 1796    Brothers, Ruth to Hooker, Joshua*
Jul 19 1790    Brotherson, Charles Moore to Stansbury, Jane*
Oct 15 1783    Brotherton, Thomas to Pickett, Blanche
Oct 14 1783    Brotherton, Thomas to Pickett, Blanche*
Jan 27 1794    Broughton, Eleanor to Gayon, Peter*
Jan 16 1795    Brower, George Henry to Wollen, Anne Margarette*
Sep 23 1795    Brown, Abraham to White, Elizabeth*
Mar 23 1795    Brown, Alexander to Jones, Ann*
Aug 30 1797    Brown, Ann to Boreing, Isaac*
Jun 10 1795    Brown, Ann to Ham, Thomas*
Dec 19 1781    Brown, Ann to Richards, Richard*
Jan 20 1792    Brown, Ann to Taylor, Edward
Jul 26 1797    Brown, Barbara to Forence, Mons*
Dec 10 1793    Brown, Barbara to Sheldecker, Joseph
Jan 16 1795    Brown, Catharine to Porter, Lewis*
May  1 1783    Brown, Catherine to Andrews, Moses*
Oct 23 1790    Brown, Charles to Owings, Micha*
Nov  5 1791    Brown, David to Elder, Jemima*
May 22 1788    Brown, Deborah to Ruddy, John
Nov 20 1798    Brown, Dennis to Porter, Rebecca*
Mar 15 1785    Brown, Edward to Richards, Sarah
Nov 11 1785    Brown, Eleanor to Wilson, Thomas
May 17 1788    Brown, Elias to Cockey, Ann*
Dec  4 1785    Brown, Elizabeth to Bayless, Augustin
Jul 13 1784    Brown, Elizabeth to Fonman, Daniel*
Jan  7 1785    Brown, Elizabeth to Hays, Aaron
Apr 14 1789    Brown, Elizabeth to Mombley, Mordecai*
Sep 11 1788    Brown, Elizabeth to Price, William*
Oct 15 1790    Brown, Elizabeth to Sappington, Jacob*
```

Sep 21 1786	Brown, Fanney to Hudson, John*
May 8 1797	Brown, Fanny to Collings, Richard*
Dec 22 1792	Brown, Frances to Forsyth, Isaac*
Feb 18 1788	Brown, Frederick to Willson, Sarah
Feb 21 1782	Brown, Henry to Holmes, Pamelia*
Feb 17 1783	Brown, Henry to Sollers, Anexa*
Oct 22 1793	Brown, Hepkabah to Perine, Maulden*
Jan 2 1781	Brown, Hugh to Rawlings, Elizabeth*
Aug 31 1795	Brown, James to Elliott, Rebecca*
Apr 13 1793	Brown, James to Jeffris, Hannah*
Dec 18 1782	Brown, James to Stansbury, Elizabeth*
Jan 2 1798	Brown, Johanna to Lisst, Henry*
Dec 2 1797	Brown, John Bigs to Gassaway, Sarah*
Oct 2 1783	Brown, John to Black, Hannah
Dec 10 1796	Brown, John to Cunningham, Betsey Ann*
Apr 30 1778	Brown, John to Davis, Elizabeth*
Nov 14 1796	Brown, John to Kelly, Mary*
Jun 16 1781	Brown, John to Lynch, Jane*
Oct 17 1798	Brown, John to Morris, Elizabeth*
Nov 27 1793	Brown, John to Parkins, Catherine*
Jul 25 1796	Brown, John to Parsons, Sarah*
Nov 23 1798	Brown, John to Rosenstell, Mary*
Jun 16 1796	Brown, John to Wilkerson, Mary*
Nov 17 1792	Brown, Joshua to Lee, Mary*
Aug 16 1790	Brown, Josiah to Kirk, Ichosheba*
May 31 1786	Brown, Kesiah to Dunn, Henry*
Dec 8 1783	Brown, Keziah to Cornstat, John
Dec 15 1783	Brown, Margaret to Madden, Thomas*
Jan 27 1781	Brown, Martha to Shakespear, Samuel*
Jan 18 1782	Brown, Mary to Davis, John*
Dec 27 1777	Brown, Mary to Everett, James*
Dec 21 1793	Brown, Mary to Howard, Henry*
Sep 16 1778	Brown, Mary to Nelson, James*
May 28 1783	Brown, Mary to Pyne, Todd*
Oct 10 1795	Brown, Mary to Todd, Thomas*
Apr 25 1797	Brown, Moses to Snowden, Mary*
Sep 12 1792	Brown, Nancy to McMann, Patrick
Dec 19 1798	Brown, Nicholas to Stoxdale, Polly
Feb 23 1793	Brown, Phebe to Harding, Godfrey
Mar 23 1790	Brown, Priscilla to Pidden, Tomas*
Nov 26 1787	Brown, Rebecca to Norwood, Samuel
Oct 30 1795	Brown, Rebecca to Warfield, George F.*
Mar 8 1793	Brown, Richard to Price, Honor
Oct 22 1782	Brown, Richard to Reece, Sarah*
Dec 19 1792	Brown, Robert to Given, Mary*
Mar 10 1788	Brown, Ruth to Cockey, Thomas*
Aug 27 1794	Brown, Sarah to Boye, Anthony*
Feb 3 1796	Brown, Sarah to Cashman, William*
Oct 17 1795	Brown, Sarah to Gosnell, Charles*
Oct 7 1796	Brown, Sarah to Hawk, Thomas*
Nov 18 1788	Brown, Sharlotte to Peck, John*
Jul 7 1790	Brown, Sophia to Davis, John*
May 26 1783	Brown, Susan to Anderson, John*
Oct 28 1794	Brown, Thomas to Camel, Jean*
Mar 4 1797	Brown, Thomas to Colgan, Mary*
Oct 6 1785	Brown, Thomas to Ellicott, Mary

Sep 27 1790	Brown, Thomas to McGregory, Ann
Mar 4 1793	Brown, Thomas to Watts, Margaret*
Jun 15 1795	Brown, William to Mattox, Mary*
Nov 15 1789	Brown, William to Parsons, Ann*
Dec 29 1785	Brown, Zachariah to Stinchcomb, Catharine*
May 11 1796	Browner, Peter to Sadler, Elizabeth*
Aug 7 1792	Browning, Elizabeth to Walker, David*
Dec 8 1796	Brownson, Fredericka to Butler, Samuel*
Jul 23 1798	Browr, Jemima Margaret to Simmon, Joseph*
Sep 29 1781	Brubecker, Mary to Isle, John*
Apr 8 1797	Brueon, Sarah to Emmitt, Philip*
Nov 25 1797	Brummel, Joseph to Fouble, Elizabeth*
Dec 2 1795	Brune, Hannah to Canby, John*
Jul 16 1794	Brunner, Andrew to Shuett, Phebe*
Jul 27 1798	Bruse, Sarah to Mills, John*
Jun 26 1790	Bryan, Ann to Imbleton, Edward
Oct 23 1797	Bryan, Biddy to Caduman, Francis*
Jun 18 1797	Bryan, Catharine to Gleeson, Roger*
Sep 2 1785	Bryan, Daniel to Sheilds, Frances*
Nov 24 1796	Bryan, Elinor to Merryman, John*
Jan 3 1797	Bryan, Elizabeth to Hopkins, John*
Dec 10 1796	Bryan, Isaac to Shock, Julianna*
Apr 4 1797	Bryan, Jemima to Grimes, Sebastian
Oct 2 1788	Bryan, John to Draves, Mary*
May 8 1793	Bryan, Margaret to Bagwell, Thomas*
Jul 28 1779	Bryan, Mary to Caldran, John Baptist
Sep 22 1796	Bryan, Mary to Etherton, Thomas*
Sep 26 1793	Bryan, Mary to Hodge, John*
May 11 1791	Bryan, Mary to Hopkins, Nicholas^
May 24 1794	Bryan, Mary to Smith, William*
Sep 18 1793	Bryan, Nicholas to Gorsuch, Deborah*
Mar 18 1796	Bryan, Peter to Cole, Margaret*
Jul 3 1790	Bryan, Polton Sarah to Ridgely, Thomas*
Feb 23 1795	Bryan, Richard to Timbull, Sarah*
Oct 21 1797	Bryan, Sarah to Grimes, James*
Jan 3 1783	Bryan, Tabitha to Roach, Michael
Nov 21 1798	Bryden, Mary to Duncan, Perry*
Apr 7 1798	Bryrne, Bartholomew C. to Hamilton, Maria*
Mar 25 1786	Bryson, John to Green, Catharine*
Nov 21 1795	Bryson, John to Stevenson, Elizabeth*
Nov 8 1797	Buchain, Elizabeth to Fort, John*
Oct 26 1790	Buchanan, Dorathy to Lowndes, Benjamin*
Jun 4 1794	Buchanan, Eleanor to Cosden, Jeremiah*
Jun 10 1783	Buchanan, Elinor to Rogers, Nicholas
Jan 1 1793	Buchanan, James A. to Calhoun, Elizabeth*
Nov 24 1787	Buchanan, James to Young, Susan
Jun 13 1797	Buchanan, Rebecca to Hagen, Abraham*
Mar 13 1790	Buchanan, Sarah to Turnbull, Robert*
Aug 26 1782	Buchanan, William to Myers, Catherine*
Oct 9 1790	Buck, Christopher to Gorsuch, Kesiah*
Mar 24 1792	Buck, Elizabeth to Green, Joel*
Nov 18 1793	Buck, John to Merryman, Catharine*
Jun 10 1778	Buck, Joshua to Crook, Sarah*
Dec 16 1793	Buck, Susanna to Porter, Robert*
Jun 30 1797	Buck, William to Price, Elizabeth*
Feb 25 1791	Buckingham, Ann to Delphy, John*

Dec 13 1797	Buckingham, Benjamin to Smith, Elizabeth*
Jul 16 1792	Buckingham, Elizabeth to Curran, William*
Feb 27 1788	Buckingham, George to Tener, Hester*
Mar 31 1790	Buckingham, Hannah to Delphia, Richard
Mar 18 1797	Buckingham, Hellen to Frizzle, William*
Sep 3 1795	Buckingham, Nancy to Wallace, John*
Jun 16 1792	Buckingham, Nathan to Leatherwood, Ruth*
Oct 23 1784	Buckingham, Obadiah to Hearmton, Ruth
Sep 21 1785	Buckingham, Thomas to Gardner, Rachael*
May 3 1793	Buckingham, Thomas to Strophel, Mary*
Aug 29 1778	Buckingham, William to Gladman, Margaret*
Nov 17 1797	Bucklers, Henry to Gilberthorp, Rachel*
May 5 1795	Buckley, Eleanor to Hathaway, Jethero*
Dec 11 1794	Buckley, Elizabeth to Harwood, Henry*
May 24 1792	Buckley, Lawrence to Conne, Catharine*
Dec 27 1798	Buckley, Margaret to Hargrove, Thomas*
Oct 30 1798	Buckley, Rachel to Black, Henry*
Oct 1 1798	Buckley, Rachel to Medley, John*
Jul 25 1796	Buckley, Thomas to Garrison, Rachel
Sep 16 1796	Budeaille, Louise F. to Boislandry, Robt. Chas. L.*
Jul 9 1785	Budiel, Elizabeth to Deagle, Lamon*
Oct 9 1784	Budrow, Margaret to Hermangs, Anthony*
May 1 1784	Buffington, Mary to Stansbury, Tobias*
Jan 20 1793	Bugan, John to Stewart, Elinor
Dec 4 1793	Bugan, Mary to Hagen, John
Oct 13 1798	Buhottz, George to Butcher, Elizabeth*
Dec 4 1797	Bukhead, Thomas to Waters, Elizabeth*
Mar 9 1797	Buldger, Henry to Price, Elizabeth*
Jan 4 1794	Bulger, Elizabeth to Borderie, Bernard*
Mar 27 1793	Bulger, Henry to Kettleman, Mary*
Apr 25 1796	Bulger, Margaret to Heath, Samuel*
Jun 12 1779	Bulger, Martin to Logue, Mary
Oct 25 1798	Bulk, Mary to Lavele, Michael*
Jan 12 1785	Bull, Jacob to Slade, Ann*
Oct 27 1791	Bull, Josias Slade to Norris, Rebecca*
Aug 27 1791	Bullen, Simon to Willson, Jane*
Apr 22 1778	Bullock, Mary to Godfrey, Bennum*
Sep 19 1795	Bunbury, Monsier Simmons to Bride, Nancy*
Jan 18 1786	Bungan, Ruth Jane to Jalland, John
Jul 28 1795	Bunker, Job to Anderson, Mary*
May 8 1798	Bunker, Moses to Franciscey, Margaret*
Sep 7 1793	Bunts, Jacob to Coleman, Rachel*
Dec 8 1798	Burch, Fanny to Eagleston, John
Nov 7 1797	Burch, John to Miles, Fanny
Jun 7 1778	Burdan, John to Squires, Elinor*
Jul 12 1779	Burdsel, Thomas to Creamour, Mary*
Aug 7 1779	Burdsel, Thomas to Whood, Mary*
Oct 25 1791	Burgen, Ann to Richards, Joseph*
Sep 22 1798	Burges, Martha to Norbury, George*
Apr 25 1782	Burgess, Alice to Hunt, John*
Jan 8 1785	Burgess, Ann to Bussey, Edward
Feb 3 1791	Burgess, Ann to Wallace, William*
Mar 8 1794	Burgess, Comfort to Pintes, James*
May 9 1791	Burgess, Eleanor to Hazzard, George*
Nov 30 1792	Burgess, Elizabeth to Israel, Bale*
Jul 5 1788	Burgess, Elizabeth to Randell, Roger*

Feb 28 1789	Burgess, Henry to James, Catharine
Feb 1 1786	Burgess, Jane to Simpson, Reagen*
Jun 29 1785	Burgess, John to Welsh, Eleanor*
Dec 18 1790	Burgess, Joshua to Burgess, Sarah*
Nov 26 1792	Burgess, Mary to Evans, Griffith*
Feb 25 1778	Burgess, Richard to Gassoway, Mary*
Dec 18 1790	Burgess, Sarah to Burgess, Joshua*
Mar 22 1796	Burgin, Elizabeth to Franklin, Garret*
Jun 17 1778	Burgiss, Ruth to Shipley, Talbott*
Apr 29 1796	Burgoine, Jacob to Gardner, Ann*
Sep 9 1798	Burgoyne, Catharine to Daster, John B.*
May 14 1796	Burgoyne, Catharine to Kilner, James*
Jul 25 1783	Burk, Deborah to Keyler, John
May 21 1791	Burk, Edward to Leatherburg, Achsah*
Feb 21 1784	Burk, Eleanor to Ritler, John*
May 7 1781	Burk, Elinor to Welsh, Walter*
May 29 1778	Burk, Jane to Morris, James*
Nov 17 1784	Burk, John to Roach, Mary*
Nov 15 1782	Burk, Margaret to Cole, Nathan*
Apr 10 1790	Burk, Margaret to Evans, John
Aug 15 1778	Burk, Michael to Woods, Mary*
Nov 7 1795	Burk, Nancy to Quay, William*
Dec 26 1780	Burk, Patty to Greene, Bednego*
Jan 19 1797	Burk, Polly to Sisler, Philip*
Apr 5 1798	Burk, Rebecca to Mortimer, Thomas*
Jan 10 1792	Burk, Richard to Dunn, Hannah*
Feb 8 1797	Burk, Sarah to Everet, John*
Nov 29 1793	Burk, Sarah to McCuminon, Joseph*
Jun 26 1795	Burk, Thomas to North, Rebecca*
Aug 22 1796	Burk, Winny to Loca, Levin*
Aug 9 1792	Burke, Charlotte to Rider, Benjamin*
Mar 1 1788	Burke, David to Murphey, Elizabeth
Apr 12 1788	Burke, Delili to Sands, Alexander
Oct 6 1797	Burke, Edward to Smith, Nancy
Aug 14 1794	Burke, Elizabeth to Osborn, Joseph*
Aug 22 1793	Burke, John to Barnes, Elizabeth*
Jan 16 1781	Burke, Mary to Connors, Dennis*
Sep 2 1793	Burke, Mary to Henigan, James*
Aug 2 1783	Burke, Mary to Miller, Samuel
Nov 17 1787	Burke, Sarah to Lemmon, Lemuel
Mar 20 1783	Burke, Theobald to Flaharty, Elizabeth*
Oct 4 1798	Burke, Thomas to Hines, Sarah*
Mar 27 1793	Burke, Thomas to Jones, Elizabeth*
Sep 18 1795	Burke, William to MacCubin, Elizabeth*
Nov 8 1784	Burkect, Ann to Waskey, Christian
Jan 14 1796	Burket, John to Kriabs, Sarah*
Mar 18 1778	Burkhead, John to Hammond, Ann*
Jan 13 1784	Burkhead, Margaret to Davis, William*
Sep 30 1790	Burland, Elizabeth to Courtnay, Robert
Jan 7 1784	Burland, Elizabeth to Wittle, Richard
Nov 10 1792	Burland, John to Neill, Mary
Oct 14 1779	Burly, John to Blake, Mary*
May 29 1792	Burn, John to McDonald, Mary Ann Dorsey*
Jan 17 1792	Burneston, Isaac to Rutter, Ann*
Aug 3 1795	Burnet, Mary to Toley, Joseph*
May 12 1789	Burnett, Barbara to Conaway, Richard*

Mar 24 1798	Burnha, Araminta to Sullivan, Andrew Moon*
Dec 14 1791	Burnham, Ann to Reed, James*
May 4 1784	Burnham, John to Davis, Rebecca*
Dec 21 1785	Burnham, Mary to Freeman, Samuel
Jan 10 1795	Burns, Adam to Ball, Mary*
Jul 13 1778	Burns, Bridget to Richardson, George*
Jan 7 1792	Burns, Hannah to Whitley, John*
Jul 27 1793	Burns, James to Cummins, Jane*
May 5 1796	Burns, Jane to Chame, Samuel*
Jun 20 1789	Burns, Juliet to Smith, Stephen*
Feb 13 1794	Burns, Margaret to Downes, William*
Jul 19 1782	Burns, Mary to Flaharty, James
Oct 11 1797	Burns, Mary to Harvey, William*
Jun 24 1782	Burns, Rebecca to Ellis, John*
Jun 25 1793	Burns, Sarah to Hotton, John*
Jul 11 1794	Burns, Simon to Knowland, Mary*
Feb 3 1778	Burns, Stephen to Shutom, Barbara*
Nov 12 1796	Burnside, Elizabeth to Mahall, Thomas*
Nov 24 1785	Burnsides, James to Slater, Margaret
Jan 31 1789	Burrell, Thomas to Adams, Mary*
Dec 15 1785	Burroughs, Thomas to Morchead, Jane
May 19 1791	Burtell, Mary to Reese, Henry*
Nov 28 1798	Burton, John to Sidden, Mary*
Dec 10 1798	Burton, Joseph to Ritter, Rebecca
Jan 4 1797	Burton, Rachel to Garman, Benjamin*
Sep 28 1785	Burton, Richard to McIntosh, Catharine
Dec 19 1795	Burton, Ruth to Yarly, Ralph*
Feb 26 1778	Burton, Thomas to Harriman, Mary*
Mar 25 1786	Burton, Thomas to Welsh, Leah*
Apr 5 1798	Burton, William to Fowler, Mary*
Feb 27 1796	Busby, Melinda to Osborn, Daniel*
Mar 8 1794	Bush, Hannah to Gibbins, James*
Jun 28 1783	Bush, Sarah to Hughes, William*
Aug 17 1796	Busk, Greenbury to Davis, Rodey*
Nov 8 1785	Busk, John to Gash, Eleanor Ridden
Feb 21 1784	Busser, Catharine to Eyon, Frederick*
Jan 8 1785	Bussey, Edward to Burgess, Ann
Dec 27 1798	Bussey, Martha to Smith, Job*
Feb 4 1796	Bussey, Thomas D. to Demmitt, Margaret*
Sep 5 1795	Buster, John to Price, Ellin*
Sep 19 1795	Butcher, Bartholomew to Plumb, Elizabeth*
Oct 13 1798	Butcher, Elizabeth to Buhottz, George*
Oct 26 1778	Butcher, John to Kinselagh, Susannah*
Jan 7 1784	Butler, Absalom to Orrick, Susannah
Jan 9 1794	Butler, Alice to Pike, James*
Feb 24 1794	Butler, Ann to Harris, John*
Aug 12 1796	Butler, Benjamin to Bentley, Harriot*
Feb 18 1783	Butler, Elisha to Martin, Elizabeth*
Feb 14 1797	Butler, Elizabeth to Davis, William*
Jul 18 1795	Butler, Elizabeth to Pitch, James*
Jun 21 1781	Butler, Elizabeth to Wallingsford, Benjamin
Apr 7 1792	Butler, John Holpin to Evans, Margaret*
Jun 22 1798	Butler, John to Robinson, Charlotte*
Apr 5 1790	Butler, John to Simpson, Rebecca*
Jan 6 1781	Butler, Joseph to Blossom, Mary*
Jul 29 1783	Butler, Joseph to Lane, Sarah*

Apr	18	1795	Butler, Margaret to Jackson, William*
Dec	11	1788	Butler, Margaret to Norris, Benjamin
Jul	8	1783	Butler, Margaret to Sittlemire, Christian
Oct	8	1793	Butler, Margaret to Whiteford, James*
Oct	19	1796	Butler, Mary to Jones, Abraham*
Dec	8	1784	Butler, Mary to Price, William*
Dec	8	1796	Butler, Samuel to Brownson, Fredericka*
Apr	5	1798	Butler, Sarah to Davis, Henry*
Feb	4	1786	Butler, Walter to Finn, Elizabeth
Apr	7	1796	Butner, John to Sherwood, Elizabeth*
Dec	4	1784	Buttengan, Thomas to Fenton, Margaret*
Jul	12	1779	Butterworth, Benjamin to Hoskins, Sarah*
Nov	10	1779	Butterworth, Benjamin to Linton, Easter
Oct	30	1779	Button, Elias to Dunkin, Mary*
Jul	8	1794	Button, Elizabeth to Hardy, William*
Aug	27	1795	Button, George to Peterson, Eve*
Aug	8	1782	Byal, William to Stafford, Elizabeth*
Oct	28	1797	Byan, Mary to Geraud, Alexander*
Oct	26	1789	Byass, Mary to Evans, John*
Jun	19	1794	Byerley, Christine to Dunlap, Charles*
Apr	6	1793	Byfield, Abraham to Corbin, Patience*
Oct	23	1783	Cable, George to Hicks, Lynda
Nov	4	1782	Cable, Mary to Krebs, Michael*
Dec	27	1798	Cabler, Mary to Pierce, Joseph
Apr	26	1788	Cables, Eleanor to Chandler, Joseph*
Nov	1	1794	Cabrera, John to Mitchell, Jane*
Feb	14	1784	Cadle, Elizabeth to Drummond, Hugh*
Nov	22	1795	Cadle, Griffith to Tevis, Agness
Mar	23	1796	Cadle, Sarah to Conway, Greenberry*
Oct	23	1797	Caduman, Francis to Bryan, Biddy*
Jun	16	1783	Cafues, Abraham to Rothrock, Elizabeth*
Dec	7	1793	Cahil, George to Murphy, Eleanor*
Aug	11	1798	Cahill, William to Farlan, Mary
Nov	29	1783	Cahill, William to Russell, Elizabeth*
May	16	1778	Cahoe, John to Bennett, Johanna*
Jan	11	1797	Cain, Margaret to Longley, John
Aug	16	1796	Caine, Henry to Grimes, Sarah
Jul	28	1779	Caldran, John Baptist to Bryan, Mary
Nov	24	1780	Caldron, Frs. to Celeston, Mary*
Jan	6	1783	Caldron, Mary to Hardy, James
May	12	1785	Caldwell, Ann to Jones, William
Nov	19	1778	Caldwell, John to Laudiger, Caterena*
Dec	11	1790	Caldwell, John to Stansbury, Lucreatia*
Feb	10	1784	Caleb, Henry to Galaush, Sarah*
Nov	17	1784	Calef, John to Knight, Achsah*
Jun	27	1778	Calep, Susannah to Mucava, Martin*
Jun	29	1789	Calffoos, Lewis to Weller, Eve*
Mar	27	1794	Calhoun, Alexander to Clemments, Sarah*
Jan	1	1793	Calhoun, Elizabeth to Buchanan, James A.*
Sep	26	1795	Calhoun, Mary to Mahon, James*
Sep	19	1784	Callahan, Catharine to Friar, John
Nov	24	1791	Callahan, Honor to Jordan, James*
Jul	14	1798	Callahan, John to Warrington, Catharine
Jun	19	1788	Callahan, Samuel to Carr, Nancy*
Sep	9	1797	Callahan, William to Davis, Susanna
Aug	28	1795	Callahan, William to Keeble, Humphrey*

Jul 31 1782	Callanan, Mary to Kennedy, Martin
Jun 2 1794	Calman, Joseph to Renuleau, Marie Martha*
Oct 5 1792	Calvert, James to Shadders, Elizabeth*
Jul 13 1786	Calvin, Priscilla to Scott, Andrew
Feb 11 1796	Calwell, John to Purle, Mary*
Nov 17 1794	Calwell, Ruth to Demangin*
Dec 9 1795	Calwell, Sally to Askew, William*
Dec 6 1782	Cambridge, Martha to Street, Benjamin
Oct 28 1794	Camel, Jean to Brown, Thomas*
Aug 4 1781	Cammell, Mary to Tracey, Bazel*
Apr 27 1796	Campbell, Aaron to Marshall, Sarah*
Nov 11 1797	Campbell, Ann to Beckley, James*
Dec 11 1787	Campbell, Ann to Scotland, Anthony*
Jun 1 1786	Campbell, Archibald to Hindmin, Elizabeth*
Mar 3 1793	Campbell, Catherine to Crawford, Seth*
Aug 21 1779	Campbell, Elizabeth to Cattle, Thomas*
Nov 22 1784	Campbell, Elizabeth to Hook, Jacob
Jan 6 1790	Campbell, James to Moody, Frances*
Jun 11 1796	Campbell, John to Howard, Sarah*
May 17 1788	Campbell, John to Maxwell, Marion*
Sep 17 1796	Campbell, John to O'Donnell, Biddy*
Jan 27 1798	Campbell, Joseph Murray to Heart, Grace*
Jun 13 1797	Campbell, Mary to Fletcher, James*
Feb 18 1792	Campbell, Nancy to Taylor, Joseph*
Nov 19 1781	Campbell, Rachel to Leef, John
Sep 18 1793	Campbell, Robert to Ranty, Catharine*
Nov 10 1791	Campbell, Robert to Smith, Catharine*
Mar 30 1797	Campbell, Thomas J. to Sinclair, Sarah*
Dec 2 1795	Canby, John to Brune, Hannah*
Feb 5 1778	Candley, Martha M. to Orsler, Charles*
Sep 19 1793	CAne, Bellinda to Hanway, Francis*
Dec 12 1795	Cann, Benjamin to Wamsley, Nancy*
Jun 1 1795	Cann, John to Helmes, Margaret*
Feb 3 1781	Cann, Mary to Jones, John*
Dec 20 1780	Cann, Susanna to Jones, Aaron*
Dec 31 1794	Cannesseke, Mary to Michael, John*
Oct 6 1791	Cannon, Airy to Stinchcomb, Nathaniel
Dec 14 1777	Cannon, Clement to Murphey, Mary*
Dec 31 1794	Cannon, Elizabeth to Mitchell, Arler*
Oct 21 1794	Cannon, Elizabeth to Ratlief, Thomas*
Aug 25 1798	Cannon, Jane to Anderson, Abraham*
Dec 2 1796	Cannon, Mary to McLaughlin, William*
Jun 4 1784	Cannon, Neomi to Morriss, William
Nov 28 1792	Cannon, Rachel to Lalanne, Frederick Raymond*
Dec 31 1789	Cannon, William to Murphy, Ann*
Aug 5 1778	Cannor, John to Hammer, Hannah*
Nov 19 1791	Canoles, Rachel to Ensor, William
Apr 11 1794	Cantler, Barnett to McLaughlin, Catharine*
Apr 15 1786	Cantwell, Ann to Hughes, William
Aug 27 1795	Cantwell, Thomas to Smith, Sally
May 22 1794	Capela, Jeanne Francoise to Badet, John Baptiste*
Mar 24 1791	Capels, Margaret to Ireland, Samuel*
Dec 23 1797	Capen, Honor to Kelly, Thomas*
Nov 11 1796	Capeta, Rebecca to Larouett, Nicholas*
Oct 8 1792	Capito, Christian to Wyant, Elizabeth*
Aug 11 1781	Caple, Abraham to Stewart, Mary*

```
Dec 18 1793    Caple, Samuel to Cole, Mary*
Dec 10 1796    Caples, Hannah to Wooden, John*
Aug 21 1793    Caples, William to Green, Elizabeth*
Aug  5 1794    Capoot, Jeremiah to Tagler, Mary*
Aug 25 1797    Carback, John to Rawlings, Jane*
May 20 1784    Carback, Temperance to Pines, William*
Nov 15 1785    Carback, William to Wright, Jane
Aug 12 1794    Carew, Thomas to Hulstrunk, Margaret Christiana*
Sep  9 1794    Carey, Dennis to Dillon, Margaret*
May  5 1798    Carey, Dennis to Moore, Judy*
Aug 28 1797    Carey, Eleanor to Hagerty, Michael*
Nov  8 1797    Carey, Elizabeth to Ganteaume, James*
Jun 30 1797    Carey, Jeremiah to Kelly, Margaret*
Feb  7 1797    Carlean, Sarah to Greenland, Nathan*
Jul  7 1797    Carlile, Agnes to Lewthwaite, Christian*
Feb 18 1790    Carlyle, John to Lane, Elizabeth
Oct 25 1797    Carmaghan, James to Miller, Catharine*
Oct 11 1797    Carmaghan, Sarah to Long, Robert, Carey*
Feb 22 1797    Carmichael, John to Landers, Elizabeth
Oct 14 1782    Carnan, Charles Ridgely to Dorsey, Priscilla*
Jan 12 1792    Carnan, Morris to Greenfield, Cordelia*
Oct  6 1778    Carnes, Catharine to Taumble, John*
Oct  3 1795    Carnes, Mary to Cheiver, Daniel*
Apr 13 1797    Carney, John to Hud, Easter*
Jan 27 1785    Carney, Mary to Collins, John*
May 16 1795    Carney, Thomas to Baxley, Sarah*
Aug 24 1784    Carnowles, Charles to Stansbury, Ruth
May  9 1795    Carpenter, Allen to Skeuse, Ann*
Jan  3 1794    Carpenter, Isaac to Reed, Lydia*
Dec 24 1793    Carpenter, John to Gwinn, Ellen*
Apr 21 1786    Carr, Aquila to Bond, Susannah*
Sep  3 1796    Carr, Daniel to Dean, Susannah*
Jun  4 1795    Carr, Felix to Figgance, Catharine*
Dec  3 1794    Carr, Isaac to Abrahams, Monarchy*
Aug 15 1797    Carr, John to Herron, Eleanor*
May 22 1781    Carr, Margaret to Marsden, Jonathan*
Sep 20 1794    Carr, Mary to Hughes, Henry*
Apr 21 1794    Carr, Mary to Ricketts, Hugh*
Jun 19 1788    Carr, Nancy to Callahan, Samuel*
Mar 29 1786    Carr, Sarah to Daw, Joseph*
Oct 30 1782    Carr, Sarah to Larch, Isaac*
May  4 1779    Carragan, Edward to Gowan, Mary
Oct 24 1793    Carre, Joseph to Deschamp, Magdaline*
Sep 30 1796    Carrick, Daniel to Farly, Bridget*
Dec 12 1796    Carrick, George to Baker, Cary*
Sep  8 1792    Carrman, John to Castle, Catherine
Feb 21 1792    Carrol, Margaret to Magrath, Michael*
Apr 14 1798    Carroll, Ann to Groves, John*
Feb 21 1783    Carroll, Hannah to Cornhaven, Jacob*
Nov  7 1789    Carroll, Henry Hill to Rogers, Sarah*
Dec 17 1787    Carroll, James to Gough, Sophia
Nov 22 1796    Carroll, Jane to Newlin, David*
May 15 1784    Carroll, Martin to _____, Mary Ann
Jun  5 1795    Carroll, Mary to Black, James*
Aug 25 1795    Carroll, Michael to Drake, Nancy*
Jul 23 1795    Carroll, Patrick to Ross, Macarit*
```

```
Aug  4 1779    Carroll, Sarah to Cunningham, George*
Dec 14 1797    Carroll, Thomas to King, Sarah*
Apr 26 1784    Carry, Andrew to Lane, Mary*
Nov 12 1798    Carson, Henry to Stricker, Louisa*
Oct 21 1797    Carson, Mary to Davis, Amos*
Mar  3 1791    Carson, Nathaniel to Creaman, Eleanor*
Feb 12 1786    Carson, William to Aldridge, Ann
Apr 10 1784    Carson, William to Taylor, Elizabeth*
Nov  8 1788    Carte, Ann to Hardriet, James*
Nov 29 1783    Cartee, Daniel to Griffee, Susannah*
Sep 24 1796    Carter, Anne to Medlicoat, Samuel*
Jun  4 1798    Carter, Charles S. to Berry, Sarah*
Jul 30 1789    Carter, Harriet Lucy to Maund, John James*
Feb 19 1791    Carter, Henry to Atherton, Elinor*
Sep 16 1797    Carter, Jane to Vaughan, James*
Jan  8 1796    Carter, John to Griffey, Jane*
Dec  1 1784    Carter, John to Scarborough, Hannah*
Dec 19 1781    Carter, Josias to Benfield, Hannah*
May 18 1778    Carter, Rebecca to Stacey, Robert*
Dec  6 1796    Carter, Sarah Fairfax to Chinn, John Yates*
Aug 25 1791    Carter, Solomon to Wall, Kitty*
Jun  4 1781    Carter, Sol. to Sindoll, Elizabeth*
Dec 23 1780    Carter, Susannah to Stevins, William*
Jan 25 1797    Carter, Thomas to Nicoll, Christina
Jun  9 1790    Carter, William M. to Keith, Sarah*
Mar 12 1781    Carter, William to Ferguson, Sarah*
Jan 20 1783    Cartright, Abraham to Hart, Mary*
Dec  8 1789    Carty, Biddy to Long, James*
Dec 21 1793    Carty, Peter to Larnott, Hannah Catherine*
Jan  4 1786    Carty, Sarah to Zoph, John
Aug 10 1779    Carver, William to Conden, Elizabeth*
Jan 29 1785    Cary, Nicholas Wilson to Smith, Margaret*
Mar 17 1779    Casey, Bridget to Couile, Michael*
Oct 21 1795    Casey, Eleanor to McGuire, Roger*
Feb 10 1798    Casey, Elizabeth to Duyer, William*
Nov 26 1787    Casey, Mary to Quinley, William*
Mar 28 1796    Casey, Robert to Davis, Elizabeth*
Jun  8 1796    Cashman, Sarah to Mahony, Thomas*
Oct 21 1795    Cashman, Timothy to Bell, Mariah*
Feb  3 1796    Cashman, William to Brown, Sarah*
Jul 16 1798    Caslow, Samuel to Marr, Catharine*
Oct 26 1784    Casment, Ann to Dorman, Cornelius*
Jun 13 1792    Cassady, Elizabeth to Clark, David*
Jan  3 1798    Cassat, Peter to Stansbury, Susan*
May 28 1778    Cassidy, Patrick to Reed, Hannah*
Nov  3 1792    Castaignet, Paul to O'Leary, Julia*
Aug 22 1797    Castille, John to Jones, Anne*
Sep  8 1792    Castle, Catherine to Carrman, John
Sep  4 1783    Castle, Mary to Peters, Henry*
Mar 15 1796    Caswell, Josiah to Scott, Nancy*
Apr 17 1795    Caswell, Thomas to Lowry, Jane*
Mar 15 1786    Catherina, Maria to Myers, Philip
Jan 29 1796    Cato, Edward to Martin, Sino*
Oct  8 1796    Caton, Eleanor to Bentley, Michael*
Jul 23 1796    Caton, Jane to Reed, Peter*
Apr 15 1798    Caton, Matthew to Barlow, Elizabeth*
```

```
Aug 21 1779    Cattle, Thomas to Campbell, Elizabeth*
Oct  8 1794    Caulk, Ann to Stevenson, Henry, Dr.
Aug  6 1795    Caulk, Frances to Dawson, John*
Apr 15 1789    Caulk, Joseph to Tripp, Ann*
May 26 1785    Caulk, Thomas Ward to Sears, Hannah*
Nov 11 1793    Cavarre, Francois to Shields, Mary*
Dec 15 1785    Cavey, John to Knight, Ann
Nov 29 1798    Cavey, Sarah to Knight, John B.*
Oct 17 1789    Cavey, Thomas to Donaldson, Elizabeth*
Mar 27 1798    Cavill, John to Perry, Ann*
Sep 19 1779    Cazy, Margaret to Williams, John*
May  1 1790    Cecil, Linday to Ireland, Richard*
Nov 24 1780    Celeston, Mary to Caldron, Frs.*
May 25 1779    Celistin, Mary to Legard, John
Aug 16 1782    Celiston, Margaret to Rondet, Francis*
Aug  3 1782    Celiston, Martha to Porce, Frs.
Aug  3 1782    Celiston, Mary to Bemon, Lewis
Jan 27 1791    Ceocte, Maria Anna to Chighizola, Evangelista*
Feb  9 1785    Chace, Thondrick to Jacobs, Mary*
Sep 29 1795    Chadders, Robert to Ridgely, Elizabeth*
Mar  5 1796    Chaddrick, Frances to Beicher, John Lambert*
Nov 19 1795    Chader, James to Jourdan, Sarah*
Nov 22 1780    Chaimberlain, John to Lynch, Elizabeth*
Jul  1 1797    Chalmers, John Jr. to Gilder, Mary*
Jun 21 1798    Chamberlain, Charles to Gutrow, Mary*
Jan 30 1794    Chamberlain, George Robins to Crookshanks, Mary*
Oct 28 1791    Chamberlain, Hoops to Stevenson, Mary*
Jul 20 1796    Chamberlain, Margaret to Kelly, Lawrence*
Oct  5 1782    Chamberlain, Mary to Stevenson, Edward
May  6 1783    Chamberlain, Priscilla to Green, Elisha*
Jul 31 1788    Chamberlain, Rebecca to Galloway, Absalom*
Nov  7 1794    Chamberlain, Susannah to Morford, John*
Feb 25 1796    Chamberlaine, Priscilla to Donaldson, William*
Apr 29 1793    Chamberlin, Rebecca to Bosley, Bazel*
Mar 11 1788    Chambers, Amos to Cramlet, Mary*
Nov 17 1791    Chambers, Daniel to Childs, Martha*
May 16 1795    Chambers, Jane to Griffin, William*
Aug 19 1782    Chambers, Martin to Miller, Mary*
Nov 27 1798    Chambers, Mary to Rackle, Thomas*
Jul 30 1783    Chambers, William to Harvey, Judy*
Jan 30 1781    Chambers, William to King, Mary*
Apr 18 1793    Chambers, William to McLaughlin, Mary*
May  5 1796    Chame, Samuel to Burns, Jane*
Sep 18 1790    Chamean, Peggy to Peach, John Battis*
Dec  6 1784    Chamillon, Joseph to Smith, Ann*
Apr 26 1788    Chandler, Joseph to Cables, Eleanor*
Sep 19 1793    Chandless, John Hurle to Anderson, Sarah*
Feb 26 1785    Chaney, Abel to Johnson, Ruth
May 15 1779    Chaney, Ann to Penn, Shaderick
Feb 24 1794    Chaney, Ann to Wimsel, Charles*
Oct 24 1796    Chaney, Joseph to Wilson, Drucilla*
Jul 14 1798    Chaney, Margaret to Proctor, Isaiah*
Jul 10 1792    Chaney, Margaret to Shirk, Peter*
Feb 14 1789    Chaney, Mordeica to Henton, Jemima*
Jun 26 1795    Changeur, Leon to Montalebor, Josephine Grissure*
Mar 17 1785    Chaplain, William to Allen, Polly
```

Dec 1 1789	Chaplin, William to Woods, Sarah*
Jun 11 1778	Chapline, Elizabeth to Reddick, James*
Apr 12 1797	Chapman, Ann to Ling, Robert*
Dec 21 1798	Chapman, Christopher to Rous, Elizabeth*
Feb 20 1781	Chapman, Elizabeth to Ditter, John*
Feb 14 1778	Chapman, Ellen to Gorsuch, Thomas*
Feb 17 1792	Chapman, Frances to Warfield, Ely*
Feb 15 1798	Chapman, James to Merryman, Rachel*
Nov 2 1780	Chapman, Jemimah to Hudson, William*
Nov 10 1778	Chapman, John to Kelly, Elizabeth*
Jun 23 1792	Chapman, Joshua to Hammel, Catherine*
Oct 5 1791	Chapman, Rebecca to Vaughan, Benjamin Gist
Jul 20 1782	Chapman, Ruth to Moore, Robert*
May 28 1790	Chargo, Susannah to Brimmer, Moses
Nov 24 1780	Charles, Abram to Pary, Judy*
Dec 17 1782	Charles to Mary (free negroes)
Jun 26 1795	Charleton, Elizabeth to Hill, William*
Jul 5 1778	Chatterback, William to Aston, Jane*
Jan 25 1796	Chattle, Nancy to Stone, Edward*
Oct 9 1797	Cheddick, Sarah to Smith, John*
Aug 12 1790	Chedick, Charlotte to Kelly, John*
Oct 3 1795	Cheiver, Daniel to Carnes, Mary*
Sep 14 1797	Cheney, Susannah to Short, Richard*
Oct 9 1783	Chenoweth, Keziah to Kempff, John Christ*
Nov 25 1791	Chenowith, Arthur to Baxter, Elizabeth*
Mar 24 1784	Chenowith, Arthur to Bosley, Cassandra*
Jul 29 1778	Chenowith, Arthur to Helm, Dellah*
Nov 19 1791	Chenowith, Catharine to Houk, Anthony*
Oct 23 1779	Chenowith, Richard to Askew, Elinor*
Sep 29 1794	Chenowith, Ruth to Wall, Michael*
Oct 6 1785	Chenowith, Samuel to Cromwell, Elizabeth*
Aug 21 1779	Chenowith, Sarah to Baxter, Samuel*
Aug 25 1798	Chenowith, Sarah to Gregory, Ralph*
Feb 12 1795	Cherves, Louisa to Shoemaker, Ignatius*
Dec 23 1797	Chesran, David to Farrell, Mary*
Apr 20 1795	Chester, Elizabeth to Shaney, John*
Nov 1 1796	Cheston, Daniel to Holland, Catharine*
Sep 18 1786	Cheston, Samuel to Harvy, Elizabeth
Feb 24 1798	Chesu, Catharine to McDowell, Thomas*
Sep 21 1791	Chew, Cassandra to Shipley, Duncan
Dec 21 1781	Chew, Richard to Scarf, Rachel*
Jul 16 1779	Chice, Rachel to Shipley, Talbott
Dec 22 1795	Chiddick, Margaret to Dykes, William*
Jan 27 1791	Chighizola, Evangelista to Ceocte, Maria Anna*
Apr 15 1782	Chilcoat, Ann to Murray, Joseph
Oct 24 1789	Chilcoat, Joshua to Arnold, Rebecca*
Apr 5 1781	Chilcoat, Robert to Webb, Joyce*
Feb 7 1789	Chilcott, Elijah to Ensor, Elizabeth*
Nov 17 1788	Chilcott, Margarett to Gill, John*
Oct 4 1792	Childes, Benjamin to Evans, Elizabeth*
Jan 31 1798	Childs, John to Wheeler, Sarah
Nov 17 1791	Childs, Martha to Chambers, Daniel*
Oct 19 1795	Childs, Mary to Pearson, Henry*
Aug 5 1794	Childs, Mary to Viseur, Francis*
Feb 27 1786	China, James to Simpson, Achsah
Nov 29 1787	China, Nathan to Mansfield, Sarah*

```
Jan 21 1783    China, Zepheniah to Lewis, Ruth*
Sep  1 1790    Chine, Mary to Galloway, James*
May  8 1788    Chineth, Ruth to Stansbury, Joseph*
Jul 27 1784    Chinia, Rachel to Deaver, William*
Dec  6 1796    Chinn, John Yates to Carter, Sarah Fairfax*
Jan  4 1783    Chinn, Sary to Howard, John*
Apr  8 1789    Chinnuth, William to Ritcherson, Elizabeth*
Jan 26 1796    Chinowith, George to Hale, Rachel*
Feb  8 1790    Chinowith, Richard to Bell, Sarah*
Aug 18 1798    Chiver, Mary to Rogin, Henry*
Jun 30 1797    Choak, John to Kindall, Cassandra*
Aug  4 1783    Choate, Richard to Lowe, Jane*
Jul  5 1791    Chord, Henry to Randall, Eleanor
Dec 12 1789    Chote, Edward to Demmitt, Elizabeth*
Mar 20 1792    Chrisholm, Thomas to Collison, Terry*
Jun 16 1798    Christian, Anthony to Welsh, Elizabeth*
Apr 26 1795    Christian, John to Jourdon, Catharine*
Jan 24 1795    Christie, Bridget to Lewis, James*
Dec 27 1785    Christie, James to Bermingham, Rebecca
Aug 23 1783    Christison, Ann to Brooks, George*
Jul 19 1796    Christman, Elizabeth to McKuven, Owen*
Apr 16 1798    Christopher, Ann to Cole, John*
Oct  6 1786    Christopher, Ann to Fulton, James
Jun  2 1798    Christopher, Susanna to Osburn, Michael*
May 17 1797    Christopher, Thomas to Tusay, Nancy*
Jun 26 1781    Christoson, Robert to James, Mary
Nov  4 1797    Chruch, Ruthe to Welden, Ebenezer*
Nov  7 1794    Chuaidi, Baptista to Hains, Rachel*
Jan 23 1790    Church, Amelia to Collins, John*
Sep  7 1797    Church, Amos to Freeman, Sina*
Sep  2 1793    Church, Rossway to Murray, Ruth
Jul 27 1793    Church, Samuel to Pitcher, Hannah*
Jul 13 1797    Churchmore, Nancy to Gillburn, William*
Jul 18 1795    Cisson, Richard to Ingrain, Mary*
Dec 20 1798    Clackner, Adam to Gill, Rebecca*
Sep 19 1795    Clackner, Lydia to Harst, William*
Sep 13 1796    Clair, Rebecca to Baker, Manning*
Jul 18 1795    Clansey, Patrick to Hogan, Hannah*
Nov  7 1793    Clapp, Stephen to Fowler, Nancy*
Jun 11 1783    Clark, Catharine to Johnson, William
Aug 29 1785    Clark, Clarissa to Gore, John
Jun 13 1792    Clark, David to Cassady, Elizabeth*
Apr  8 1790    Clark, Edward to Addison, Jemima
Nov 24 1790    Clark, Elisha to Porter, Elizabeth
Jun 10 1784    Clark, Jesse to Mackinhamer, Catherine
Feb 22 1796    Clark, John to Bobbin, Charlotte*
Mar 13 1797    Clark, John to Elston, Ann*
Apr 28 1783    Clark, John to Maydwell, Hannah*
Jan 21 1786    Clark, Joseph to O'Brian, Nancy*
Aug 12 1779    Clark, Margaret to Jackson, Daniel
Jan 12 1792    Clark, Patrick to Mitchell, Sarah*
Aug  8 1797    Clark, Raphael to Patterson, Martha
Oct 26 1778    Clark, Richard to Berry, Margaret*
Feb 28 1785    Clark, Samuel to Lucas, Mary*
Dec 24 1789    Clark, William to Fitzs, Darkes*
Oct 19 1778    Clarke, Ambrose to Neat, Barbara*
```

```
Dec  4 1790      Clarke, Ann to Nevis, Hezekiah*
Jan 21 1795      Clarke, Bailey E. to Vanhorn, Elizabeth*
Oct  2 1793      Clarke, Catharine to Helms, John*
Apr 17 1795      Clarke, Elizabeth to Philips, Nathan*
Feb  7 1798      Clarke, Henry to Davey, Charlotte*
May 18 1797      Clarke, James to Birmingham, Mary Ann*
Dec 16 1784      Clarke, James to Rock, Barbary*
Jan 10 1798      Clarke, John to Bombarger, Margaret
Dec 31 1796      Clarke, John to Cleary, Catharine*
Aug 12 1797      Clarke, John to Dodd, Priscilla*
Oct  3 1779      Clarke, John to Greene, Sarah*
Dec  4 1787      Clarke, John to McKlevane, Ann*
May  4 1793      Clarke, John to Waley, Mary*
Mar 28 1796      Clarke, Judith to McNamar, John*
Nov  2 1790      Clarke, Mary to Hammond, Philip*
Sep  2 1795      Clarke, Oliver to North, Sophia*
Jul  3 1781      Clarke, Peter to Wadley, Elizabeth*
Aug  5 1779      Clarke, Richard to Benbo, Mary*
Nov 24 1798      Clarke, Sarah to Stewart, John*
Sep 14 1798      Clarke, Thomas to Peoins, Drucilla
Apr 22 1789      Clarke, William to Gough, Frances*
Jan  3 1798      Clarke, William to Grimes, Rachel*
Apr 15 1786      Clarke, William to Reese, Mary*
Jul 19 1785      Clarkson, Thomas to Tompanks, Elizabeth
Aug 27 1798      Clashe, Patrick to Reading, Margaret*
Nov 12 1795      Clauherty, Patrick to Faherty, Honour*
Feb 14 1778      Clay, Mary to German, Thomas*
Sep 29 1798      Clay, Nancy to Hanson, Dory
Dec 22 1795      Clay, Rachel to Jackson, Abel*
Aug 20 1782      Clayor, Mary to Fite, Peter
Aug 18 1796      Clayton, Joseph to Wells, Sarah*
Sep 18 1798      Clayton, Mary to Pipperman, Anthony*
Jun 19 1779      Clayton, Tabitha to Mosser, Kid*
Dec  7 1796      Cleamer, Mary to Gutchers, David*
Dec 31 1796      Cleary, Catharine to Clarke, John*
May 21 1794      Cleaves, Elizabeth to Thompson, James*
Jul 22 1797      Clebe, Charlotte to Salter, Thomas*
Dec 20 1794      Cleburn, George With to Hellen, Mary King*
Nov 28 1795      Clement, Sidney to Primrose, Robert*
Nov 27 1782      Clements, Edward to Morris, Elizabeth*
Mar  4 1796      Clements, Edward to Wade, Charlotte*
Sep  3 1794      Clements, James to Landrakin, Mary*
Aug 30 1783      Clements, Mary to Eagan, John
Aug 13 1785      Clemins, Thomas to Malone, Mary
Apr 10 1790      Clemments, Elizabeth to McSherry, Patrick*
Mar 27 1794      Clemments, Sarah to Calhoun, Alexander*
Sep 19 1794      Clerage, Elizabeth to Pennington, Nathan*
Dec 26 1792      Clery, Michael to Rust, Mary*
Oct  3 1794      Cline, Sarah to Howard, John*
May 25 1798      Clinefitter, John to McClung, Letitia*
Dec 15 1797      Clingan, John to Wise, Ann*
Mar  2 1786      Clopper, John to Stansbury, Elizabeth*
Sep 11 1794      Clopper, Peter to Goulding, Mary*
Nov  1 1797      Close, David to Bentley, Mary*
Mar 15 1778      Cloud, Elizabeth to McIlvain, Andrew*
Mar 22 1783      Clouse, Mary to Danach, John*
```

```
May 24 1793    Clouse, Stephen to Rowlana, Rosend
Sep 21 1797    Clower, Elizabeth to Kellen, John*
Jun 22 1797    Clower, Polly to Williams, Jacob*
May 20 1778    Clun, Mary M. to Squires, Peter*
Apr 17 1797    Clusby, Polly to West, Simeon*
Oct  8 1794    Coal, George to Biddison, Sarah*
Mar 23 1793    Coale, Charles C. to Rhodes, Sarah*
May 18 1779    Coale, John to Stevens, Elizabeth
Apr 23 1794    Coale, William to Boiven, Elizabeth*
Mar  8 1793    Coates, James to Jackson, Rachel*
Dec 22 1794    Coats, Francis to Linton, Charlotte*
Feb 20 1798    Cobben, Joseph to Scocofer, Catharine*
Jul  9 1798    Cobenhufer, Elizabeth to Albright, Andrew*
Jul  8 1795    Cochran, Mary to Kitten, Theophilus*
May 18 1797    Cochran, Polly to Mills, Joseph*
Sep  9 1798    Cochran, Sally to Watts, John G.*
Dec 15 1796    Cochran, Susanna to Hendrickson, Joseph*
Apr  3 1798    Cock, Lydia to French, Samuel*
Dec 19 1781    Cockey, Actions to Ford, Thomas Cockey Dye*
May 17 1788    Cockey, Ann to Brown, Elias*
Jan  7 1789    Cockey, Caleb to Rutler, Sally*
Feb 18 1793    Cockey, Eleanor to Groff, Sebastine*
Jan 10 1788    Cockey, Elizabeth to Cockey, Thomas Deye*
Jan  1 1783    Cockey, Elizabeth to Cole, Philip*
Apr 18 1778    Cockey, Hannah to Stone, William*
Aug 17 1785    Cockey, John to Cole, Mary*
Dec 20 1797    Cockey, Joshua Frederick to Fouble, Elizabeth*
Feb 21 1782    Cockey, Joshua to Cromwell, Henrietta*
Apr 17 1793    Cockey, Joshua to Jones, Polly*
May  9 1792    Cockey, Penelope Dye to Gist, Thomas*
Mar 22 1791    Cockey, Ruth to Owings, Samuel*
Jan 10 1788    Cockey, Thomas Deye to Cockey, Elizabeth*
Mar 25 1793    Cockey, Thomas Deye to Ristean, Ann
Mar 10 1788    Cockey, Thomas to Brown, Ruth*
Sep 26 1795    Cockey, Thomas to Owings, Elizabeth*
Dec 23 1780    Cockran, George to Shaw, Elinor*
Jun  5 1782    Cockran, Mary to Norman, Henry*
Jun 21 1788    Cockran, Thomas to Lemmon, Hannah*
May 11 1783    Cockran, William to McGill, Ann*
Mar  2 1798    Cockrill, Thomas to Wiley, Sarah*
Oct 10 1797    Coe, Elizabeth to Simmons, James
Jan 31 1798    Coe, James to Hart, Sarah*
Jan 12 1791    Coe, William to Barber, Hannah*
May 16 1798    Coffee, John to Woodward, Elizabetts Jemima*
Nov 24 1795    Coffel, Mariah to Johnston, Edward*
Nov 30 1798    Coffers, Judy to Errickson, Bernard*
Sep 28 1793    Coghan, Nancy to Townsend, Elijah*
Nov 10 1794    Coghlan, William to Kisk, Catharine*
Aug  9 1797    Cohen, Isaac to Moore, Peggy*
Oct 26 1779    Coher, James to Lere, Margaret*
Dec 13 1796    Cohoun, Moses to Leecoumpt, Sarah E.*
Apr 27 1784    Cohown, Moses to Welsh, Elinor*
Apr 17 1778    Coil, Samuel to Brady, Catharine*
Aug  3 1797    Colbertson, Deborah to Ganer, John*
Dec 12 1790    Cole, Abraham Jr. to Gist, Ceal*
Nov 22 1781    Cole, Abram to Ensor, Honour
```

```
Jun  5 1779    Cole, Ann to Deaver, Philip*
Aug 22 1785    Cole, Ann to Spurrier, John
Aug  1 1794    Cole, Anthony to Fifer, Maria*
Sep 17 1794    Cole, Arabella to Devonsher, Henry*
Jun  4 1781    Cole, Dealy to Crocker, Thomas*
Jan 23 1796    Cole, Eleanor to Renshaw, James
Feb  3 1792    Cole, Elijah to Phillips, Patsy
Jul  9 1796    Cole, Elizabeth to Baxley, Thomas*
Feb 25 1782    Cole, Elizabeth to Green, Abraham*
Apr 12 1796    Cole, Elizabeth to Smith, Bazel*
Jul 30 1796    Cole, Elizabeth to Willima, Nicholas*
Feb 15 1791    Cole, Giles to Osborne, Sarah*
May 23 1789    Cole, Godfrey to Keener, Elizabeth*
Feb  2 1786    Cole, Honour to Wheeler, James*
Aug 12 1790    Cole, James to Ensor, Eleanor*
Jul  9 1796    Cole, Jane to Evans, Edward*
Apr 16 1798    Cole, John to Christopher, Ann*
May  4 1782    Cole, John to Cullison, Elizabeth*
Dec 27 1782    Cole, John to Cunningham, Margaret*
Nov  8 1785    Cole, John to Maratle, Eleanor
Sep 25 1782    Cole, John to McCoon, Sarah*
Feb  4 1797    Cole, John to McDonogh, Mary*
Jun  1 1797    Cole, John to Young, Rachel*
Dec 24 1788    Cole, Joseph to Osborn, Sophia*
Oct 13 1789    Cole, Joshua to Lee, Ann*
Jun 19 1794    Cole, Lydia to Dorsey, Archibald*
Mar 18 1796    Cole, Margaret to Bryan, Peter*
Mar 13 1795    Cole, Margaret to George, Henry*
Dec 18 1793    Cole, Mary to Caple, Samuel*
Aug 17 1785    Cole, Mary to Cockey, John*
May  5 1791    Cole, Mary to Enloes, David*
Sep  8 1783    Cole, Mary to Ford, Barny*
Sep 12 1778    Cole, Mary to Ford, Joshua*
Feb 24 1797    Cole, Mary to Johnston, James
Oct 15 1794    Cole, Mordecai to Murray, Rachel*
May  4 1778    Cole, Mordecai to Price, Hatridge*
Sep  9 1782    Cole, Nancy to Bosley, John
Nov 15 1782    Cole, Nathan to Burk, Margaret*
Mar 15 1790    Cole, Nathan to Tudor, Darcus*
Jan  1 1783    Cole, Philip to Cockey, Elizabeth*
Nov 25 1789    Cole, Sarah to Anderson, Robert*
Mar 21 1795    Cole, Sarah to Eislin, Frederick*
Jun 10 1786    Cole, Sarah to Ford, Joshua
Jan 12 1791    Cole, Sarah to Gosnell, Mordecai*
Oct  1 1795    Cole, Sarah to Halfpenny, Patrick*
Jun  2 1789    Cole, Sarah to Pitts, Lewis*
Jan 14 1783    Cole, Sarah to Wyley, Walter*
Nov  3 1792    Cole, Stephen to Gorsuch, Rachel*
Oct 14 1786    Cole, Temperance to Green, Nicholas
Jan 13 1790    Cole, Thomas to Bosley, Rebecca*
Dec 17 1783    Cole, Thomas to Ford, Allatha*
Feb 15 1797    Cole, Thomas to Gardner, Rachel*
May 18 1782    Cole, Thomas to Hart, Jean
Mar 14 1792    Cole, Thomas to Hunter, Ann*
Dec 11 1798    Cole, Thomas to Tracey, Martha
May 14 1792    Coleby, Charles to Bind, Rachel*
```

```
Jan 20 1791    Colegate, Ann Eliz. Partridge to Emmerson, John*
Oct 26 1782    Colegate, Elizabeth to Prosser, Charles*
Feb 17 1781    Colegate, John to Ashman, Eleanor*
Jul 13 1798    Colegate, John to Stewart, Elizabeth*
Mar 11 1797    Coleman, Elizabeth to Riggen, Edmond*
Dec  8 1783    Coleman, John to Goodwin, Pleasance
Sep 16 1783    Coleman, John to Rainer, Mary
Dec  5 1787    Coleman, John to Springfield, Leah*
Jan 30 1793    Coleman, Joseph to McMeckin, Mary*
May  7 1795    Coleman, Pese Ann to Millerman, George*
Sep  7 1793    Coleman, Rachel to Bunts, Jacob*
Jun 12 1793    Coleman, William to Allen, Sinah*
Jul 27 1784    Coleman, William to Lebanus, Ann*
Mar  4 1797    Colgan, Mary to Brown, Thomas*
Oct  5 1798    Colgar, Margaret to Bradbury, Stephen*
Aug 30 1794    Collard, Sarah to Murphey, Peter*
May 23 1796    Collentine, Rebecca to Miller, Daniel*
Nov  1 1794    Coller, John to Cortz, Elizabeth*
Jan 20 1782    Collert, Joseph to Hammer, Catherine*
Dec 15 1781    Collett, Abraham to Curtis, Hannah*
Jan 29 1782    Collett, Jacob to Wyley, Elizabeth*
Oct  8 1778    Collier, John to Hardly, Esther*
Aug 30 1798    Collings, James to Donnellan, Mary*
Nov 21 1794    Collings, James to Moonshot, Sarah*
May  8 1797    Collings, Richard to Brown, Fanny*
Jul 16 1785    Collins, Ann to Thralls, Samuel*
May  5 1795    Collins, Diannah to Weaver, Daniel*
Nov  4 1784    Collins, Frances to Hill, James
Dec 23 1790    Collins, George to Bailey, Sarah*
Feb  8 1786    Collins, Hannah to Trimble, William*
Jan 27 1785    Collins, John to Carney, Mary*
Jan 23 1790    Collins, John to Church, Amelia*
Feb  4 1795    Collins, Lydia to McKubbin, James*
Mar  5 1783    Collins, Mary to Fowler, Richard
Jun 25 1796    Collins, Mary to Parks, Mayberry*
Aug  9 1792    Collins, Mary to Spiller, Timothy*
Nov 19 1796    Collins, Patsy to Brest, Clement*
Feb  5 1784    Collins, Sarah to Roulison, Moses*
Apr 21 1778    Collins, Timothy to McFee, Elizabeth*
Dec 27 1784    Collins, William to Waters, Judah
Mar 20 1792    Collison, Terry to Chrisholm, Thomas*
Dec 31 1792    Colvin, Philip to Desramcaus, Rossetta Martin*
Oct  5 1798    Combesh, Elizabeth to Noland, Peregrine*
Jan 15 1798    Comen, Catharine to McGrath, James*
Feb 16 1792    Comley, Mary to Merryman, Nicholas*
May 23 1783    Comryngham, Robert to Adams, Elizabeth*
Jun 11 1785    Comyn, Patrick to Deaver, Nancy
May 12 1789    Conaway, Richard to Burnett, Barbara*
Dec 20 1785    Conchlin, John to Merritt, Mary
May 29 1784    Concilman, Catherine to Hush, John
Aug 10 1779    Conden, Elizabeth to Carver, William*
May 12 1797    Conden, John to McDonogh, Sarah*
Oct 26 1779    Conden, Mary to Rheabottom, Thomas*
May 10 1788    Conden, Mary to Worrell, Thomas*
Nov  3 1785    Condreu, Ann to Sin, Edward
Jan  4 1798    Conely, Margaret to Windlake, Lawrence*
```

Sep 4 1778	Conkaway, Sarah to Smith, Henry*
May 20 1790	Conklan, Rachel to Deforrest, Henry*
Nov 6 1797	Conley, Philip to Reed, Sally*
Aug 11 1781	Conly, John to Kemp, Honor
Jan 13 1783	Conn, Elizabeth to Rhea, Joseph*
May 6 1784	Conn, Sarah to Duvall, Daniel*
Oct 10 1793	Connally, Ann to Arnoh, Joseph*
Jan 3 1795	Connally, Ceile Ann to St Clair, George*
Nov 25 1795	Connally, Eleanor to McClain, Roddy*
Jul 13 1790	Connally, Sarah to Loughhead, Adam*
Dec 17 1793	Connaway, America to Sadler, Mary*
Sep 5 1785	Connaway, Catharine to Smith, Aquila
May 6 1784	Connaway, Charles to Gardner, Catherine*
May 17 1792	Connaway, Samuel to Henry, Sarah*
May 24 1792	Conne, Catharine to Buckley, Lawrence*
Nov 20 1778	Connelly, Elizabeth to Arry, James*
Oct 7 1783	Connelly, John to Conner, Mary
Sep 8 1794	Conner, Catharine to Flaherty, Patrick*
Aug 26 1790	Conner, Jane to Willson, Matthew*
Oct 7 1783	Conner, Mary to Connelly, John
Jan 13 1795	Conner, Sarah to Monro, Jonathan*
Apr 14 1796	Conner, William to Meredith, Mary*
Jul 12 1794	Conners, Mary to Hughes, Henry*
Sep 13 1791	Connolly, Lucy to Little, Robert*
Dec 12 1785	Connor, Arthur to Loney, Mary
May 30 1795	Connor, Jane to Smith, John*
Jan 16 1781	Connors, Dennis to Burke, Mary*
Mar 19 1778	Connough, Mary to Taylor, William*
Jun 11 1793	Connoway, Pamelia to Ensor, William Burton*
Aug 12 1797	Connoway, Rebecca to Lee, William*
Sep 11 1788	Connoway, Susannah to Banks, William*
Dec 13 1783	Conor, Edward to Forbes, Rachel*
Sep 25 1794	Conoway, Deborah to Penn, William*
Apr 14 1781	Conoway, John to Banks, Elizabeth
Jan 6 1791	Conrad, Matthias to Fisher, Philepin*
May 29 1784	Conrod, John to Enloes, Sarah*
Jul 17 1781	Conroy, Barneby to Spicer, Jean
Aug 18 1795	Constable, Cassandra to Holbrooks, Thomas*
Jan 27 1791	Constable, Charles to Baker, Ann*
Jul 29 1794	Constable, Elizabeth to Keaton, William*
Nov 13 1793	Constable, Mary to Harris, William*
Jul 12 1796	Constable, Priscilla to Morrison, Patrick*
Aug 20 1788	Constantine, Edward to Demmitt, Catharine
Mar 23 1796	Conway, Greenberry to Cadle, Sarah*
Nov 24 1792	Conway, James to Atkinson, Amelia Elizabeth*
Jan 6 1797	Conway, John to Steele, Sarah*
Nov 10 1795	Conway, Rachel to Lytle, John*
Aug 25 1792	Conway, William to Atkinson, Sarah*
Apr 11 1795	Conway, William to Stewart, Hannah*
Oct 25 1797	Coogle, John to Green, Ann*
Jul 28 1792	Cook, Absolam to Wilson, Violet*
Jan 23 1795	Cook, Ann to Frizzle, Absalom*
Apr 19 1783	Cook, Elizabeth to Lockard, Matthew
Feb 20 1797	Cook, Emanuel to Gosnell, Ann*
Oct 18 1788	Cook, Greenbury to Basman, Arice*
Jan 10 1784	Cook, James to Bailey, Rachel

Dec 2 1793	Cook, James to Mappet, Margaret*
Mar 6 1786	Cook, John to Black, Elizabeth
Oct 21 1784	Cook, John to Curnoles, Sarah*
Oct 17 1798	Cook, Mary to Lee, John*
Oct 31 1778	Cook, Rebecca to Stansbury, Caleb*
Jul 14 1797	Cook, Susanna to Taron, William*
Jun 13 1778	Cook, Thomas to Simpson, Mary*
Nov 30 1791	Cook, Urith to Sindell, David*
Nov 9 1797	Cook, Zany to Linard, John*
Dec 12 1787	Cooke, Hannah to Meldrum, James
Jul 26 1792	Cooke, Samuel to Holland, Charlotte*
Sep 12 1798	Cooper, Agnes to Lourey, Samuel*
Jan 17 1795	Cooper, Anney to Odell, John*
Jun 1 1784	Cooper, George to Murphey, Susannah
Mar 24 1794	Cooper, John to Beach, Susannah*
May 18 1784	Cooper, John to Davison, Agnes*
Apr 29 1797	Cooper, John to McClellan, Elizabeth*
Mar 16 1791	Cooper, John to Shaffer, Apeloni
Feb 4 1790	Cooper, Juliet to Hale, Christian*
Mar 23 1785	Cooper, Juliet to Waggoner, George
Jan 28 1786	Cooper, Keziah to Taylor, William*
Apr 21 1798	Cooper, Margaret to McGill, Zachariah*
Nov 9 1796	Cooper, Margaret to Polk, David*
Oct 12 1796	Cooper, Mary to Fitzgerrald, Thomas*
Nov 30 1797	Cooper, Mary to McCurtz, George*
May 14 1795	Cooper, Rebecca to Dudley, James*
Dec 13 1793	Cooper, Robert Clark to Griffen, Rebecca*
Nov 22 1797	Cooper, Sarah to Forsyth, Jacob*
Dec 8 1797	Cooper, Sarah to Mason, Benjamin*
Jun 20 1798	Cooper, Stephen to Harting, Nancy*
Oct 6 1778	Cooper, Thomas to Gill, Catharine*
Jul 5 1781	Cooper, Thomas to Summers, Margaret*
Mar 30 1795	Cooper, William to Sample, Sarah*
Apr 22 1788	Copeland, Rachael to Ross, Hams*
Nov 11 1778	Copinger, Elinor to Enright, John*
Apr 28 1783	Corban, Joseph to Corban, Mary*
Apr 28 1783	Corban, Mary to Corban, Joseph*
Dec 6 1794	Corbet, Marie to Barbann, Louis*
Oct 1 1798	Corbin, Abraham to Bosley, Eleanor*
Feb 16 1785	Corbin, Elijah to Kelly, Sarah*
Mar 21 1797	Corbin, Elinor to Marsh, Beal*
Oct 3 1798	Corbin, Elizabeth to Parks, William*
Aug 4 1784	Corbin, Mary to Perdue, Walter*
Oct 5 1785	Corbin, Nathan to Anderson, Susannah
Apr 6 1793	Corbin, Patience to Byfield, Abraham*
May 6 1794	Corbin, Sayne to MacCreery, Nathaniel*
May 5 1795	Corbin, Thomas to Sinwal, Elinor*
Sep 19 1778	Corbin, Unity to McDaniel, Cornelius*
Jul 14 1792	Corbin, William to Leary, Catharine Maryann*
Dec 13 1777	Corbit, Patrick to Cunningham, Mary*
Nov 20 1790	Corbley, Nicholas to Kneass, Hannah*
Oct 22 1798	Cord, Abraham to Ford, Mary*
Feb 27 1790	Cord, Ann to Stinchcomb, Victory*
Feb 9 1798	Cord, Catharine to Hudson, John
Jun 15 1792	Cord, Elizabeth to Johnson, Thomas*
Mar 18 1778	Cord, John M. to Hendricks, Mary*

```
Nov 29 1794    Cord, John to Wilson, Mary*
Dec 29 1783    Cord, Mary to Hooper, Jacob*
Mar  1 1779    Cord, Rebecca to Randall, Aquilla*
Sep 27 1788    Cord, Sarah to Rowles, Ely*
May 20 1779    Corgonton, Mary to Sutton, Thomas
Jan 29 1782    Corilter, Elizabeth to Tate, James*
Apr  2 1784    Corn, Mary to Warren, Thomas*
May 29 1798    Cornelius, Hidey to Davidson, William*
Jul  5 1796    Corney, Elizabeth to Flinn, James*
Feb 21 1783    Cornhaven, Jacob to Carroll, Hannah*
Apr 24 1797    Cornical, Mary to Hay, James*
Feb  1 1781    Cornish, Joseph Rouse to Tooly, Abigail Harper*
Sep 28 1793    Cornish, Levin to Govax, Milly*
Oct  3 1792    Cornmiller, Jacob to Robinson, Jane*
Dec  8 1783    Cornstat, John to Brown, Keziah
May 26 1796    Corrie, Elizabeth to Savage, Patrick*
Oct 22 1798    Corrie, Margaret to Fitzgerald, Richard*
Jul  2 1798    Corrie, Patience to Flinn, James
Nov 29 1783    Corrigan, Edward to Scott, Mary*
Apr 27 1785    Corsuch, Mary to Perrigoy, Joseph
Jun 20 1778    Corter, Hannah to Lewis, James*
Jun  1 1778    Corty, Mary to Reynolds, Robert*
Nov  1 1794    Cortz, Elizabeth to Coller, John*
Jun  4 1794    Cosden, Jeremiah to Buchanan, Eleanor*
Sep 12 1798    Cosh, Joseph to White, Polly*
Feb  4 1792    Coskery, Patty to O'Brian, Charles*
Jan 19 1797    Cosset, Catharine to Starkins, Thomas*
May 16 1782    Costin, James to Wandiford, Rebecca
Apr 24 1788    Cotrell, Rachael to Holland, Daniel*
May 20 1795    Cotteral, James to Harryman, Charity*
Mar 27 1779    Cottom, William to Edwards, Elizabeth*
Dec 10 1783    Cottonal, Frances to Hews, James*
Mar 15 1785    Cottonal, Mary to Davis, Ezekiel
Jan 20 1796    Cottrel, Ruth to Tucksworth, Robert*
Oct 19 1796    Cottrell, Thomas to Hughes, Margaret
Jul  3 1783    Couch, Ann to Nash, John*
Dec 24 1795    Coughlin, Frances to Smith, Edward*
May 25 1786    Coughran, John to Dunavin, Mary*
Mar 17 1779    Couile, Michael to Casey, Bridget*
Apr  4 1778    Couling, James to Sullers, Elizabeth*
Dec 10 1784    Coulon, John Baptist to Mangee, Mary*
Mar 29 1792    Coulter, Alexander to McCaskey, Hetty*
Jan 26 1797    Coulter, Alexander to McCoon, Jane*
Feb  2 1788    Coulter, John to McCasky, Mary*
Nov  3 1796    Coulter, John to Muckleroy, Margaret*
Jun 11 1798    Councilman, George to Fitch, Sarah*
Jul 25 1778    Councilman, John to Turnpaugh, Mary*
May 31 1786    Councilman, Margaret to Franklain, Thomas*
Dec 22 1781    Councilman, Margaret to May, Benjamin
Apr 25 1792    Counsilman, Catherine to Franklin, Charles
Sep  3 1796    Courtenay, Elizabeth to Geddes, David*
Nov 18 1794    Courtenay, James to Mitcheson, Mary*
Sep 30 1790    Courtnay, Robert to Burland, Elizabeth
Oct 16 1790    Courtney, Hercules to Drury, Mary*
Oct 13 1798    Cousins, Mary to Peterson, Lawrence*
May  2 1794    Cousron, Olivier to Troure, Jane Faurline*
```

Feb 16 1790	Covel, Jonathan to Forrest, Ann
Aug 29 1785	Covenhoon, William to Pindell, Eleanor*
May 18 1795	Covinton, Levin to Green, Mary*
Jun 17 1795	Cowan, Alexander to Hubbert, Rody*
Sep 15 1785	Cowan, Elizabeth to McClain, James*
Dec 29 1783	Cowan, Elizabeth to Stevenson, John*
Nov 30 1777	Cowan, James to McDonald, Elizabeth*
Jan 2 1783	Cowan, Lewis to Banks, Milly*
Aug 28 1793	Cowan, Mary to Middleton, John*
Mar 10 1796	Cowan, Susannah to Sharp, William*
Jul 13 1796	Cowan, Thomas to Venny, Margaret*
Nov 17 1787	Cowan, William to Stewart, Catherine*
Nov 4 1796	Coward, Jemina to Taylor, James*
Apr 1 1794	Coward, Naomi to Favery, Thomas*
Oct 5 1781	Coward, Richard to Goldsbury, Elizabeth
Sep 2 1797	Coward, William to Tuines, Sophia*
Dec 16 1780	Cowden, John to Peters, Frances*
Sep 30 1779	Cox, Abraham to Tipton, Cassanna*
Oct 13 1796	Cox, Catharine to Allen, Jesse*
Jul 1 1790	Cox, Catharine to McCoy, Charles*
Apr 16 1785	Cox, Dinah to Young, William Price*
Apr 25 1783	Cox, Elijah to Gill, Elizabeth*
May 29 1797	Cox, George to Lewis, Biddy*
Nov 9 1785	Cox, Israel to Hopkins, Elizabeth
Dec 8 1796	Cox, James to Fulford, Catharine*
Jan 30 1790	Cox, Jane to Quinland, Edmund*
Sep 24 1789	Cox, Matthew to McMechen, Rebecca*
Sep 15 1791	Cox, Robert to Johnston, Jannet*
Jan 13 1795	Cox, Sally to Waddle, William*
Jun 11 1795	Cox, Samuel to Fowler, Eleanor*
Sep 6 1797	Cox, Sarah to Tracey, George*
Sep 17 1783	Cox, William to Bosley, Susanah*
Feb 2 1798	Cox, William to Tipton, Rebecca*
Aug 19 1789	Cox, William to West, Mary*
Dec 23 1797	Cracroft, Luke to Hall, Alice*
Apr 10 1797	Cradock, Mary to Cromwell, Stephen*
Jan 20 1798	Craff, Jacob to Taylor, Averilla
Aug 1 1782	Crag, Sarah to Drake, John*
Dec 11 1787	Crage, Mary to Fitchwick, James
Apr 16 1794	Craig, Collin to Hill, Sarah*
Jan 23 1797	Craig, Grace to Hall, William J.*
Jul 31 1794	Craig, Mary to Joice, Pearce*
Jul 2 1795	Craig, Nancy to Patterson, William*
Feb 10 1795	Craig, Sarah to Himes, James*
Dec 29 1796	Craig, Thomas to Thomas, Bethia*
Sep 12 1793	Craigh, Stephen to Allen, Mary*
Sep 30 1790	Cramblet, Henry to Dunham, Martha*
Oct 14 1786	Cramblet, Michael to Randall, Ruth*
May 7 1796	Cramblet, Stephen to Day, Avis*
Aug 30 1794	Cramer, Edward to Britt, Mary*
Mar 7 1798	Cramer, Philip to McKean, Peggy*
Feb 5 1789	Cramlet, Ann to Howard, Joshua*
Mar 11 1788	Cramlet, Mary to Chambers, Amos*
May 14 1783	Cramphin, Polly to Griffin, George*
Jun 8 1793	Crane, William to Henshaw, Nancy
Feb 21 1789	Cranford, John to Seargant, Priscila*

Mar 9 1783	Crapper, Sarah to Hays, Joel*
Oct 23 1781	Craton, Ann to Johnson, David*
Oct 16 1786	Craton, Deborah to Brian, Daniel
Jun 13 1786	Craton, Nancy to Hooper, Henry*
Jan 13 1796	Crawford, Alexander to Ryan, Sarah*
Jun 13 1793	Crawford, Ann to Longfield, George*
Mar 2 1795	Crawford, Richard to Bolahouse, Margaret*
Feb 21 1794	Crawford, Samuel to Parker, Ann*
Mar 3 1793	Crawford, Seth to Campbell, Catherine*
Nov 27 1795	Crawley, Eleanor to Zeckley, William*
Nov 5 1796	Cray, John to Divier, Mary*
Mar 3 1791	Creaman, Eleanor to Carson, Nathaniel*
Aug 19 1793	Creamer, Edward to Fokey, Eleanor*
Apr 24 1792	Creamer, Elizabeth to Mencer, George*
Jul 12 1784	Creamer, Mary to Vian, John
Jun 2 1785	Creamer, Valuntine to Bancks, Rachael*
Jul 12 1779	Creamour, Mary to Burdsel, Thomas*
Feb 11 1783	Creggel, Charlotte to Wells, Cornelius
Nov 16 1796	Creigh, Ann to Bagford, William*
Dec 4 1783	Creighton, John to Flood, Elizabeth*
Oct 11 1797	Cremore, Susannah to Pine, Thomas*
Oct 16 1798	Crips, Sarah to Gums, Manuel*
Oct 5 1790	Crisall, Peter to Richards, Margaret*
Sep 27 1782	Criss, Sarah to Granger, Joseph*
Oct 12 1793	Crissman, Mary to Stigar, Matthias*
Sep 2 1797	Criswell, Ann to Miller, Nicholas*
Apr 9 1791	Criswell, James to Wages, Elizabeth*
Oct 27 1797	Criswell, Richard to Lane, Elizabeth*
Jul 2 1785	Crocker, Casper to Achenbaugh, Nancy
Jun 4 1781	Crocker, Thomas to Cole, Dealy*
Feb 18 1784	Crocket, Henry to Merrick, Ann*
Mar 8 1785	Crockett, Benjamin to Donnallin, Jane
Oct 3 1786	Crockett, Elizabeth to Skinner, Thomas
Aug 10 1778	Crockett, Jane to Fulton, John*
Sep 14 1795	Crockett, Margaret to Johnson, Francis*
Oct 1 1791	Crockley, Polly to Dorsey, Levin*
Jun 28 1789	Croghan, James to Waitman, Elizabeth
Apr 12 1783	Crohan, Matthew to Armstrong, Jane*
Oct 12 1791	Crombrie, Elizabeth Aber to Manus, Joseph*
Nov 3 1784	Cromey, Mary Abbey to French, Benjamin*
Sep 19 1794	Cromley, Mary to Miller, Christian*
Jun 21 1798	Cromwell, Ann to Bagnell, Michael*
Apr 23 1794	Cromwell, Ann to Herring, Langford*
Dec 23 1783	Cromwell, Ann to Stevenson, Sater*
Apr 12 1793	Cromwell, Comfort to Dunkill, George A.*
Oct 13 1796	Cromwell, Eleanor to Lee, Thomas*
Feb 2 1790	Cromwell, Elizabeth to Ash, James*
Oct 6 1785	Cromwell, Elizabeth to Chenowith, Samuel*
Nov 14 1785	Cromwell, Elizabeth to Merryman, Elijah
Jan 9 1794	Cromwell, Frances to Messersmith, William*
Feb 21 1782	Cromwell, Henrietta to Cockey, Joshua*
Dec 6 1787	Cromwell, John to Owings, Urath*
Sep 12 1793	Cromwell, John to Rowles, Elizabeth (widow)*
Feb 1 1788	Cromwell, John to Williams, Ruth*
Dec 10 1780	Cromwell, Joseph to Stansbury, Keziah*
May 23 1785	Cromwell, Lydia to Logue, John Smith

Oct 8 1796	Cromwell, Margaret to Pumphrey, Cockey*
May 1 1794	Cromwell, Margaret to Stevenson, George*
Sep 18 1782	Cromwell, Mary to Pumphrey, William
Mar 21 1782	Cromwell, Oliver to Pumphrey, Margaret*
Feb 21 1797	Cromwell, Philemon to Fisher, Mary
Feb 24 1778	Cromwell, Ruth to Williams, Brown*
Jan 10 1792	Cromwell, Sarah to Linthicum, Amasa*
Aug 11 1794	Cromwell, Sarah to Longley, Edmund*
Nov 6 1778	Cromwell, Sarah to Miles, Thomas*
Apr 10 1797	Cromwell, Stephen to Cradock, Mary*
Nov 3 1796	Cromwell, Susannah to Bond, William*
May 24 1784	Cromwell, Thomas to Waters, Ann
Mar 21 1793	Cromwell, William to Walker, Anne
Jun 23 1779	Cron, Margaret to Jain, Samuel
Sep 24 1796	Cronan, Catharine to Blair, John*
Jun 20 1783	Crone, Kitty to Onion, Stephen*
Jun 12 1792	Croner, Frederick to Watkins, Rebecca Gassaway*
Nov 17 1796	Croney, James to Rowles, Alice*
Oct 29 1791	Cronmiller, Philip to Myer, Margaret*
Mar 7 1786	Crook, Catherine to Dallas, Walter Riddle
May 26 1795	Crook, George to Morrow, Jane*
Dec 22 1787	Crook, Margaret to Wood, Thomas*
Jun 10 1778	Crook, Sarah to Buck, Joshua*
May 22 1793	Crook, Walter to Atler, Mary*
Nov 13 1778	Crook, William to Walsh Mary
Oct 16 1781	Crooks, John to Owings, Rachel
Jan 30 1794	Crookshanks, Mary to Chamberlain, George Robins*
Mar 22 1797	Crosby, Mary to Howard, Philip*
Aug 30 1794	Crosillant, Joackim to Round, Charlotte*
Nov 3 1790	Cross, Barton to Cross, Ruth*
Nov 15 1797	Cross, Bridget to Henry, Samuel*
Dec 15 1781	Cross, Gabriel to Jackson, Agness*
Dec 21 1795	Cross, Jemima to Murphey, Bazel*
Jun 30 1785	Cross, Jemimah to West, William
Jan 12 1798	Cross, John to Williams, Mary*
Jan 11 1793	Cross, Levina to Hollingsworth, Henry*
Mar 25 1796	Cross, Margery to Jean, Joseph*
Jan 7 1794	Cross, Nicodemus to Gladman, Barbary*
Jan 22 1783	Cross, Rebecca to Norris, Abraham*
Mar 3 1795	Cross, Robert to Hilderbrand, Catharine*
Jun 11 1794	Cross, Robert to Lewis, Charlotte*
Nov 3 1790	Cross, Ruth to Cross, Barton*
Mar 7 1797	Cross, Sarah to Foster, Nicholas
Aug 23 1778	Crouder, Ealy to Woolf, Lovep*
Oct 4 1794	Crouse, Christian to Zegland, Catherine*
May 30 1789	Crow, James to Tevis, Rachael*
Dec 21 1797	Crow, Thomas to Galloway, Eleanor*
Feb 28 1785	Crow, William to McCoy, Sarah
Apr 6 1778	Crowe, Margaret to Thomas, James*
Apr 8 1778	Crowe, Margaret to Thomas, James*
Apr 26 1779	Crowley, Margaret to Marten, William
Feb 5 1794	Crowley, Mary to Hooper, William*
Mar 14 1786	Crowse, George to King, Nancy
Jun 12 1781	Croxall, Charles to Morris, Mary*
Mar 11 1788	Croxall, James to Gittings, Eleanor*
Nov 26 1791	Croxall, John to Hannah, Isabella*

Aug 19 1784	Cruise, Catherine to Toole, James*
Dec 10 1789	Cruse, Jacob to Hoffman, Mary*
Aug 4 1794	Cruses, Elizabeth to Fisher, Joseph*
Aug 7 1783	Crust, Elizabeth to Fisher, Michael*
Sep 28 1784	Cryer, Jacob to Willoughby, Sarah
Apr 19 1778	Culbertson, William to Robinson, Harriott*
Jul 13 1791	Cullerson, Margaret to Applegarth, James*
Feb 7 1797	Cullidon, George to File, Catharine*
May 10 1797	Cullin, Travers to Hall, Ellinor*
Dec 20 1797	Cullings, Isaac to Downey, Martha*
Nov 14 1793	Cullison, Ann to Hughes, Young Samuel*
Feb 13 1795	Cullison, Delile to Malonee, James*
May 4 1782	Cullison, Elizabeth to Cole, John*
Aug 30 1784	Cullison, Jesse Stansbury to Pickett, Susannah
Apr 3 1779	Cullison, Joshua to Wheeler, Elizabeth
May 15 1795	Culverwell, Mary to Keppler, John T.*
Jul 29 1786	Culverwell, Richard to Randell, Rebecca
Apr 16 1795	Cummins, Elizabeth to Pearce, Thomas*
Jul 27 1793	Cummins, Jane to Burns, James*
Jun 27 1797	Cummins, Mary to Long, Samuel*
Oct 11 1798	Cunningham, Andrew to Black, Elizabeth*
Dec 10 1796	Cunningham, Betsey Ann to Brown, John*
Jul 27 1786	Cunningham, Elizabeth to Duvitt, Thomas
Aug 4 1779	Cunningham, George to Carroll, Sarah*
Dec 10 1794	Cunningham, John to Leary, Catharine*
Dec 25 1795	Cunningham, John to Peola, Mary*
Nov 3 1783	Cunningham, Judith to Brady, John*
Dec 27 1782	Cunningham, Margaret to Cole, John*
Dec 13 1777	Cunningham, Mary to Corbit, Patrick*
Dec 21 1782	Cunningham, Michael to Rowles, Leah
Dec 10 1795	Curnan, Frances Todd to Wilkinson, Robert*
Oct 21 1784	Curnoles, Sarah to Cook, John*
Dec 31 1777	Curran, Mary to Ruliff, Gilbert*
Jul 16 1792	Curran, William to Buckingham, Elizabeth*
Feb 28 1793	Curren, John to Walsh, Mary*
Sep 12 1786	Currey, Elizabeth to Taylor, Hugh
Sep 10 1796	Currough, Sarah to Weaver, John*
Feb 12 1784	Curry, Ann to Moore, John*
Aug 12 1786	Curry, John to Soreah, Sarah
Mar 13 1794	Curson, Richard to Moale, Elizabeth*
Jul 5 1798	Curtain, James to Hay, Ann*
Jan 6 1798	Curteain, Sarah to Fossey, John*
Sep 5 1795	Curtfield, Mary to Shane, Joseph*
Feb 21 1797	Curtin, Thomas to Graves, Jane*
Jun 28 1790	Curtis, Benjamin to Perigo, Deborah*
Feb 27 1796	Curtis, Edmund to Kirby, Elizabeth*
Sep 5 1788	Curtis, Eleazer to Karns, Bridget*
Feb 26 1794	Curtis, Elizabeth to Hines, William*
Dec 15 1781	Curtis, Hannah to Collett, Abraham*
Jan 5 1784	Curtis, John to Edwells, Peggy*
Oct 18 1784	Curtis, Joseph to Walker, Mary*
Jul 30 1798	Curtis, Urith to Bennet, Richard
Apr 17 1793	Curtis, William to Sheppherd, Ann
Feb 8 1794	Curtis, William to Turine, Mary*
Jun 25 1789	Cushion, Robert to Shipley, Susannah*
May 30 1795	Cushion, Thomas to Smith, Catharine*

May 14 1782	Daffin, Mary to Mitchell, John*
Oct 20 1798	Dafourneq, A.J. St. Martin to Delaprade, Jean T.C.*
Dec 14 1795	Dagan, Elizabeth to Russell, William*
Aug 12 1793	Dagon, Peter to McCuming, Sarah
Jan 31 1798	Dailey, John to Keefe, Ally*
Jun 23 1795	Dailey, Margaret to Selbrue, Louis*
Jan 3 1798	Dailey, Mary to Deshaw, Peter*
Oct 15 1798	Dais, Joseph A.L. to Ducasse, Marie F.*
Jan 11 1781	Daizell, Elizabeth to Roe, James*
Jul 7 1795	Dakings, Joseph to Mannings, Eliza*
Dec 27 1798	Daley, Daniel to Killum, Elizabeth*
Nov 18 1795	Daley, Mary to Myers, Nicholas*
Nov 20 1794	Dall, James to Holliday, Sarah Brooke*
Jan 19 1790	Dall, James to Lane, Charlotte*
Mar 7 1786	Dallas, Walter Riddle to Crook, Catherine
Feb 10 1781	Dallis, Catherine to Galloway, Thomas*
Jan 20 1798	Dalton, George to Vinny, Catharine*
Oct 21 1784	DalZivcount, Peter Antony Balne to Bassow, Louise
Mar 22 1783	Danach, John to Clouse, Mary*
May 19 1795	Dance, Mary to Davidson, Robert*
Sep 15 1798	Dancer, William to Brien, Susannah*
Mar 21 1797	Danecole, Jac Bernard to Evans, Sally*
Dec 2 1797	Danfary, Barthazan Maurice to Mureno, Catharine E.*
Dec 1 1795	Dangston, Mary to Wetherstrand, Thomas*
Jan 27 1783	Daniley, Michael to Sadler, Catherine*
Mar 2 1782	Danily, Dolly to Fenton, Charles*
Apr 16 1795	Dannenberg, Frederick William to Koenig, Dorothea*
Jan 23 1796	Danososte, Guilliaume to Murray, Elizabeth*
Feb 12 1795	Daplan, Marie Caterine to Panterr, Antoine*
Dec 16 1795	Darbin, Polly to Talbot, James*
Aug 9 1792	Darel, Annaa to Keens, Joseph*
Apr 27 1790	Darier, Susanna to Epaugh, George*
Sep 16 1788	Darley, Michael to Miller, Caroline*
Dec 14 1798	Darnale, Francis to Fidings, Margaret*
Apr 25 1792	Darrell, Elizabeth to Keys, John*
Aug 9 1796	Darton, Sarah to Simmons, William*
Sep 3 1796	Dashield, Daniel to Dashield, Polly*
Oct 30 1798	Dashield, Margaret to Anthony, Joseph*
Sep 3 1796	Dashield, Polly to Dashield, Daniel*
Aug 3 1795	Dashiell, Christy to Story, George L.*
Sep 9 1798	Daster, John B. to Burgoyne, Catharine*
Jun 8 1790	Daughaday, Joseph to Taylor, Sarah*
May 10 1798	Daughaday, Mary to Norris, John*
Jul 30 1793	Daughady, Abraham to Wheeler, Susannah*
Sep 20 1794	Daughady, John to Hales, Mary
Oct 21 1795	Daughady, John to Leakins, Rachel*
Dec 5 1798	Daughady, Johnsey to Owings, Susanna*
Aug 3 1797	Daugherty, Catharine to Manson, William*
Mar 3 1791	Daugherty, Hugh to Steitz, Ann*
May 23 1796	Daugherty, Joseph to Holmes, Joyce*
Sep 23 1794	Daugherty, Neal to Green, Mary*
Nov 9 1796	Daugherty, Neal to James, Mary*
Nov 14 1798	Daugherty, Susanna to Deale, Henry*
Apr 27 1790	Daugherty, William to Towson, Ruth*
Jul 10 1794	Daull, Susannah to Harris, James*
Aog 30 1796	Dauphin, Elizabeth to Matthews, James*

```
Dec 21 1780    Daus, Josiah to Hallock, Margaret*
Aug 14 1798    Dava, Sarah to Saul, Christian*
Jul  9 1778    Davage, Mary to Elder, Elijah*
Jun 19 1779    Davage, Sarah to Joice, William
Jun 18 1779    Davage, Sarah to Joice, William
Oct 26 1794    Davenport, Elizabeth to Rice, James*
Jul 20 1785    Davey, Catherine Sarah to McKim, Alexander
Feb  7 1798    Davey, Charlotte to Clarke, Henry*
Dec  3 1789    Davey, Elizabeth to Evans, Joseph*
Oct 11 1783    Davey, Henrietta Mariah to James, John
Feb 25 1786    Davey, Michael to Knowland, Ann
May 23 1791    David, Lucy to Haskan, Josiah*
Mar 17 1788    Davidson, Alexander to Young, Mary
Nov 13 1795    Davidson, Andrew to Somerville, Mary*
Jun 19 1792    Davidson, Elizabeth to Lambert, Richard*
Jul  4 1798    Davidson, James to O'Cay, Elizabeth*
May 17 1778    Davidson, Job to Miller, Elizabeth*
Sep 29 1798    Davidson, John to Lowman, Lydia*
May 19 1795    Davidson, Robert to Dance, Mary*
Nov 24 1787    Davidson, Samuel to Dunbar, Jane*
Mar 11 1797    Davidson, Sarah to Denmeade, John*
May 29 1798    Davidson, William to Cornelius, Hidey*
Oct 10 1796    Davies, Mary Ann to Bail, Robert P.*
May  1 1778    Davis, Alexander to Doyle, Elizabeth*
Aug  6 1785    Davis, Ambrou to Grover, Elizabeth*
Oct 21 1797    Davis, Amos to Carson, Mary*
Oct  3 1783    Davis, Andrew to Robinson, Elizabeth*
Nov  3 1788    Davis, Ann to Scott, Burrage*
Nov 12 1778    Davis, Avis to Smith, Bazil*
Aug 27 1796    Davis, Barny to Mitchell, Mary*
May 15 1792    Davis, Benjamin to McClown, Ann*
Sep 20 1798    Davis, Betsy to Hassard, John
Sep  3 1783    Davis, Betsy to Welsh, John*
Jan 28 1796    Davis, Catharine to Jackson, Isaiah*
Jul 25 1784    Davis, Christian to Sweeting, Mary
Jan 15 1784    Davis, Daniel to Jorden, Elizabeth
Feb  4 1786    Davis, Daniel to Leech, Mary
May  2 1785    Davis, Edward to Londiman, Catherine
Jun  1 1797    Davis, Elias to Smith, Catharine*
Apr 30 1778    Davis, Elizabeth to Brown, John*
Mar 28 1796    Davis, Elizabeth to Casey, Robert*
Jul 27 1785    Davis, Elizabeth to Enloes, Thomas
Jul  7 1795    Davis, Elizabeth to Law, James*
Dec  3 1796    Davis, Elizabeth to Musgrove, Samuel*
May  5 1792    Davis, Elizabeth to Undewood, John*
Jul 28 1786    Davis, Elizabeth to Wooderd, John
May 10 1794    Davis, Eloha to Stansbury, Hannah*
Mar 15 1785    Davis, Ezekiel to Cottonal, Mary
Nov  2 1796    Davis, Francis to Bennett, Milly*
Nov 19 1783    Davis, Gilbert to Ratcliff, Elizabeth
Sep 23 1794    Davis, Harriot to Sumblin, William*
Jan 21 1795    Davis, Henry Ferguson to Britt, Elizabeth*
Apr  5 1798    Davis, Henry to Butler, Sarah*
Jan 22 1785    Davis, Ichabod to Randall, Delilah*
Aug 27 1791    Davis, James to Hudson, Elizabeth*
Dec 22 1798    Davis, John to Beatty, Eleanor
```

Jun 16 1795	Davis, John to Bordan, Mary*
Dec 10 1782	Davis, John to Bosley, Mary*
Jan 18 1782	Davis, John to Brown, Mary*
Jul 7 1790	Davis, John to Brown, Sophia*
Feb 20 1789	Davis, John to Dorsey, Elinor*
Dec 14 1784	Davis, John to Vaughan, Sarah
Aug 27 1784	Davis, Joseph to Rowles, Catharine*
Dec 24 1792	Davis, Kiddwallader to Potter, Margaret*
May 7 1784	Davis, Luke to Shepherd, Ann
Apr 11 1795	Davis, Marmaduke to Forrest, Dravsilla*
May 5 1778	Davis, Mary to Gardener, Richard*
Aug 21 1790	Davis, Mary to Harding, Matthew*
Aug 17 1784	Davis, Mary to Smith, James*
Jul 19 1782	Davis, Moses to Dun, Catherine
Mar 29 1785	Davis, Nancy to Lague, Aquila
Feb 16 1785	Davis, Nathaniel to Hutson, Margaret*
Nov 15 1797	Davis, Polly to Bond, John Pitts*
Jun 19 1797	Davis, Polly to McDonald, Alexander*
Dec 24 1793	Davis, Presilla to McCaine, James*
May 4 1784	Davis, Rebecca to Burnham, John*
Mar 15 1797	Davis, Rebeccah to Shaw, William*
Oct 4 1779	Davis, Richard to Johns, Rachel*
Mar 20 1782	Davis, Robert to Ratcliff, Susannah
Aug 17 1796	Davis, Rodey to Busk, Greenbury*
Oct 16 1790	Davis, Ruth to Randall, Nathan*
Oct 8 1795	Davis, Samuel to Renshaw, Deborah*
Mar 30 1796	Davis, Samuel to Rust, Hannah*
Apr 14 1781	Davis, Sarah to Hardin, Ignations
Dec 17 1798	Davis, Sarah to Mason, Thomas*
Oct 9 1791	Davis, Sarah to McConnell, Alexander*
Aug 1 1781	Davis, Sarah to Rowles, David*
Sep 9 1797	Davis, Susanna to Callahan, William
Nov 17 1778	Davis, Susannah to Dent, George*
Apr 9 1794	Davis, Susannah to Talbott, Henry*
Dec 8 1782	Davis, Thomas to Tippet, Margaret
Aug 2 1795	Davis, Thomas to Young, Margaret*
May 8 1795	Davis, William L. to Stubbs, Sarah*
Jan 13 1784	Davis, William to Burkhead, Margaret*
Feb 14 1797	Davis, William to Butler, Elizabeth*
Dec 11 1794	Davis, William to McMahon, Mary*
Jun 30 1796	Davis, William to Owings, Ruth*
Apr 9 1794	Davis, William to Wells, Rachel*
Jul 16 1779	Davisen, Andrew to Stokes, Ann
May 18 1784	Davison, Agnes to Cooper, John*
Jan 21 1783	Davison, Andrew to Donnal, Miszey*
Jul 3 1779	Davisson, Peter to Kelly, Mary
Mar 29 1786	Daw, Joseph to Carr, Sarah*
Jul 31 1783	Dawbridge, Jane to York, William
Sep 24 1796	Dawney, John to Blaney, Jane*
Sep 10 1796	Dawney, William to Green, Elizabeth*
Dec 29 1784	Daws, Meral to Johnson, Israel Hendrick
Jun 16 1781	Dawson, Elizabeth to Selman, Jonathan
Feb 20 1782	Dawson, Hannah to Jones, David Smith*
Sep 25 1795	Dawson, Henne to Laying, Thomas*
Aug 6 1795	Dawson, John to Caulk, Frances*
May 22 1794	Dawson, Philemon to Henderson, Jane*

```
Mar 23 1779    Dawson, Rebecca to Aitherton, James*
Aug 27 1785    Dawson, Sarah to Jenny, Nathaniel
Mar 19 1795    Dawson, William to Robertson, Ann*
Jan 28 1793    Day, Anne to Amergist, Christian*
May  7 1796    Day, Avis to Cramblet, Stephen*
Nov 11 1787    Day, Edward to Presbury, Mary
May 26 1778    Day, James to Jonston, Elizabeth*
May 10 1792    Day, John to Kitley, Providence*
Feb  5 1794    Day, Lydia to Geddes, David*
Apr 23 1796    Day, Sarah to Hale, Joseph*
Dec  8 1785    Day, Sarah to Wetherall, James
Aug 27 1778    Day, Thomas to Dean, Hannah*
Jan  2 1796    Day, William to Dells, Alice*
Jun 23 1797    De Boydene, Marie to Reo, Peter*
Oct  9 1797    De Breelin, Aramintha to McGonagall, Rowland
Dec 27 1794    De Carnass, Jasper to Richardson, Elizabeth*
Apr  7 1785    de la Mark, John F. C. B. to Brooks, Elizabeth
May 19 1794    De Ladebat, Auguste P.S. to Vallerot, Jeanne S.L.A.*
May 15 1794    De Margueret, Tourneroche to Morton, Adalin*
Feb  2 1798    De Narbes, Jeaune J.R. to Leclaire, Lewis Sebast
Oct  4 1794    de Rabar de Bomale, Marie Claire to Montonroy, Louis*
Jul  9 1785    Deagle, Lamon to Budiel, Elizabeth*
Nov 14 1793    Deagle, Mary to Berru, Jacob Michael*
Nov 26 1783    Deal, Christian to Stiles, Hannah*
May 27 1794    Deal, Michael to Agnew, Nancy*
Nov 14 1798    Deale, Henry to Daugherty, Susanna*
Feb 18 1795    Deale, Mary to Pecker, Joseph*
Aug 21 1794    Dean, Ann to Duvall, Beal*
Nov  5 1790    Dean, Barney to Ratcliff, Catherine
Mar 12 1778    Dean, Ezekiah to Lownea, Rebecca*
Aug 27 1778    Dean, Hannah to Day, Thomas*
Sep 18 1790    Dean, Joshua to Jones, Nanny*
Jan  7 1790    Dean, Lydia to Phalan, Jepe*
Jun 28 1785    Dean, Martha to Odenbaugh, Charles*
Sep 10 1790    Dean, Milcah to Shipley, Elijah*
Jan 12 1798    Dean, Nancy to Ensor, James*
Oct 10 1791    Dean, Prudence to Kirby, James*
Jun 10 1782    Dean, Rebecca to Dunn, Patrick
Dec 10 1791    Dean, Robert to Young, Margaret*
Mar  7 1791    Dean, Sarah to Allen, William
Oct  5 1784    Dean, Sarah to Taylor, John
Sep  3 1796    Dean, Susannah to Carr, Daniel*
Jun  7 1794    Dean, Thomas to Armand, Peggey*
Oct 21 1791    Dean, Thomas to Jackson, Elizabeth*
Jan 26 1781    Dear, Elizabeth to Lugar, Jacob*
Jan 15 1794    Dear, John Kean to Ellis, Mary*
Feb  2 1778    Dearfield, Godfrey to Bloom, Clorcy*
Sep  4 1790    Dearmona, Catharine to Merrick, William*
May 25 1779    Deavannah, Seater to Ropkins, Samuel
Dec 19 1796    Deaver, Ann to Tipton, Brian*
Feb 15 1798    Deaver, Hugh to Holbrooks, Darky
Dec 13 1777    Deaver, Jemima to Pickett, William*
Jan 11 1797    Deaver, John to Hunt, Sarah*
Jun  9 1778    Deaver, Martha to Talbot, Benjamin R.*
Jan  9 1793    Deaver, Mary to Stinchcomb, John*
Jun 11 1785    Deaver, Nancy to Comyn, Patrick
```

Jun 5 1779	Deaver, Philip to Cole, Ann*
Oct 6 1790	Deaver, Richard to Pierce, Deborah*
Mar 11 1778	Deaver, Susannah to Wright, Daniel*
Jul 27 1784	Deaver, William to Chinia, Rachel*
Sep 4 1786	Deavour, Jonas to Scott, Temperance
Aug 26 1783	Debauler, William to Kitely, Hannah*
Jul 24 1784	Deblegey, Elizabeth to Low, John*
Sep 20 1797	Debraudon, Theresa to Rousseau, Charles*
May 5 1791	Dechamp, Elizabeth to Glarany, Francis Henry
Aug 16 1792	Decker, George to Forney, Susannah*
May 9 1788	Decker, Jacob to Turnpaugh, Margaret*
Jun 8 1796	Decourse, Sarah to Kirby, James*
May 10 1798	Deddep, John to Stoxdale, Rachel*
Mar 6 1790	Deffidaffer, Elizabeth to Barry, John*
Nov 3 1783	Deffin, Delila to Powell, Richard*
May 20 1790	Deforrest, Henry to Conklan, Rachel*
Sep 15 1794	DeGoff, Sophia to Delisle, John Baptiste Godart*
Jun 25 1791	Deigers, Rachel to Stewart, James*
Aug 25 1778	Deisdel, Peggy to Armstrong, James*
Jun 15 1795	Deiter, Margaret to Menson, Gabriel*
Jun 4 1795	Deiter, Susannah to Gisse, Peter*
Jan 8 1794	Delahay, Sophia to Ward, Charles*
Nov 26 1782	Delahon, Margaret to Ammery, William
Sep 26 1778	Delany, Peter to Fitzgerald, Bridget*
Oct 20 1798	Delaprade, Jean T.C. to Dafourneq, A.J. St. Martin*
Apr 20 1784	Delasera, Barbier Chevellier to Dulany, Nancy
Feb 11 1786	Delat, Augustine to Ross, Frances
Nov 25 1790	Delaunay, Jacque A. to Lebourdais, Therese C.M.H.*
Jun 4 1779	Delay, Catharine to Smith, John
Feb 12 1794	Delevet, Peter to Jones, Ann*
Sep 19 1795	Deliquit, _____ to McSherry, Elizabeth*
Sep 15 1794	Delisle, John Baptiste Godart to DeGoff, Sophia*
May 6 1797	Delisle, John Godart to Laroche, Elizabeth*
Nov 18 1785	Delisle, John to Blieze, Mary
Feb 19 1785	Delislle, Hillaire to Poreura, Mara Rose*
Jan 24 1782	Delker, Christiana to March, Nicholas*
Oct 21 1795	Dell, Esther to Walker, Thomas*
Oct 29 1796	Dell, John to Norton, Mary*
Nov 28 1793	Dell, Peter to Kelley, Nancy*
Aug 16 1779	Dellero, Thomas to Lynch, Elizabeth*
Jan 2 1796	Dells, Alice to Day, William*
Oct 1 1789	Dells, Ann to Gue, Joseph*
Aug 15 1797	Dells, Elizabeth to Thompson, Jonathan*
Dec 13 1792	Delord, Sophia Francois to Breard, Michael Augustus
Mar 31 1790	Delphia, Richard to Buckingham, Hannah
Feb 25 1791	Delphy, John to Buckingham, Ann*
May 11 1791	Deluce, Francis to Hallock, Elizabeth*
Nov 17 1794	Demangin to Calwell, Ruth*
Sep 6 1793	Demarick, Frances to Despo, Joseph*
Jan 14 1797	Demmitt, Burch to Legness, Catharine*
Aug 20 1788	Demmitt, Catharine to Constantine, Edward
Dec 12 1789	Demmitt, Elizabeth to Chote, Edward*
Apr 15 1786	Demmitt, Hollin to Irgrig, John*
Feb 4 1796	Demmitt, Margaret to Bussey, Thomas D.*
Jan 9 1796	Demmitt, Margaret to Low, David*
Sep 7 1791	Demmitt, Rachel to Devenport, Nicholas*

```
Feb 15 1794    Demmitt, Thomas to Wright, Rachel*
Aug 30 1796    Demmitt, William to Traplin, Nancy*
Nov 23 1798    Demmott, Elisha to Jessop, Delilah
Jun  3 1788    Dempsey, Luke to Scott, Sarah*
Aug 27 1796    Dempsey, Mary to Leary, Andrew*
Jan 23 1796    Dempsey, Patrick to McDermot, Elizabeth*
Jun  2 1781    Demsey, Elizabeth to Worthington, William*
Jun 29 1781    Denion, Ann to Hatton, China
Mar 11 1797    Denmeade, John to Davidson, Sarah*
Dec 26 1796    Denning, Oliver to Flowers, Mary*
Nov 30 1793    Denning, Peggy to Mitchell, John*
Jul 22 1797    Dennis, James to Jones, Polly*
May 20 1779    Dennis, Margaret to Mahue, Samuel*
Mar 24 1797    Dennis, Martha to Hewitt, Eli*
Jan 22 1785    Denny, Elizabeth to Risteau, John Talbott*
Aug 16 1790    Denny, Hanny to Robeson, Thomas
Jun 12 1788    Denny, William to Biays, Elizabeth*
Jan 30 1798    Densel, Elizabeth to Selvers, John*
Nov 17 1778    Dent, George to Davis, Susannah*
Jan 22 1784    Dentling, Elizabeth to Lavely, Andrew*
Jan 21 1795    Denton, Darcus to Green, Ezekiel*
Sep 15 1779    Denton, Elizabeth to Raby, Richard*
Dec 23 1796    Denton, Hannah to Gray, Lyncy*
Apr 17 1795    Denton, James to Green, Temperance*
Apr  4 1795    Denton, John to Beamer, Susannah*
Apr  2 1783    Denton, John to Hendrickson, Ann*
Nov 10 1784    Denton, John to May, Margaret*
Aug  8 1783    Denton, Rachael to Hodges, William*
Nov 24 1796    Deny, Neal to Anderson, Rebecca*
Jan  4 1794    Derga, Pearl to Gaile, Jonna*
Jul 15 1784    Derick, David to Griffin, Jemimah*
Jul  2 1790    Derochbroom, Lewis to Walmsley, Rachael*
Dec 14 1795    Desbordes, Antoine G.L. to Tilly, Marie Claire LG.*
Oct 24 1793    Deschamp, Fanny to Isoard, Joseph*
Oct 24 1793    Deschamp, Magdaline to Carre, Joseph*
Jan  3 1798    Deshaw, Peter to Dailey, Mary*
Dec 26 1795    Deshayes, Lucy Jane to Salvan, Joseph Lewis*
Nov  3 1793    Desize, Jean Baptiste A.M. to Baron, Marie L.V.*
Sep  6 1793    Despo, Joseph to Demarick, Frances*
Dec 31 1792    Desramcaus, Rossetta Martin to Colvin, Philip*
Jul 20 1782    Desshiels, Polly to Latreyte, John
Sep 12 1796    Deterly, Peter to Reese, Elizabeth*
Mar 22 1798    Deuham, Robert to Hunt, Eliza*
Jul 18 1794    DeValcourt, Alexander to Gold, Margaret*
Feb 15 1796    Devall, Thompsa to Wells, Thomas*
Mar  6 1793    Deveney, Darcus to Ogston, Henry*
Sep  7 1791    Devenport, Nicholas to Demmitt, Rachel*
Aug 28 1782    Deverex, Sarah to Thorpe, Benjamin*
May  5 1788    Devers, John to Eagleston, Belinda*
Nov  9 1797    Device, John Darch Livel to Summers, Margaret*
Oct  7 1784    Devilbiss, Frederick to Shultz, Polly*
Apr 16 1798    Devin, Cain to Shrurick, Elizabeth*
Oct 20 1794    Devine, Elizabeth to Elwood, Thomas*
Sep 17 1794    Devonsher, Henry to Cole, Arabella*
Apr  4 1793    Dew, Mary to Evans, Nathaniel
Jul 23 1796    Dew, Robert to Stansbury, Elizabeth
```

```
Feb  2 1793    Dewall, Jeremiah to Warfield, Elizabeth*
Sep 29 1798    Dewhurch, Hannah to Lane, Elijah
Aug 17 1785    Dewley, Catherine to Truck, Esau
Jun 21 1792    Dexter, James to Bouer, Ann*
Jan 31 1783    Dey, Rebecca to Weston, John*
May 16 1797    Diamond, Ann to Gorsuch, Joshua*
Nov 13 1778    Dicas, James to Mushaw, Elizabeth*
Jan  3 1778    Dicas, John to Leatherwood, Sarah*
Jul 20 1797    Dicke, Maria to James, Abraham*
Mar 26 1783    Dickinson, Ann to Sharp, Peter*
Mar 25 1794    Dickinson, David to Hickey, Eleanor*
Jul 14 1796    Dickinson, Gideon to Leister, Priscilla*
Feb 15 1794    Dickinson, Sarah to Wright, Samuel*
Aug 13 1782    Dicks, Ann to Pruet, Sylvester*
Mar  1 1783    Dicks, Catherine to Ensor, Abraham*
Dec 24 1785    Dickson, Eleanor to Williams, John
Nov 12 1798    Dickson, Isaac to Sarah, Susannah
Sep 19 1798    Dickson, Sarah to Ryan, Philip*
Feb 21 1795    Dicus, Jacob to Riddle, Sarah*
Jun 11 1785    Dieter, Jacob to Hitterpraugh, Susannah
Jul  8 1794    Diffenderffer, Mary to Klein, Jacob*
Jun 19 1783    Diffenderffer, Samuel to Messersmith, Elizabeth*
Jan  3 1798    Diffendirffer, Eve to Albers, Luider*
Sep  4 1792    Diffindolph, Catherine to Herther, Nathan
Apr 20 1798    Digabeau, John to Holmes, Magdelane*
Jul 21 1797    Dilhelms, Henrietta to Henninger, Philip*
Apr 22 1796    Dilley, Henry to Gaul, Catharine*
Jan  2 1796    Dillihunt, John to Newman, Harriet*
Sep  9 1794    Dillon, Margaret to Carey, Dennis*
Jan  4 1792    Dillon, Margaret to Elms, Samuel*
Jan 21 1793    Dills, Sarah to Ridgely, Beale
Jun 17 1795    Dilworth, Amos to Randall, Margaret*
Nov  6 1784    Dilworth, Joseph to Allen, Ann
Jul 15 1789    Dilworth, Letitia to James, John*
Sep 11 1788    Dilworth, William to Greenfield, Kezia*
Nov 15 1796    Dimmet, Henry to Bond, Elizabeth*
Dec 22 1784    Dimmett, Dealley to Gorsuch, Charles
Dec  9 1783    Dimmitt, Richard to Merryman, Rebecca*
Nov 18 1780    Dine, Magdalain to Landry, George*
Jan  9 1798    Dinemore, Thomas to Dodds, Hannah*
May 18 1796    Dines, Mary to Wheeler, Philip*
Nov  3 1798    Dinsmore, Margaret to Dodds, John*
Feb 25 1795    Disnee, Elizabeth to Whittle, Zachariah*
Jun 11 1796    Disney, Benjamin to Abbet, Sarah*
May  3 1796    Disney, Solomon to Fitz, Rachal*
Mar 16 1792    Ditleff, Christian to Henly, Ann*
Feb 20 1781    Ditter, John to Chapman, Elizabeth*
Sep 22 1796    Diverbaugh, Jacob to Horn, Catharine*
Jan 22 1793    Divers, Sarah to Lucas, John*
Nov  5 1796    Divier, Mary to Cray, John*
Jun 12 1794    Divirce, Ann to Remage, Nicholas*
Sep 23 1779    Dixen, John to Roberts, Clovander*
Nov  2 1791    Dixon, Raphael to Parks, Rachael*
Aug 31 1782    Dixon, Thomas to Frazier, Elizabeth*
Mar 22 1796    Doah, James to Gribel, Sarah*
Sep 14 1796    Doah, James to Myers, Polly*
```

```
Mar 20 1797    Dodd, Abraham to Smith, Elizabeth*
Jun  6 1782    Dodd, John to Bond, Ann
Aug 12 1797    Dodd, Priscilla to Clarke, John*
Jan  9 1798    Dodds, Hannah to Dinemore, Thomas*
Nov  3 1798    Dodds, John to Dinsmore, Margaret*
Oct 10 1793    Dodge, Samuel to Stansbury, Ann*
Oct 10 1778    Doe, Joseph to Jones, Mary*
Jun 15 1798    Doions, Margaret to Downey, William
Jun 16 1778    Dolphin, Peter to Hults, Elizabeth*
Oct 17 1789    Donaldson, Elizabeth to Cavey, Thomas*
Jun 28 1791    Donaldson, James to Berbine, Elizabeth*
Apr  8 1797    Donaldson, John to Philips, Priscilla*
Feb 25 1796    Donaldson, William to Chamberlaine, Priscilla*
Sep 21 1796    Donavan, Elizabeth to Bitlers, John*
Apr 17 1795    Donlind, John to Gilberthorp, Ann*
Jan 21 1783    Donnal, Miszey to Davison, Andrew*
Mar  8 1785    Donnallin, Jane to Crockett, Benjamin
Jun 19 1794    Donnallin, Nehemiah to Mull, Mary*
Mar 16 1793    Donnalls, Anthony to Mincoy, Anna Mana*
May 15 1794    Donnavan, Valentine to McKenzie, Eleanor*
Aug 30 1798    Donnellan, Mary to Collings, James*
Nov 28 1782    Donnellan, Mary to Loney, Amos
Apr  2 1798    Donnelly, James to McKinzie, Mary*
Jun  1 1778    Donnigan, Catherine to Donnigan, John*
Jun  1 1778    Donnigan, John to Donnigan, Catherine*
Feb 12 1784    Donning, John to Stull, Margaret*
Aug  6 1794    Donoran, Mary to Jack, John*
May 27 1785    Donovan, Catherine to Watts, Samuel
Aug  8 1782    Donovan, Sarah to Gorsuch, Robert*
Jan  3 1793    Donsheath, Mary to Goghan, John
Sep 20 1784    Donwilly, Robert to Kidd, Eleanor*
Nov  8 1796    Dooley, Sarah to Ulary, Anst*
Apr 15 1796    Dopp, Henry to Martin, Rachel*
Oct 26 1784    Dorman, Cornelius to Casment, Ann*
May 10 1794    Dorman, William B. to Gorsuch, Julian*
Nov  8 1797    Dorsen, Mable to Barnes, James*
Jan  1 1784    Dorsey, Achsah to Dorsey, Thomas Beale*
Dec 10 1787    Dorsey, Achsah to Gwinn, Edward*
Mar 13 1794    Dorsey, Achsah to Owings, Isaac*
May  8 1784    Dorsey, Amos to Dorsey, Polly*
Sep 14 1782    Dorsey, Ann to Worthington, John*
Jun 19 1794    Dorsey, Archibald to Cole, Lydia*
May 15 1788    Dorsey, Arianna to Owings, Samuel*
Sep  6 1786    Dorsey, Bazel John to Hanes, Dolley*
Dec  7 1784    Dorsey, Bazel to Odel, Rachel*
Nov 30 1784    Dorsey, Benjamin to Sellman, Pamelia
Aug 24 1789    Dorsey, Charles to Anchors, Elizabeth
Feb 18 1794    Dorsey, David to Porter, Mary*
Dec  4 1790    Dorsey, Deborah to Wilson, Joshua*
Nov  8 1788    Dorsey, Dennis to Elder, Tarisha*
Nov 30 1797    Dorsey, Derias to Talbott, Mary*
Mar 25 1786    Dorsey, Edward to Dorsey, Elizabeth*
Feb 21 1786    Dorsey, Edward to Lawrence, Susannah*
Jun  8 1781    Dorsey, Edward to McCubbin, Deborah*
Feb 13 1788    Dorsey, Elias to Lawrence, Polly
Jun  2 1779    Dorsey, Elias to Snoden, Susannah*
```

Feb 20 1789	Dorsey, Elinor to Davis, John*
May 15 1788	Dorsey, Elizabeth Goodwin to Scott, John Jr.*
Mar 25 1786	Dorsey, Elizabeth to Dorsey, Edward*
Feb 13 1790	Dorsey, Elizabeth to Frost, John*
Apr 27 1795	Dorsey, Elizabeth to Hawkins, John*
Nov 14 1798	Dorsey, Ellin to Ruckle, John*
Feb 21 1778	Dorsey, Ely to Barnes, Ellis*
Dec 1 1791	Dorsey, George to Ridgely, Rachel*
Oct 14 1797	Dorsey, Henrietta to Dorsey, Owen*
Feb 21 1786	Dorsey, Henry to Mackubbin, Mary
Dec 8 1798	Dorsey, Hezekiah to Talbott, Mary*
Mar 14 1797	Dorsey, Jemima to Warfield, Alexander*
Jun 18 1783	Dorsey, John Lawrence to Selmon, Ann*
Nov 30 1792	Dorsey, John to Gist, Jemima*
Sep 28 1791	Dorsey, John to Stocksdale, Airy*
May 30 1778	Dorsey, John W. to Worthington, Cornford*
Feb 16 1789	Dorsey, Joshua to Hammond, Henrietta
Oct 1 1791	Dorsey, Levin to Crockley, Polly*
Jan 26 1797	Dorsey, Lloyd to Green, Anna*
Oct 25 1788	Dorsey, Lucy to Stevenson, Samuel*
Dec 11 1790	Dorsey, Mary to Hopkins, David*
Dec 4 1795	Dorsey, Mary to Ingram, Clark*
May 23 1795	Dorsey, Mary to Lawrence, Levin*
Apr 15 1788	Dorsey, Mary to Norwood, Samuel*
Feb 1 1794	Dorsey, Nancy to Elder, Owen*
Jan 26 1786	Dorsey, Nancy to Grover, Benjamin*
Apr 8 1797	Dorsey, Nicholas to Lindsey, Kassandra*
Oct 14 1797	Dorsey, Owen to Dorsey, Henrietta*
May 23 1782	Dorsey, Patt to Hobbs, Margaret
Dec 13 1787	Dorsey, Philip to Joyce, Elizabeth*
May 8 1784	Dorsey, Polly to Dorsey, Amos*
Oct 14 1782	Dorsey, Priscilla to Carnan, Charles Ridgely*
Oct 8 1781	Dorsey, Prissilla to Wilmott, Robert
Oct 19 1791	Dorsey, Rachel to Glover, Joshua*
Feb 17 1786	Dorsey, Rebecca to Mercer, Peregrine
Feb 18 1790	Dorsey, Ruth to Owings, Beale*
Jan 23 1795	Dorsey, Samuel to Preston, Clementine*
Aug 19 1786	Dorsey, Sarah to Lawrence, Leaven
Jan 1 1784	Dorsey, Thomas Beale to Dorsey, Achsah*
Mar 14 1786	Dorsey, Vachael to Ireland, Clementina*
Feb 24 1778	Dorsey, Vachel to Batty, Elizabeth*
Sep 17 1791	Dorter, Archibald to Fowler, Elizabeth*
Aug 11 1783	Dorum, Ann to Wilson, Thomas*
Sep 29 1784	Dougherty, John to McCormick, Margaret*
Feb 23 1791	Dougherty, John to Woolerick, Mary*
Apr 3 1786	Dougherty, Sarah to Isour, Joshua*
May 29 1781	Douglass, Elizabeth to Heswell, John Jona Vanden*
May 23 1795	Douglass, George to Boucher, Frances*
Mar 13 1779	Douglass, Rebecca to McLure, John*
Jan 20 1785	Dounhour, Jacob to Foulk, Elizabeth*
Nov 26 1798	Dowdd, Charles to Moore, Margaret*
Apr 27 1786	Dowdel, Barbara to Emmitt, David*
Mar 2 1781	Dower, Elizabeth to Liscum, John*
May 30 1778	Dowlan, Charles to Brannigan, Ann*
Oct 6 1792	Dowlen, James to Neilson, Mary
Jun 10 1794	Downes, Thomas to Marsh, Susannah*

Feb 13 1794	Downes, William to Burns, Margaret*
Jun 3 1791	Downes, William to Jones, Sarah*
May 29 1784	Downey, John to Ptoxall, Emey*
Feb 18 1797	Downey, Margaret to Tracy, John*
Dec 20 1797	Downey, Martha to Cullings, Isaac*
Jul 3 1783	Downey, Matthias to Jones, Elizabeth*
Jul 1 1788	Downey, Philip to Wright, Sarah*
Nov 17 1796	Downey, Sarah to Hawkins, Joseph*
Jun 15 1798	Downey, William to Doions, Margaret
Sep 23 1796	Downey, William to Parks, Dorothy*
Dec 14 1798	Downie, Thomas to Tracy, Margaret*
Apr 6 1792	Downing, Mary to Maxfield, Hezekiah*
Sep 29 1792	Downs, Robert to Witzell, Allafar
Jan 22 1783	Doyel, Mary to Baker, John*
Apr 29 1786	Doyle, Cynthia to Merryman, Benjamin of William*
Sep 5 1792	Doyle, Elizabeth to Armorgost, Peter*
May 1 1778	Doyle, Elizabeth to Davis, Alexander*
May 24 1798	Doyle, Elizabeth to McKinzie, Archibald*
Jun 4 1798	Doyle, Elizabeth to Slebe, Thomas*
Apr 18 1786	Doyle, John to Grafton, Sarah*
Mar 18 1788	Doyle, Margaret to Murray, Ephraim
Dec 11 1790	Doyle, Margaret to Powell, Thomas*
Dec 28 1782	Doyle, Nancy to Floyd, Joseph
Jun 5 1794	Doyle, Nicholas to McDaniel, Nancy*
Aug 19 1794	Doyne, John to Myers, Mary*
Oct 24 1797	Doyne, Robert to Hamilton, Jane Flemming*
Dec 8 1784	Drain, John to Sollers, Barbara*
Aug 1 1782	Drake, John to Crag, Sarah*
Jun 2 1795	Drake, Mary to Fitzgerald, John*
Aug 25 1795	Drake, Nancy to Carroll, Michael*
Dec 31 1790	Drane, Rachael to Richardson, James*
Apr 30 1789	Drane, Rebecca to Gray, Joshua
Oct 2 1788	Draves, Mary to Bryan, John*
Feb 20 1794	Draynan, Sarah to Kelly, John*
Jun 16 1792	Drepbert, Christian to Forney, Mary*
Dec 27 1788	Dreppard, Andrew to Ilger, Katharine
Oct 1 1796	Dresser, Alfred to Powers, Rachel*
Jul 14 1785	Dresson, Katharine to Westrum, Andrew*
Dec 19 1785	Drew, Anthony to Nelson, Priscilla*
Jan 5 1793	Drinan, Thomas to Pinson, Mary*
Dec 5 1796	Drisher, Kitty to Hare, John*
Oct 21 1779	Driskell, Mary to Healy, John*
May 3 1792	Driver, James to Hobbs, Lucy*
Apr 6 1779	Drumbo, Conrad to Neff, Caterena*
Feb 14 1784	Drummond, Hugh to Cadle, Elizabeth*
Oct 16 1790	Drury, Mary to Courtney, Hercules*
Jul 26 1796	Dubread, Maria Rose to Wante, Chas. Stephen Peter*
Oct 15 1798	Ducasse, Marie F. to Dais, Joseph A.L.*
May 21 1795	Ducatel, Edna to Pineau, Anne*
Jan 9 1793	Duckeman, Francis to Mongean, Margaret*
Jun 23 1781	Ducker, Elizabeth to Sappinton, John
Aug 2 1794	Duckier, Elizabeth to Frazier, William*
May 14 1795	Dudley, James to Cooper, Rebecca*
Apr 9 1778	Dudley, Joseph to Loten, Ann*
Aug 26 1785	Dudley, Sarah to Martin, Isaac
Sep 10 1791	Duff, John to Green, Sarah*

Oct 18 1796	Duffey, John to Grimes, Hannah
Mar 29 1788	Duffey, Owen to Williams, Mary*
Oct 31 1786	Dugan, Cumberland to Kelsoe, Margaret
Aug 22 1789	Dugan, James to Gutry, Ann*
Jun 7 1783	Dugan, James to Masterson, Honor*
Oct 2 1798	Dugan, Margaret to Smith, William R.*
Jan 21 1796	Dugan, Nancy to Henry, William*
Dec 30 1793	Dugan, Peter to Tully, Elizabeth*
Aug 25 1783	Dugan, Thomas to Fowler, Rebecca*
Jun 3 1778	Dugmore, Isabella to Flisher, John*
Jan 9 1782	Dugmore, Martha to Edwards, William*
Jul 25 1798	Duharty, Susanna Catharine to Stupery, Pierce*
Jun 15 1792	Duhig, Oliver to Headekin, Catherine*
Mar 23 1797	Duke, Christian to Duke, Jane*
Mar 23 1797	Duke, Jane to Duke, Christian*
Apr 15 1795	Duke, Rebecca to Hopkins, John*
May 26 1794	Duke, Rebecca to Hopkins, Nicholas*
Oct 21 1790	Dukehart, Elizabeth to Ball, William*
Sep 20 1784	Dukehart, Henry to Dutroe, Elizabeth*
Oct 7 1784	Dukehart, Satah to Riley, Benjamin*
Aug 1 1785	Dukes, Christopher to Graves, Jane
Jun 12 1779	Dukes, Elizabeth to Whigley, Isaac
Jul 23 1783	Dulany, Kitty to Belt, Horatio Sharp
Apr 6 1798	Dulany, Mary to Raynaud, Francis R.B.*
Apr 20 1784	Dulany, Nancy to Delasera, Barbier Chevellier
Sep 26 1793	Duln, Elizabeth to Shryock, Jacob*
Nov 25 1783	Duloy, Nancy to Benno, Matthew*
May 1 1792	Dulshary, John to Franklin, Catherine*
Nov 6 1778	Dumatz, John to Galloway, Mary*
Sep 3 1779	Dumont, John to Bauk, Ann
Jul 19 1782	Dun, Catherine to Davis, Moses
May 25 1786	Dunavin, Mary to Coughran, John*
Nov 24 1787	Dunbar, Jane to Davidson, Samuel*
Jan 9 1798	Dunbar, William to Wells, Martha
Jul 3 1778	Dunbo, Elizabeth to Witson, Thomas*
Nov 25 1790	Duncan, Easter to Leahy, John*
Aug 24 1793	Duncan, nancy to Scott, Samuel*
Nov 21 1798	Duncan, Perry to Bryden, Mary*
Aug 12 1778	Duncan, Perry to Hook, Elizabeth*
Sep 4 1790	Duncan, William to Talbot, Martha*
Aug 21 1794	Duncin, Elizabeth to Elston, Thomas*
Jul 22 1795	Dunderson, Allie to Britt, Humphrey*
Dec 8 1796	Dungan, Benjamin to French, Elizabeth*
Aug 22 1797	Dungan, Benjamin to Rusk, Anne*
Feb 20 1796	Dungan, Easter to Armstrong, William*
Feb 13 1796	Dungan, Elizabeth to Anderson, Andrew*
JUl 16 1794	Dungan, Elizabeth to Rowles, Jacob*
Jun 26 1794	Dungan, Mary to Baker, John*
Sep 28 1797	Dungan, Thomas to Gray, Mary*
Sep 30 1790	Dunham, Martha to Cramblet, Henry*
Nov 8 1798	Dunington, Handley to McGale, Margaret S.*
Apr 12 1793	Dunkill, George A. to Cromwell, Comfort*
Jul 18 1789	Dunkin, Ann to McColin, Dennis*
Dec 2 1791	Dunkin, Elizabeth to Highjoe, Philip*
Sep 22 1789	Dunkin, Hester to Taylor, Joseph*
Oct 30 1779	Dunkin, Mary to Button, Elias*

```
Jul 21 1788    Dunkin, Mary to Dunkin, William*
Jun 28 1794    Dunkin, Sarah to Hook, William*
Dec 10 1793    Dunkin, Sarah to Lock, Thomas*
Dec 23 1791    Dunkin, Susannah to Robb, John*
Dec 10 1791    Dunkin, Thomas to Wright, Mary*
Jul 21 1788    Dunkin, William to Dunkin, Mary*
Feb  1 1794    Dunkin, William to Rice, Bridget*
Jun 19 1794    Dunlap, Charles to Byerley, Christine*
Apr 28 1795    Dunn, Ann to Smith, Leakin*
Nov  8 1783    Dunn, Catherine to Gregory, John*
Jun 14 1794    Dunn, Edward to O'Hagan, Mary*
Oct  3 1794    Dunn, Elizabeth to Floyd, Charles*
Jan 10 1792    Dunn, Hannah to Burk, Richard*
May 31 1786    Dunn, Henry to Brown, Kesiah*
Dec 24 1782    Dunn, James to Hodges, Sarah
May 16 1783    Dunn, Jane to Wood, Robert*
Oct 19 1793    Dunn, Mary to Thompson, Edward*
Jul  9 1788    Dunn, Michael to McGuire, Mary*
Jun 10 1782    Dunn, Patrick to Dean, Rebecca
Jun 20 1790    Dunnavan, Pierce to Harris, Nelly*
Oct 18 1794    Dunnaway, Nancy to Riney, John*
Sep 24 1789    Dunning, Dennis to Dutton, Nancy*
Sep  9 1798    Dunning, James to Plueburn, Mary*
Oct 20 1798    Dunns, Daniel to Park, Elizabeth*
Aug 10 1784    Dunsheaf, Jane to Workman, Robert
Sep 24 1789    Dunwick, Isaac to Ray, Jane*
Apr 14 1791    Dunwoody, Ann to Eccles, Samuel*
Feb 27 1796    Dunwoody, Robert to McCann, Ann*
Jun 20 1797    Dupeiy, Helene F.J. to Amie, Jean B. Jos. A.*
Mar 15 1797    Durka, Pearl to Hankey, Mary*
Jun 25 1782    Durmeste, John to Keeports, Elizabeth
Dec 22 1792    Dutro, George to Stansbury, Elizabeth
Sep 20 1784    Dutroe, Elizabeth to Dukehart, Henry*
Sep 24 1789    Dutton, Nancy to Dunning, Dennis*
Feb  2 1798    Duvall, Airy to Yerrington, Richard*
Aug 21 1794    Duvall, Beal to Dean, Ann*
May  6 1784    Duvall, Daniel to Conn, Sarah*
Jun 18 1783    Duvall, Frances to Duvall, John*
Nov 24 1798    Duvall, Job to Hands, Margaret*
Jun 18 1783    Duvall, John to Duvall, Frances*
Feb 12 1793    Duvall, Richard to Baker, Elizabeth
Sep 19 1797    Duvernous, Louise to Placide, Paul*
Jul 27 1786    Duvitt, Thomas to Cunningham, Elizabeth
Feb 10 1798    Duyer, William to Casey, Elizabeth*
Mar 23 1796    Dwier, Eleanor to Andrews, Edmond Burns*
Feb  2 1798    Dwyer, Mary Ann to Williams, Hugh*
Jan 20 1797    Dycas, Isaac to Williams, Susannah*
Oct  7 1782    Dyer, Esther to Henderson, Gilbert*
Dec 22 1795    Dykes, William to Chiddick, Margaret*
Oct 18 1792    Dysart, James to Ellender, Catherine*
Jul 18 1794    Dysort, Catharine to Sampson, George*
Apr 10 1795    D'Alban, Anne Francoise to Faune, Joseph*
Mar 16 1781    Eaden, Robert to Poole, Minah
Oct 16 1782    Eades, John to Holton, Sarah
Nov 17 1796    Eagan, Catharine to Key, Abner*
Aug 30 1783    Eagan, John to Clements, Mary
```

```
Nov  1 1797   Eagleston, Abraham to Hughes, Rebecca
Jan 30 1784   Eagleston, Ann to Fitch, Henry*
May  5 1788   Eagleston, Belinda to Devers, John*
Nov 29 1784   Eagleston, Charity to French, Otho*
Sep 25 1793   Eagleston, Delinah to Smith, John*
Jan 23 1793   Eagleston, Eleanor to Wood, Charles*
Dec  8 1798   Eagleston, John to Burch, Fanny
Sep  2 1783   Eagleston, Mary to Wigley, Edward*
Feb 20 1784   Eaglestone, Elizabeth to Reese, George*
Feb  2 1785   Eaglestone, Mary to Harryman, John*
Oct  3 1786   Eakley, Sarah to Haslep, Rezin
Aug 31 1779   Eames, Luke to Barry, Catherine*
Nov  1 1791   Eara, Elizabeth to Teret, Valentine*
Oct 10 1793   Earnest, George to Both, Rachel*
May 22 1784   Earp, Elizabeth to Jones, Jacob*
Jan 17 1795   Eastburn, Hetty to Murehert, John*
Feb  2 1781   Eaton, Biddy to King, Michael*
Dec 16 1797   Ebbeck, John Frederick to Fry, Catharine*
Mar 30 1778   Ebbert, John to Hitejus, Catharina*
Apr 12 1782   Ebbert, John to Ritter, Caterena
Aug 14 1790   Eberhart, Jacob to Block, Catherine*
Sep  3 1779   Ebert, George to Jackson, Margaret
Dec  6 1788   Ebert, John to Odle, Elizabeth*
Nov 17 1791   Eccles, Margaret to Watkins, William*
Apr 14 1791   Eccles, Samuel to Dunwoody, Ann*
Nov 23 1792   Eccleston, Abraham to Austin, Jane*
Mar 21 1778   Eckard, Barbara to Jordan, Thomas*
Oct 19 1791   Ecle, Philip to Tinges, Mary*
Oct  8 1789   Eden, Elizabeth to Smith, John*
Jun  2 1797   Eden, Garret to Watson, Agness
Sep  6 1786   Edgar, Mark to Lone, Abagail*
Feb 17 1796   Edger, Abigail to Strawbridge, Theophelus*
Jun 20 1791   Edmonston, Alexander to Jones, Cassandra*
May 30 1785   Edwards, Catherine to Edwards, Joseph*
Aug  3 1785   Edwards, David to Kettle, Elizabeth*
Mar 27 1779   Edwards, Elizabeth to Cottom, William*
May 19 1785   Edwards, Ephraim to Sinclair, Elizabeth*
Jul 15 1784   Edwards, Heathcoat to Towson, Dorcas
Jan 15 1791   Edwards, John to Greenfield, Dinah*
Dec  7 1796   Edwards, Jonathan to Middleton, Mary S.*
May 30 1785   Edwards, Joseph to Edwards, Catherine*
Oct 21 1783   Edwards, Margaret to Fonerdan, John
Aug 15 1795   Edwards, Margaret to Pease, Dennis*
Mar  1 1779   Edwards, Mary to Kelly, Michael*
Sep 18 1792   Edwards, Paul to Snidorff, Mary*
Sep 10 1785   Edwards, Paul to Travolet, Sarah*
Mar 28 1793   Edwards, Philip to Rollins, Ann*
Aug 27 1796   Edwards, Polly to Adair, Abraham*
Sep 18 1798   Edwards, Thomas to Gordan, Anne*
Jan  9 1782   Edwards, William to Dugmore, Martha*
May 21 1794   Edwards, William to McCollom, Ann*
Jan  5 1784   Edwells, Peggy to Curtis, John*
Dec 25 1794   Egleston, Sarah to Thompson, David*
Oct 18 1785   Eichelberger, Jacob to Barneston, Elizabeth*
May 10 1781   Eichelberger, Martin to Welsh, Elizabeth*
Nov 26 1788   Eiglehart, Edward to Herrine, Sophia*
```

Apr	19	1791	Elphenston, David to Hambleton, Lydia*
Mar	21	1795	Eislin, Frederick to Cole, Sarah*
Jun	8	1791	Elcon, Eve to Batline, Joseph*
Nov	7	1798	Elder, Deliah to Lindsey, Sarah*
Jun	30	1781	Elder, Delilah to Tonstell, Henry
Jul	9	1778	Elder, Elijah to Davage, Mary*
Mar	1	1779	Elder, Elinor to Ridges, Jonathan*
Apr	7	1798	Elder, Elizabeth to Beasman, Joshua*
Nov	5	1791	Elder, Jemima to Brown, David*
Sep	6	1794	Elder, John to Greenwood, Margaret*
Dec	31	1793	Elder, Michael to Petticoat, Pleasant*
Feb	1	1794	Elder, Owen to Dorsey, Nancy*
Feb	27	1789	Elder, Providence to Shipley, Robert*
Nov	8	1788	Elder, Tarisha to Dorsey, Dennis*
Sep	22	1797	Eldon, Charles to Howard, Sarah*
Feb	10	1792	Elender, George to Grimes, Sarah*
Nov	28	1792	Elfry, Mary to Reed, Hugh*
Jul	4	1781	Elivil, Samuel to Riddy, Margaret*
Jan	17	1785	Elizabeth, Mariah to Sligh, John*
Aug	7	1794	Elkins, Catharine to Sanger, Seth*
Nov	7	1780	Elkins, Ellen to Berneston, Thomas*
Aug	10	1797	Elkins, Joseph to Fonts, Nancy*
Oct	26	1795	Elkins, Margaret to LeBaren, Leonard*
Oct	18	1792	Ellender, Catherine to Dysart, James*
Sep	23	1793	Ellerton, Ann to Higgins, Edward*
Aug	4	1792	Ellick, Ann to McFadon, William*
Jun	30	1778	Ellicott, David to Evans, Martha*
Sep	5	1790	Ellicott, Elizabeth to Ellicott, Nathaniel
Jun	22	1778	Ellicott, Latissa to Evans, John*
Oct	6	1785	Ellicott, Mary to Brown, Thomas
Sep	5	1790	Ellicott, Nathaniel to Ellicott, Elizabeth
Oct	22	1796	Ellicott, Tacey to McPherson, Isaac*
Jan	16	1789	Elliert, Harlman to Vernet, Elizabeth*
Sep	28	1784	Elliot, Susannah to Neil, James
Feb	16	1781	Elliot, William to Bosley, Rachel*
Jan	4	1786	Elliott, Betsy Ann to Sharp, Shratio
Apr	7	1779	Elliott, John to Hopkins, Cassandra*
Aug	29	1783	Elliott, Precilla to Reid, Emmanuel*
Aug	31	1795	Elliott, Rebecca to Brown, James*
Oct	12	1785	Elliott, Tarah Chew to O'Donnell, John
Oct	27	1798	Ellirt, James to Quidane, Nancy*
Jun	24	1782	Ellis, John to Burns, Rebecca*
Oct	22	1796	Ellis, John to McCoone, Sarah*
Jan	15	1794	Ellis, Mary to Dear, John Kean*
Oct	5	1795	Ellis, Mary to McGray, John*
Mar	16	1791	Ellis, Stephen to Shak, Margaret*
Apr	2	1782	Ellis, Susannah to Fosset, John*
Jun	23	1781	Ellison, Matthew to Miller, Mary
Jan	31	1782	Ellitt, Karenhappah to McBroom, John
Jan	4	1792	Elms, Samuel to Dillon, Margaret*
Jun	27	1795	Elsey, Isaac to Kornish, Rachel*
Sep	2	1790	Elson, Henry to Low, Rachael*
Mar	13	1797	Elston, Ann to Clark, John*
Aug	21	1794	Elston, Thomas to Duncin, Elizabeth*
Sep	12	1795	Elvans, William to Rogers, Elizabeth*
Oct	20	1794	Elwood, Thomas to Devine, Elizabeth*

Oct 11 1797	Elwood, Thomas to Wila, Eleanor*
Jan 13 1797	Emench, Philip to Miller, Elizabeth*
Apr 13 1795	Emick, Nicholas to Inch, Elizabeth*
Jan 20 1791	Emmerson, John to Colegate, Ann Eliz. Partridge*
Apr 4 1797	Emmert, Catharine to Allen, Lucas
Apr 27 1786	Emmitt, David to Dowdel, Barbara*
Mar 7 1782	Emmitt, Issabella to Folger, Frederick*
Jan 15 1791	Emmitt, Mary to Ridgely, John
Apr 8 1797	Emmitt, Philip to Brueon, Sarah*
Mar 14 1798	Emmitt, William to Zimmerman, Sarah*
Oct 25 1783	England, Joseph to Rowland, Elizabeth*
Aug 15 1794	Engle, Thomas to Hurst, Margaret*
May 2 1785	Englebright, John to Wood, Margaret
May 8 1779	English, Margaret to Palmer, Thomas*
Mar 15 1782	English, Margaret to Tobit, James
Apr 26 1779	Engram, John to Hutcheson, Sarah
May 5 1791	Enloes, David to Cole, Mary*
May 29 1784	Enloes, Sarah to Conrod, John*
Jul 27 1785	Enloes, Thomas to Davis, Elizabeth
Aug 17 1782	Ennin, Mary to Mason, John Peter*
May 2 1785	Ennis, Joshua to Peterkin, Sarah
Oct 17 1781	Ennis, Mary to Salmon, Benjamin
Nov 11 1778	Enright, John to Copinger, Elinor*
May 25 1785	Ensloe, Joseph to McGackey, Mary
Dec 18 1787	Ensor, Abraham Jr. to Brooks, Barthia
Mar 1 1783	Ensor, Abraham to Dicks, Catherine*
Feb 26 1783	Ensor, Ann to Holland, John
Nov 30 1792	Ensor, Darby to Hunter, Rachel*
Feb 5 1778	Ensor, Deborah to Merryman, Nicholas*
Aug 12 1790	Ensor, Eleanor to Cole, James*
Feb 7 1789	Ensor, Elizabeth to Chilcott, Elijah*
Dec 9 1795	Ensor, George to Smith, Sarah*
Mar 18 1797	Ensor, Honor to Myers, Patrick
Nov 22 1781	Ensor, Honour to Cole, Abram
Jan 12 1798	Ensor, James to Dean, Nancy*
May 11 1779	Ensor, John to Gorsuch, Urith*
Dec 16 1797	Ensor, John to Smith, Eleanor*
Feb 20 1783	Ensor, Jonathan P. to Ensor, Sarah*
Nov 20 1784	Ensor, Mary to Oldham, Edward*
Mar 12 1796	Ensor, Mary to Stonall, William*
Feb 20 1783	Ensor, Sarah to Ensor, Jonathan P.*
Dec 4 1797	Ensor, Temperance to Brigg, James*
Jun 11 1793	Ensor, William Burton to Connoway, Pamelia*
Nov 19 1791	Ensor, William to Canoles, Rachel
Apr 27 1790	Epaugh, George to Darier, Susanna*
Oct 12 1795	Epiron, Louisa to Ollives, John B.*
Jul 3 1794	Ermon, Francis to Lebat, Peggy*
Oct 6 1797	Errickson, Barnet, Schlieper, Hannah*
Nov 30 1798	Errickson, Bernard to Coffers, Judy*
Nov 30 1797	Erskin, Edward to Martin, Lucy*
Apr 14 1784	Esam, James to Watts, Frances*
Aug 22 1795	Esseck, Susannah to Purdon, William*
Sep 22 1796	Etherton, Thomas to Bryan, Mary*
Dec 24 1795	Etling, Eliza to MIckle, Robert*
Mar 8 1793	Etling, Frances to Taylor, Robert*
Aug 24 1797	Etow, Elizabeth to Harvey, William*

Jun 22 1784	Ettybum, Catharine to Gibson, James*
Nov 27 1798	Etzberger, Adam to Etzberger, Eve*
Nov 27 1798	Etzberger, Eve to Etzberger, Adam*
Jul 9 1796	Evans, Edward to Cole, Jane*
Oct 4 1792	Evans, Elizabeth to Childes, Benjamin*
Apr 15 1797	Evans, Elizabeth to Selby, Loyd
Dec 2 1778	Evans, Elizabeth to Taylor, Thomas*
Aug 28 1790	Evans, Evan to Noon, Mary*
Mar 23 1796	Evans, Francis to Porter, Ann*
Nov 26 1792	Evans, Griffith to Burgess, Mary*
Jul 5 1788	Evans, Griffith to Hewitt, Sarah*
Dec 14 1796	Evans, Jemimah to Bowen, Benjamin*
Apr 10 1790	Evans, John to Burk, Margaret
Oct 26 1789	Evans, John to Byass, Mary*
Jun 22 1778	Evans, John to Ellicott, Latissa*
Feb 20 1782	Evans, John to Hartman, Mary*
Nov 11 1795	Evans, John to Shaffer, Elizabeth*
Dec 3 1789	Evans, Joseph to Davey, Elizabeth*
Apr 7 1792	Evans, Margaret to Butler, John Holpin*
Jun 30 1778	Evans, Martha to Ellicott, David*
Dec 6 1792	Evans, Mary to Boyle, William*
Sep 16 1795	Evans, Mary to Price, Richard*
Mar 11 1797	Evans, Molly to Yeatman, Henry Lewis*
Nov 21 1789	Evans, Naomi to Stocksdale, Edmund H.*
Apr 4 1793	Evans, Nathaniel to Dew, Mary
Apr 11 1792	Evans, Rebecca to Rogers, Allen*
Mar 21 1797	Evans, Sally to Danecole, Jac Bernard*
Oct 24 1795	Evans, Sally to Loyd, Peregrine*
Sep 25 1783	Evans, Sarah to Shears, Richard*
Sep 29 1794	Evans, Waller to Barger, Barbary*
Nov 14 1781	Evans, William to Powell, Susanna
Feb 8 1797	Everet, John to Burk, Sarah*
Dec 27 1777	Everett, James to Brown, Mary*
Mar 8 1793	Everitt, John to Taylor, Eleanor*
Feb 14 1795	Everson, Elizabeth to Shipley, Edward*
Aug 1 1795	Everson, Nathaniel to Nash, Elsbeth*
Aug 23 1792	Everson, Richard to Lonhart, Mary*
Jul 22 1783	Everton, Daniel to Stringer, Elizabeth
Nov 23 1782	Eves, William to Hubbard, Sarah
Sep 3 1788	Evins, William to Fowler, Rebecca*
Dec 23 1785	Ewing, Eleanor to Stewart, James
Feb 21 1784	Eyon, Frederick to Busser, Catharine*
Feb 13 1795	Fabre, Lewis Augustin to Ferrier, Henrietta*
Nov 12 1795	Faherty, Honour to Clauherty, Patrick*
Jan 5 1789	Fairbanks, John to Harmon, Ann*
Jun 16 1783	Fallon, James to Baker, Ann*
Oct 29 1796	Fallows, Ann to Waters, William*
Dec 10 1785	Falls, Moor to Biddle, Abagal
Sep 24 1796	Falls, Moore to Wilson, Rebecca*
Jul 5 1792	Fanning, James to Allen, Susannah*
Oct 29 1788	Fannon, Lawrence to Kenseller, Ann*
Jan 23 1790	Farel, Ann to Harvey, Thomas*
Feb 4 1797	Farely, James to Whittle, Elizabeth*
Dec 13 1796	Farien, John to Thompson, Mary*
Oct 23 1790	Farker, John to Branagan, Mary*
Aug 11 1798	Farlan, Mary to Cahill, William

May 15 1792	Farlana, Joseph to Frazier, Mary*
Sep 30 1796	Farly, Bridget to Carrick, Daniel*
Sep 2 1794	Farmer, Catharine to Freeman, Patrick*
Sep 12 1788	Farmer, John to Galbraith, Hesther*
Aug 31 1782	Farnworth, James to Murphey, Jane*
Feb 8 1797	Farquson, Eleanor to Wilson, John*
Dec 15 1777	Farran, Joseph to Sutton, Alice*
May 20 1797	Farrar, Peter to Hickson, Margaret*
May 24 1783	Farrel, Rebecca to McGee, Joseph*
Dec 23 1797	Farrell, Mary to Chesran, David*
Oct 10 1793	Farrell, Timothy to Blake, Catharine*
Apr 10 1795	Faune, Joseph to D'Alban, Anne Francoise*
Jan 29 1794	Faure, Jariet Ann to Thomas, William*
Dec 19 1792	Faurice, Jacob to Amy, Mary*
Jan 2 1786	Fauster, Margery to Petty, John*
Jan 4 1792	Fauxall, Thomas to French, Elizabeth*
Apr 1 1794	Favery, Thomas to Coward, Naomi*
Jun 30 1797	Favory, Neomia to Willey, Joseph*
Nov 16 1798	Fawzer, Jonathan to McCallister, Mary*
May 28 1791	Fearson, Jesse to Wells, Hannah*
Dec 17 1798	Fee, John to Simpson, Elizabeth*
Dec 24 1796	Feit, Henry to Segan, Elizabeth*
May 7 1791	Fell, Elijah to Galloway, Priscilla*
Dec 17 1780	Fellon, John to Summers, Mary*
May 22 1797	Fellows, Edward to Higgins, Jenny*
Dec 24 1783	Fellows, Richard to Barloro, Mary*
Jan 19 1789	Feltner, Rebecca to Macunkey, William*
Jan 11 1793	Fenn, William to Harris, Elizabeth*
Apr 25 1778	Fenn, William to Quay, Susannah*
Dec 30 1782	Fennell, Mary to Goodwin, Thomas
Dec 30 1782	Fennell, Sarah to Lowery, Joseph
Jun 2 1792	Fennill, Ruth to Johnson, Thomas*
May 25 1791	Fenning, Thomas to Thompson, Mary*
Mar 2 1782	Fenton, Charles to Danily, Dolly*
Dec 4 1784	Fenton, Margaret to Buttengan, Thomas*
May 19 1798	Ferguson, Eleanor to Banke, Thomas*
Oct 6 1784	Ferguson, Robert to Vanhorn, Elizabeth
Mar 12 1781	Ferguson, Sarah to Carter, William*
Aug 9 1798	Ferley, William to White, Elizabeth*
Nov 11 1796	Ferraud, Marian to Bonnet, Joseph*
Feb 13 1795	Ferrier, Henrietta to Fabre, Lewis Augustin*
Feb 6 1796	Ferring, William to Geating, Elizabeth*
Sep 26 1798	Fessen, Elizabeth to Morie, Benedictus*
Oct 27 1797	Fesset, Jemima to Plowman, Jonathan*
Jan 7 1790	Fete, Eve to Reinicker, Conrad*
Nov 2 1795	Few, Catharine to Kennard, Isaac*
Dec 14 1798	Fidings, Margaret to Darnale, Francis*
Sep 2 1790	Field, Martin to Hogan, Jane*
Feb 27 1797	Field, Mary to Perling, Peter*
Feb 11 1797	Field, Thomas to Thomas, Rebecca*
Jun 7 1794	Fields, Ann to Miller, Henry*
Dec 22 1797	Fields, Anne to McCallister, John*
Feb 27 1798	Fields, Comfort to Glede, James*
Sep 7 1796	Fields, Eleanor to Miller, Richard*
Mar 31 1779	Fields, John to Silverwood, Hannah*
Sep 9 1786	Fields, William to Londerman, Elizabeth

```
Jul 22 1786    Fifer, John to Wallass, Sarah*
Aug  1 1794    Fifer, Maria to Cole, Anthony*
Jun 28 1794    Fifer, Rachel to Stoare, John*
Jun  4 1795    Figgance, Catharine to Carr, Felix*
May 12 1791    Fightmaster, Frederick to Kennedy, Sarah*
Feb  7 1797    File, Catharine to Cullidon, George*
Aug 26 1779    Filer, Mary to Wallis, Aron*
Aug 30 1798    Fill, Achsah to Ingleos, John*
Sep 28 1778    Fin, Mary Ann to O'Brian, Daniel*
Aug 25 1796    Finagan, Ariana to Renaud, John*
May 23 1795    Finch, George to Fleishal, Rosina*
Dec 13 1783    Finch, Thomas to Stevens, Alice*
Aug 11 1788    Finlay, Hugh to Hughes, Sarah
Sep 19 1798    Finley, James to Gantz, Catharine*
Jun  9 1778    Finley, William to Whinrite, Ann*
Feb  4 1786    Finn, Elizabeth to Butler, Walter
Oct 28 1782    Finn, Peter to Wheeler, Mary*
Jul  2 1794    Fish, Ann to Hedwicks, James*
Apr  7 1785    Fish, Benjamin to Ridgely, Harriot
Oct 11 1791    Fish, James to Hunter, Nancy*
Aug 27 1796    Fish, Joseph to Martin, Jemima*
Jul 13 1797    Fishburn, Catharine to Mummey, Thomas*
Jun  2 1779    Fisher, Ann Harden to Norsou, Philip Olle
Jun  3 1791    Fisher, Ann to Warden, John*
Mar 26 1796    Fisher, Barbary to Baughman, George*
Dec 29 1787    Fisher, Basil to Paradise, Sophia*
Jun  2 1794    Fisher, Catharine to Aukerman, Philip*
Oct 23 1793    Fisher, Catharine to Grallot, Francis*
May 21 1798    Fisher, Catharine to Hamlin, Jacob*
Oct 14 1794    Fisher, Daniel to Wolslager, Elizabeth*
Jun  8 1797    Fisher, Hannah to Price, Joseph*
Jul 23 1796    Fisher, Jacob to Sowers, Mary*
Oct  5 1791    Fisher, Jemimah to Hinks, William*
Sep 25 1789    Fisher, John to Fisher, Susannah*
Feb  8 1791    Fisher, John to Hobbs, Airy
Aug  4 1794    Fisher, Joseph to Cruses, Elizabeth*
May 19 1798    Fisher, Martin to Forrester, Rody*
Feb 21 1797    Fisher, Mary to Cromwell, Philemon
Jun 29 1795    Fisher, Mary to Kirkman, Thomas*
Aug  7 1783    Fisher, Michael to Crust, Elizabeth*
Dec 26 1794    Fisher, Phebe to Waggoner, Valentine*
Jan  6 1791    Fisher, Philepin to Conrad, Matthias*
Dec 20 1791    Fisher, Robert to Baker, Hannah*
Dec 29 1790    Fisher, Ruth to Gilbert, Thomas Priar*
Sep 25 1789    Fisher, Susannah to Fisher, John*
Dec 19 1792    Fishpaw, Henry to Isher, Ruth*
Aug 11 1798    Fishpaw, John to Haile, Ann*
Jan 30 1784    Fitch, Henry to Eagleston, Ann*
Jun 11 1798    Fitch, Sarah to Councilman, George*
Jan  9 1790    Fitch, William to Turner, Elizabeth*
Dec 11 1787    Fitchwick, James to Crage, Mary
Mar 10 1791    Fite, Jacob to Reinicker, Nancy*
Aug 20 1782    Fite, Peter to Clayor, Mary
Feb  3 1796    Fitz, Elizabeth to Turner, Nathaniel*
May  3 1796    Fitz, Rachal to Disney, Solomon*
Oct  3 1795    Fitzgerald, Ann to Gavin, Matthew*
```

```
Nov 20 1779    Fitzgerald, Ann to Minutan, Charles*
Sep 26 1778    Fitzgerald, Bridget to Delany, Peter*
May  2 1794    Fitzgerald, Garret to Mackew, Jane*
Mar  3 1794    Fitzgerald, Garrett to Myers, Margaret*
Jun 28 1786    Fitzgerald, Jane to Jacob, William
Jun  2 1795    Fitzgerald, John to Drake, Mary*
Nov 20 1779    Fitzgerald, Margaret to Warren, Thomas
Nov 19 1778    Fitzgerald, Mary to Thompson, Edward*
Jul  1 1796    Fitzgerald, Polly to Barnet, James*
Oct 22 1798    Fitzgerald, Richard to Corrie, Margaret*
Sep 25 1797    Fitzgerald, Susannah to Booth, Michael*
Oct  7 1796    Fitzgerald, Margaret to Howard, Francis*
Oct 12 1796    Fitzgerrald, Thomas to Cooper, Mary*
Aug 13 1794    Fitzpatrick, Hugh to Slater, Julia*
Aug 25 1786    FitzPatrick, James to Yates, Lucy
May  8 1797    Fitzpatrick, Mary to Noonan, Edward*
Dec 24 1789    Fitzs, Darkes to Clark, William*
Jun  1 1798    Fitzsimmon, Pierce to Freeman, Ann
May 12 1784    Fivcash, Peter to Parks, Charlotte*
Mar 20 1783    Flaharty, ELizabeth to Burke, Theoblad*
Apr 12 1779    Flaharty, James to Brand, Mary
Jul 19 1782    Flaharty, James to Burns, Mary
Sep  8 1794    Flaherty, Patrick to Conner, Catharine*
Nov 25 1784    Flanagan, Alazane to Ogle, George*
Mar 26 1796    Flanagan, Mary to Bosler, John*
Nov  9 1791    Flanteroy, Sarah to Travers, William Briscoe*
Jul 14 1781    Flattery, James to Hannan, Elizabeth
May 14 1796    Flattery, Mary to O'Brian, Joseph D.*
Oct 19 1786    Flax, Margaret to Geddes, James
Dec 11 1794    Fleetwood, Nancy to Small, Jacob*
May 23 1795    Fleishal, Rosina to Finch, George*
Dec 18 1778    Flemman, David to McNeall, Mary*
Aug 27 1796    Flemming, Joseph to Williams, Nancy*
Jan  2 1783    Flemmon, Elizabeth to Tumbletown, Henry
Jul 16 1794    Flemmon, James to Kibble, Elizabeth*
Jun 21 1785    Fletcher, Ann to Billmyer, Leonard*
Jun 13 1797    Fletcher, James to Campbell, Mary*
Aug 27 1795    Fletcher, Mary to Hall, William*
Apr 17 1784    Fletcher, Philip to Wolfe, Catherine
Oct 11 1794    Fleury, Mr. to Young, Clara*
Jun  3 1786    Fleury, Sebastien to Sapen, Magdeline
Sep 10 1779    Fling, Margaret to Price, James*
Jan 24 1793    Flinn, Alice to Loney, Amos
Dec 31 1793    Flinn, Eleanor to Strike, Nicholas*
Oct 21 1795    Flinn, Eliza to Pritchard, William*
Jul  5 1796    Flinn, James to Corney, Elizabeth*
Jul  2 1798    Flinn, James to Corrie, Patience
Nov 30 1793    Flinn, John to McMahan, Judith*
Feb 23 1796    Flinn, Margaret to Babcock, Clark*
Dec 19 1798    Flintz, Polly to Hostetter, David*
Jun  3 1778    Flisher, John to Dugmore, Isabella*
Jul 22 1779    Flood, Catharine to Smith, William*
Jul 14 1791    Flood, Eleanor to Henley, Robert*
Dec  4 1783    Flood, Elizabeth to Creighton, John*
Jul  4 1795    Flood, Elizabeth to Gaikes, Samuel*
Jul  9 1778    Flood, Elizabeth to Roberts, Levy*
```

```
Jul 23 1796    Flood, Obediah to Whips, Sarah*
Jul 26 1797    Florence, Mons to Brown, Barbara*
Aug 19 1783    Flosence, Nicholas to Woolen, Pamelia*
Dec 26 1796    Flowers, Mary to Denning, Oliver*
May 31 1793    Floyd, Caleb to Lee, Eleanor*
Oct  3 1794    Floyd, Charles to Dunn, Elizabeth*
Jul 20 1791    Floyd, Elizabeth to Reynolds, Robert*
Dec 28 1782    Floyd, Joseph to Doyle, Nancy
Dec  8 1794    Floyd, Joseph to Logue, Catherine*
Nov 21 1787    Floyd, Joseph to Wheeler, Nancy*
Jun 15 1793    Floyd, Samuel to Somclin, Fanny*
Sep 23 1795    Floyd, Thomas to Todd, Ann*
Jan 12 1791    Flud, Deborah to Peck, Nicholas*
Mar 17 1796    Flueker, Sarah Lyons to Beaumez, Bon Albert Briois*
Nov 15 1798    Foard, Elinor to Howard, Samuel*
Mar 11 1797    Foche, Anthony to Sullivan, Biddy*
Oct 28 1797    Foharty, Edward to Mekin, Judy*
Aug 19 1793    Fokey, Eleanor to Creamer, Edward*
Mar  7 1782    Folger, Frederick to Emmitt, Issabella*
Jun 15 1779    Folinger, Mary to Keler, Jacob*
Dec  7 1798    Foller, Mary to Wilson, David*
Aug 29 1795    Follmar, Martin to Penman, Martha Fredericka C.*
Dec 28 1785    Fonday, Abraham to Grimes, Margaret
Jul 28 1798    Fonder, Abigail to Robinson, Robert*
Oct 21 1783    Fonerdan, John to Edwards, Margaret
Feb 13 1794    Fonerden, Martha to Bonsal, Robert*
Jul 13 1784    Fonman, Daniel to Brown, Elizabeth*
Aog 10 1797    Fonts, Nancy to Elkins, Joseph*
Nov  5 1785    Foos, Philip to Barton, Dorothy*
Dec 25 1794    Foose, Mary to Reily, William*
Nov  3 1798    Foose, William to Merritt, Martha*
Oct  9 1783    Forbes, James to Foster, Elizabeth*
Dec  4 1788    Forbes, James to Smith, Ann*
Jul 14 1788    Forbes, Matthew to Bevans, Polly*
Dec 13 1783    Forbes, Rachel to Conor, Edward*
Dec 17 1783    Ford, Allatha to Cole, Thomas*
Sep  8 1783    Ford, Barny to Cole, Mary*
Aug 10 1789    Ford, Carline to Haile, Samuel*
Oct 19 1793    Ford, Charity to Ambrose, James*
Sep  7 1784    Ford, Edmund to Bond, Catherine
Dec 16 1795    Ford, Eleanor to Hadson, Daniel*
Dec 10 1781    Ford, Elinor to Todd, Benjamin
Nov  6 1779    Ford, Elinor to Wyley, Joshua*
Oct 14 1797    Ford, James to Wood, Sarah*
Oct 15 1778    Ford, John to Beavin, Elizabeth*
Sep 12 1778    Ford, Joshua to Cole, Mary*
Jun 10 1786    Ford, Joshua to Cole, Sarah
Dec 14 1796    Ford, Joshua to Johnston, Mary*
Oct 22 1798    Ford, Mary to Cord, Abraham*
Dec  7 1796    Ford, Mary to Griffith, James*
Oct 23 1795    Ford, Nathaniel to Stacey, Rebecca*
Jan 13 1784    Ford, Ollive to Moffett, John*
May 28 1784    Ford, Romman to Poddewang, Peggy*
Apr 18 1795    Ford, Ruth to Lockerd, Thomas*
Jan 14 1791    Ford, Susannah to Penny, Alexander*
Dec 19 1781    Ford, Thomas Cockey Dye to Cockey, Actions*
```

```
Dec 24 1782    Ford, Thomas to White, Hannah*
May  5 1785    Ford, Thomas to Wood, Nancy*
Aug  6 1795    Ford, William to Barton, Fanny*
Aug 10 1798    Ford, William to Holmes, Jane*
Dec 31 1796    Foreman, Christina to Paine, John*
Mar 23 1782    Foreman, Ludwig to Mattox, Rachael
May  3 1783    Forester, George to Oram, Rachel*
Jul 30 1778    Forkner, Sidney to Murphy, Thomas*
Nov 20 1790    Forman, William Loe to Spear, Jane*
Apr 26 1797    Forney, John to Boyce, Sarah*
Jun 16 1792    Forney, Mary to Drepbert, Christian*
Jul  7 1794    Forney, Mary to Sharpe, Jacob*
Jul  4 1798    Forney, Nicholas to Potter, Charlotte*
Aug 16 1792    Forney, Susannah to Decker, George*
Feb 16 1790    Forrest, Ann to Covel, Jonathan
Apr 11 1795    Forrest, Dravsilla to Davis, Marmaduke*
Dec 16 1785    Forrest, Josiah to Stone, Ann
Oct  2 1782    Forrest, Nicholas to Oram, Ruth
Dec 22 1792    Forrest, Sarah to Ashwell, Barnet*
Nov 17 1778    Forrest, Vincent to Mewshaw, Sarah*
Jul 30 1779    Forrester, Alexander to Pontenay, Sarah*
Sep  1 1791    Forrester, Cassandra to Ricketts, Benjamin*
Apr  8 1789    Forrester, George to Gardner, Cassandra
Sep 28 1778    Forrester, Margaret to Lanto, George*
May 19 1798    Forrester, Rody to Fisher, Martin*
Jun 22 1791    Forrester, William to Reynolds, Hetty*
Jun 10 1796    Forse, John to Biddle, Augustine*
Dec 22 1792    Forsyth, Isaac to Brown, Frances*
Nov 22 1797    Forsyth, Jacob to Cooper, Sarah*
Nov 19 1795    Forsyth, Jane to Thompson, Josias*
Jun 22 1796    Forsyth, John to Suyman, Catharine*
Nov  9 1785    Forsythe, Sarah to Pringle, James
Nov  8 1797    Fort, John to Buchain, Elizabeth*
Sep 11 1798    Fosoler, Ann to Apples, Christian*
Apr  2 1782    Fosset, John to Ellis, Susannah*
Jan  6 1798    Fossey, John to Curteain, Sarah*
Jan 24 1798    Fossey, John to Mitchell, Elizabeth*
Nov 26 1798    Fossham, Mary to Taylor, Matthew*
Jan  1 1789    Foster, Absalom to Meredith, Agness*
Jul 25 1798    Foster, Ann to Roberts, George*
Jun  2 1783    Foster, Comfort to Bennett, Hannah
Oct 15 1793    Foster, Comfort to Lemmon, Thomas*
Nov 23 1797    Foster, Elijah to Singary, Anne*
Oct  9 1783    Foster, Elizabeth to Forbes, James*
Oct  7 1794    Foster, Elizabeth to Powel, Peter*
Feb  2 1782    Foster, George to Myers, Elizabeth*
Dec  7 1782    Foster, John to Liddel, Elizabeth*
Dec 20 1782    Foster, Joseph to Tull, Sarah*
Apr 26 1792    Foster, Lucy to Gray, John*
Dec 22 1795    Foster, Millison to Lemmon, John*
Mar  7 1797    Foster, Nicholas to Cross, Sarah
Jun  8 1782    Foster, Patience to Walker, Christopher*
Apr  2 1782    Foster, William to Walker, Sarah*
Nov 20 1779    Foteman, Rebecca to Garret, Samuel*
Nov 25 1797    Fouble, Elizabeth to Brummel, Joseph*
Dec 20 1797    Fouble, Elizabeth to Cockey, Joshua Frederick*
```

Sep 10 1789	Fouble, Jasper to Watson, Elizabeth*
Oct 13 1792	Fouble, Peter to Painter, Elizabeth
Aug 3 1792	Foucackon, Mary Theresse to Trouin, Andrew*
Jan 30 1795	Foulds, James to Hammond, Ann*
Jan 20 1785	Foulk, Elizabeth to Dounhour, Jacob*
Apr 14 1796	Fous, Theobald to Shoeman, Catharine*
Jul 20 1782	Fouse, Ann to Williamson, William
Jun 18 1795	Foute, Jacob to Fowble, Catharine*
Jun 18 1795	Fowble, Catharine to Foute, Jacob*
Aug 15 1797	Fowble, Mary to Vogel, James*
Jul 23 1781	Fowle, Mary to Way, Michael*
Jan 6 1789	Fowler, Ann to Hardisty, Charles*
Mar 24 1796	Fowler, Benjamin to Hughes, Mary*
May 18 1782	Fowler, Christiana to Grimes, George
Jun 11 1795	Fowler, Eleanor to Cox, Samuel*
Sep 17 1791	Fowler, Elizabeth to Dorter, Archibald*
Apr 16 1791	Fowler, George to Hammond, Eleanor*
Apr 11 1786	Fowler, Henrietta Marion to Stansbury, David*
Aug 13 1795	Fowler, Isaac to Head, Nancy*
May 21 1796	Fowler, Jacob to Hafleigh, Margaret*
Apr 20 1795	Fowler, James to Moore, Elizabeth*
Dec 21 1791	Fowler, John to Johnston, Ann*
Apr 5 1798	Fowler, Mary to Burton, William*
Nov 7 1793	Fowler, Nancy to Clapp, Stephen*
Aug 25 1783	Fowler, Rebecca to Dugan, Thomas*
Sep 3 1788	Fowler, Rebecca to Evins, William*
Mar 5 1783	Fowler, Richard to Collins, Mary
Apr 12 1796	Fowler, Samuel to Adams, Ann Carey*
Jun 3 1794	Fowler, Samuel to Love, Rebecca*
Nov 26 1794	Fowler, Samuel to Reese, Mary*
May 5 1790	Fowler, Sarah to League, John*
Oct 10 1793	Fowler, Thomas to Barton, Sarah*
Mar 17 1792	Fowler, William to Watkins, Rebecca*
Sep 17 1782	Fowler, Zacharia to Jones, Elizabeth
Aug 16 1782	Fox, Anthony to Kemp, Sarah*
Mar 21 1796	Fox, Hannah to Tomblinson, Samuel*
Dec 20 1794	Fox, John Hopkins to Johnson, Elizabeth*
May 25 1796	Foy, Catharine to Liddle, John*
Dec 22 1783	Foy, Elizabeth to Martin, Joseph
May 15 1782	Frances, Renick to Roddy, Ann*
Dec 31 1784	Francis, William to Bosman, Sarah*
May 8 1798	Franciscey, Margaret to Bunker, Moses*
Nov 19 1793	Francoisi, Elizabeth to Bramont, John*
May 31 1786	Franklain, Thomas to Councilman, Margaret*
May 1 1792	Franklin, Catherine to Dulshary, John*
Apr 25 1792	Franklin, Charles to Counsilman, Catherine
Mar 22 1796	Franklin, Garret to Burgin, Elizabeth*
Dec 30 1797	Franklin, Hannah to Maddox, Richard*
Apr 5 1782	Franklin, Lydia to Sellman, Mordecai*
Jul 22 1784	Frankling, Kitty to Hood, James*
Nov 21 1781	Fravis, Matthew to Travis, Mary
Mar 26 1798	Frazer, Charlotte to Seigfried, Charles Lewis*
Aug 29 1793	Frazier, Ann to Griffith, William*
Jan 23 1790	Frazier, Ann to Smith, Bazel Lowman*
Aug 31 1782	Frazier, Elizabeth to Dixon, Thomas*
Mar 22 1791	Frazier, Lilly to Reese, George*

May 15 1792	Frazier, Mary to Farlana, Joseph*
Jul 11 1798	Frazier, Mary to Walker, Joseph*
Oct 11 1794	Frazier, Peggy to Miller, George*
Aug 2 1794	Frazier, William to Duckier, Elizabeth*
Oct 27 1798	Frederick, Michael to Sholl, Catharine*
Oct 19 1792	Free, Babby to Mason, Bingley*
Oct 22 1792	Free, Babby to Mason, Bingley*
May 6 1794	Freeberger, Henry to Miller, Margaret*
Jan 17 1794	Freeland, Juliet to Townsend, Robert*
Oct 2 1793	Freeland, Rebeccah to Robbins, Roger*
Jun 1 1798	Freeman, Ann to Fitzsimmon, Pierce*
May 18 1797	Freeman, Ann to Kemp, James*
Jul 23 1795	Freeman, Dorcus to Bartlet, Samuel*
Nov 5 1795	Freeman, Elizabeth to McNutty, Thomas*
Sep 2 1794	Freeman, Patrick to Farmer, Catharine*
Dec 21 1785	Freeman, Samuel to Burnham, Mary
Sep 7 1797	Freeman, Sina to Church, Amos*
Nov 2 1798	Freeman, Sinney to Smith, Richard*
Nov 26 1784	Freeman, William to Mason, Ann*
Nov 27 1797	Freir, John to League, Chloe*
Aug 15 1795	Fremaine, William to Beltson, Catharine*
Nov 3 1784	French, Benjamin to Cromey, Mary Abbey*
Nov 3 1781	French, Daniel to Wilson, Rachel
Dec 29 1792	French, Dominick to Shillingsburgh, Mary
Jan 27 1785	French, Elinor to Stansbury, Richard*
Dec 8 1796	French, Elizabeth to Dungan, Benjamin*
Jan 4 1792	French, Elizabeth to Fauxall, Thomas*
Oct 11 1796	French, John to Welsh, Margaret*
May 16 1795	French, Mary to McClane, Hugh Charles*
Nov 12 1788	French, Othea to Waters, Ellennor*
Nov 29 1784	French, Otho to Eagleston, Charity*
Apr 3 1798	French, Samuel to Cock, Lydia*
Mar 29 1786	French, Simon to Ingram, Sarah*
Jan 4 1797	Freport, Mary to Branson, Balset*
Mar 9 1778	Fresh, Catharina to Inseler, Valerius*
Dec 12 1781	Fresh, Catherine to Plowman, Edward*
Sep 19 1784	Friar, John to Callahan, Catharine
Dec 5 1792	Frick, Mary to Smith, George*
Nov 19 1791	Frigate, Temperance to Tudor, Salathiel*
Apr 19 1788	Frigele, Margaret to Mitchell, Gideon
Jul 20 1793	Friggot, Sarah to Gold, Pollish*
Oct 21 1790	Frigle, Mary to Gosjean, John James*
Sep 12 1789	Frigle, Ruth to Wilson, Nicholas*
Oct 2 1784	Frish, Mary to Kittinger, Jacob*
Jun 2 1784	Frits, Christiana to Hederick, Thomas*
Jun 29 1798	FritzPatrick, Elizabeth to Johnson, William*
Sep 5 1798	Frizele, William D. to Win, Jane*
Dec 19 1782	Frizzel, Absalom to Porter, Rachel*
Jan 22 1791	Frizzel, Catherine to Phillips, James*
Jan 23 1795	Frizzle, Absalom to Cook, Ann*
Feb 17 1795	Frizzle, Elizabeth to Shipley, Groves*
Apr 4 1795	Frizzle, John to Sank, Achsah*
Mar 23 1796	Frizzle, Nancy to Wages, William*
Mar 18 1797	Frizzle, William to Buckingham, Hellen*
Apr 20 1789	Froft, George to Mahar, Ann*
Feb 24 1796	Frog, Elizabeth to Griffen, John*

```
Oct 15 1796    Frog, Susanna to Barlow, Joseph
Apr 17 1793    Froggett, Mary to Gocchea, Charles*
Sep  9 1785    Frolick, Jacobina to Metzler, Nicholas*
Dec 30 1788    Fromiller, Kitty to Moore, Jacob*
Jan 26 1791    Frost, Caleb to Mansell, Elizabeth*
Nov  6 1781    Frost, James to Simpson, Sarah
Feb 13 1790    Frost, John to Dorsey, Elizabeth*
Jan  4 1783    Frost, Margaret to Shipley, Lloyd*
Apr 27 1784    Frost, Rachel to Shipley, Adam*
Oct 22 1790    Frost, Ruth to Owings, Joshua*
Mar  2 1784    Frost, Susannah to Shipley, George*
Aug 19 1791    Frost, William to Shipley, Mary Ogg*
Dec  3 1789    Fry, Barbary to Gore, George*
Dec 16 1797    Fry, Catharine to Ebbeck, John Frederick*
Jan 10 1781    Frymiller, Elizabeth to Weaver, Casper*
Jun 27 1798    Frymiller, John to Walter, Elizabeth*
Oct 19 1793    Frymiller, Mary F. to Grafflin, Jacob*
Jun 15 1796    Fugate, Alice to Patterson, Samuel*
Feb  4 1782    Fugate, Ann to Pocock, James
Jan  4 1786    Fugate, Elizabeth to Pattison, John
May 22 1783    Fugate, Martin to Pocock, Mary*
Jan  6 1796    Fugate, Mary to Johnson, Charles*
Apr 17 1795    Fugate, Sarah to Tudor, John*
Dec  8 1796    Fulford, Catharine to Cox, James*
Jan 30 1794    Fulford, John to Hughes, Sarah*
Apr  2 1794    Fulford, Mary to Lorman, William*
May 29 1795    Fulhart, Elizabeth to Beazoe, Richard*
Aug  4 1797    Fulhart, Philip to Lynch, Elizabeth*
Apr  7 1783    Fuller, Samuel to Sheers, Elizabeth
Dec 15 1777    Fullhart, Mary to Armitage, John*
May  2 1782    Fullom, George to King, Dorathy*
Oct  6 1786    Fulton, James to Christopher, Ann
Aug 10 1778    Fulton, John to Crockett, Jane*
May 16 1793    Furby, John to Turner, Margaret*
Jul 27 1786    Furgason, Elizabeth to Presbury, George Gould
May  5 1791    Furlong, William to Johnson, Sally*
Dec 15 1781    Furney, Hannah to Jones, Thomas*
Jul 28 1784    Furst, Elizabeth to Lambough, Ephraim*
Aug 12 1795    Fush, Michael to Henry, Margaret*
Aug 18 1795    Gable, Susannah to Willing, William*
Dec 10 1777    Gaddis, George to Hays, Isabella*
Jan  2 1796    Gahogan, Elizabeth to Anderson, Jabez*
Jul  4 1795    Gaikes, Samuel to Flood, Elizabeth*
Jan  4 1794    Gaile, Jonna to Derga, Pearl*
Mar 25 1779    Gailer, Delila to Kirk, Thomas*
May 24 1783    Gaither, Actions to Ridgely, Basil*
Jan 18 1791    Gaither, Elinor to Becknell, Thomas*
Jun  3 1797    Gaither, James to Gray, Susannah V.*
Dec  5 1798    Gaither, James to Hale, Patience*
Dec 24 1793    Gaither, John to Hipsley, Ruth*
Jun 28 1783    Gaither, Razin to Ridgely, Sarah*
Feb 10 1784    Galaush, Sarah to Caleb, Henry*
Sep 12 1788    Galbraith, Hesther to Farmer, John*
Jul 27 1797    Gale, Susanna to Barton, Charles*
Dec 24 1798    Gallaher, John to Anna, Alec*
Jul 23 1796    Gallentine, Barbara to Hosselbaugh, John George*
```

Sep 28 1792	Gallop, Hannah to Smith, Daniel*
Jul 31 1788	Galloway, Absalom to Chamberlain, Rebecca*
Feb 18 1792	Galloway, Acquila to Barton, Nancy*
Dec 21 1797	Galloway, Eleanor to Crow, Thomas*
Mar 23 1790	Galloway, Francis to Shockny, Margaret*
Nov 6 1797	Galloway, Jalathiel to Galloway, Mary
Sep 1 1790	Galloway, James to Chine, Mary*
May 13 1793	Galloway, Jane to Moore, Robert*
Sep 2 1786	Galloway, Marshall to Watlin, Hannah*
Sep 12 1797	Galloway, Martha to Baterman, John*
Feb 22 1781	Galloway, Mary Ann to Shepherd, John*
Feb 11 1794	Galloway, Mary to Andrew, William Holland*
Nov 6 1778	Galloway, Mary to Dumatz, John*
Nov 6 1797	Galloway, Mary to Galloway, Jalathiel
Aug 29 1797	Galloway, Mary to Presbury, Walter
Mar 6 1782	Galloway, Moses to Owings, Pamelia*
May 7 1791	Galloway, Priscilla to Fell, Elijah*
Dec 19 1795	Galloway, Sarah to Gorsuch, John*
Feb 10 1781	Galloway, Thomas to Dallis, Catherine*
Dec 13 1783	Galloway, William to Brian, Scisley*
Jun 6 1792	Galloway, William to Waller, Ann (nee Taylor)*
Aug 14 1790	Gamble, Margaret to Johnson, Elijah
Oct 29 1795	Gamble, Thomas to McPellon, Mary*
Feb 7 1793	Gambrill, Margaret to Jacob, Zachariah*
Aug 24 1797	Gambrill, William to Jacob, Elizabeth*
Aug 3 1797	Ganer, John to Colbertson, Deborah*
Nov 8 1797	Ganteaume, James to Carey, Elizabeth*
Sep 19 1798	Gantz, Catharine to Finley, James*
Dec 17 1796	Gantz, Elizabeth to Georgia, John*
Apr 17 1783	Garar, Peter to Momillan, Magdaline*
May 5 1778	Gardener, Richard to Davis, Mary*
Feb 8 1797	Gardiner, Anne to King, Richard*
Oct 27 1783	Gardiner, Margaret to Holston, Robert
Dec 2 1796	Gardiner, Mary to Mainster, Jacob*
Nov 5 1792	Gardiner, Mary to Rea, William*
Oct 18 1782	Gardiner, Mary to Wheeler, William*
Jun 3 1791	Gardiner, Obed to Gottier, Deborah*
Aug 28 1786	Gardiner, Priscila to Brooks, Joseph*
Nov 8 1785	Gardiner, Sarah to Smith, Jacob
Nov 7 1788	Gardiner, William to Porter, Tabitha*
Nov 15 1784	Gardinner, Cathrine to Myers, Henry
Apr 29 1796	Gardner, Ann to Burgoine, Jacob*
Apr 8 1789	Gardner, Cassandra to Forrester, George
May 6 1784	Gardner, Catherine to Connaway, Charles*
Dec 5 1793	Gardner, Catherine to Parrish, James
Apr 10 1797	Gardner, Elizabeth to Lewis, John*
Aug 18 1796	Gardner, Hannah to Brooks, William*
Sep 3 1779	Gardner, Helen to Gardner, William*
Aug 22 1798	Gardner, Isaac to Ibusson, Rachel*
Mar 10 1794	Gardner, John to Hoofman, Margaret*
Dec 16 1797	Gardner, John to Sadler, Ann*
Nov 24 1781	Gardner, Martha to Brooks, James
Dec 24 1795	Gardner, Mary to Morean, Jonas*
Mar 29 1794	Gardner, Polly to Bellinger, Jean Phillipes E.*
Sep 21 1785	Gardner, Rachael to Buckingham, Thomas*
Feb 15 1797	Gardner, Rachel to Cole, Thomas*

Mar 19 1793	Gardner, Sarah to Jewell, Lewis*
Nov 23 1790	Gardner, Sarah to Jordan, Samuel*
Jun 2 1796	Gardner, Sybel to Waters, Philip
Sep 3 1779	Gardner, William to Gardner, Helen*
Feb 2 1798	Gardner, William to Stewart, Rachel*
Jul 27 1778	Garer, John Valentine to Kelly, Mary*
Nov 19 1788	Garetson, Mary to Hammond, Abraham George*
Feb 27 1797	Garland, George to Nisser, Martha
Nov 11 1790	Garland, John to Lyston, Mary Ann*
Jan 4 1797	Garman, Benjamin to Burton, Rachel*
Feb 24 1778	Garman, Elizabeth to Parlett, William*
May 20 1793	Garn, William to Goodwin, Sarah*
Jun 5 1782	Garner, Ann to Shipley, Vachel*
Feb 5 1794	Garner, Flinn to Parrish, Carey*
Feb 13 1794	Garnes, William to Tane, Jane*
Nov 20 1797	Garns, Elizabeth to Watts, Thomas*
Oct 14 1784	Garoin, William to Ager, Jane
Nov 20 1779	Garret, Samuel to Foreman, Rebecca*
Jan 26 1782	Garretson, Cornelius to Henderson, Mary
May 25 1793	Garretson, Sarah to Hands, Ephraim*
Jun 21 1784	Garretson, Shadrick to Andrews, Mary*
May 22 1790	Garrett, Nancy to Grimes, John*
May 23 1798	Garrettson, Rebecca to Alburger, Samuel*
Oct 23 1789	Garrettson, Thomas to Roberts, Rachel*
Jan 2 1792	Garrison, Elizabeth to Halfpenny, William*
Nov 13 1792	Garrison, Margaret to Hendrickson, Joseph
Jul 25 1778	Garrison, Martha to Worthington, Samuel
Jul 25 1796	Garrison, Rachel to Buckley, Thomas
Apr 14 1791	Garts, Elizabeth to Robb, William*
Feb 9 1793	Garty, Mary to Lidiard, John*
Sep 12 1795	Garvey, Bridget to Lynch, James*
Nov 21 1793	Garvey, George to Botts, Jemima*
Dec 10 1794	Gary, Sarah to Sank, Samuel*
Feb 26 1794	Gash, Benjamin to Taylor, Ruth*
Nov 8 1785	Gash, Eleanor Ridden to Busk, John
Sep 12 1781	Gash, Nicholas to Hiss, Mary*
Feb 15 1797	Gassaway, Anne to Warfield, James*
Feb 9 1785	Gassaway, Nicholas to Randell, Cassandra*
Dec 2 1797	Gassaway, Sarah to Brown, John Bigs*
Feb 25 1778	Gassoway, Mary to Burgess, Richard*
Jun 3 1786	Gatch, Elizabeth to Hiss, Jacob
Oct 18 1796	Gatchel, Samuel H. to Gray, Anne*
Dec 16 1780	Gater, Thomas to Hickins, Lyde*
Feb 11 1794	Gates, Jane to Towson, Abraham*
Jun 27 1795	Gath, John Henry to Schlocman, Johanna Franciocus*
Apr 22 1796	Gaul, Catharine to Dilley, Henry*
Nov 19 1796	Gaulisa, John Baptista to Leuder, Pauline Justine*
Nov 14 1793	Gauterot, Anne to Rinoudet, Pierre Abraham*
Oct 3 1795	Gavin, Matthew to Fitzgerald, Ann*
Jan 27 1794	Gayon, Peter to Broughton, Eleanor*
May 14 1796	Geary, Mary to Harris, Elias*
Feb 6 1797	Geating, Elizabeth to Ferring, William*
Sep 3 1796	Geddes, David to Courtenay, Elizabeth*
Feb 5 1794	Geddes, David to Day, Lydia*
Oct 19 1786	Geddes, James to Flax, Margaret
Feb 13 1798	Geisenderfer, Jacob to Nicodemus, Elizabeth*

```
May 28 1778    Geiter, Elizabeth to Trimble, Cornelous*
Nov 29 1785    Gelhampton, Catharine to Iams, Thomas
Nov 19 1785    Gelhampton, Mary to Ijams, William*
Jun  1 1796    Gent, Thomas to Landers, Judith*
Oct  8 1794    Gentille, Hamot Perry to Racine, Daniel*
Feb 15 1798    Geoghagen, Elizabeth to Goodwin, Moses*
Mar  3 1778    Geoghegan, Ambross to Selman, Mary*
Jul 10 1788    Geoghegan, George to Wonder, Elizabeth
May  3 1779    Geoghegan, John to Harris, Deanar*
Jul 18 1796    Geoghegan, Mary to Storey, John*
Aug  6 1778    Geoghen, Mary to Bennett, Joel*
Mar 13 1795    George, Henry to Cole, Margaret*
Dec 17 1796    Georgia, John to Gantz, Elizabeth*
Mar 26 1795    Georgia, Mary to Williamea, John Nicholas*
Jun 18 1796    Gerand, Jam John to Wheeler, Ann Harret*
Oct 28 1797    Geraud, Alexander to Byan, Mary*
Apr  7 1796    Gerlach, John to Keilholtz, Mary*
Feb 17 1784    German, Benjamin to Parlet, Rachael*
Jan  9 1786    German, Elizabeth to West, William*
Mar 27 1784    German, Hosannah to Parlett, David*
Dec 21 1782    German, John to Barney, Sarah
Aug  7 1792    German, Margaret to Holmes, John*
Mar 21 1784    German, Ruth to Renshaw, Philip*
Feb 13 1798    German, Sally to Russell, Samuel*
Oct  5 1785    German, Thomas to Bevin, Zana
Feb 14 1778    German, Thomas to Clay, Mary*
Jun  4 1778    Gerrish, Francis to Lyon, Mary*
Oct 10 1786    Gerry, James to Low, Florah
Nov 14 1787    Gerthrell, Ruth to Howard, Brice*
Dec 24 1794    Gervey, Mary to Orrick, John*
Aug  1 1792    Getie, Henry to Barnover, Mary*
Feb  6 1797    Gette, Marie Charlotte to Norquey, Magnus*
Feb  7 1792    Gettings, Susannah to Goe, Henry Bateman*
Apr  8 1797    Gevane, Mary to Owings, Samuel*
Feb  5 1785    Ghequin, Charles to Haily, Harriet*
May 20 1779    Gib, James to Mattison, Catharine*
Mar  8 1794    Gibbins, James to Bush, Hannah*
Aug 23 1781    Gibbons, Jane to Barns, Aquila
Feb  3 1784    Gibbons, Margaret to Round, John*
Oct 21 1779    Gibbs, Joseph to Brawton, Elizabeth*
May 19 1782    Gibson, Elizabeth to Sterling, James
Jun 22 1784    Gibson, James to Ettybum, Catharine*
Oct  7 1778    Gibson, Jane to Grier, Aaron*
May  9 1795    Gibson, John to Joyce, Elizabeth*
Nov 23 1789    Gibson, John to Pearson, Lucy*
Oct 28 1783    Gibson, Joseph to Jones, Susanna*
Mar  8 1778    Gibson, Thomas to Porter, Caroline*
Feb 24 1789    Gilbert, Benjamin to Hudson, Eleanor*
May 21 1783    Gilbert, Catharine to Knight, Thomas*
Dec 29 1790    Gilbert, Thomas Priar to Fisher, Ruth*
Apr 17 1795    Gilberthorp, Ann to Donlind, John*
Apr 18 1798    Gilberthorp, Francis to Pratt, Sarah*
Nov 14 1796    Gilberthorp, Francis to Sunderlun, Mary*
Mar 17 1797    Gilberthorp, Mary to Berry, Andrew*
Nov 17 1797    Gilberthorp, Rachel to Bucklers, Henry*
Aug  6 1792    Gilberthorp, Thomas to Joy, Rachel*
```

```
Jul  1 1797    Gilder, Mary to Chalmers, John Jr.*
Oct  5 1790    Gilder, Reuben to Alken, Mary Ashberry*
May 22 1794    Giles, Anne to Johnson, Thomas*
May  9 1785    Giles, George to Hollings, Mary
Sep 18 1784    Giles, Robert to Oatmer, Elizabeth*
Dec 11 1790    Giles, Samuel to Phields, Dorothy*
Apr  2 1793    Giles, Sarah to Gover, Gerrard*
Dec 19 1795    Giles, Susannah to Alter, John*
Dec  4 1794    Giles, Susannah to Moore, Philip*
Apr  5 1796    Giles, William to Israel, Nancy*
Dec 18 1798    Gilfoy, Nancy to Hagan, Henry*
Feb  2 1795    Gill, Ann to Matthews, Thomas*
Nov 28 1792    Gill, Benjamin to Murray, Jamima*
Oct  6 1778    Gill, Catharine to Cooper, Thomas*
May 13 1779    Gill, Edward to Jones, Mary
Oct  4 1782    Gill, Edward to Parish, Ann*
Aug  8 1793    Gill, Eleanor to Sellman, Vachel*
Apr 25 1783    Gill, Elizabeth to Cox, Elijah*
May 13 1794    Gill, Elizabeth to Gill, Nicholas*
Feb 24 1786    Gill, Hugh to Russell, Emsey
May 20 1779    Gill, James to Matison, Catharine
Nov 29 1792    Gill, John Price to Kirby, Providence*
Oct 30 1781    Gill, John to Barney, Leah
Nov 17 1788    Gill, John to Chilcott, Margarett*
Mar  7 1798    Gill, Martha to Green, Eleander*
Jun 15 1793    Gill, Mary to Gill, William*
May  1 1795    Gill, Mary to Keeler, Joseph*
May 13 1794    Gill, Nicholas to Gill, Elizabeth*
Dec 20 1798    Gill, Rebecca to Clackner, Adam*
Jun 27 1790    Gill, Stephen G. to Gill, Urath
Apr  2 1789    Gill, Susannah to Hager, John*
Jun 27 1790    Gill, Urath to Gill, Stephen G.
Jun 15 1793    Gill, William to Gill, Mary*
Dec  3 1795    Gill, William to Haile, Susannah*
May 12 1783    Gill, William to Wooden, Rachel*
Jul 13 1797    Gillburn, William to Churchmore, Nancy*
May 11 1793    Gilley, Susannah to Hamphrey, Nathan
Jul 12 1778    Gilling, James to Wates, Elizabeth*
Sep 23 1791    Gillingham, Thomas to Williams, Mary*
Oct 25 1788    Gillings, Mary to Gones, Abraham*
Dec  8 1797    Gilliss, Arraminta to Shipley, John*
Jul 23 1792    Gilliss, John to Shipley, Susannah*
Oct 25 1798    Gilmore, Eliza to Sherlock, John*
Jan 11 1796    Gilmore, John to Smith, Jane*
Mar 22 1786    Gilson, Morris to McDonald, Mary
May 16 1795    Ginnings, William to Hoppom, Mary*
Oct  1 1796    Gipson, Mary to Martin, Alexander*
Jun  4 1795    Gisse, Peter to Deiter, Susannah*
Dec 12 1790    Gist, Ceal to Cole, Abraham Jr.*
Jun  4 1785    Gist, David to Hammond, Rebecca*
Nov 30 1792    Gist, Jemima to Dorsey, John*
Nov 13 1783    Gist, John Elder to Trip, Frances*
Jan 21 1778    Gist, Mordecai to Sterrett, Mary*
Nov 13 1779    Gist, Sarah to Richards, John*
Jul  2 1778    Gist, Sarah to Smith, Joseph*
May  9 1792    Gist, Thomas to Cockey, Penelope Dye*
```

Jul 29 1785	Gist, Thomas to Kelly, Ruth
Jul 11 1785	Gittelman, John to Maydwell, Mary
Mar 11 1788	Gittings, Eleanor to Croxall, James*
Nov 3 1792	Gittings, Elizabeth to Smith, Lambert*
Oct 5 1779	Gittings, James to Gorsuch, Mary*
Apr 22 1793	Gittings, James to Sterett, Harriott*
Feb 9 1795	Gittings, Mary to Ringold, Thomas*
Nov 20 1788	Gittings, Richard to Sterett, Mary*
Dec 6 1794	Given, James to Green, Elizabeth*
Dec 19 1792	Given, Mary to Brown, Robert*
Oct 25 1782	Givin, John to McClung, Mary*
Jan 7 1794	Gladman, Barbary to Cross, Nicodemus*
Jun 9 1792	Gladman, Cassandra to Maddox, George*
Aug 29 1778	Gladman, Margaret to Buckingham, William*
Mar 30 1779	Gladman, Michael to Porter, Aminer*
Aug 14 1798	Gladman, Rachel to Baker, Morris
Dec 12 1788	Gladman, Rachel to Robinson, William
Apr 28 1792	Gladman, Thomas to Weir, Eleanor*
May 31 1798	Glanvile, Stephen to Stevenson, Sarah*
Jun 15 1793	Glaply, Nancy to McNamarak, Matthew*
May 5 1791	Glarany, Francis Henry to Dechamp, Elizabeth
Feb 27 1798	Glede, James to Fields, Comfort*
Aug 13 1793	Gledine, Mary to Prudheimme, John Baptiste*
Feb 11 1795	Gleede, Caroline to Grant, William*
Jun 18 1797	Gleeson, Roger to Bryan, Catharine*
Sep 22 1797	Gleeson, Winiford to Spellard, Matthias*
Feb 5 1785	Glen, Jean to Miles, Joshua*
May 29 1782	Glen, Samuel to Rone, Ann*
May 23 1795	Glenn, Hanson William to Penn, Catharine*
May 19 1798	Glodin, Juliana to Sharp, Andrew*
Oct 19 1791	Glover, Joshua to Dorsey, Rachel*
Nov 13 1790	Glover, Sally to Beasman, George*
Oct 19 1798	Glovers, Charlotte to Smith, Barnet*
Apr 6 1779	Glynn, James to Roberts, Elizabeth*
Nov 26 1798	Goalin, Thomas to Baxter, Hesther*
Apr 17 1793	Gocchea, Charles to Froggett, Mary*
Jun 24 1786	Goddard, William to Larew, Elizabeth*
Jun 23 1783	Goddard, William to Rockholt, Ann
Apr 22 1778	Godfrey, Bennum to Bullock, Mary*
Mar 27 1781	Godfrey, Mary to Jacob, William
Apr 17 1797	Godfrey, Mary to Norman, Levy*
Nov 17 1796	Godin, Francis to Meek, Margaret
Mar 27 1798	Godman, Elizabeth to Bayley, Thomas
Feb 7 1792	Goe, Henry Bateman to Gettings, Susannah*
Oct 5 1790	Goe, William to Jones, Cassandra*
Aug 23 1794	Goetz, John to Nondenborg, Rachel*
Jan 3 1793	Goghan, John to Donsheath, Mary
Jul 18 1794	Gold, Margaret to DeValcourt, Alexander*
Aug 4 1785	Gold, Mary to Meak, William
Jul 20 1793	Gold, Pollish to Friggot, Sarah*
Oct 5 1781	Goldsbury, Elizabeth to Coward, Richard
Oct 26 1778	Golligen, Mary to Mucmen, Nathaniel*
Oct 25 1788	Gones, Abraham to Gillings, Mary*
Feb 4 1790	Good, Samuel to White, Eleanor*
Oct 30 1794	Goodfellow, Mary to Tracey, Joshua*
Aug 26 1778	Goodinn, Margaret to Nabbs, Thomas*

Apr 21 1778	Goodman, Elizabeth to Hipsilly, Joshua*
Aug 26 1779	Goodman, Sarah to Ward, Francis*
Dec 28 1790	Goodridge, Mary to Willey, Harry
Aug 5 1794	Goodwin, Achsah to Wilkins, William*
Jul 14 1798	Goodwin, James to Vincent, Lilly*
Sep 22 1781	Goodwin, James to Williams, Catherine*
Mar 15 1779	Goodwin, Lyde to Leiy, Abigail*
Feb 15 1798	Goodwin, Moses to Geoghagen, Elizabeth*
Dec 8 1783	Goodwin, Pleasance to Coleman, John
May 20 1793	Goodwin, Sarah to Garn, William*
Dec 30 1782	Goodwin, Thomas to Fennell, Mary
Sep 18 1798	Gordan, Anne to Edwards, Thomas*
Jul 7 1796	Gordon, George to Ober, Elizabeth*
Mar 25 1778	Gordon, James to Barkever, Mary*
Aug 1 1778	Gordon, James to Skinner, Jane*
Feb 10 1795	Gordon, John to Myers, Sophia*
Mar 25 1797	Gordon, John to Wilson, Eleanor*
Dec 13 1787	Gordon, Mary to King, Michael*
Jul 5 1794	Gordon, Michael to Savage, Frances*
Nov 27 1795	Gordon, Philip to Williams, Silby*
May 12 1781	Gordon, Sarah to Jones, William*
Apr 18 1788	Gordon, William to Pocock, Elizabeth
May 5 1784	Gordon, William to White, Tomison*
Dec 3 1789	Gore, George to Fry, Barbary*
Aug 29 1785	Gore, John to Clark, Clarissa
Oct 29 1790	Gore, Richard to Mondgomery, Letty*
Nov 7 1794	Gore, Richard to Sandillend, Allay*
Jan 21 1778	Gorman, Mary to Bolton, Richard*
Oct 20 1788	Gorman, Mary to Miles, Daniel*
Sep 17 1796	Gormley, Cornelius to O'Brian, Mary*
Mar 5 1782	Gorsuch, Aberilla to Warrell, John*
Jun 5 1783	Gorsuch, Benjamin to Holland, Mary
Jan 20 1781	Gorsuch, Charity to Kelly, Thomas*
Dec 22 1784	Gorsuch, Charles to Dimmett, Dealley
Oct 30 1786	Gorsuch, David to Gorsuch, Rebecca
Sep 18 1793	Gorsuch, Deborah to Bryan, Nicholas*
Mar 24 1794	Gorsuch, Dickinson to Talbott, Mary
Apr 25 1793	Gorsuch, Eleanor to Merryman, Joseph*
Feb 21 1778	Gorsuch, Elizabeth to Bond, Henry*
Jan 29 1794	Gorsuch, Elizabeth to Merryman, Luke*
Nov 15 1783	Gorsuch, Elizabeth to Stansbury, Elijah*
Dec 7 1785	Gorsuch, Elizabeth to Weatherby, Daniel
Jan 21 1796	Gorsuch, Jacob to Hitherton, Elizabeth*
Feb 7 1789	Gorsuch, Jemima to Stansbury, James*
Dec 19 1795	Gorsuch, John to Galloway, Sarah*
Oct 3 1791	Gorsuch, John to McClung, Mary*
Oct 22 1791	Gorsuch, John to Price, Elizabeth*
Nov 29 1797	Gorsuch, John to Riley, Mary
May 16 1797	Gorsuch, Joshua to Diamond, Ann*
Jun 24 1795	Gorsuch, Joshua to Smith, Ann*
May 10 1794	Gorsuch, Julian to Dorman, William B.*
Oct 9 1790	Gorsuch, Kesiah to Buck, Christopher*
Jun 25 1794	Gorsuch, Keziah to Heddington, Nathan*
Nov 8 1790	Gorsuch, Kitty to Gorsuch, Norman*
Jun 30 1790	Gorsuch, Margaret to Pindell, Thomas*
Oct 5 1779	Gorsuch, Mary to Gittings, James*

Apr 12 1786	Gorsuch, Mary to Jessop, Charles*
Feb 9 1793	Gorsuch, Mary to Rhode, George*
Sep 13 1779	Gorsuch, Nathan to Pearce, Balasha*
Nov 8 1790	Gorsuch, Norman to Gorsuch, Kitty*
Jan 20 1789	Gorsuch, Prudence to Williams, Benjamin*
Nov 4 1783	Gorsuch, Rachael to Hooper, James*
Nov 3 1792	Gorsuch, Rachel to Cole, Stephen*
Jan 16 1796	Gorsuch, Rachel to Griffith, Abednigo*
May 26 1790	Gorsuch, Rachel to Worrell, Caleb
Oct 30 1786	Gorsuch, Rebecca to Gorsuch, David
Aug 8 1782	Gorsuch, Robert to Donovan, Sarah*
Jun 15 1785	Gorsuch, Ruth to Perrigoy, Charles
Aug 11 1795	Gorsuch, Ruth to Perrigoy, James*
Nov 26 1791	Gorsuch, Ruth to Williams, John*
Mar 12 1781	Gorsuch, Sarah to Hicks, Abraham*
Jan 19 1791	Gorsuch, Sarah to Hurst, Benedict*
Feb 14 1778	Gorsuch, Thomas to Chapman, Ellen*
Dec 15 1787	Gorsuch, Thomas to McClung, Rachael*
Mar 29 1779	Gorsuch, Thomas to Wheelar, Keziah*
May 11 1779	Gorsuch, Urith to Ensor, John*
Jan 9 1783	Gorsuch, William to Tipton, Caroline*
Nov 14 1787	Gorsuch, William to Tipton, Penelope*
Jun 6 1793	Gorsuch, William to Vaughan, Aberellah*
Oct 21 1790	Gosjean, John James to Frigle, Mary*
Feb 5 1785	Goslin, Ann to Israel, Ely*
Sep 30 1795	Goslin, Mary to Poole, Benjamin*
Mar 31 1778	Goslin, Mordecai to Seabrooks, Lippy*
Dec 13 1788	Goslin, Sarah to Wattles, Chandler
Mar 21 1789	Gosnel, Rachel to Israel, Robert*
Mar 8 1788	Gosnel, Rachel to Parker, William
Feb 20 1797	Gosnell, Ann to Cook, Emanuel*
Oct 17 1795	Gosnell, Charles to Brown, Sarah*
Oct 13 1779	Gosnell, Elizabeth to Brooks, Thomas*
Oct 1 1792	Gosnell, Greenberry to Pinbarton, Ruth*
Jan 19 1778	Gosnell, Margaret to Ware, John*
Jan 12 1791	Gosnell, Mordecai to Cole, Sarah*
Jan 21 1791	Gosnell, Peter to Shipley, Nancy*
May 29 1798	Gosnell, Rachel to Israel, Robert*
Jan 25 1797	Gosnell, Sarah to Wilmott, John*
Jan 19 1785	Gotset, Anne to Sutton, Thomas*
Mar 2 1785	Gott, Achsah Green to Allen, William Towson*
Nov 12 1779	Gott, Ann to Bosley, Joshua
Dec 13 1791	Gott, Edward to Bond, Mary*
Sep 19 1797	Gott, Elizabeth to Riland, Arthur*
Dec 16 1795	Gott, Richard to Bailey, Ruth*
Jun 23 1778	Gott, Sarah to Stevenson, John*
Jun 8 1793	Gott, Susannah to Hunt, Phinias*
Jun 3 1791	Gottier, Deborah to Gardiner, Obed*
Apr 28 1794	Gough, Frances Philips to Stansbury, Joseph of John*
Apr 22 1789	Gough, Frances to Clarke, William*
May 16 1788	Gough, Harry to Onion, Patty*
Dec 17 1787	Gough, Sophia to Carroll, James
Aug 8 1794	Goujaud, Joseph to Guarique, Susane*
Mar 12 1796	Gould, John to Wheeler, Margaret*
Oct 23 1788	Gould, Martha to Goulding, John*
Dec 15 1791	Gould, Pete to White, Mary*

```
Oct 22 1795    Goulding, Elizabeth to Todd, Philip*
Oct 23 1788    Goulding, John to Gould, Martha*
Sep 11 1794    Goulding, Mary to Clopper, Peter*
May  6 1794    Goulding, Patrick to Young, Arabella*
Jan 30 1781    Gouldsbury, Mark to Kennedy, Judeah*
Nov 19 1792    Gouldsmith, Martha to Taylor, George*
Oct 26 1797    Gouldsmith, Mary Ann to Kell, Thomas*
Oct 25 1798    Govan, Mary W. to Howard, James G.*
Sep 28 1793    Govax, Milly to Cornish, Levin*
Apr  2 1793    Gover, Gerrard to Giles, Sarah*
May 26 1792    Gow, John Hammond to Barnett, Ursula*
May  4 1779    Gowan, Mary to Carragan, Edward
Aug  8 1778    Grace, Margaret to Grimes, Vincent*
Oct 19 1793    Grafflin, Jacob to Frymiller, Mary F.*
Sep 20 1784    Grafft, William to Meake, Catharine*
Apr 18 1786    Grafton, Sarah to Doyle, John*
Feb  3 1785    Graham, James to Sorivenor, Mary*
Jun 28 1778    Graham, William to Robinson, Liba*
Oct 12 1784    Grainger, Ann to Peshaw, Joseph*
Oct 23 1793    Grallot, Francis to Fisher, Catharine*
Apr  6 1786    Graner, Daniel to Shartel, Margaret*
Sep 27 1782    Granger, Joseph to Criss, Sarah*
Nov 22 1784    Granger, Margaret to Labatt, John Baptist
Apr 17 1783    Granger, Mary Ann to Millesh, Cosin Constinate
Jan 26 1795    Granget, Mary to Morton, John Andrew*
Mar 20 1783    Grant, Alexander to Johnson, Mary*
Dec 12 1782    Grant, Ann to Maxwell, James*
Aug  7 1794    Grant, Daniel to Nelson, Isabella*
Jan  1 1788    Grant, Jane to Hacket, John*
Mar 31 1798    Grant, John to Seaver, Elizabeth*
Feb 18 1797    Grant, Nancy to Smith, George*
Feb 11 1795    Grant, William to Gleede, Caroline*
May 19 1798    Grarish, Francis to Holbrook, Rachel*
Sep 12 1778    Grasmith, Maydelena to Wille, Frederick C.*
Apr 22 1795    Grate, Abigail to Reeves, William*
Feb  1 1796    Graves, Ann to Ivory, John*
Aug 21 1797    Graves, Ebenezer to Anderson, Mary*
Feb 21 1797    Graves, Jane to Curtin, Thomas*
Aug  1 1785    Graves, Jane to Dukes, Christopher
Sep 24 1794    Graves, Mary to Roberson, George*
Sep 12 1797    Graves, Nero to Benson, Alice*
Mar  2 1796    Graves, William to Williams, Margaret*
Feb 16 1788    Gray, Ann to Rice, Joseph
Oct 18 1796    Gray, Anne to Gatchel, Samuel H.*
Jun  1 1796    Gray, Arabella to Boreing, Absalom*
Oct 17 1798    Gray, Elizabeth to Kimisler, John*
Feb 27 1798    Gray, Elizabeth to Migarnty, Thomas*
Dec 28 1792    Gray, James to Bowen, Ann
Apr 26 1792    Gray, John to Foster, Lucy*
Sep  3 1795    Gray, Joseph to Wilson, Elizabeth*
Apr 30 1789    Gray, Joshua to Drane, Rebecca
Dec 23 1796    Gray, Lynch to Denton, Hannah*
Jun 23 1790    Gray, Lynch to McLaughlin, Catherine*
Jul  2 1783    Gray, Lynch to Rutter, Sarah*
Jul 11 1793    Gray, Mary Ann to Leonard, Philip
Sep 28 1797    Gray, Mary to Dungan, Thomas*
```

Oct 14 1784	Gray, Mary to Sullivan, Daniel*
Jun 14 1791	Gray, Mary to Williams, Christian
Nov 14 1792	Gray, Nancy to Ashbaw, John*
Aug 12 1794	Gray, Nancy to Robertson, Joseph*
Mar 22 1798	Gray, Peter to Bradburn, Mary*
Nov 21 1781	Gray, Richard to Brewer, Elizabeth
Oct 28 1789	Gray, Sarah to Wilcocks, James*
Jun 3 1797	Gray, Susannah V. to Gaither, James*
Feb 19 1781	Gray, Zachariah to Holmes, Sophia*
Nov 17 1787	Graybill, Mary to Rutler, Thomas Jr.
Aug 12 1798	Graydy, Jane to McCormick, John*
Jul 13 1782	Grear, Catherine to Lambden, Thomas*
Feb 25 1782	Green, Abraham to Cole, Elizabeth*
Feb 2 1798	Green, Allwaturs Thompson to Holbrooks, Delilah
Feb 11 1797	Green, Ann Pamelia to Ball, William*
Oct 25 1797	Green, Ann to Coogle, John*
May 24 1798	Green, Ann to Maidwell, John*
Jan 26 1797	Green, Anna to Dorsey, Lloyd*
Nov 10 1798	Green, Bennett to Jones, Ann*
Mar 25 1786	Green, Catharine to Bryson, John*
Jul 30 1790	Green, Catherine to Rotch, George*
Mar 14 1798	Green, Charles to Lane, Ann*
Mar 19 1796	Green, Clement to Todd, Rebecca*
Jul 2 1783	Green, Delilah to Tibbet, Walter*
Mar 7 1798	Green, Eleander to Gill, Martha*
Nov 9 1793	Green, Eleanor to Jones, William*
May 6 1783	Green, Elisha to Chamberlain, Priscilla*
Aug 21 1793	Green, Elizabeth to Caples, William*
Sep 10 1796	Green, Elizabeth to Dawney, William*
Dec 6 1794	Green, Elizabeth to Given, James*
Apr 7 1798	Green, Elizabeth to Lawson, Charles*
Jan 21 1795	Green, Ezekiel to Denton, Darcus*
Jun 21 1788	Green, Henry to Boering, Elizabeth*
Jan 14 1794	Green, Henry to Walters, Elizabeth*
Apr 14 1778	Green, James to McGloughlin, Catharine*
Oct 27 1792	Green, James to Painter, Ann*
Mar 24 1792	Green, Joel to Buck, Elizabeth*
Nov 6 1790	Green, John to McKinsley, Alice*
Mar 24 1792	Green, John to Wheeler, Rachel*
Mar 25 1789	Green, Joseph to Stansbury, Catharine*
May 31 1786	Green, Joshua to Kelly, Rebecca*
Nov 24 1796	Green, Josias to Moseh, Mary*
Jun 25 1789	Green, Mary to Baldry, William*
May 18 1795	Green, Mary to Covinton, Levin*
Sep 23 1794	Green, Mary to Daugherty, Neal*
Jun 28 1794	Green, Mary to Shay, James*
May 16 1788	Green, Mary to Streney, Nicholas*
Nov 3 1784	Green, Millison to Ricketts, Edward*
Oct 14 1786	Green, Nicholas to Cole, Temperance
Nov 30 1797	Green, Rebecca to Pittengill, James
Jul 23 1796	Green, Samuel to Nailor, Hannah*
Sep 10 1791	Green, Sarah to Duff, John*
Apr 28 1798	Green, Sarah to Kilman, James*
Oct 13 1786	Green, Susannah to Perrigoy, Joseph*
Apr 17 1795	Green, Temperance to Denton, James*
Mar 27 1781	Green, Thomas to Barry, Ann

```
Aug 29 1795    Green, Thomas to Harryman, Ann*
Dec 20 1792    Green, William to Beset, Susannah*
Dec 21 1795    Green, William to League, Chloe*
Nov 17 1792    Green, William to Stinchcomb, Achsah*
Dec 26 1780    Greene, Bednego to Burk, Patty*
Mar 30 1782    Greene, Cloe to Parks, William*
Oct  3 1779    Greene, Sarah to Clarke, John*
Jun 25 1793    Greenfield, Ashberry to Kemmell, Sarah*
Jan 12 1792    Greenfield, Cordelia to Carnan, Morris*
Jan 15 1791    Greenfield, Dinah to Edwards, John*
May 25 1778    Greenfield, Elizabeth to Hannah, John*
Jan  5 1793    Greenfield, Elizabeth to Turner, Robert
Oct 28 1790    Greenfield, Joanna to Robinson, John*
Sep 11 1788    Greenfield, Kezia to Dilworth, William*
Feb 12 1791    Greenfield, Nathaniel to Hatton, Elizabeth*
Oct 17 1790    Greenfield, Patty to Teer, Owen
Jul  1 1784    Greenfield, Thomas Truman to Taler, Frances*
Feb  7 1797    Greenland, Nathan to Carlean, Sarah*
Sep 19 1795    Greenwood, Benjamin to Briggs, Ann*
Sep  6 1794    Greenwood, Margaret to Elder, John*
Sep  3 1782    Greenwood, Thomas to Peddicord, Sopiah*
Aug 30 1796    Greenwood, Thomas to Stansbury, Keziah*
Jul 30 1782    Greer, Catherine to Lamden, Thomas*
Oct 13 1794    Gregler, Elizabeth to Lepress, Joseph*
Dec 29 1798    Gregory, Anne to Jones, William
Jun  6 1789    Gregory, David to Williams, Elizabeth*
Dec  2 1795    Gregory, Elizabeth to Arnel, Peter*
May  5 1796    Gregory, James to Bond, Sarah*
Nov  8 1783    Gregory, John to Dunn, Catherine*
Jan 13 1790    Gregory, John to Grimes, Elizabeth*
Sep 15 1779    Gregory, Margaret to Smith, Joseph*
Aug 25 1798    Gregory, Ralph to Chenowith, Sarah*
Apr 13 1797    Gregory, Rebecca to O'Haben, David*
Oct 23 1790    Greogery, James to Wigley, Jane*
May 29 1789    Gressman, Agnes to Small, James*
Mar 22 1796    Gribel, Sarah to Doah, James*
Oct  7 1778    Grier, Aaron to Gibson, Jane*
Nov 29 1783    Griffee, Susannah to Cartee, Daniel*
Jul 30 1781    Griffen, Charles to Kelley, Rebecca*
Feb 24 1796    Griffen, John to Frog, Elizabeth*
Mar  5 1778    Griffen, John to Ridgely, Elizabeth*
Dec 13 1793    Griffen, Rebecca to Cooper, Robert Clark*
Nov  7 1792    Griffen, Sarah to Boone, John*
Apr 17 1784    Griffen, Thomas to Jones, Elizabeth*
Apr  7 1796    Griffen, Walter to Pearson, Elizabeth*
Jan  8 1796    Griffey, Jane to Carter, John*
Aug 10 1793    Griffin, Abraham to Miller, Mary*
Nov  6 1787    Griffin, Ann to Bivans, Joseph*
May 14 1783    Griffin, George to Cramphin, Polly*
May  4 1786    Griffin, Jemima to Henderson, George
Jul 15 1784    Griffin, Jemimah to Derick, David*
Dec  1 1784    Griffin, Joseph to Hughes, Ruth
Jan 31 1784    Griffin, Luke to Board, Ann*
Dec  6 1792    Griffin, Margaret to Armstrong, Solomon*
Jan 27 1794    Griffin, Peter to Hacket, Helin*
Feb 14 1784    Griffin, Rebecca to Mahanah, Daniel*
```

```
Dec 31 1777    Griffin, Rebecca to Weston, Josephus*
May 16 1795    Griffin, William to Chambers, Jane*
May 24 1790    Griffin, York to Belt, Susannah
May 10 1778    Griffis, Martha to Bard, James*
Jan 16 1796    Griffith, Abednigo to Gorsuch, Rachel*
Mar 26 1790    Griffith, Achsah to Boon, Robert*
Jan  6 1795    Griffith, Benjamin to Worrell, Rachel*
Jan 16 1792    Griffith, Elizabeth to Worthington, James*
Dec 21 1789    Griffith, Ely Ridgely to Spurrier, Sarah*
Dec 23 1783    Griffith, George to Lane, Dianna*
Aug  1 1782    Griffith, Greenberry to Manning, Lydia*
Dec  7 1796    Griffith, James to Ford, Mary*
Sep 12 1795    Griffith, James to Malonee, Margaret*
Oct  4 1798    Griffith, John to Jeffries, Sarah*
Nov 13 1779    Griffith, Kinsey to Porine, Jane*
Oct  6 1783    Griffith, Martha to Tador, William*
May  2 1783    Griffith, Mary to Slingsby*
Oct 22 1792    Griffith, Milky to Pierpoint, Benedict*
Oct 26 1779    Griffith, Nathan to Ogg, Catharine*
Mar 22 1794    Griffith, Nathan to Thomas, Susannah*
Feb 23 1778    Griffith, Owen to Haile, Ann*
Nov 14 1787    Griffith, Rachel to Bell, John Sprigg*
May  3 1792    Griffith, Rachel to Hiede, George*
Nov 18 1796    Griffith, Rachel to Parks, Nathan*
May 12 1790    Griffith, Rebecca to Steffee, Harman*
Sep  6 1796    Griffith, Ruth to Kelly, Samuel*
Jul 27 1785    Griffith, Sarah to Reynolds, Tobias*
Aug 29 1793    Griffith, William to Frazier, Ann*
Mar 19 1796    Grigley, William to Tanner, Nancy*
Oct 27 1790    Grimes, Aery to Macklefresh, Ely*
Nov  1 1780    Grimes, Ann to Sutton, Isaac*
Jan 13 1790    Grimes, Elizabeth to Gregory, John*
Oct 14 1789    Grimes, Elizabeth to Hilton, Abraham
Oct 28 1786    Grimes, Elizabeth to Wilson, Joshua
May 18 1782    Grimes, George to Fowler, Christiana
Oct 18 1796    Grimes, Hannah to Duffey, John
Oct 21 1797    Grimes, James to Bryan, Sarah*
Oct 23 1779    Grimes, James to Horsler, Sarah*
Oct 19 1782    Grimes, Jenny to Shipley, Charle*
May 22 1790    Grimes, John to Garrett, Nancy*
Jan 13 1778    Grimes, John to Hendon, Delia*
Oct  2 1790    Grimes, John to Morrison, Mary*
Dec 28 1785    Grimes, Margaret to Fonday, Abraham
Jan  3 1798    Grimes, Rachel to Clarke, William*
Feb 11 1795    Grimes, Rezin to Macklefish, Susannah*
Aug 16 1796    Grimes, Sarah to Caine, Henry
Feb 10 1792    Grimes, Sarah to Elender, George*
Apr  4 1797    Grimes, Sebastian to Bryan, Jemima
Aug  8 1778    Grimes, Vincent to Grace, Margaret*
Dec 22 1785    Grimes, William to Shipley, Sarah*
Dec 23 1794    Groce, John Antoine to Le Monnur, Catharine Marie*
Nov 17 1790    Groff, Henry to Long, Elizabeth*
Feb 18 1793    Groff, Sebastine to Cockey, Eleanor*
Dec  2 1797    Grooen, Priscilla to Proctor, Hugh*
Apr  5 1795    Groom, William to Miller, Isabella*
Aug 25 1792    Gross, Barbara to Weiss, Felia
```

Sep 26 1794	Gross, Henry to Isaacks, Elizabeth*
Oct 4 1794	Gross, Polly to Boyle, Thomas*
Jan 22 1798	Gross, Simon to Allison, Ann Job
Dec 17 1795	Grosse, Louis to Wise, Catharine*
May 18 1782	Grouev, Sarah to Hardin, Nicholas*
Jul 1 1790	Grove, Hannah to McClan, Robert*
Apr 21 1790	Groven, Jemima to Mockbee, William*
Jan 26 1786	Grover, Benjamin to Dorsey, Nancy*
Nov 4 1788	Grover, Drusilla to Talbott, Richard Colegate*
Aug 6 1785	Grover, Elizabeth to Davis, Ambrou*
Jan 26 1782	Grover, Elizabeth to Talbott, Jeremiah
Apr 4 1798	Grover, George to Benton, Elizabeth*
Jun 29 1796	Grover, Jenny to Weelon, Henry*
Oct 12 1791	Grover, Mary to Allen, John*
Oct 31 1789	Grover, William to Bosley, Sarah*
Oct 31 1798	Groverman, Anthony to La Dadus, Henrietta*
Oct 11 1796	Groves, Ezekiel to Ireland, Linny*
Apr 14 1798	Groves, John to Carroll, Ann*
Aug 8 1789	Groves, Mary to Sexsmith, Simoin*
Sep 21 1798	Grub, Conrad to Block, Sophia*
Jul 7 1796	Grunnor, John to Baker, Barbara*
Aug 8 1794	Guarique, Susane to Goujaud, Joseph*
Mar 30 1792	Gudgeon, Elizabeth to Boyce, Benjamin*
Jul 6 1791	Gudgeon, Elizabeth to Hughes, John*
Dec 3 1795	Gudgeon, Mary to Howland, John Wilks*
Oct 1 1789	Gue, Joseph to Dells, Ann*
Jul 2 1796	Guersois, Louisa to Bouti, John*
Dec 29 1795	Guffey, Ann to Bevan, Richard*
Nov 25 1793	Guilman, Suzanne to L'Engledene, Jean*
Sep 21 1793	Guiron, Johnna to Hurley, Michael*
Mar 4 1789	Guishard, David to Patterson, Rachel*
Feb 22 1796	Guishard, Mark to McCabe, Catharine*
Nov 27 1792	Gultry, Joshua to Keener, Elizabeth*
Oct 16 1798	Gums, Manuel to Crips, Sarah*
May 3 1796	Gunby, Stephen to Stansbury, Ann*
Dec 7 1796	Gutchers, David to Cleamer, Mary*
Aug 31 1779	Guth, Rebecca to Bocklob, Charles*
Sep 1 1779	Guth, Rebecca to Bocklob, Charles*
May 13 1797	Gutlerow, John to Joiner, Rebecca*
Jan 10 1785	Gutridge, Sarah to Leech, Benjamin*
Jun 21 1798	Gutrow, Mary to Chamberlain, Charles*
Aug 22 1789	Gutry, Ann to Dugan, James*
Dec 6 1783	Guttery, Joshua to Keener, Susannah
Mar 23 1797	Gutthrey, William to Bateman, Mary*
May 2 1797	Guyer, Dennis to Oldfield, Jane*
Apr 29 1784	Guyer, John to Hull, Elizabeth*
May 24 1788	Guyton, Elizabeth to Steward, William*
May 31 1796	Guyton, Ruth to Watkins, John*
Dec 10 1787	Gwinn, Edward to Dorsey, Achsah*
Dec 24 1793	Gwinn, Ellen to Carpenter, John*
Feb 8 1797	Gwynn, Elizabeth to Gwynn, Robert*
Feb 8 1797	Gwynn, Robert to Gwynn, Elizabeth*
Mar 18 1794	Hablestin, Bartholomew to Machana, Harriott*
Mar 5 1794	Hacket, Barshalea to Inloes, James*
Jan 27 1794	Hacket, Helin to Griffin, Peter*
Jan 1 1788	Hacket, John to Grant, Jane*

Feb 28 1797	Hackey, Mary to McLinsy, Michael*
Nov 28 1787	Haddaway, Prudence to Larrimore, James*
Dec 16 1795	Hadson, Daniel to Ford, Eleanor*
May 21 1796	Hafleigh, Margaret to Fowler, Jacob*
Dec 18 1798	Hagan, Henry to Gilfoy, Nancy*
Jan 7 1782	Hagan, Hugh to McDonough, Margaret*
Jun 13 1797	Hagen, Abraham to Buchanan, Rebecca*
Dec 4 1793	Hagen, John to Bugan, Mary
Apr 2 1789	Hager, John to Gill, Susannah*
Apr 23 1795	Hagerthy, Matthew to Brat, Juiny*
Sep 16 1778	Hagerty, Catharine to Smith, Francis*
Feb 26 1794	Hagerty, Elizabeth to McElroy, William*
Oct 3 1796	Hagerty, Mary to Barrett, John*
Aug 28 1797	Hagerty, Michael to Carey, Eleanor*
Apr 13 1796	Hagsman, Samuel to Wooden, Rebecca*
Dec 26 1791	Hague, Hugh to McCoy, Catherine*
Sep 15 1794	Hahn, John Adam to Auckerman, Catherine*
Dec 3 1785	Hahn, Mariah to Turnpaugh, William
May 4 1791	Hahn, Nany to Kirby, Godfrey*
Apr 9 1798	Hahn, Peter to Smith, Eve
Sep 17 1785	Hail, Abednego to Hail, Ruth*
Sep 17 1785	Hail, Ruth to Hail, Abednego*
Aug 11 1798	Haile, Ann to Fishpaw, John*
Feb 23 1778	Haile, Ann to Griffith, Owen*
Nov 7 1794	Haile, Lydia to Peters, Conrod*
Jun 17 1782	Haile, Mary to Norwood, John*
Sep 1 1781	Haile, Neale to Hicks, Ruth
Mar 14 1795	Haile, Robert to Mitchell, Mary*
Sep 3 1783	Haile, Ruth to Baxter, Barnett
Aug 10 1789	Haile, Samuel to Ford, Carline*
Dec 3 1795	Haile, Susannah to Gill, William*
Mar 19 1798	Haile, Thomas to Neighbours, Sarah Edmondson*
Nov 27 1790	Hailey, Peter to Leary, Margaret*
Feb 5 1785	Haily, Harriet to Ghequin, Charles*
Feb 13 1793	Haines, Ann to Hansler, Philip
Jan 24 1782	Haines, Daniel to Sollers, Ann*
Oct 30 1798	Hains, Benjamin to Sisannick, Rose*
Mar 6 1782	Hains, Elizabeth to Watters, Alexander*
Nov 7 1794	Hains, Rachel to Chuaidi, Baptista*
Dec 10 1798	Hains, Rose to Stevenson, George*
Aug 23 1794	Hainsworth, Aaron to Rider, Eve*
Sep 15 1783	Halbert, Sarah to Rogers, Joseph
Feb 4 1790	Hale, Christian to Cooper, Juliet*
Oct 7 1795	Hale, Delila to Rowland, Thomas*
Jun 16 1791	Hale, Elizabeth to Boon, John Cockey Robert Bailey*
Jun 23 1795	Hale, Elizabeth to Shurred, Matthew*
Apr 23 1796	Hale, Joseph to Day, Sarah*
Dec 5 1798	Hale, Patience to Gaither, James*
Nov 1 1789	Hale, Rachael to Strong, Joseph*
Jan 26 1796	Hale, Rachel to Chinowith, George*
Sep 20 1794	Hales, Mary to Daughady, John*
Jul 15 1794	Haley, Ann to Myers, Patrick*
Apr 8 1786	Haley, Eleanor to Osborn, James*
May 15 1783	Haley, Frances to Hamilton, George*
Dec 3 1795	Haley, Mary to Aldridge, Abraham*
Nov 19 1795	Haley, Mary to Hathway, James*

Aug 8 1797	Haley, Peggy to McKeay, William*
Dec 18 1794	Haley, Peter to Larey, Elizabeth*
Oct 1 1795	Halfpenny, Patrick to Cole, Sarah*
Jan 2 1792	Halfpenny, William to Garrison, Elizabeth*
Dec 8 1780	Hall, Actions to Wheeler, William*
Jan 20 1794	Hall, Alasanah to Hotchkiss, Solomon*
Dec 23 1797	Hall, Alice to Cracroft, Luke*
Oct 31 1795	Hall, Ann to Bond, Joseph*
Mar 24 1798	Hall, Ann to Johnson, James*
Feb 28 1786	Hall, Elijah to Wheeler, Constance
Jun 23 1788	Hall, Elisha to Todd, Mary*
Apr 10 1788	Hall, Elizabeth to Howard, Charles
May 10 1797	Hall, Ellinor to Cullin, Travers*
Nov 2 1796	Hall, Ezekiel to Hammond, Elizabeth*
May 9 1788	Hall, George to Robinson, Elizabeth
Aug 5 1797	Hall, Henry to Porter, Kettuel*
Oct 30 1792	Hall, James to McGreggory, Rebecca*
Feb 2 1784	Hall, Jesse to Jacob, Patience*
Nov 16 1795	Hall, John to Lynch, Susannah*
Feb 7 1798	Hall, John to Townsend, Julian*
Sep 30 1786	Hall, Jonathan to Miller, Ann
Apr 2 1782	Hall, Mary to Irish, John*
Nov 6 1792	Hall, Nicholas to Howard, Martha*
Jun 9 1796	Hall, Sophia to Key, Philip*
May 16 1798	Hall, Susanna to Harris, John*
Sep 5 1778	Hall, Thomas to Ravelling, Ann*
Jan 9 1778	Hall, Thomas to Wheeler, Mary*
Jun 14 1786	Hall, Welthy to Perrigoy, Elisha*
Jan 23 1797	Hall, William J. to Craig, Grace*
Aug 27 1795	Hall, William to Fletcher, Mary*
Aug 6 1783	Hall, William to Steed, Sarah*
Mar 26 1796	Hallan, Hannah to Adams, William*
May 10 1798	Hallock, Anna to Welsh, John*
May 11 1791	Hallock, Elizabeth to Deluce, Francis*
Dec 21 1780	Hallock, Margaret to Daus, Josiah*
Nov 19 1779	Halmoney, ELizabeth to Street, Samuel
Aug 31 1798	Halton, Aquilla to Lee, Keziah*
Dec 27 1792	Ham, Daniel to Hamilton, Sidney
Jul 26 1783	Ham, John to Sprigg, Mary
Jun 10 1795	Ham, Thomas to Brown, Ann*
Oct 29 1778	Ham, Thomas to Merriett, Sarah
Oct 6 1798	Hambleton, Benjamin to Thomas, Sarah
Mar 25 1778	Hambleton, Jane to Tumblison, William*
Apr 19 1791	Hambleton, Lydia to Eiphenston, David*
Jul 11 1798	Hamilton, Agnes to Hawk, Stephen
Oct 20 1790	Hamilton, Ann to Merrick, Patrick*
Oct 29 1796	Hamilton, Charles to Sinklair, Elizabeth*
Jan 14 1793	Hamilton, Ephraim to Hanies, Sarah*
May 15 1783	Hamilton, George to Haley, Frances*
Apr 14 1796	Hamilton, George to Williams, Rachel*
Jun 10 1796	Hamilton, James to Bailey, Catharine
Jun 27 1788	Hamilton, James to Bond, Cassandra*
Oct 13 1779	Hamilton, James to McCracken, Elizabeth*
Oct 24 1797	Hamilton, Jane Flemming to Doyne, Robert*
Aug 8 1782	Hamilton, John Agnu to Shepherd, Margaret*
Apr 13 1790	Hamilton, John to Reith, Margaret*

Jun 26 1795	Hamilton, Margaret to Morrison, John*
Jul 4 1791	Hamilton, Margaret to Welsh, Henry
Apr 7 1798	Hamilton, Maria to Bryne, Bartholomew C.*
Dec 7 1797	Hamilton, Pliney to Barry, Abigail*
Jan 4 1786	Hamilton, Samuel to Baker, Elizabeth
Dec 27 1792	Hamilton, Sidney to Ham, Daniel
May 21 1798	Hamlin, Jacob to Fisher, Catharine*
Jun 23 1792	Hammel, Catherine to Chapman, Joshua*
Jan 20 1782	Hammer, Catherine to Collert, Joseph*
Aug 5 1778	Hammer, Hannah to Cannor, John*
Jun 22 1792	Hammer, Henry to Miller, Mary*
May 11 1791	Hammersley, Thomas to Thompson, Prudence
Sep 12 1795	Hammitt, Thomas to Stine, Mariah Rosannah*
Apr 14 1783	Hammon, Thomas to Hoppom, Eleanor*
Nov 19 1788	Hammond, Abraham George to Garetson, Mary*
Mar 18 1778	Hammond, Ann to Burkhead, John*
Jan 30 1795	Hammond, Ann to Foulds, James*
Nov 14 1798	Hammond, Ann to Woods, William
Jun 16 1792	Hammond, Avir to Jub, William*
May 20 1785	Hammond, Charles to Smith, Providence*
Apr 16 1791	Hammond, Eleanor to Fowler, George*
Aug 4 1784	Hammond, Elizabeth Ann to King, William
Nov 2 1796	Hammond, Elizabeth to Hall, Ezekiel*
Jun 11 1779	Hammond, George to Wells, Elizabeth
Feb 16 1789	Hammond, Henrietta to Dorsey, Joshua
Mar 13 1778	Hammond, Isaac to Bond, Susanna*
Mar 4 1795	Hammond, John to Anderson, Elizabeth*
Nov 25 1783	Hammond, John to McConnell, Elizabeth*
Dec 24 1783	Hammond, Mary to Stiles, Lawrence*
May 5 1796	Hammond, Mary to Willey, Isaac*
Sep 12 1778	Hammond, Nancey to Labesius, John
Nov 2 1790	Hammond, Philip to Clarke, Mary*
Mar 23 1785	Hammond, Rachel to Morris, John
Jun 4 1785	Hammond, Rebecca to Gist, David*
Mar 13 1790	Hammond, Rebecca to Young, Richard*
Jan 8 1793	Hammond, Rezin to Joyce, Nancy*
May 11 1793	Hamphrey, Nathan to Gilley, Susannah
Aug 15 1783	Hams, Jacob to Tarmer, Elizabeth*
Aug 23 1783	Hancock, Joseph to Iams, Milla*
Dec 23 1797	Hancock, Mary to Waters, Aquila*
Jul 29 1797	Hancock, Nancy to Boon, Robert*
Feb 17 1778	Hancock, Stephen to Ridgely, Belinda*
Jul 14 1798	Hancock, William to Waters, Elizabeth*
Mar 29 1791	Hand, Amelia to Lock, Nathaniel*
Jun 15 1786	Hand, Thomas to Hanward, Mary*
Jul 22 1781	Hand, William to Sillet, Sarah*
Feb 12 1798	Handles, James to Kelly, Catharine*
Jun 28 1798	Handling, Patrick to James, Jane*
May 25 1793	Hands, Ephraim to Garretson, Sarah*
May 31 1783	Hands, Lydia to Robinson, Richard
Nov 24 1798	Hands, Margaret to Duvall, Job*
Sep 9 1789	Hands, Mary to Vincent, Samuel*
Sep 6 1786	Hanes, Dolley to Dorsey, Bazel John*
Jan 14 1793	Hanies, Sarah to Hamilton, Ephraim*
Jun 4 1795	Hanken, Elizabeth to Miller, Matthew*
Mar 15 1797	Hankey, Mary to Durka, Pearl*

Dec 21 1797	Hankin, Ann to Myers, Jacob*
Feb 10 1785	Hanley, Mary to Rix, Robert
Dec 30 1784	Hanley, Sarah to Archman, Henry
Dec 30 1784	Hanley, Susannah to Mitchell, William
Jun 21 1798	Hanna, Andrew to Mayra, Ann*
Nov 7 1797	Hannah, Edward to McLure, Rebecca*
Nov 26 1791	Hannah, Isabella to Croxall, John*
May 25 1778	Hannah, John to Greenfield, Elizabeth*
Jan 29 1793	Hannah, John to Linkens, Hannah*
Oct 16 1784	Hannah to Prout, Richard (negroes)
Jul 14 1781	Hannan, Elizabeth to Flattery, James
Feb 10 1789	Hannan, Elizabeth to Host, Michael*
Aug 18 1792	Hannan, Elizabeth to Towers, John*
Jan 16 1796	Hannan, James to Thomas, Eliza*
Jan 3 1795	Hannan, John to Towers, Margaret*
May 5 1785	Hannen, George to Pack, Rosannah
Feb 13 1793	Hansler, Philip to Haines, Ann
Sep 29 1798	Hanson, Dory to Clay, Nancy
Jan 1 1783	Hanson, Eleanor to Boyd, James*
Feb 23 1782	Hanson, James to Biven, Aberilla*
Apr 25 1791	Hanson, James to Skipper, Rachael*
Apr 13 1784	Hanson, Peter to Smith, Ann*
Jun 20 1797	Hanson, Peter to Yepson, Hannah*
Feb 4 1778	Hanuf, Stophel to Hook, Barbara*
Feb 6 1778	Hanuf, Stophel to Hook, Barbara*
Oct 28 1781	Hanum, Christian to Roles, Ara
Jun 15 1786	Hanward, Mary to Hand, Thomas*
Sep 19 1793	Hanway, Francis to Cane, Bellinda*
Mar 9 1793	Harbest, Frederick to Lucas, Mary*
Nov 21 1778	Hard, Ruth to Williamson, Thomas
Feb 25 1794	Harden, John Borton to Hughes, Nancy*
Oct 13 1785	Hardesty, Levy to Tennant, Phebe
Mar 22 1788	Hardesty, Nancy to Wells, Richard*
Apr 14 1781	Hardin, Ignations to Davis, Sarah
May 18 1782	Hardin, Nicholas to Grouev, Sarah*
Feb 23 1793	Harding, Godfrey to Brown, Phebe
Dec 26 1792	Harding, Joseph to Hederick, Delilah
Aug 29 1795	Harding, Mary to Majors, Thomas*
Aug 21 1790	Harding, Matthew to Davis, Mary*
Jun 5 1795	Harding, Nicholas to Hobbs, Ruth*
Jan 6 1789	Hardisty, Charles to Fowler, Ann*
Feb 23 1789	Hardisty, Joshua to Bell, Ruth
Feb 13 1789	Hardisty, Rezin to King, Ann*
Dec 2 1795	Hardisty, Robert to Hopkins, Ann*
Oct 8 1778	Hardly, Esther to Collier, John*
Nov 8 1788	Hardriet, James to Carte, Ann*
Jan 6 1783	Hardy, James to Caldron, Mary
Jul 8 1794	Hardy, William to Button, Elizabeth*
Dec 5 1796	Hare, John to Drisher, Kitty*
Sep 4 1783	Hargan, Mary to McLellan, John
Apr 22 1783	Harget, Mary to Price, Peter*
Dec 27 1798	Hargrove, Thomas to Buckley, Margaret*
Apr 22 1794	Harker, Mary to Sanders, John*
Apr 13 1797	Harker, Richard to Lynch, Jemima*
Jun 28 1794	Harman, Andrew to Reynolds, Rebecca*
Jun 21 1784	Harman, Henry to Biddinger, Mary*

Nov 7 1793	Harman, James to Sorter, Mary*
Nov 12 1796	Harman, Martin to Wood, Elizabeth*
Jan 5 1789	Harmon, Ann to Fairbanks, John*
Apr 13 1785	Harmon, Mary to Reynolds, Benedicet*
May 7 1779	Harn, Mary to Pattan, Thomas*
Nov 22 1794	Harner, Daniel to Knight, Elizabeth*
Sep 8 1778	Harnett, James to Summersby, Sarah*
Jul 19 1795	Harp, Catharine to Summers, Andrew*
May 13 1794	Harp, Eleanor to Jones, William*
Feb 18 1791	Harp, James to Jones, Susannah*
Apr 21 1785	Harp, Joshua to McKinsey, Eleanor
Apr 19 1794	Harp, Mary to Sladsmon, Michael*
Mar 11 1789	Harp, Rachael to McKinsey, Aaron*
Dec 6 1777	Harp, Sarah to Jones, Jeremiah*
Mar 9 1779	Harper, Elephel to Shellim, William*
Mar 17 1779	Harper, Eliphel to Shellin, William*
Aug 19 1789	Harper, Mary to West, Elijah*
Oct 29 1778	Harriman, Caleb to Hawkins, Nancy*
Feb 26 1778	Harriman, Mary to Burton, Thomas*
Dec 9 1783	Harriman, Temperence to Marsh, Joshua*
Jun 2 1781	Harrington, Thomas to Howard, Biddy
Sep 25 1779	Harris, Ann to Rush, George*
Mar 18 1795	Harris, Asact to Orrick, Anna*
Jan 22 1788	Harris, David to Moale, Frances Halton*
May 3 1779	Harris, Deanar to Geoghegan, John*
Aug 31 1790	Harris, Edward to Sullivan, Margaret*
May 14 1796	Harris, Elias to Geary, Mary*
Jan 11 1793	Harris, Elizabeth to Fenn, William*
Jul 10 1794	Harris, James to Daull, Susannah*
Jan 28 1795	Harris, James to Moore, Eleanor*
Feb 24 1794	Harris, John to Butler, Ann*
May 16 1798	Harris, John to Hall, Susanna*
Mar 7 1779	Harris, Mary to Hill, John*
Mar 6 1786	Harris, Nancy to McCliesh, Alexander
Jun 20 1790	Harris, Nelly to Dunnavan, Pierce*
Jul 27 1793	Harris, Roseanah to Phillips, Samuel*
Feb 18 1797	Harris, Sarah to Shearly, Thomas*
Nov 13 1793	Harris, William to Constable, Mary*
Jan 6 1778	Harrison, Charles to Luton, Isabella*
Mar 3 1796	Harrison, Daniel to Hollingsworth, Eleanor*
Apr 1 1796	Harrison, Elizabeth to Marchant, John*
Apr 12 1783	Harrison, George to Shipley, Agness*
Apr 4 1785	Harrison, John to Lucas, Catherine
Oct 5 1781	Harrison, John to Merritt, Sarah
Mar 14 1783	Harrisson, Thomas to Inloes, Elizabeth*
Feb 2 1792	Harrowod, Elizabeth Ann to Smith, Zachariah*
Sep 18 1779	Harry, David to Rush, Mary
Aug 29 1795	Harryman, Ann to Green, Thomas*
May 20 1795	Harryman, Charity to Cotteral, James*
Aug 4 1797	Harryman, Elizabeth to Bond, Thomas*
Feb 8 1788	Harryman, George to Bond, Rachel
Feb 2 1785	Harryman, John to Eaglestone, Mary*
Jan 13 1785	Harryman, Joshua to Willey, Sarah*
Nov 8 1785	Harryman, Nancy to Worrington, William
Oct 7 1796	Harryman, Nathaniel to Oliver, Catharine*
Aug 17 1790	Harryman, Nathaniel to Oram, Mary

Dec 19 1785	Harryman, Sarah to Bond, Barnett*
Oct 11 1794	Harrywood, Robert to Parker, Barbara*
Sep 19 1795	Harst, William to Clackner, Lydia*
Mar 23 1779	Hart, Ann to Blackford, Isaac*
Aug 10 1786	Hart, Ann to Sire, James*
Dec 9 1797	Hart, Catharine to Snuggrass, William*
Apr 19 1786	Hart, Charles to Taylor, Mary*
Jan 16 1778	Hart, Daniel to Beucard, Sarah*
Aug 7 1789	Hart, Henry to Ayres, Ruth*
May 18 1782	Hart, Jean to Cole, Thomas
Jan 20 1783	Hart, Mary to Cartright, Abraham*
Apr 15 1784	Hart, Mary to White, James*
Jan 31 1798	Hart, Sarah to Coe, James*
Jun 20 1798	Harting, Nancy to Cooper, Stephen*
Jan 25 1786	Hartman, Mary to Barbini, Charles*
Feb 20 1782	Hartman, Mary to Evans, John*
May 8 1797	Hartnet, James to Brillain, Mary*
Aug 4 1796	Hartong, Godfrey to Valentine, Elizabeth*
Mar 28 1797	Hartzot, George to Zeinsor, Dorothy*
Oct 23 1790	Harvey, Cassandra to Wall, John*
Dec 2 1796	Harvey, Joseph to Thompson, Mary*
Apr 21 1797	Harvey, Joshua to Patrick, Elizabeth*
Jul 30 1783	Harvey, Judy to Chambers, William*
Jun 5 1790	Harvey, Margaret to Hook, Joseph*
Apr 28 1783	Harvey, Patrick to Smith, Mary*
Jan 23 1790	Harvey, Thomas to Farel, Ann*
Dec 31 1787	Harvey, Thomas to Thornton, Hannah*
Oct 11 1797	Harvey, William to Burns, Mary*
Aug 24 1797	Harvey, William to Etow, Elizabeth*
Jun 7 1788	Harvey, William to Jackson, Eleanor*
Sep 18 1786	Harvy, Elizabeth to Cheston, Samuel
Nov 30 1793	Harwood, Blanckey to Night, David*
Dec 11 1794	Harwood, Henry to Buckley, Elizabeth*
Mar 7 1789	Hasen, Jessey to McCallister, Mary*
Jul 2 1783	Hashley, Beatrix to Willis, John
May 23 1791	Haskan, Josiah to David, Lucy*
Oct 3 1786	Haslep, Rezin to Eakley, Sarah
Oct 17 1797	Haslet, Rebecca Mercer to Bourm, Sylvanus*
Feb 14 1798	Haslett, Alexander to Highjeh, Elizabeth
Oct 31 1785	Haslett, Kesiah to McClain, Alexander
Jan 3 1793	Hasolton, Abigail to Solomon, Elkin*
Sep 20 1798	Hassard, John to Davis, Betsy
Oct 13 1797	Hatch, Nancy to Wright, John*
May 5 1795	Hathaway, Jethero to Buckley, Eleanor*
Nov 19 1795	Hathway, James to Haley, Mary*
Oct 31 1794	Hattier, Henry to Perenne, Magdalen
May 12 1791	Hatton, Ann to Weaver, Casper*
Aug 4 1796	Hatton, Anne to Bateman, Benjamin*
Jun 16 1798	Hatton, Aquilla to Parks, Delia*
Jun 29 1781	Hatton, China to Denion, Ann
Feb 12 1791	Hatton, Elizabeth to Greenfield, Nathaniel*
Oct 15 1785	Hatton, John to Magnus, Mary
Oct 18 1798	Hatton, Mary to Stansbury, Thomas*
Feb 7 1783	Hatton, Sarah to Stevens, Nathaniel
Aug 7 1797	Hatton, Susannah to Tydings, Richard*
Aug 30 1784	Hatton, Thomas to Ward, Mary*

Jul 11 1798	Hawk, Stephen to Hamilton, Agnes
Oct 7 1796	Hawk, Thomas to Brown, Sarah*
Dec 7 1778	Hawkins, Aaron to Roles, Susannah*
Jul 14 1797	Hawkins, Daniel to Sweeny, Biddy*
Mar 30 1798	Hawkins, George to Barton, Margaret*
Apr 27 1795	Hawkins, John to Dorsey, Elizabeth*
Nov 17 1796	Hawkins, Joseph to Downey, Sarah*
Apr 30 1778	Hawkins, Mary to Shaw, John*
Apr 17 1798	Hawkins, Mary to Smith, Sabritt
Oct 29 1778	Hawkins, Nancy to Harriman, Caleb*
Dec 19 1792	Hawkins, Ralph to Jacobs, Susannah*
Sep 11 1795	Hawkins, Rebecca to Plishow, Nicholas*
May 6 1794	Hawkins, Robert to Missee, Mary*
Nov 20 1787	Hawkins, Samuel to Pumphrey, Catherine*
May 11 1797	Hawkins, Sarah to Spurrier, Thomas*
Mar 11 1786	Hawksworth, Mary to Riddell, Robert
Feb 26 1798	Hawley, Thomas to Ridgely, Ann
Jul 27 1796	Hay, Alexander to Miller, Juliet*
Jul 5 1798	Hay, Ann to Curtain, James*
Jul 12 1794	Hay, Jacob to Shally, Elizabeth*
Apr 24 1797	Hay, James to Cornical, Mary*
Nov 13 1794	Hay, Janet to James, William*
May 12 1791	Hay, William to Steitz, Ann*
Sep 6 1784	Haycock, William to Miles, Fealey*
Dec 20 1798	Hayden, James to Nussen, Elizabeth*
Feb 14 1795	Hayden, Samuel to Mahoney, Elizabeth*
Oct 5 1778	Hayes, Arche to Smith, Hannah*
Oct 22 1798	Hayes, Edward to Brian, Abigail*
Jul 12 1793	Hayes, Elizabeth to Thompson, Amos*
Jul 20 1796	Hayes, John to Langston, Mary*
Apr 9 1789	Hayes, Mary to Steel, John*
Dec 14 1798	Hayes, Sarah to Hess, Peter*
Apr 24 1798	Hayes, Sarah to Kryder, John*
Oct 7 1791	Hayes, William Jr. to Stockett, Mary*
Jun 28 1798	Haymaker, Mary to Mooney, William*
Sep 9 1792	Hayman, Henry F. to Hellmens, Rebecca
Mar 14 1794	Haynes, Michael to Nicodemus, Esther*
Jan 7 1786	Hays, Aaron to Brown, Elizabeth
Dec 10 1777	Hays, Isabella to Gaddis, George*
Mar 26 1785	Hays, Jemina to Hutchins, Joshua
Mar 9 1783	Hays, Joel to Crapper, Sarah*
Dec 15 1791	Hays, Joseph to Weldon, Jane*
Mar 15 1796	Hays, Margaret to McFall, John*
Jun 18 1794	Hays, Mary to Richardson, John*
Sep 18 1782	Hays, Sarah to Mason, Abraham
Jan 10 1781	Hayward, Rachel to Hussey, George*
Dec 8 1787	Hayworth, Jonathan to Randall, Rebecca*
Oct 28 1783	Hazleton, Sarah to Mark, John Peterson*
May 9 1791	Hazzard, George to Burgess, Eleanor*
Aug 3 1796	Heackley, Sebastian to White, Catharine*
May 27 1795	Head, John to Bond, Elizabeth*
Aug 13 1795	Head, Nancy to Fowler, Isaac*
Jun 15 1792	Headekin, Catherine to Duhig, Oliver*
Dec 8 1783	Headington, Mary to Ogg, George*
Nov 15 1798	Headington, Ruth to Blake, Ebenezer*
Apr 28 1796	Healds, Phebe to Peters, John*

Oct 21 1779	Healy, John to Driskell, Mary*
Oct 23 1784	Hearmton, Ruth to Buckingham, Obadiah
Nov 17 1794	Hearn, Anthony to Jenkins, Sarah*
Apr 2 1793	Hearn, Mary to Jones, Isaac
Jan 27 1798	Heart, Grace to Campbell, Joseph Murray*
May 19 1794	Heath,, James to Langley, Mary*
Apr 25 1796	Heath, Samuel to Bulger, Margaret*
Feb 12 1789	Heath, Samuel to Joyce, Eleanor*
Feb 7 1793	Heathrington, Thomas to Pollock, Sarah*
Jun 28 1797	Hebert, John Baptiste to Tassey, Elizabeth*
Aug 3 1784	Heckholt, Henry to Brett, Rachael*
Jul 9 1793	Heddinger, Michael to Herman, Juley Catharine*
Aug 30 1794	Heddington, Eleanor to Heddington, Laben*
Aug 30 1794	Heddington, Laben to Heddington, Eleanor*
Jun 25 1794	Heddington, Nathan to Gorsuch, Keziah*
Dec 15 1792	Heddington, Nicholas to Baxter, Delia*
Dec 11 1781	Heddington, Zebulon to Bosley, Sarah
Dec 26 1792	Hederick, Delilah to Harding, Joseph
Jun 2 1784	Hederick, Thomas to Frits, Christiana*
May 5 1798	Hedley, Anthony to Lewis, Susanna*
Jul 2 1794	Hedwicks, James to Fish, Ann*
Jul 25 1798	Heide, Henry to Lauhar, Elizabeth*
Nov 19 1794	Heiecke, Frederick to Shroeder, Anna Doratha*
Apr 13 1791	Heir, Jemima to Sullivan, Thomas*
Apr 27 1791	Heirmance, Jacob I. to Wootton, Maria Sprigg
Apr 9 1792	Heirs, Elizabeth to Murray, John*
Mar 28 1793	Heiser, Susannah to Sweeting, John*
Apr 19 1793	Hellen, Ann to Jenkins, William*
Dec 20 1794	Hellen, Mary King to Cleburn, George With*
Sep 9 1792	Hellmens, Rebecca to Hayman, Henry F.
Jan 6 1784	Helm, Ann to Arnest, Caleb*
Apr 4 1795	Helm, Ann to McKeen, John*
Jul 29 1778	Helm, Dellah to Chenowith, Arthur*
Jun 17 1791	Helm, Leonard to Horsman, Mary*
Apr 25 1785	Helm, Mary to Loubies, Philipe
Dec 26 1795	Helm, Nancy to Swann, Joshua*
Jun 1 1795	Helmes, Margaret to Cann, John*
Oct 2 1793	Helms, John to Clarke, Catharine*
Sep 22 1790	Helms, Patience to Logsden, Jeb*
Nov 22 1796	Hemling, Magdaline to Bond, Philip*
Sep 7 1793	Hendericks, Ann to Barkman, Anthony
May 4 1786	Henderson, George to Griffin, Jemima
Oct 7 1782	Henderson, Gilbert to Dyer, Esther*
May 22 1794	Henderson, Jane to Dawson, Philemon*
Jun 18 1778	Henderson, Marthen to Thomas, John*
Jan 26 1782	Henderson, Mary to Garretson, Cornelius
Jun 8 1778	Henderson, Mary to Sulivan, Daniel*
Dec 27 1797	Henderson, Phebe to Perry, Peter*
May 21 1794	Henderson, William to Stansbury, Hannah*
Jun 7 1788	Hendon, Benjamin to Marsh, Sophia*
Jan 13 1778	Hendon, Delia to Grimes, John*
Feb 28 1784	Hendricks, Eldret to Shaw, Jane*
Jan 13 1796	Hendricks, Jane to Plumber, Charles*
Mar 18 1778	Hendricks, Mary to Cord, John M.*
Oct 7 1796	Hendricks, Mette Loua to Undusst, Nicholas*
Apr 2 1783	Hendrickson, Ann to Denton, John*

```
Dec 15 1796    Hendrickson, Joseph to Cochran, Susanna*
Nov 13 1792    Hendrickson, Joseph to Garrison, Margaret
Dec 29 1780    Hendrickson, Joseph to Pearce, Mary*
Oct  1 1782    Hendrickson, Mary to Roach, Thomas*
Sep  1 1788    Hendrickson, Ruth to Parks, John*
May 13 1786    Hendrickson, Sarah to Lenton, James*
Sep  2 1793    Henigan, James to Burke, Mary*
Aug 28 1783    Heninger, JOhn to Post, Elizabeth*
Apr 29 1789    Henlet, Margaret to Weaver, John*
Nov  5 1798    Henley, Hannah to Myers, Philip*
Jul 13 1793    Henley, Rebecca to Tague, Thomas
Jul 14 1794    Henley, Robert to Flood, Eleanor*
Feb  2 1792    Henley, Thomas to Holoraft, Charlotte*
Mar 16 1792    Henly, Ann to Ditleff, Christian*
May  2 1791    Henly, Letitia to Smith, Jeremiah*
Jun 23 1784    Hennen, James to Waters, Ann*
Dec 27 1790    Hennesy, Johanna to Berry, Redmond*
Jul 21 1797    Henninger, Philip to Dilhelms, Henrietta*
Jun  8 1797    Henry, Ann to Howard, John*
Aug  2 1798    Henry, John to Shipley, Catharine*
Apr 13 1796    Henry, John to Wright, Elizabeth*
Aug 12 1795    Henry, Margaret to Fush, Michael*
Nov 18 1796    Henry, Maria to Johnson, Joseph*
Sep 17 1778    Henry, Robert Jenkins to Stevenson, Patty
Nov 15 1797    Henry, Samuel to Cross, Bridget*
May 17 1792    Henry, Sarah to Connaway, Samuel*
Nov 19 1795    Henry, Sarah to Mackey, Hugh*
Oct 24 1797    Henry, Sophia to Miller, Adam*
Jan 21 1796    Henry, William to Dugan, Nancy*
Jul 18 1795    Hensey, Michael to Wooden, Rachel*
Jan 21 1782    Henshaw, Basil to Kilman, Mary*
Jun  8 1793    Henshaw, Nancy to Crane, William
Feb 14 1789    Henton, Jemima to Chaney, Mordeica*
Sep 12 1795    Henwood, Elizabeth to Thompson, Nathan Sylvester*
Nov 30 1797    Henwood, Robert to Richards, Nancy*
Oct 29 1793    Herach, Jacob to Stein, Rebecca*
Sep 26 1794    Herbert, Mary to Place, John*
Jul 21 1785    Herbert, Rebecca to Swain, Jeremiah
Dec  6 1782    Herd, John to Shields, Mary
Nov 23 1798    Herlick, Margaret to Wedge, Simon*
Jul  9 1793    Herman, Juley Catharine to Heddinger, Michael*
Oct  9 1784    Hermangs, Anthony to Budrow, Margaret*
Jun  9 1785    Hermon, John to Anderson, Mary
Oct  2 1797    Herrick, Thomas to Wooden, Margaret*
Aug 10 1785    Herrin, Judah to Boas, Benjamin*
Nov 26 1788    Herrine, Sophia to Eiglehart, Edward*
Jun 10 1789    Herring, Elizabeth to Birmingham, William*
Apr 23 1794    Herring, Langford to Cromwell, Ann*
Mar 11 1779    Herring, Mary to Lick, Peter
Sep  4 1794    Herring, Robert to Lavely, Susannah*
Oct 19 1798    Herrlin, Elizabeth to Honig, Henry*
Aug 15 1797    Herron, Eleanor to Carr, John*
Sep  4 1783    Herron, Timothy to O'Brian, Ann*
Sep  5 1792    Hershberger, Catherine to Phile, Charles
Nov  4 1797    Herston, Charles to Sprigg, Delilah
Sep  4 1792    Herther, Nathan to Diffindolph, Catherine
```

Dec 10 1796	Heshogan, Catharine to Saglekin, John*
Dec 14 1798	Hess, Peter to Hayes, Sarah*
May 29 1781	Heswell, John Jona Vanden to Douglass, Elizabeth*
Jan 19 1785	Heter, Jacob to Miller, Susannah*
Jul 21 1789	Hethrington, Elizabeth to Bowen, William*
Oct 21 1789	Hettinger, Michael to Lower, Elizabeth
May 11 1793	Hettlestem, Thomas to Ross, Elizabeth
Aug 30 1791	Heuiler, Maximillien to Bernard, Marie*
Jul 6 1786	Hewett, Caleb to Hull, Mary*
Aug 19 1778	Hewit, Hannah to Low, John*
May 15 1794	Hewitt, Caleb to Wilkinson, Sarah*
Mar 24 1797	Hewitt, Eli to Dennis, Martha*
Aug 5 1795	Hewitt, Emelia to McMechen, Hugh*
Sep 7 1779	Hewitt, Nichel to Leatherwood, Ann
Nov 25 1790	Hewitt, Rachel to Linthicum, Zachariah*
Dec 4 1792	Hewitt, Rebecca to Jordan, William*
Jul 5 1788	Hewitt, Sarah to Evans, Griffith*
Dec 10 1783	Hews, James to Cottonal, Frances*
Sep 17 1794	Heyser, Sarah to Hook, Frederick*
Dec 30 1797	Hick, Elizabeth to Anderson, Robert*
Mar 10 1779	Hick, Lewis to Towson, Elizabeth
Dec 18 1788	Hickens, Ann to Murray, Elan
Mar 25 1794	Hickey, Eleanor to Dickinson, David*
Apr 18 1782	Hickey, Johannah to Thompson, James*
Oct 25 1797	Hickey, Peter to Aires, Margaret*
Dec 16 1780	Hickins, Lyde to Gater, Thomas*
Jul 8 1783	Hickman, Barbara to Mumma, David
Mar 12 1781	Hicks, Abraham to Gorsuch, Sarah*
Apr 2 1784	Hicks, Dalsey to Simpson, James*
Mar 24 1784	Hicks, Hannah to Miller, Joshua*
Nov 22 1796	Hicks, Joshua to Sollers, Rebecca*
Aug 2 1792	Hicks, Louisa to Miercken, David*
Oct 23 1783	Hicks, Lynda to Cable, George
Jul 1 1778	Hicks, Nehemiah to Marshall, Hannah*
Sep 1 1781	Hicks, Ruth to Haile, Neale
May 20 1797	Hickson, Margaret to Farrar, Peter*
May 3 1792	Hiede, George to Griffith, Rachel*
Oct 17 1779	Higgenbottom, John to Kain, Elizabeth*
Sep 7 1790	Higginbothom, Elizabeth to McKenny, Roddey*
Mar 10 1796	Higginbothom, Elizabeth to Murray, George William*
Aug 13 1792	Higginbottom, Arthur to Wilson, Eleanor*
Sep 23 1793	Higgins, Edward to Ellerton, Ann*
May 22 1797	Higgins, Jenny to Fellows, Edward*
Apr 16 1788	Higgins, John to Hutchins, Gracey*
Jan 18 1792	Higgins, Joseph to Warfield, Amelia*
Apr 16 1779	High, James to Stafford, Hannah*
Oct 16 1783	High, Jean to Hill, Joses
Feb 1 1788	Higham, Abraham L. to Morgan, Sarah*
Feb 14 1798	Highjeh, Elizabeth to Haslett, Alexander
Dec 2 1791	Highjoe, Philip to Dunkin, Elizabeth*
Jun 25 1789	Higson, George to Hubbard, Sarah*
May 29 1782	Hiland, George to Smith, Catharine*
Jan 21 1785	Hildebrand, Polly to Boyer, Lewis*
Mar 3 1795	Hilderbrand, Catharine to Cross, Robert*
Jul 25 1789	Hilderbrant, Jacob to Pomp, Catherine
Jan 28 1796	Hill, Christian to Schriver, Julianna*

```
Oct 29 1791    Hill, Eleanor to Wellsford, George William*
Jan 30 1794    Hill, Hannah to Wilson, Hugh*
Nov  4 1784    Hill, James to Collins, Frances
Mar  7 1779    Hill, John to Harris, Mary*
Sep  6 1788    Hill, John to Wallace, Deborah*
Oct 16 1783    Hill, Joses to High, Jean
Oct 28 1785    Hill, Mary to Strong, Ludwick
Dec 12 1798    Hill, Nancy to Willis, John*
Sep  4 1797    Hill, Rebekah to Jackson, John*
Nov 11 1797    Hill, Richard to Adams, Ann*
Apr 16 1794    Hill, Sarah to Craig, Collin*
Apr 14 1795    Hill, William to Baker, Keturah*
Jun 26 1795    Hill, William to Charleton, Elizabeth*
Feb  9 1789    Hillen, Jane Paron to Smith, John Jacob*
Nov 23 1784    Hillen, John to Rusk, Catharine*
May 14 1793    Hillen, Mary to Armour, David
Oct 14 1789    Hilton, Abraham to Grimes, Elizabeth
May 22 1794    Hilton, Abraham to Thompson, Catharine*
Aug 13 1782    Hilton, John to Sicamore, Lydia*
Jun  2 1794    Hilton, Patience to Bishop, William*
Dec 13 1794    Hilton, Thomas to McHaffe, Robina Kennedy*
Dec 13 1781    Hilton, William to Mechannah, Elizabeth*
Feb 10 1795    Himes, James to Craig, Sarah*
Jan  2 1791    Himmelbright, Samuel to Shriver, Mary*
Sep  9 1789    Hinchs, Nelly to Waters, Philip*
Jun 29 1797    Hinder, Thomas to Townsend, Nancy*
Jun  1 1786    Hindmin, Elizabeth to Campbell, Archibald*
Dec  4 1797    Hindon, Elizabeth to Kenecker, Frederick*
May  7 1795    Hiner, Frances to Jackson, Hezekiah*
Feb  4 1796    Hiner, Joseph to Hollaway, Ann*
Mar 26 1796    Hines, Betsey to Travelet, Francis*
Oct  4 1798    Hines, Sarah to Burke, Thomas*
Feb 26 1794    Hines, William to Curtis, Elizabeth*
Oct  5 1791    Hinks, William to Fisher, Jemimah*
Oct 18 1798    Hinton, Thomas to Turner, Eleanor*
Aug  3 1779    Hipitey, Patience to Beasings, James
Apr 21 1778    Hipsilly, Joshua to Goodman, Elizabeth*
Nov 20 1788    Hipsler, Benjamin to Bishop, Elizabeth*
Sep  6 1797    Hipsley, Caleb to Shipley, Margaret*
Jun 25 1783    Hipsley, Caleb to Shipley, Sarah Hood*
Dec 24 1793    Hipsley, Ruth to Gaither, John*
Sep 15 1779    Hiritt, John to McCaslin, Barbary*
Apr  6 1786    Hisdale, Catharine to Swindall, Peter*
Jul 14 1795    Hiser, David to Sweeting, Charlotte*
Oct 15 1795    Hislet, Mary to Shute, Henry*
Jun  3 1786    Hiss, Jacob to Gatch, Elizabeth
Sep 12 1781    Hiss, Mary to Gash, Nicholas*
Jul 17 1783    Hissey, Caleb to Hissey, Rebecca*
Feb  9 1788    Hissey, Catharine to Barnett, Jacob
Nov  2 1797    Hissey, Charles to Zimmerman, Hannah*
Jun 15 1798    Hissey, Mary to Zimmerman, John*
Jul 17 1783    Hissey, Rebecca to Hissey, Caleb*
Oct 25 1783    Hissey, Rebecca to Smith, Nicholas
Jan  3 1784    Hissey, William to Kettle, Mary*
Oct 22 1793    Hisson, Cornelius to Weaver, Elizabeth*
Nov 18 1778    Hist, Gideon to Ryan, Ann*
```

Mar 30 1778	Hitejus, Catharina to Ebbert, John*
Jan 21 1796	Hitherton, Elizabeth to Gorsuch, Jacob*
Jun 11 1785	Hitterpraugh, Susannah to Dieter, Jacob
Nov 17 1783	Hively, Elizabeth to Reese, William*
Aug 13 1791	Hobb, Amelia to Shipley, Benjamin*
Feb 8 1791	Hobbs, Airy to Fisher, John
Nov 23 1795	Hobbs, Ally to Boulin, John
Oct 8 1785	Hobbs, Amelia to Peddicoart, Jasper
Dec 3 1788	Hobbs, Aserieth to Warfield, John*
Sep 7 1790	Hobbs, Beall to Smith, Eleanor*
Nov 9 1793	Hobbs, Caleb to Norwood, Hannah*
Nov 19 1791	Hobbs, Denton to Norwood, Mary
Nov 5 1788	Hobbs, Elizabeth to Peddicoart, William*
Jul 30 1798	Hobbs, Elizabeth to Russell, Robert*
Jan 22 1791	Hobbs, Hanson to Shipley, Mary*
Dec 23 1790	Hobbs, James to Knox, Ann*
Aug 27 1785	Hobbs, Joseph to Randell, Nancy
May 3 1792	Hobbs, Lucy to Driver, James*
May 23 1782	Hobbs, Margaret to Dorsey, Patt
Apr 16 1793	Hobbs, Ruspar to Howard, Brice*
Jun 5 1795	Hobbs, Ruth to Harding, Nicholas*
Dec 22 1794	Hobbs, Sarah to Hood, James*
Jan 7 1784	Hodg, Joseph to Phields, Elizabeth*
Nov 21 1778	Hodge, Jane to Wannell, Henry
Sep 26 1793	Hodge, John to Bryan, Mary*
Jul 28 1791	Hodge, Martha to Bayler, Andrew*
Sep 26 1778	Hodges, Ann to Rayner, Benjamin*
Dec 24 1782	Hodges, Sarah to Dunn, James
Aug 8 1783	Hodges, William to Denton, Rachael*
Sep 28 1791	Hodghin, Barbara to Riley, William
Jan 28 1783	Hodgkin, Mary to Slade, Ezekiel*
Jul 3 1788	Hodgson, Mary to Young, Benjamin*
Jun 30 1794	Hoffer, John to Peterson, Ann*
Jan 18 1786	Hoffman, Adam to Lane, Elizabeth*
Nov 4 1783	Hoffman, Barbara to Perry, John*
Feb 24 1784	Hoffman, Jacob to Swingler, Barbara*
Dec 10 1789	Hoffman, Mary to Cruse, Jacob*
Dec 12 1778	Hoffstetter, Cartrout to Smith, Adam*
Jul 18 1796	Hogan, Catharine to McCoy, Richard*
Sep 1 1791	Hogan, Dennis to Lucas, Elizabeth*
Jul 18 1795	Hogan, Hannah to Clansey, Patrick*
Sep 2 1790	Hogan, Jane to Field, Martin*
Oct 27 1797	Hogan, John to Keaton, Eleanor*
May 12 1798	Hogan, Kitty to Barley, George*
Jul 1 1797	Hoggins, Martha to Williams, John*
Feb 27 1781	Hohn, Peter to Brodbech, Loys
Nov 21 1798	Hoit, Israel to McGoiff, Sarah*
May 19 1798	Holbrook, Ann to Arnolde, John*
May 19 1798	Holbrook, Rachel to Grarish, Francis*
Dec 28 1793	Holbrooke, Jacob to Bauzel, Elizabeth*
Feb 15 1798	Holbrooks, Darky to Deaver, Hugh
Dec 23 1797	Holbrooks, Sarah to Arnold, Peter*
Aug 18 1795	Holbrooks, Thomas to Constable, Cassandra*
Feb 13 1790	Holebrooks, Elinder Roon to Barton, Thomas*
Jun 19 1794	Holems, Eleanor to Wright, Joshua*
Nov 1 1796	Holland, Catharine to Cheston, Daniel*

```
Jan 12 1790    Holland, Catherine to Laverty, James*
Oct  6 1783    Holland, Charles to Joyce, Ann
Jul 26 1792    Holland, Charlotte to Cooke, Samuel*
Apr 24 1788    Holland, Daniel to Cotrell, Rachael*
Dec 20 1785    Holland, Elizabeth to Moxley, William
Aug  8 1778    Holland, Elizabeth to Roland, Samuel*
May 18 1797    Holland, Francis to West, Sybel*
Aug  2 1778    Holland, George to Allender, Margaret*
Jul 23 1781    Holland, Jacob to Riggs, Carline*
Feb 26 1783    Holland, John to Ensor, Ann
Aug 23 1790    Holland, Margaret to Penn, Shadrack*
Jun  5 1783    Holland, Mary to Gorsuch, Benjamin
Mar  7 1798    Holland, Sarah to Allen, James*
Feb  4 1789    Holland, Sarah to Taylor, Acquila*
Dec 20 1797    Holland, Thomas to O'Conner, Margaret
Feb  4 1796    Hollaway, Ann to Hiner, Joseph*
Feb  2 1798    Hollbrooks, Delilah to Green, Allwaturs Thompson
Feb 24 1778    Holler, Francis to Pangle, Elizabeth*
Dec 24 1788    Holler, Philip to Almark, Mary*
Nov  5 1795    Holliday, Achsah Chamier to Beatly, Thomas Johnson*
May  9 1796    Holliday, John to Rareton, Margaret*
Nov 20 1794    Holliday, Sarah Brooke to Dall, James*
May  9 1785    Hollings, Mary to Giles, George
Mar 16 1792    Hollingsworth, Ann to Willis, Henry*
Mar  3 1796    Hollingsworth, Eleanor to Harrison, Daniel*
Jan 11 1793    Hollingsworth, Henry to Cross, Levina*
Sep 30 1790    Hollingsworth, Jesse to Parkin, Rachael Lyde*
Feb 22 1781    Hollingsworth, Mary to Yellott, Jeremiah
Apr 22 1790    Hollingsworth, Zebulon to Ireland, Elizabeth*
Sep 24 1794    Hollins, John to Mahony, Charlotte*
Dec 30 1785    Hollins, John to Smith, Jane*
Oct 27 1782    Hollins, Margaret to Hull, Samuel*
Jul 16 1785    Holliwell, James to Aspin, Hannah
Mar 14 1796    Hollow, Mary to Bords, Adam*
Aug 23 1794    Holloway, Ann to Newshaw, Nathan*
Jul 31 1789    Holmes, Ann to Robinson, Samuel*
Jul  6 1795    Holmes, Anthony to Reeves, Margaret*
Nov 19 1791    Holmes, Elizabeth to Moore, Robert*
May  6 1797    Holmes, Elizabeth to Robinson, John*
Feb  2 1793    Holmes, Gabriel to Bacon, Mary*
Aug 10 1798    Holmes, Jane to Ford, William*
Aug  7 1792    Holmes, John to German, Margaret*
Dec 24 1783    Holmes, Joshua to Sellman, Ann*
May 23 1796    Holmes, Joyce to Daugherty, Joseph*
Apr 20 1798    Holmes, Magdelane to Digabeau, John*
Feb 21 1782    Holmes, Pamelia to Brown, Henry*
Jun  2 1798    Holmes, Sarah to Lovitt, William*
Feb 19 1781    Holmes, Sophia to Gray, Zachariah*
Jun  1 1786    Holmes, William James to Wells, Ann*
Feb  2 1792    Holoraft, Charlotte to Henley, Thomas*
Jun 18 1795    Holston, Margaret to Rosell, Charles*
Oct 27 1783    Holston, Robert to Gardiner, Margaret
Oct 16 1782    Holton, Sarah to Eades, John
Apr 12 1784    Holton, Sarah to Leach, John*
May 26 1797    Holton, William to Bowles, Jane*
Oct 11 1791    Homan, Mary to Beard, William*
```

```
Oct 19 1798    Honig, Henry to Herrlin, Elizabeth*
Apr  4 1795    Honser, John to Roe, Barbara*
Jul 22 1784    Hood, James to Frankling, Kitty*
Dec 22 1794    Hood, James to Hobbs, Sarah*
May 18 1798    Hood, Mary to McDonnell, John*
Jan  9 1788    Hood, Ruth to Pigman, Joseph Waters
Sep 12 1786    Hood, Sarah to Worthington, Walter
Apr  9 1788    Hoofman, Daniel to O'Brian, Biddy
Jan 28 1793    Hoofman, Daniel to Shrote, Mary*
Mar 10 1794    Hoofman, Margaret to Gardner, John*
Jul 12 1779    Hoofman, William to Sighsurger, Rosannah
Mar 17 1786    Hoofnagle, George Jr. to Stringer, Mary*
Jun 26 1783    Hoofstetter, Catherine to Hull, John*
Feb  6 1778    Hook, Barbara to Hanuf, Stophel*
Feb  4 1778    Hook, Barbara to Hanuf, Stophel*
May 21 1795    Hook, Barbara to Taylor, Thomas*
Apr  1 1793    Hook, Barbara to Wallon, John*
Apr 24 1786    Hook, Catharine to Orban, Henry*
Aug 12 1778    Hook, Elizabeth to Duncan, Perry*
Oct 20 1788    Hook, Elizabeth to Irwin, Philip*
Nov 24 1787    Hook, Elizabeth to Pickerin, Peter
Sep 17 1794    Hook, Frederick to Heyser, Sarah*
Mar 13 1791    Hook, Jacob to Boone, Susannah
Nov 22 1784    Hook, Jacob to Campbell, Elizabeth
Apr 20 1795    Hook, John to Horke, Sophia*
Jun  5 1790    Hook, Joseph to Harvey, Margaret*
May 22 1794    Hook, Joseph to Hudge, Barbara*
Dec  1 1791    Hook, Margaret to O'Brian, Michael*
May 12 1784    Hook, Margarett to Knight, Benjamin*
Jan  2 1783    Hook, Mary to Riley, Stephen*
Jul 18 1789    Hook, Priscilla to Sweeny, Hugh*
Jan 14 1778    Hook, Rudolph to Ritter, Catharine*
Apr  2 1779    Hook, Sophiah to Verdelett, John Ely
Jun 28 1794    Hook, William to Dunkin, Sarah*
Mar 28 1781    Hook, William to Stocksdale, Hannah
Feb  7 1781    Hooker, Debora to Wyley, John*
Jun 13 1783    Hooker, Jacob to Parish, Mary*
Nov 29 1796    Hooker, Joshua to Brothers, Ruth*
Dec 10 1789    Hooker, Mary to Ogg, Benjamin*
Sep 22 1786    Hooker, Mary to Roiston, Joshua*
Dec 15 1784    Hooker, Samuel to Belt, Rachael*
Feb 16 1789    Hooker, Susannah to Hutson, Joshua*
Sep 19 1793    Hooks, Jane to Warrier, William*
Oct 10 1790    Hooper, Elinor to Taylor, John
Jun 13 1786    Hooper, Henry to Craton, Nancy*
Oct 28 1797    Hooper, Isaac to Kirkwood, Jane*
Dec 29 1783    Hooper, Jacob to Cord, Mary*
Nov  4 1783    Hooper, James to Gorsuch, Rachael*
Sep 20 1786    Hooper, John Ashcom to Parrot, Mary Ann*
May 30 1778    Hooper, Orpah to Treakle, Stephen*
Dec  7 1785    Hooper, Patty to Ritchie, William
Jun 31 1790    Hooper, Rachel to Wooden, John*
Dec  7 1796    Hooper, Samuel to Kitely, Mary
Sep 28 1791    Hooper, Sarah to Wooden, Thomas*
Feb  5 1794    Hooper, William to Crowley, Mary*
Aug  6 1792    Hoopman, Christian to Baughman, Elizabeth*
```

Dec	2	1795	Hopkins, Ann to Hardisty, Robert*
Apr	7	1779	Hopkins, Cassandra to Elliott, John*
Dec	11	1790	Hopkins, David to Dorsey, Mary*
Jul	25	1781	Hopkins, David to Howard, Mary
Mar	25	1794	Hopkins, Eliza to Small, Jacob*
Nov	9	1785	Hopkins, Elizabeth to Cox, Israel
Apr	18	1789	Hopkins, Gerrard of R. to Luce, Elizabeth*
Jan	3	1797	Hopkins, John to Bryan, Elizabeth*
Apr	15	1795	Hopkins, John to Duke, Rebecca*
Nov	29	1791	Hopkins, Joseph to Hopkins, Sally*
Nov	7	1796	Hopkins, Joseph to Hughes, Mary*
Jul	18	1795	Hopkins, Lydia to Kliffora, James*
May	11	1791	Hopkins, Nicholas to Bryan, Mary*
May	26	1794	Hopkins, Nicholas to Duke, Rebecca*
Nov	29	1791	Hopkins, Sally to Hopkins, Joseph*
Dec	28	1790	Hopkins, William to Barton, Prescilla*
Mar	22	1785	Hoppen, Ruth to Taylor, Levin
Apr	14	1783	Hoppom, Eleanor to Hammon, Thomas*
May	16	1795	Hoppom, Mary to Ginnings, William*
Apr	20	1795	Horke, Sophia to Hook, John*
Sep	22	1796	Horn, Catharine to Diverbaugh, Jacob*
Feb	25	1792	Horn, Phillip to Litler, Catherine*
Jun	26	1783	Horner, Mary to Waters, Charles*
Nov	28	1788	Hornes, Michael to Waupole, Flora*
Apr	12	1797	Hornsby, John to Wilson, Unity*
Oct	23	1779	Horsler, Sarah to Grimes, James*
Jun	17	1791	Horsman, Mary to Helm, Leonard*
May	24	1778	Horton, Ann to Shaw, Thomas*
May	19	1778	Horton, Ann to Shaw, Thomas"
Sep	18	1778	Horton, Elizabeth to Lindle, Philip*
Feb	12	1795	Hose, Catharine to Levillain, Michael*
Oct	13	1786	Hoskins, Dolley to Aldridge, John
Jul	12	1779	Hoskins, Sarah to Butterworth, Benjamin*
Jul	23	1796	Hosselbaugh, John George to Gallentine, Barbara*
Jun	3	1784	Hossleboch, John to Bridenhart, Mary*
Feb	10	1789	Host, Michael to Hannan, Elizabeth*
Dec	19	1798	Hostetter, David to Flintz, Polly*
Jan	20	1794	Hotchkiss, Solomom to Hall, Alasanah*
Jun	25	1793	Hotton, John to Burns, Sarah*
Nov	19	1791	Houk, Anthony to Chenowith, Catharine*
Apr	17	1794	Houk, Catherine to Smith, Michael*
Jan	17	1786	Houlton, John to Soles, Eleanor
May	15	1797	Houregan, Patrick to Barry, Sarah*
Sep	27	1783	House, Susanna to Parsons, John*
Nov	2	1780	House, Thomas to Sulivan, Hannah*
Apr	1	1793	Householder, Mary to Swingle, George*
Apr	10	1797	Hover, Sebastian to Mintz, Rebecca*
Feb	4	1795	Howard, Bethia to Warren, William*
Jun	2	1781	Howard, Biddy to Harrington, Thomas
Nov	14	1787	Howard, Brice to Gerthrell, Ruth*
Apr	16	1793	Howard, Brice to Hobbs, Ruspar*
Sep	21	1791	Howard, Charles to Bailey, Sarah*
Apr	10	1788	Howard, Charles to Hall, Elizabeth
Nov	4	1778	Howard, Denoon to Anderson, Ann*
Nov	6	1793	Howard, Eliza G. to Sadler, Thomas*
Mar	30	1798	Howard, Elizabeth to Kearly, James*

```
Dec 11 1795    Howard, Elizabeth to Leech, John*
Nov 23 1791    Howard, Elizabeth to Rowan, John*
Feb  8 1783    Howard, Elizabeth to Smith, Joshua*
Oct  7 1796    Howard, Francis to Fitzgerrald, Margaret*
Dec 21 1793    Howard, Henry to Brown, Mary*
Oct 25 1798    Howard, James G. to Govan, Mary W.*
Mar 10 1796    Howard, Jemimah to Norwood, Edward*
Jan  4 1783    Howard, John to Chinn, Sary*
Oct  3 1794    Howard, John to Cline, Sarah*
Jun  8 1797    Howard, John to Henry, Ann*
Sep  9 1789    Howard, Joseph to Howard, Mary*
Feb  5 1789    Howard, Joshua to Cramlet, Ann*
Nov  6 1792    Howard, Martha to Hall, Nicholas*
Jul 25 1781    Howard, Mary to Hopkins, David
Sep  9 1789    Howard, Mary to Howard, Joseph*
Nov 17 1797    Howard, Mary to Perine, Peter*
Feb 20 1797    Howard, Mary to Stratton, William*
Jan 18 1791    Howard, Nancy to Mockbee, John*
Jan 12 1791    Howard, Patience to Norwood, Samuel*
Mar 22 1797    Howard, Philip to Crosby, Mary*
Jun 17 1785    Howard, Ruth to Johnson, Jeremiah Jr.*
Sep 11 1782    Howard, Ruth to Shipley, Henry*
Nov 15 1798    Howard, Samuel to Foard, Elinor*
Jun 11 1796    Howard, Sarah to Campbell, John*
Sep 22 1797    Howard, Sarah to Eldon, Charles*
Mar  5 1792    Howard, Sarah to Stinchcomb, Enoch*
Apr  1 1793    Howard, Thomas Gassaway to Tally, Martha*
Dec  1 1784    Howard, Violetta to West, Joseph*
May 10 1784    Howell, James to Trotten, Mary*
Dec  3 1795    Howland, John Wilks to Gudgeon, Mary*
Aug  2 1783    Howland, Mary to Bain, William
May  1 1793    Howlett, John to Johnson, Druvilla*
Jun  2 1783    Hoy, Ann to Sullivan, Jeremiah
Mar 27 1783    Hubbard, Mary to Scampen, Antony*
Nov 23 1782    Hubbard, Sarah to Eves, William
Jun 25 1789    Hubbard, Sarah to Higson, George*
Jun 10 1782    Hubbert, John to Mewshaw, Elizabeth
Jun 17 1795    Hubbert, Rody to Cowan, Alexander*
Jun 11 1796    Hubbert, William to Nice, Elizabeth*
Mar 30 1790    Hubbort, Elizabeth to Rutler, Moses*
Aug  1 1796    Hubon, Marie Anna to Beaudu, William*
Apr 13 1797    Hud, Easter to Carney, John*
May 22 1794    Hudge, Barbara to Hook, Joseph*
Dec 11 1778    Hudless, Ann to Tear, Ignatius*
Jul 22 1778    Hudless, Mary to Kelly, Hugh*
Oct 29 1791    Hudson, Edward to Porter, Providence*
Feb 24 1789    Hudson, Eleanor to Gilbert, Benjamin*
Aug 27 1791    Hudson, Elizabeth to Davis, James*
Sep  8 1796    Hudson, James to MacNamarah, Johnannah*
Sep 21 1786    Hudson, John to Brown, Fanney*
Feb  9 1798    Hudson, John to Cord, Catharine
Jan 30 1794    Hudson, Priscilla to Porter, Caleb*
Nov  2 1780    Hudson, William to Chapman, Jemimah*
Apr 30 1784    Huett, Catherine to Marsh, John*
Nov 22 1779    Huety, Vachel to Rady, Ann
Apr 30 1796    Hughes, Abraham to Norris, Belinda*
```

```
Mar 22 1797    Hughes, Ann to Maddox, William
Aug 24 1797    Hughes, Anna Bella to Little, Peter*
Jan  2 1790    Hughes, Catherine to Oliver, John*
Jun  7 1778    Hughes, Christopher to Sanderson, Peggy
Oct  3 1798    Hughes, Eleanor to Ruil, William A.*
Aug 19 1794    Hughes, Elizabeth to Maddox, William*
Jun 14 1790    Hughes, Elizabeth to Rady, Joshua
Dec 29 1781    Hughes, Frs. to Mildews, Mary*
Jan 24 1795    Hughes, George to Jones, Cassandra*
Oct  3 1796    Hughes, Hannah to Bond, Mordecai*
Sep 20 1794    Hughes, Henry to Carr, Mary*
Jul 12 1794    Hughes, Henry to Conners, Mary*
Nov  5 1794    Hughes, Hugh to Bond, Ann*
Oct  7 1791    Hughes, James to Stansbury, Mary
Jul  6 1791    Hughes, John to Gudgeon, Elizabeth*
May 14 1796    Hughes, John to Todd, Rachel*
Oct 19 1796    Hughes, Margaret to Cottrell, Thomas
Nov  2 1797    Hughes, Margaret to Rankin, Hugh*
Apr 27 1782    Hughes, Martha to Wheeler, Wayson*
Mar 24 1796    Hughes, Mary to Fowler, Benjamin*
Nov  7 1796    Hughes, Mary to Hopkins, Joseph*
Feb 25 1794    Hughes, Nancy to Harden, John Borton*
Jun 17 1797    Hughes, Polly to Page, Daniel*
Nov  1 1797    Hughes, Rebecca to Eagleston, Abraham
Jan 12 1790    Hughes, Ruth to Bond, Barnet*
Dec  1 1784    Hughes, Ruth to Griffin, Joseph
Aug 11 1788    Hughes, Sarah to Finlay, Hugh
Jan 30 1794    Hughes, Sarah to Fulford, John*
Oct 11 1783    Hughes, Sarah to Strobe, Jacob*
Oct 20 1790    Hughes, Susannah to Riston, Abraham*
Mar 29 1798    Hughes, Susannah to Stains, William*
Jun 28 1783    Hughes, William to Bush, Sarah*
Apr 15 1786    Hughes, William to Cantwell, Ann
Nov 19 1789    Hughes, William to McKirdy, Elizabeth*
Nov 14 1793    Hughes, Young Samuel to Cullison, Ann*
Apr 28 1778    Hugin, Barbara to Loose, Johann A.
Oct 18 1798    Hugo, Julia to Trimble, John*
Feb  1 1783    Huitt, William to Mackie, Susannah*
Apr 25 1798    Hulk, Catharine to Bakerven, Peter
Apr 29 1784    Hull, Elizabeth to Guyer, John*
Jun 26 1783    Hull, John to Hoofstetter, Catherine*
Jul  6 1786    Hull, Mary to Hewett, Caleb*
Aug  1 1779    Hull, Richard to Swan, Mary*
Oct 27 1782    Hull, Samuel to Hollins, Margaret*
Nov  5 1783    Hull, Susan to Bankson, James*
Aug 12 1784    Hulstrunk, Margaret Christiana to Carew, Thomas*
Jun 16 1778    Hults, Elizabeth to Dolphin, Peter*
Jan  4 1792    Humphrey, Elizabeth to Bowen, Sabrel*
Nov  3 1798    Hunby, John to Perry, Anne*
Mar 22 1798    Hunt, Eliza to Deuham, Robert*
Nov  9 1795    Hunt, James to Rogers, Elizabeth*
Apr 25 1782    Hunt, John to Burgess, Alice*
Mar 29 1788    Hunt, Mary to Miller, John
Jun  8 1793    Hunt, Phinias to Gott, Susannah*
Jan 11 1797    Hunt, Sarah to Deaver, John*
Apr 17 1782    Hunt, Thomas to Rush, Elizabeth*
```

Dec 5 1798	Hunt, William to Nicolls, Sarah*
Feb 10 1786	Hunt, William to Standiford, Rachel
Dec 24 1784	Hunt, William to Whaland, Elizabeth*
Mar 14 1792	Hunter, Ann to Cole, Thomas*
Sep 29 1796	Hunter, James to Inloes, Jemima*
Oct 11 1791	Hunter, Nancy to Fish, James*
Feb 18 1792	Hunter, Nancy to Parish, Benjamin*
Apr 21 1795	Hunter, Peter to Rogers, Elizabeth*
Nov 30 1792	Hunter, Peter to Scott, Esther*
Feb 24 1796	Hunter, Peter to Vaughan, Elizabeth*
Nov 30 1792	Hunter, Rachel to Ensor, Darby*
Jan 9 1786	Hurley, Bridget to Hurley, Patrick
Dec 5 1789	Hurley, Dennis to Woolf, Margaret*
Aug 24 1782	Hurley, Mary to Peat, Claude*
May 5 1786	Hurley, Mary to Tuffts, James*
Sep 21 1793	Hurley, Michael to Guiron, Johnna*
Jan 9 1786	Hurley, Patrick to Hurley, Bridget
Jan 19 1791	Hurst, Benedict to Gorsuch, Sarah*
Aug 15 1794	Hurst, Margaret to Engle, Thomas*
Jan 9 1784	Hurst, William to Woodlin, Betsey*
Apr 22 1797	Hurtzot, William to Barnett, Elizabeth*
Dec 4 1778	Hush, Conrod to Puntney, Elinor*
May 29 1784	Hush, John to Concilman, Catherine
Oct 20 1779	Hush, Mary to Pierpoint, John
Jan 10 1781	Hussey, George to Hayward, Rachel*
Jun 9 1795	Huston, John to Peck, Elizabeth*
Jan 12 1798	Hutchem, Ann Eleanor Shew to Languell, Thomas*
Aug 14 1779	Hutchenson, Robert to McCabe, Pheby*
Apr 26 1779	Hutcheson, Sarah to Engram, John
Nov 12 1785	Hutchings, Alice to Shaw, Joshua
Feb 15 1793	Hutchins, Elizabeth to Bosley, Isaac
Apr 16 1788	Hutchins, Gracey to Higgins, John*
Mar 26 1785	Hutchins, Joshua to Hays, Jemina
Jun 14 1782	Hutchins, Martha to Blake, William Hopper*
Jun 9 1796	Hutchins, Samuel to Justis, Mary*
Mar 21 1792	Hutchins, Sarah to Magun, John*
Jul 19 1790	Hutchins, William to Jackson, Darcus*
Feb 16 1789	Hutson, Joshua to Hooker, Susannah*
Feb 16 1785	Hutson, Margaret to Davis, Nathaniel*
Jun 20 1796	Hutton, Henry to Sadler, Sarah*
Sep 15 1795	Hutton, Jane to Murray, Francis*
Jan 22 1798	Hyatt, Aquila to Hyatt, Rachel*
Jan 22 1798	Hyatt, Rachel to Hyatt, Aquila*
Dec 12 1783	Hyner, Joseph to Sthall, Elizabeth*
May 24 1796	Hynson, Nathaniel to Owings, Kitty*
Feb 28 1784	Hynum, Thomas to White, Mary*
Dec 9 1780	Hyson, Josiah to Smith, Sarah*
Oct 13 1779	Iams, Elizabeth to Barcalow, Volentine*
Aug 23 1783	Iams, Milla to Hancock, Joseph*
Nov 29 1785	Iams, Thomas to Gelhampton, Catharine
Aug 22 1798	Ibusson, Rachel to Gardner, Isaac*
Jan 5 1785	Idle, Frederick to Johnstone, Mary*
Jun 6 1793	Ifler, Mary to Linkert, Frederick*
Mar 23 1791	Igo, Comfort to Jourdan, Richard
Apr 8 1788	Ijams, Mary to Penn, William*
Nov 19 1785	Ijams, William to Gelhampton, Mary*

Aug 12 1797	Ilessen, Elizabeth to Morrison, James*
Dec 27 1788	Ilger, Katharine to Dreppard, Andrew
Apr 27 1795	Ilker, Sarah to Tinges, Henry Walker*
Jun 26 1790	Imbleton, Edward to Bryan, Ann
Oct 9 1793	Impford, Titus to Thomas, Elizabeth*
Apr 13 1795	Inch, Elizabeth to Emick, Nicholas*
Jul 18 1795	Ingle, John to Witcomb, _____*
Aug 30 1798	Ingleos, John to Fill, Achsah*
Jul 18 1795	Ingrain, Mary to Cisson, Richard*
Dec 4 1795	Ingram, Clark to Dorsey, Mary*
Nov 16 1779	Ingram, John to Bell, Sarah*
Apr 13 1784	Ingram, Mary to Martin, William
Jul 21 1797	Ingram, Nancy to Stevens, Joseph*
Oct 10 1786	Ingram, Samuel to McNight, Mary
Mar 29 1786	Ingram, Sarah to French, Simon*
Oct 30 1789	Inkster, James to Mahon, Elizabeth*
Oct 18 1792	Inkston, Elizabeth to Long, Thomas*
Mar 14 1783	Inloes, Elizabeth to Harrisson, Thomas*
Sep 6 1786	Inloes, Henry to Peddicord, Elizabeth
Mar 5 1794	Inloes, James to Hacket, Barshalea*
Sep 29 1796	Inloes, Jemima to Hunter, James*
Nov 26 1791	Inloes, Thomas to Weller, Catharine*
Mar 9 1778	Inseler, Valerius to Fresh, Catharina*
Feb 17 1794	Ireland, Catherine to Bennett, John*
Mar 14 1786	Ireland, Clementina to Dorsey, Vachael*
Apr 22 1790	Ireland, Elizabeth to Hollingsworth, Zebulon*
Oct 11 1796	Ireland, Linny to Groves, Ezekiel*
Nov 27 1794	Ireland, Margaret to Boyer, Nicholas*
May 1 1790	Ireland, Richard to Cecil, Linday*
Mar 24 1791	Ireland, Samuel to Capels, Margaret*
Apr 15 1786	Irgrig, John to Demmitt, Hollin*
Dec 30 1795	Irick, Mary to Lemmon, Valentine*
Apr 2 1782	Irish, John to Hall, Mary*
Dec 3 1795	Irons, Thomas to Scott, Delila*
Aug 8 1798	Irvin, Henry to Jones, Frances*
Mar 28 1798	Irvin, Mary to Bailey, Evan*
Oct 5 1784	Irwin, Elizabeth H. to Leakin, John
Oct 20 1788	Irwin, Philip to Hook, Elizabeth*
Oct 6 1798	Isaac, Isaac to Mulligan, Henrietta*
Mar 22 1794	Isaac, Rachel to Belk, James*
Sep 26 1794	Isaacks, Elizabeth to Gross, Henry*
Apr 18 1796	Isabey, Francis to Wilson, Martha*
Nov 30 1780	Iser, Elizabeth to Shirock, John
Aug 9 1781	Iser, Margaret to Vetz, Jacob*
Jan 20 1795	Iser, Nicholas to Rutler, Sophia*
Nov 5 1788	Isgrig, Temperance to Pocock, John*
Dec 19 1792	Isher, Ruth to Fishpaw, Henry*
Sep 29 1781	Isle, John to Brubecker, Mary*
Oct 24 1793	Isoard, Joseph to Deschamp, Fanny*
Feb 23 1793	Isor, Nicholas to Parks, Ann*
Oct 16 1779	Isor, Richard to Shall, Barbara
Apr 3 1786	Isour, Joshua to Dougherty, Sarah*
Nov 30 1792	Israel, Bale to Burgess, Elizabeth*
Jul 17 1784	Israel, Casper to Wyley, Mary
Feb 5 1785	Israel, Ely to Goslin, Ann*
Jan 22 1788	Israel, Joseph to Thompson, Hester*

Apr	5	1796	Israel, Nancy to Giles, William*
Mar	21	1789	Israel, Robert to Gosnel, Rachel*
May	29	1798	Israel, Robert to Gosnell, Rachel*
Feb	2	1791	Israel, Robert to Williams, Nancy*
Sep	3	1796	Ives, James to Mann, Martha*
Feb	1	1796	Ivory, John to Graves, Ann*
Feb	24	1783	Izzard, Elizabeth to Ridgely, William*
Aug	6	1794	Jack, John to Donoran, Mary*
Dec	22	1795	Jackson, Abel to Clay, Rachel*
Dec	15	1781	Jackson, Agness to Cross, Gabriel*
Apr	17	1794	Jackson, Ann to Jemison, Joseph*
Mar	27	1784	Jackson, Ann to Lannum, Lewis*
May	30	1795	Jackson, Ann to Martin, George*
Aug	29	1792	Jackson, Ann to Smith, John*
Feb	24	1796	Jackson, Collin to Nicoll, Jane*
Aug	12	1779	Jackson, Daniel to Clark, Margaret
Jul	19	1790	Jackson, Darcus to Hutchins, William*
Jun	7	1788	Jackson, Eleanor to Harvey, William*
Oct	21	1791	Jackson, Elizabeth to Dean, Thomas*
Apr	24	1793	Jackson, Elizabeth to Phell, William*
Jul	28	1792	Jackson, Elizabeth to Thompson, Nathaniel G.*
May	7	1795	Jackson, Hezekiah to Hiner, Frances*
Jan	28	1796	Jackson, Isaiah to Davis, Catharine*
Sep	4	1797	Jackson, John to Hill, Rebekah*
Sep	3	1779	Jackson, Margaret to Ebert, George
May	23	1791	Jackson, Mary to Jones, Levin*
Apr	10	1794	Jackson, Mary to Lee, Samuel*
Nov	23	1798	Jackson, Mary to McKinzie, George*
Dec	26	1796	Jackson, Mary to Pickard, William*
Mar	8	1793	Jackson, Rachel to Coates, James*
Dec	9	1797	Jackson, Rosannah to Smith, John*
Nov	15	1794	Jackson, Sally to Bennet, John*
Jan	24	1798	Jackson, Sally to Tyson, Nathan*
Jun	8	1784	Jackson, Sarah to Bias, James
Feb	2	1796	Jackson, Thomas to Allender, Elizabeth*
Mar	19	1794	Jackson, Thomas to O'Brian, Mary*
Sep	8	1797	Jackson, Thomas to Reily, Elizabeth*
Apr	18	1795	Jackson, William to Butler, Margaret*
Oct	8	1794	Jackson, William to Smith, Sarah*
Dec	31	1789	Jacob, Anna to Philips, Parker*
Sep	5	1798	Jacob, Benjamin to Oursler, Elizabeth*
Aug	24	1797	Jacob, Elizabeth to Gambrill, William*
Jul	18	1785	Jacob, Elizabeth to Roles, John
Sep	26	1796	Jacob, Ellinor Fair to Appleby, John*
Feb	2	1784	Jacob, Patience to Hall, Jesse*
Dec	11	1790	Jacob, Rachael to Linthicum, Abner*
Jun	28	1786	Jacob, Sarah to Merrikin, John*
Jun	28	1786	Jacob, William to Fitzgerald, Jane
Mar	27	1781	Jacob, William to Godfrey, Mary
Oct	31	1785	Jacob, William to Williams, Rachel
Feb	7	1793	Jacob, Zachariah to Gambrill, Margaret*
Jun	9	1796	Jacobs, George to Moore, Jane*
Jan	25	1783	Jacobs, Joseph to Steward, Rachael*
Feb	9	1785	Jacobs, Mary to Chace, Thondrick*
Jun	1	1796	Jacobs, Mary to Topham, Matthew*
Mar	18	1784	Jacobs, Rachel to Royston, Samuel*

```
Dec 22 1795    Jacobs, Ruth to Stevens, Messer*
Apr 30 1778    Jacobs, Samuel to Macker, Catharine*
Dec 19 1792    Jacobs, Susannah to Hawkins, Ralph*
Jun 15 1796    Jaffray, Frances to Smith, Doman*
Aug  6 1791    Jaffray, Mary to Spence, John
Sep 16 1793    Jaffris, John to Tea, Sarah*
Jun 23 1779    Jain, Samuel to Cron, Margaret
Jan 18 1786    Jalland, John to Bungan, Ruth Jane
Jul 20 1797    James, Abraham to Dicke, Maria*
Jan 12 1797    James, Ann to Walsh, John*
Feb 28 1789    James, Catharine to Burgess, Henry
Jul 16 1785    James, Dinah to Parkinson, Edward*
Sep 27 1793    James, Elie Akeum to Leggett, Amelia*
Nov 10 1797    James, Elizabeth to James, William*
Nov 13 1793    James, Elizabeth to Lawrence, Richard
Sep 13 1782    James, Elizabeth to Sharpe, William*
Nov  7 1791    James, George to Lemmon, Mary*
Jan  7 1796    James, Henry to Ross, Elizabeth*
Jun 28 1798    James, Jane to Handling, Patrick*
Oct 11 1783    James, John to Davey, Henrietta Mariah
Jul 29 1789    James, John to Dilworth, Letitia*
May  9 1795    James, John to Johns, Mary*
Mar 21 1792    James, Lydia to Billmaker, William*
Jun 26 1781    James, Mary to Christoson, Robert
Nov  9 1796    James, Mary to Daugherty, Neal*
Feb 12 1795    James, Mary to Myers, Robert*
Apr 28 1791    James, Sarah to Newman, Henry*
Nov 29 1792    James, Sarah to Randell, William*
Aug 10 1782    James, Temperance to Wheeler, William*
Feb 13 1797    James, William to Alexandria, Flora*
Nov 13 1794    James, William to Hay, Janet*
Nov 10 1797    James, William to James, Elizabeth*
Nov 23 1785    James, William to Landon, Susannah
Sep  9 1786    Jameson, Adam to Johnston, Mary
Jun 20 1792    Jameson, Anne to Louderman, George*
Oct 17 1798    Jaqut, John P. to Stran, Rebecca*
Aug 23 1792    Jardon, James to Smith, Sarah*
Dec  7 1787    Jarvis, Aquila to Rowles, Elizabeth
Sep 29 1796    Jarvis, Averilla to Palmer, William*
Sep 12 1781    Jarvis, Edward to Brooks, Mary*
Dec 23 1793    Jarvis, Edward to Oram, Nancy*
Jun  3 1795    Jarvis, John to Williams, Nancy*
Apr 19 1794    Jarviss, Robert to Stinchcomb, Rebecca*
Jun 18 1796    Jay, Joseph to Williams, Ann*
Mar 25 1796    Jean, Joseph to Cross, Margery*
Jan 11 1786    Jean, William to Miller, Ruth
Nov 30 1789    Jeffery, Sarah to Sloan, John*
Dec  7 1790    Jeffery, William to Puntany, Mary*
Jan 28 1796    Jeffords, George to Robinson, Catharine*
May 22 1778    Jeffrey, Thomas to Barkhouse, Catharine*
Dec 31 1798    Jeffrey, Thomas to Litchfield, Rachel*
Oct  4 1798    Jeffries, Sarah to Griffith, John*
Apr 13 1793    Jeffris, Hannah to Brown, James*
Apr 17 1794    Jemison, Joseph to Jackson, Ann*
Dec 28 1782    Jemmison, Mary to Sincklair, Moses
Oct 22 1795    Jenkins, Elizabeth to Winkle, James*
```

Sep 1 1792	Jenkins, George to Wilson, Eleanor*
Jan 28 1796	Jenkins, Henrietta to Stone, Thomas*
Nov 17 1794	Jenkins, Sarah to Hearn, Anthony*
Apr 19 1793	Jenkins, William to Hellen, Ann*
Sep 16 1798	Jenks, Henry to Webb, Jane*
Jan 6 1786	Jennet, Eleanor to Ludwick, Charles
Jan 23 1792	Jennings, Elizabeth to Brooks, William*
Sep 28 1797	Jennings, James to McGoivan, Eleanor*
Nov 2 1793	Jennings, John to Kough, Elizabeth*
Dec 5 1793	Jennings, John to Shryock, Rachel
Apr 7 1798	Jennings, Mary to Malonee, Alexander*
Jun 9 1794	Jennings, Peter to Lombard, Elizabeth*
Feb 4 1790	Jenny, Ebenezer to Tulheln, Rebecca*
Aug 27 1785	Jenny, Nathaniel to Dawson, Sarah
May 26 1798	Jenny, Sarah to Baldwin, Abraham*
Jul 27 1798	Jervis, Elizabeth to Reese, Joseph*
Jul 20 1789	Jervis, Hannah to Allender, John*
Aug 2 1798	Jervis, Mary to Roaker, Samuel
Jun 4 1778	Jervis, Philip to Alguire, Sarah*
Oct 12 1797	Jessop, Abraham to Wells, Achsah*
Apr 12 1786	Jessop, Charles to Gorsuch, Mary*
Nov 23 1798	Jessop, Delilah to Demmott, Elisha
Jan 4 1798	Jessop, Elizabeth to Lewis, William*
Apr 12 1797	Jessop, Mary to Meads, Benjamin*
Sep 11 1788	Jewell, Aloe to McClaskey, Joseph*
Mar 19 1793	Jewell, Lewis to Gardner, Sarah*
Apr 16 1794	Jewell, William to Arnold, Nancy*
May 19 1798	Jiami, Benjamin to Mitchell, Mary*
Jul 1 1795	Joffray, Mary Theresa to Ricker, Nicholas Augustine*
Aug 11 1797	John, James to Alexandria, Mary Ann*
Apr 12 1779	Johns, Anne to Millard, Kingsby
Oct 21 1785	Johns, Cassandra to Jones, John*
Dec 22 1794	Johns, Hosea to Slade, Penelope*
May 9 1795	Johns, Mary to James, John*
Oct 4 1779	Johns, Rachel to Davis, Richard*
Apr 14 1789	Johns, Richard to Luce, Mary*
Aug 15 1795	Johnson, Amelia to Beaman, James*
Dec 25 1777	Johnson, Ann to Ashmead, Joseph*
Jan 4 1790	Johnson, Ann to McCan, John*
Nov 4 1796	Johnson, Ann to Ozard, Robert*
Jun 12 1782	Johnson, Basil to Long, Elizabeth
Nov 7 1793	Johnson, Caleb, Revd. to Shields, Jame*
Jan 6 1796	Johnson, Charles to Fugate, Mary*
Feb 18 1794	Johnson, Charles to Richardson, Elizabeth*
Apr 28 1794	Johnson, Daphne to Roberts, Richard*
Oct 23 1781	Johnson, David to Craton, Ann*
Jun 21 1796	Johnson, David to Lanon, Bridget*
May 1 1793	Johnson, Druvilla to Howlett, John*
May 31 1798	Johnson, Edward to Mackubin, Elizabeth*
Mar 31 1791	Johnson, Edward to Plowman, Ann*
Aug 14 1790	Johnson, Elijah to Gamble, Margaret
Mar 17 1794	Johnson, Elijah to Oram, Elizabeth*
May 26 1779	Johnson, Elizabeth to Bosul, James
Dec 20 1794	Johnson, Elizabeth to Fox, John Hopkins*
Apr 30 1793	Johnson, Elizabeth to Joyce, Joshua*
Aug 8 1797	Johnson, Elizabeth to Lester, William*

```
Dec  8 1792    Johnson, Elizabeth to Parrish, Nicholas*
Nov 16 1796    Johnson, Elizabeth to Philpot, Bryan*
Dec 27 1794    Johnson, Elizabeth to Stansbury, John Dixon*
May 20 1779    Johnson, Esther to McCartney, James
Sep 14 1795    Johnson, Francis to Crockett, Margaret*
Dec 10 1796    Johnson, Frederick to Weisner, Mary*
Feb 19 1781    Johnson, Henry Augustine to Wells, Sarah
Nov 20 1794    Johnson, Horatio to Warfield, Elizabeth*
May  8 1793    Johnson, Houkman to Sollers, Ann*
Dec 29 1784    Johnson, Israel Hendrick to Daws, Meral
Oct 15 1798    Johnson, Israel to Whiteford, Margaret*
Dec 17 1796    Johnson, Jacob Jr. to Wiley, Catharine*
Mar 24 1798    Johnson, James to Hall, Ann*
Nov 29 1794    Johnson, James to Oval, Catharine*
Apr  7 1798    Johnson, Jemima to Shraden, James*
Jun 17 1785    Johnson, Jeremiah Jr. to Howard, Ruth*
Apr  7 1798    Johnson, John to Kirk, Elizabeth*
Aug 18 1796    Johnson, John to Smith, Susannah*
Nov 18 1796    Johnson, Joseph to Henry, Maria*
Oct  4 1794    Johnson, Joseph to Lacely, Julia*
Jun 17 1795    Johnson, Lake to Sherrud, Elizabeth*
Jun  5 1798    Johnson, Martha to Young, James
Mar 20 1783    Johnson, Mary to Grant, Alexander*
Aug 28 1779    Johnson, Mary to Reed, John*
Apr 20 1796    Johnson, Mary to Shreader, Jacob*
Mar  2 1798    Johnson, Matthew to Vashen, Annestica*
May  9 1793    Johnson, Metilida to Nelson, Thomas*
Nov  4 1795    Johnson, Patience to Ridgely, Mordecai*
Aug 15 1793    Johnson, Penia to O'Brian, Patrick*
Oct 28 1797    Johnson, Peter to White, Priscilla*
Jul 28 1792    Johnson, Rachel to Woodard, John*
Oct 29 1783    Johnson, Rebecca to Peters, Thomas
Sep 29 1790    Johnson, Rebecca to Stran, John*
Apr  3 1790    Johnson, Rezin to Bennett, Lydia
Feb 26 1785    Johnson, Ruth to Chaney, Abel
May  5 1791    Johnson, Sally to Furlong, William*
Dec 11 1790    Johnson, Sarah to Merryman, John
Jun 11 1779    Johnson, Sarah to Oram, Henry
May 17 1793    Johnson, Sarah to Reynolds, James*
Dec 22 1787    Johnson, Sarah to Wescost, John*
Jan 30 1796    Johnson, Sophia to Anderson, James*
Oct 26 1797    Johnson, Susannah to Bishop, John*
Jun 15 1792    Johnson, Thomas to Cord, Elizabeth*
Jun  2 1792    Johnson, Thomas to Fennill, Ruth*
May 22 1794    Johnson, Thomas to Giles, Anne*
Jul 16 1779    Johnson, Thomas to Odle, Mary
Oct  1 1795    Johnson, Thomas to Russell, Eliza*
Aug 23 1797    Johnson, William to Askins, Eleanor*
Jun 11 1783    Johnson, William to Clark, Catharine
Jun 29 1798    Johnson, William to FitzPatrick, Elizabeth*
Mar  8 1797    Johnson, William to Piper, Grace*
Jan 23 1782    Johnston, Absolom to Wooden, Ruth*
Dec 21 1791    Johnston, Ann to Fowler, John*
Jan 14 1796    Johnston, Barney to Smith, Catharine*
Mar 31 1795    Johnston, Daniel to Wright, Ann*
Nov 24 1795    Johnston, Edward to Coffel, Mariah*
```

```
Feb 24 1797    Johnston, James to Cole, Mary
Nov 19 1794    Johnston, James to Spencer, Sarah*
Sep 15 1791    Johnston, Jannet to Cox, Robert*
Dec 14 1796    Johnston, Mary to Ford, Joshua*
Sep  9 1786    Johnston, Mary to Jameson, Adam
Oct 13 1794    Johnston, Nancy to West, Edward*
Jan  5 1785    Johnstone, Mary to Idle, Frederick*
Dec  6 1798    Joice, Nathan to Ryal, Martha*
Jul 31 1794    Joice, Pearce to Craig, Mary*
Oct 24 1778    Joice, Peter Anthony to Patience - negro*
Dec 21 1782    Joice, Stephen to Kinkade, Elizabeth
Jun 19 1779    Joice, William to Davage, Sarah
Jun 18 1779    Joice, William to Davage, Sarah
May 13 1797    Joiner, Rebecca to Gutlerow, John*
Mar  8 1790    Joiner, Sarah to Lanahan, Charles*
Dec 20 1780    Jones, Aaron to Cann, Susanna*
Oct 19 1796    Jones, Abraham to Butler, Mary*
Aug 26 1783    Jones, Amos to Lewin, Ann*
Mar 23 1795    Jones, Ann to Brown, Alexander*
Feb 12 1794    Jones, Ann to Delevet, Peter*
Nov 10 1798    Jones, Ann to Green, Bennett*
Sep  6 1790    Jones, Ann to Ringrow, Aaron*
Aug 22 1797    Jones, Anne to Castille, John*
Mar 20 1788    Jones, Benjamin to Jones, Sarah*
Jun 20 1791    Jones, Cassandra to Edmonston, Alexander*
Oct  5 1790    Jones, Cassandra to Goe, William*
Jan 24 1795    Jones, Cassandra to Hughes, George*
Feb 16 1797    Jones, Charles to Spicer, Temperance*
Nov  3 1798    Jones, Chloe to Mace, Moses*
Aug 30 1794    Jones, Daniel to Messersmith, Catharine*
Feb 20 1782    Jones, David Smith to Dawson, Hannah*
Sep 27 1783    Jones, Eleanor to Parks, Benjamin*
Oct 16 1784    Jones, Elisha to White, Sarah*
May  3 1798    Jones, Elizabeth to Balden, John*
Apr 30 1785    Jones, Elizabeth to Bell, Lloyd
Dec 14 1793    Jones, Elizabeth to Boswell, Joseph*
Mar 27 1793    Jones, Elizabeth to Burke, Thomas*
Jul  3 1783    Jones, Elizabeth to Downey, Matthias*
Sep 17 1782    Jones, Elizabeth to Fowler, Zacharia
Apr 17 1784    Jones, Elizabeth to Griffen, Thomas*
Jun  4 1790    Jones, Elizabeth to Lease, William*
Aug 21 1797    Jones, Elizabeth to Shepherd, Josias*
May 21 1795    Jones, Elizabeth to Shipley, Richard*
Dec 24 1795    Jones, Elizabeth to Sinners, Elijah R.*
Jan 20 1796    Jones, Elizabeth to Wheeler, James*
Apr 19 1794    Jones, Ester to Stevenson, Meshach*
Aug  8 1798    Jones, Frances to Irvin, Henry*
Nov 25 1784    Jones, Francis to Maidscou, Barbara*
Dec 18 1790    Jones, Hannah to Miller, John*
Mar 21 1793    Jones, Hannah to Wall, Jacob*
Jan  2 1783    Jones, Hannah to Wingard, Abraham*
Oct  4 1794    Jones, Isaac to Banks, Eleanor*
Apr  2 1793    Jones, Isaac to Hearn, Mary
May 22 1784    Jones, Jacob to Earp, Elizabeth*
Jun  7 1786    Jones, Jacob to Perrigoe, Elizabeth*
Sep 12 1795    Jones, Jacob to Streeback, Rachel*
```

Sep 8 1797	Jones, James to Murphey, Frances*
Dec 6 1777	Jones, Jeremiah to Harp, Sarah*
Aug 14 1797	Jones, John to Bishop, Nancy*
Feb 3 1781	Jones, John to Cann, Mary*
Oct 21 1785	Jones, John to Johns, Cassandra*
Feb 28 1797	Jones, John to Roberts, Mary*
May 5 1781	Jones, John to Trott, Sarah*
Aug 5 1786	Jones, John to Young, Rachel
Nov 26 1791	Jones, Joshua Merrican to Baker, Hellin
May 5 1798	Jones, Joshua to Sands, Mary*
May 23 1791	Jones, Levin to Jackson, Mary*
Jun 13 1781	Jones, Lucy to Owings, Stephen Jr.
Nov 11 1788	Jones, Magdaline to Renshaw, Martin*
Jun 19 1784	Jones, Margaret to Britton, Joseph*
Oct 10 1778	Jones, Mary to Doe, Joseph*
May 15 1779	Jones, Mary to Gill, Edward
Sep 2 1797	Jones, Mary to Low, John*
May 21 1785	Jones, Mary to Miller, Charles
Sep 9 1792	Jones, Mary to Mintz, Absalom*
Sep 3 1796	Jones, Mary to Philips, Samuel*
Jun 15 1784	Jones, Mary to Taylor, James*
Jun 25 1783	Jones, Mary to Winters, John
Sep 18 1790	Jones, Nanny to Dean, Joshua*
Jun 30 1795	Jones, Pheby to Moutre, James*
Apr 17 1793	Jones, Polly to Cockey, Joshua*
Jul 22 1797	Jones, Polly to Dennis, James*
Sep 11 1790	Jones, Precilla to Parks, Peter*
Dec 9 1777	Jones, Rachel to Lemmon, Alexis*
Dec 5 1783	Jones, Richard to Wile, Cassandra*
Apr 28 1789	Jones, Salsbury to Loney, Eleanor*
Aug 3 1782	Jones, Samuel to Young, Martena*
May 28 1781	Jones, Sarah to Battle, John
Apr 4 1779	Jones, Sarah to Berry, Lawrence
Jun 3 1791	Jones, Sarah to Downes, William*
Mar 20 1788	Jones, Sarah to Jones, Benjamin*
Apr 15 1797	Jones, Sarah to Ryland, John Burk*
Dec 15 1781	Jones, Solomon to Still, Lydia*
Oct 28 1783	Jones, Susanna to Gibson, Joseph*
Nov 27 1788	Jones, Susanna to Roads, Andrew*
Feb 18 1791	Jones, Susannah to Harp, James*
Jan 14 1792	Jones, Susannah Watts to Watts, Edward Allison
Dec 15 1781	Jones, Thomas to Furney, Hannah*
May 12 1785	Jones, William to Caldwell, Ann
May 12 1781	Jones, William to Gordon, Sarah*
Nov 9 1793	Jones, William to Green, Eleanor*
Dec 29 1798	Jones, William to Gregory, Anne
May 13 1794	Jones, William to Harp, Eleanor*
Mar 24 1789	Jones, William to McClung, Elizabeth*
Jan 26 1786	Jones, William to McKinze, Mary*
Nov 13 1790	Jones, William to Thomas, Ann
May 26 1778	Jonston, Elizabeth to Day, James*
Dec 4 1797	Jordan, Esmy to McDermot, Henry*
Oct 26 1778	Jordan, Henry to Murfort, Elizabeth*
Nov 24 1791	Jordan, James to Callahan, Honor*
May 20 1797	Jordan, Mary to Robinson, John*
Nov 23 1790	Jordan, Samuel to Gardner, Sarah*

Jul 24 1783	Jordan, Sarah to Bond, Thomas*
Mar 21 1778	Jordan, Thomas to Eckard, Barbara*
Dec 4 1792	Jordan, William to Hewitt, Rebecca*
Jan 15 1784	Jorden, Elizabeth to Davis, Daniel
Aug 11 1798	Jordon, Caleb to Wagers, Rachel*
Mar 24 1798	Jordon, Hugh to Pollock, Susannah*
Nov 24 1781	Jourdan, Jane to Williams, Thomas*
Mar 23 1791	Jourdan, Richard to Igo, Comfort
Nov 19 1795	Jourdan, Sarah to Chader, James*
Aug 23 1785	Jourdan, Thomas to Orrick, Sarah
Apr 26 1795	Jourdon, Catharine to Christian, John*
Aug 6 1792	Joy, Rachel to Gilberthorp, Thomas*
Oct 6 1783	Joyce, Ann to Holland, Charles
Sep 18 1797	Joyce, Catharine to McDarmott, John*
Feb 12 1789	Joyce, Eleanor to Heath, Samuel*
Jan 1 1795	Joyce, Elisha to Raven, Elizabeth*
Dec 13 1787	Joyce, Elizabeth to Dorsey, Philip*
May 9 1795	Joyce, Elizabeth to Gibson, John*
Dec 2 1789	Joyce, Elizabeth to King, John*
Jun 25 1797	Joyce, Elizabeth to Tillon, Thomas*
Dec 10 1793	Joyce, Jacob to Williams, Nancy*
Apr 30 1793	Joyce, Joshua to Johnson, Elizabeth*
Jan 8 1793	Joyce, Nancy to Hammond, Rezin*
Jul 23 1789	Joyce, Nathan to Bassage, Hannah*
Oct 7 1791	Joyce, Nicholas to Lansdale, Deborah Sanders
May 30 1793	Joyce, Rachel to McCoy, William*
Feb 23 1786	Joyce, Richard to _____, Elizabeth
Jul 28 1789	Joyce, Sarah to Bacon, John*
Apr 19 1794	Joyce, Sarah to Louderman, George*
Apr 11 1786	Joyce, Thomas to Shields, Rebecca
Apr 14 1781	Joyce, Zachariah to Reighnor, Sarah
Jun 16 1792	Jub, William to Hammond, Avir*
Jul 13 1788	Jube to Annes, Ruth--free negroes
Jan 9 1783	Judah, Hannah to Taylor, William*
Apr 22 1779	Judah, Jacob to Overy, Mary
Aug 28 1779	Judy, Elizabeth to Wilson, Charles*
Aug 29 1795	Judy, Frances to Wilson, Solomon*
Apr 22 1786	Jurdan, Elizabeth to Shea, Daniel
Mar 7 1783	Jury, Ann to Wattle, Joseph
May 3 1788	Justice, Elizabeth to McNamee, John*
Jun 9 1796	Justis, Mary to Hutchins, Samuel*
Dec 12 1789	Justis, Rebecca to Wallace, Robert*
Jan 8 1782	Kailland, Hamutril to Logan, Michael*
Oct 17 1779	Kain, Elizabeth to Higgenbottom, John*
Jan 6 1782	Kain, Mariah to Potter, Andrew*
Aug 6 1793	Kandley, Joseph to Stevens, Sophia*
Dec 16 1791	Kaney, Elizabeth to Minchen, William*
Sep 6 1790	Kannady, Ann to Archibold, James*
Jul 11 1779	Kannady, John to Perry, Ann
May 22 1788	Kapolt, Lewis to Bahm, Hannah
Sep 5 1788	Karns, Bridget to Curtis, Eleazer*
Jun 27 1789	Karr, Christiana to McConnal, John
Mar 30 1798	Kearly, James to Howard, Elizabeth*
Aug 26 1797	Kearney, Richard to McCaskey, Ann*
Sep 17 1791	Kearns, Charles to Long, Hannah*
Jun 20 1790	Kearns, Susannah to Murphy, Patrick

Feb	9	1798	Keaslen, George Dederick to Wenberry, Elizabeth*
May	12	1789	Keath, Jane to Patterson, James*
Oct	27	1797	Keaton, Eleanor to Hogan, John*
Jul	29	1794	Keaton, William to Constable, Elizabeth*
Jan	2	1781	Kedie, James to Turner, Sarah*
Sep	29	1794	Keeble, Humphrey to Berry, Lucy*
Aug	28	1795	Keeble, Humphrey to Callahan, William*
Jan	31	1798	Keefe, Ally to Dailey, John*
May	1	1795	Keeler, Joseph to Gill, Mary*
May	23	1789	Keener, Elizabeth to Cole, Godfrey*
Nov	27	1792	Keener, Elizabeth to Gultry, Joshua*
Jul	9	1798	Keener, Margaret to Bordely, William C.*
Dec	13	1777	Keener, Margaret to Swoope, Benedict Jr.*
May	17	1783	Keener, Michael to Strebeck, Christiana*
Dec	6	1783	Keener, Susannah to Guttery, Joshua
Aug	9	1792	Keens, Joseph to Darel, Anna*
Jan	2	1791	Keens, Susannah to Night, Joseph
Jul	29	1779	Keephost, Michael to Sutton, Ann*
Dec	20	1780	Keeports, Catharine to Bantulau, Paul*
Jun	25	1782	Keeports, Elizabeth to Durmeste, John
Aug	11	1784	Keerl, Henry to Myers, Polly*
Jan	26	1781	Kees, Elizabeth to Keller, John*
May	16	1794	Keifle, Nicholas to Philling, Mary M.*
Jul	13	1798	Keighler, Daniel to Ashburner, Mary
Aug	25	1796	Keilholtz, Margaret to Smallwood, Robert*
Apr	7	1796	Keilholtz, Mary to Gerlach, John*
Mar	22	1790	Keirl, Michael to Maroil, Mary*
Jan	24	1797	Keirn, Christina to Morris, Augustus*
Dec	23	1783	Keistord, Jane to Stevens, Richard*
Dec	25	1777	Keith, Ann to Woodhouse, George*
Jun	9	1790	Keith, Sarah to Carter, William M.*
Apr	20	1798	Keith, William to Stitford, Mary*
Jun	15	1779	Keler, Jacob to Folinger, Mary*
Mar	1	1792	Kell, Pamela to Andrew, Maddox*
Oct	26	1797	Kell, Thomas to Gouldsmith, Mary Ann*
Jan	30	1790	Kelleham, Johannes to Willis, George*
Sep	21	1797	Kellen, John to Clower, Elizabeth*
Dec	20	1783	Kellen, John to Triplet, Polly
Jan	26	1781	Keller, John to Kees, Elizabeth*
Nov	28	1793	Kelley, Nancy to Dell, Peter*
Jul	30	1781	Kelley, Rebecca to Griffen, Charles*
Aug	18	1792	Kelley, Thomas to Arters, Rachel
Mar	23	1793	Kelly, Butler to Kitely, Anne*
Feb	12	1798	Kelly, Catharine to Handles, James*
Dec	30	1794	Kelly, Edward to Taylor, Grace*
Dec	5	1785	Kelly, Eleanor to Smith, William
Oct	18	1783	Kelly, Elinor to Reese, John*
Nov	10	1778	Kelly, Elizabeth to Chapman, John*
Sep	10	1794	Kelly, Emanuel to Leach, Sarah*
Jul	22	1778	Kelly, Hugh to Hudless, Mary*
Oct	7	1794	Kelly, James to Rose, Rachell*
Aug	12	1790	Kelly, John to Chedick, Charlotte*
Feb	20	1794	Kelly, John to Draynan, Sarah*
May	4	1789	Kelly, Joseph to Bagford, Rachael
Jul	20	1796	Kelly, Lawrence to Chamberlain, Margaret*
Jun	30	1797	Kelly, Margaret to Carey, Jeremiah*

```
Jul  3 1778    Kelly, Margaret to McClughan, James*
Jan 20 1798    Kelly, Margaret to Wagers, Elijah*
Nov 14 1796    Kelly, Mary to Brown, John*
Jul  3 1779    Kelly, Mary to Davisson, Peter
Jul 27 1778    Kelly, Mary to Garer, John Valentine*
Jul 10 1797    Kelly, Mary to Lansfield, George*
Jun 19 1778    Kelly, Mary to Young, John*
Mar  1 1779    Kelly, Michael to Edwards, Mary*
Feb 15 1786    Kelly, Nancy to Morfoot, John
Jan 28 1794    Kelly, Patrick to Williams, Sarah*
Mar  9 1797    Kelly, Phebe to Prestman, Thomas*
May 31 1786    Kelly, Rebecca to Green, Joshua*
Jul 29 1785    Kelly, Ruth to Gist, Thomas
Dec 31 1788    Kelly, Ruth to Plowman, Richard*
Sep  6 1796    Kelly, Samuel to Griffith, Ruth*
Feb 16 1785    Kelly, Sarah to Corbin, Elijah*
Mar 20 1786    Kelly, Stephen to Moore, Ann*
Jun  1 1796    Kelly, Susannah to Matthews, John*
Aug 28 1794    Kelly, Susannah to Myers, Benjamin*
Dec 23 1797    Kelly, Thomas to Capen, Honor*
Jan 20 1781    Kelly, Thomas to Gorsuch, Charity*
Dec 26 1777    Kelly, William Jr. to Loveall, Martha*
Mar 27 1786    Kelly, William to Wallace, Margaret*
Jan  7 1797    Kelso, Ann to Sprucebunk, Abraham*
Aug  1 1793    Kelso, James to Standiford, Elizabeth*
Dec 31 1792    Kelso, James to Walker, Mary*
Apr 22 1789    Kelso, Thomas to Rutledge, Penelope*
Oct 31 1786    Kelsoe, Margaret to Dugan, Cumberland
Dec 25 1793    Kelsoe, Sarah to Moore, Nicholas Ruxton*
Jun 25 1793    Kemmell, Sarah to Greenfield, Ashberry*
Aug 11 1781    Kemp, Honor to Conly, John
May 18 1797    Kemp, James to Freeman, Ann*
Aug 16 1782    Kemp, Sarah to Fox, Anthony*
Oct  9 1783    Kempff, John Christ to Chenoweth, Keziah*
Dec 12 1795    Kendal, Vachel to Barnes, Ursely*
Apr  2 1796    Kendal, Vachel to Shipley, Rachel*
Oct 28 1789    Kendell, Elizabeth to Kennerly, Samuel*
Dec  4 1797    Kenecker, Frederick to Hindon, Elizabeth*
May 10 1794    Kenedy, Ann to Skerret, John*
Sep  8 1791    Kennard, George to Lane, Providence*
Nov  2 1795    Kennard, Isaac to Few, Catharine*
May 26 1783    Kennedy, John to Pierson, Bridget*
Jan 30 1781    Kennedy, Judeah to Gouldsbury, Mark*
Jul 31 1782    Kennedy, Martin to Callanan, Mary
May 12 1791    Kennedy, Sarah to Fightmaster, Frederick*
Apr 20 1797    Kennedy, William to Peake, Eleanor*
Oct 28 1789    Kennerly, Samuel to Kindell, Elizabeth*
Feb 27 1783    Kenney, Alice to Ware, Charles
Dec 21 1785    Kenocken, Matte to Shean, David*
Oct 29 1788    Kenseller, Ann to Fannon, Lawrence*
Jun 19 1788    Kent, Emanuel to Barneston, Eleanor*
Jan  6 1798    Kent, Robert to Myers, Margaret*
Jun 21 1784    Kentlemyer, John Mike to Partle, Peggy*
May 11 1793    Kepp, Sarah to Shryar, Lewis
Mar 22 1797    Keppard, Louis to Slaughter, Elizabeth*
May 15 1795    Keppler, John T. to Culverwell, Mary*
```

Jul 29 1790	Kerby, Joshua to Murray, Elizabeth*
Jan 3 1792	Kerns, Margaret to Apple, Christian
Nov 4 1779	Kerns, Mary to Speck, Henry
May 27 1784	Kerr, William to Rush, Agness
Feb 11 1786	Kerwan, John to Sewell, Mary
Nov 16 1795	Kessuck, Roger to Thomas, Milcha*
Dec 13 1783	Ketcham, Sarah to Smith, Joseph
Aug 3 1785	Kettle, Elizabeth to Edwards, David*
Jan 3 1784	Kettle, Mary to Hissey, William*
Nov 21 1797	Kettleman, Elizabeth to Archer, John*
Feb 21 1793	Kettleman, Elizabeth to Arnold, Peter*
Nov 14 1793	Kettleman, Elizabeth to Thornburgh, Robert*
Mar 27 1793	Kettleman, Mary to Bulger, Henry*
Oct 18 1793	Kettler, Mary to Sapet, John Francis*
Nov 17 1796	Key, Abner to Eagan, Catharine*
Mar 21 1791	Key, David to Richardson, Cloe*
Apr 24 1794	Key, James E. to Smith, Elizabeth*
Apr 22 1791	Key, Mary to Ritter, Richard*
Jun 9 1796	Key, Philip to Hall, Sophia*
Jul 25 1783	Keyler, John to Burk, Deborah
Dec 3 1788	Keys, Ann to Sigler, John*
Aug 25 1784	Keys, Charlotte to Tritely, Freak
Sep 4 1788	Keys, Elizabeth to Kraner, Henry*
Apr 25 1792	Keys, John to Darrell, Elizabeth*
May 24 1785	Keys, Margaret to Pilling, Jonathan*
Jul 16 1794	Kibble, Elizabeth to Flemmon, James*
Jul 31 1786	Kidd, Bridget to Shean, Dennis
Sep 20 1784	Kidd, Eleanor to Donwilly, Robert*
Sep 7 1797	Kiersted, Luke to Allison, Jane*
Jun 15 1796	Kilbourn, Elizabeth to Teague, Laban*
Sep 28 1797	Kilbreath, Elizabeth to Scott, David*
Sep 28 1795	Killion, Jacob to Newman, Mary*
Oct 18 1797	Killman, Priscila to Stewart, Mark*
Dec 27 1798	Killum, Elizabeth to Daley, Daniel*
Oct 29 1791	Kilman, Edward to Stevens, Dolly*
Apr 28 1798	Kilman, James to Green, Sarah*
Nov 7 1795	Kilman, John to Riley, Alice*
Jan 21 1782	Kilman, Mary to Henshaw, Basil*
May 14 1796	Kilner, James to Burgoyne, Catharine*
Jul 25 1781	Kilsomor, Frs. to Myers, Margaret*
Oct 17 1798	Kimble, Patty to Switzer, John*
Jan 30 1798	Kimbs, Mary Ann to Pearson, David*
Oct 17 1798	Kimisler, John to Gray, Elizabeth*
Mar 16 1786	Kimmell, Mary to Swartz, George*
Jun 30 1797	Kindall, Cassandra to Choak, John*
Dec 17 1791	Kindell, Sarah to Shipley, John
Feb 13 1789	King, Ann to Hardisty, Rezin*
Jan 15 1791	King, Ann to Louderman, John Christian
Oct 29 1798	King, Comfort to Bennett, Thomas*
Feb 3 1796	King, David to King, Martha*
May 2 1782	King, Dorathy to Fullom, George*
Feb 1 1783	King, Fanny to Martin, Peter
Dec 2 1789	King, John to Joyce, Elizabeth*
Dec 2 1794	King, Margaret to McCandley, Neale*
Feb 3 1796	King, Martha to King, David*
Jan 30 1781	King, Mary to Chambers, William*

May	7	1784	King, Mary to Linigan, John*
Feb	2	1781	King, Michael to Eaton, Biddy*
Dec	13	1787	King, Michael to Gordon, Mary*
Mar	14	1786	King, Nancy to Crowse, George
Feb	8	1797	King, Richard to Gardiner, Anne*
Oct	9	1793	King, Samuel to Rea, Sarah*
Dec	14	1797	King, Sarah to Carroll, Thomas*
Sep	4	1783	King, Thomas to Barnes, Ann
Aug	4	1784	King, William to Hammond, Elizabeth Ann
Oct	18	1798	Kingan, John to Alorafts, Martha*
Sep	20	1788	Kingdon, Mary to Mitcheson, Henry
Apr	29	1786	Kingslane, Clarinda to Zuill, William
Dec	21	1782	Kinkade, Elizabeth to Joice, Stephen
Oct	26	1778	Kinselagh, Susannah to Butcher, John*
Jan	7	1797	Kinsly, Alice to Purdin, Michael*
Oct	7	1794	Kiplinger, Catherine to Steigar, John
Jun	26	1782	Kirby, Amey to Treacle, William
Sep	11	1786	Kirby, Catey to McGrah, Thomas*
Feb	27	1796	Kirby, Elizabeth to Curtis, Edmund*
May	4	1791	Kirby, Godfrey to Hahn, Nany*
Oct	10	1791	Kirby, James to Dean, Prudence*
Jun	8	1796	Kirby, James to Decourse, Sarah*
Jan	9	1790	Kirby, John to Porter, Amana*
Jan	30	1778	Kirby, Patience to Warfield, Silvanus*
Nov	29	1792	Kirby, Providence to Gill, John Price*
Apr	25	1789	Kirby, Sarah to Lewis, John*
May	20	1784	Kirby, Sarah to Trimble, John*
Mar	2	1797	Kirivan, Bryan to Mills, Jane
Apr	7	1798	Kirk, Elizabeth to Johnson, John*
Aug	16	1790	Kirk, Ichosheba to Brown, Josiah*
Nov	19	1778	Kirk, Mary to Richards, William*
Mar	25	1779	Kirk, Thomas to Gailer, Delila*
Jun	29	1795	Kirkman, Thomas to Fisher, Mary*
Oct	28	1797	Kirkwood, Jane to Hooper, Isaac*
Nov	10	1794	Kisk, Catharine to Coghlan, William*
Jun	11	1798	Kiteley, Elizabeth to Whalen, William*
Nov	14	1797	Kitely, Abraham to Tenis, Sarah*
Mar	23	1793	Kitely, Anne to Kelly, Butler*
Aug	26	1783	Kitely, Hannah to Debauler, William*
Dec	7	1796	Kitely, Mary to Hooper, Samuel
May	10	1792	Kitley, Providence to Day, John*
Oct	2	1786	Kitten, Catharine to Barret, Edward
Jul	12	1791	Kitten, John to Towson, Rachel*
Jul	8	1795	Kitten, Theophilus to Cochran, Mary*
Jan	18	1797	Kitting, Mary to Wooden, Benjamin*
Oct	2	1784	Kittinger, Jacob to Frish, Mary*
Jul	8	1794	Klein, Jacob to Diffenderffer, Mary*
Jul	18	1795	Kliffora, James to Hopkins, Lydia*
Jul	21	1792	Kline, Elizabeth to Totten, Joseph*
Oct	15	1796	Kline, Margaret to Shrebeck, William*
Aug	7	1784	Knap, Jacob to Pendon, Katharine
Nov	20	1790	Kneass, Hannah to Corbley, Nicholas*
Nov	17	1784	Knight, Achsah to Calef, John*
Dec	15	1785	Knight, Ann to Cavey, John
Jun	2	1795	Knight, Basha to Borkelt, John*
May	12	1784	Knight, Benjamin to Hook, Margarett*

Nov 22 1794	Knight, Elizabeth to Harner, Daniel*
Aug 4 1783	Knight, Hannah to Bosley, William*
Dec 11 1782	Knight, Jacob to Anderson, Mary*
Sep 3 1779	Knight, Jacob to ------------*
Nov 29 1798	Knight, John B. to Cavey, Sarah*
Jan 31 1793	Knight, Joshua to Anderson, Sarah*
May 21 1783	Knight, Thomas to Gilbert, Catharine*
Feb 13 1795	Knopwood, John to Lyons, Mary*
Dec 24 1793	Knott, Ann to Neighbours, Henry
Apr 17 1784	Knoutten, Elizabeth to Summers, Martin*
Feb 25 1786	Knowland, Ann to Davey, Michael
Jul 11 1794	Knowland, Mary to Burns, Simon*
Sep 4 1788	Knowland, Mary to Palmer, Edward*
Dec 23 1790	Knox, Ann to Hobbs, James*
Feb 3 1781	Knox, William to Page, Elizabeth*
Apr 16 1795	Koenig, Dorothea to Dannenberg, Frederick William*
Jul 14 1792	Kogt, Jane to Booth, William*
Jun 10 1785	Koh, Elizabeth to Myers, Christian*
Apr 28 1791	Koniche, Nicholas to Thomas, Catherine*
Jun 27 1795	Kornish, Rachel to Elsey, Isaac*
Nov 2 1793	Kough, Elizabeth to Jennings, John*
Sep 4 1788	Kraner, Henry to Keys, Elizabeth*
Nov 14 1787	Kraner, Michael to Nice, Susanna*
Jan 7 1784	Krebs, Elizabeth to Somevault, Philip*
Nov 18 1797	Krebs, John to Sumvalt, Mary*
Oct 26 1793	Krebs, Michael to Berry, Sarah*
Nov 4 1782	Krebs, Michael to Cable, Mary*
Jul 20 1794	Krems, Joseph to Shultz, Christiana*
Mar 26 1795	Kreps, Sarah to Bockins, Peter*
Jan 14 1796	Kriabs, Sarah to Burket, John*
Feb 28 1778	Krider, Sophia to Bencil, Balcer*
Apr 24 1798	Kryder, John to Hayes, Sarah*
Oct 31 1798	La Dadus, Henrietta to Groverman, Anthony*
Jul 12 1779	La Gibson, John to Wheeler, Mary
Mar 5 1783	Labat, Sarah to Willis, George*
Nov 22 1784	Labatt, John Baptist to Granger, Margaret
Sep 12 1778	Labesius, John to Hammond, Nancey
Jan 29 1791	LaBlonig, Mary Magdalen to Blossom, Peter*
May 15 1784	Laborde, Bernard to Landry, Modeste*
Apr 1 1779	Laborett, Thebe to Witherson, Robert*
Feb 27 1797	Labough, Christina to Stillinger, Jacob*
Oct 4 1794	Lacely, Julia to Johnson, Joseph*
Oct 19 1790	Ladler, Susannah to Stack, Samuel
Jan 29 1794	Lafen, Barnard to Morine, Susannah*
Mar 29 1785	Lague, Aquila to Davis, Nancy
Apr 10 1794	Lake, Michael to McLaughlin, Sarah*
May 24 1783	Lakin, Robert to Langley, Mary
Nov 28 1792	Lalanne, Frederick Raymond to Cannon, Rachel*
Mar 24 1794	Laman, James to Taylor, Mary*
Nov 25 1784	Lamar, William to Worthington, Margaret*
Jul 11 1795	Lamb, Rebecca to Parker, John*
Jul 5 1779	Lambath, Daniel to Bennett, Mary*
Jul 13 1782	Lambden, Thomas to Grear, Catherine*
Oct 8 1798	Lambert, Lewis to Trottenberg, Maria*
Jun 19 1792	Lambert, Richard to Davidson, Elizabeth*
Jul 28 1784	Lambough, Ephraim to Furst, Elizabeth*

Jul 30 1782	Lamden, Thomas to Greer, Catherine*
Aug 6 1792	Lamecole, Hannah to Matzen, Henry*
Jan 13 1784	Laming, Benjamin to Ridgely, Eleanor*
Jun 6 1795	Lammot, Elizabeth to Lower, Samuel*
Feb 20 1798	Lamosne, Peter to Munge, Elizabeth
Mar 8 1790	Lanahan, Charles to Joiner, Sarah*
Jul 15 1783	Lanahan, Lewis to Sullivan, Hannah
Jun 13 1798	Lanahan, Timothy to Ryan, Mary*
Aug 25 1783	Lancaster, Nathan to Parsons, Rebecca
Oct 30 1792	Landerkin, John to Bouser, Nell*
Feb 22 1797	Landers, Elizabeth to Carmichael, John
Jun 1 1796	Landers, Judith to Gent, Thomas*
Apr 21 1796	Landers, William to Taylor, Elizabeth*
Sep 19 1793	Landin, Alexander to Beachgood, Sarah*
Nov 23 1785	Landon, Susannah to James, William
Sep 3 1794	Landrakin, Mary to Clements, James*
Aug 2 1783	Landre, Mary to Pumesho, Joseph*
Feb 14 1794	Landres, Peter to Simpson, Lydia*
Nov 18 1780	Landry, George to Dine, Magdalain*
May 15 1784	Landry, Modeste to Laborde, Bernard*
Nov 12 1784	Landsdale, Richard to Waters, Sarah Arnold
Mar 14 1798	Lane, Ann to Green, Charles*
Jan 19 1790	Lane, Charlotte to Dall, James*
Nov 6 1790	Lane, Deriah to Read, George*
Dec 23 1783	Lane, Dianna to Griffith, George*
Sep 29 1798	Lane, Elijah to Dewhurch, Hannah
Feb 26 1784	Lane, Elisha to Manin, Tacy*
Feb 18 1790	Lane, Elizabeth to Carlyle, John
Oct 27 1797	Lane, Elizabeth to Criswell, Richard*
Jan 18 1786	Lane, Elizabeth to Hoffman, Adam*
Jan 12 1788	Lane, James to Mason, Lydia*
Aug 13 1796	Lane, John to Milliron, Mary*
Apr 26 1784	Lane, Mary to Carry, Andrew*
Sep 8 1791	Lane, Providence to Kennard, George*
Aug 4 1791	Lane, Providence to Lane, Samuel*
Aug 4 1791	Lane, Samuel to Lane, Providence*
Jul 29 1783	Lane, Sarah to Butler, Joseph*
Apr 29 1794	Lanes, Christopher to Little, Polly*
Nov 28 1783	Langdon, Joseph to Lynch, Sarah*
May 19 1794	Langley, Mary to Heath, James*
May 24 1783	Langley, Mary to Lakin, Robert
Jul 20 1796	Langston, Mary to Hayes, John*
Oct 12 1784	Langston, Nehemiah to Osborn, Cordelia
Jan 12 1798	Languell, Thomas to Hutchem, Ann Eleanor Shew*
Jun 9 1798	Langwall, Mary to Perry, Samuel*
Mar 27 1784	Lannum, Lewis to Jackson, Ann*
Mar 29 1786	Lannum, Lewis to Mitchell, Martha*
Jun 21 1796	Lanon, Bridget to Johnson, David*
Oct 7 1791	Lansdale, Deborah Sanders to Joyce, Nicholas
Nov 15 1780	Lansdell, Sarah to Turner, Jeremiah*
Jul 10 1797	Lansfield, George to Kelly, Mary*
Sep 28 1778	Lanto, George to Forrester, Margaret*
Oct 30 1782	Larch, Isaac to Carr, Sarah*
Jun 24 1786	Larew, Elizabeth to Goddard, William*
Dec 18 1794	Larey, Elizabeth to Haley, Peter*
Jul 10 1783	Largeau, George James to Adams, Rachel*

Dec 21 1793	Larnott, Hannah Catherine to Carty, Peter*
May 6 1797	Laroche, Elizabeth to Delisle, John Godart*
Oct 16 1786	Laroche, Elizabeth to _____*
Nov 11 1796	Larouett, Nicholas to Capeta, Rebecca*
Nov 28 1787	Larrimore, James to Haddaway, Prudence*
Feb 24 1781	Larsh, Elenor to Shaver, Balser*
Mar 31 1781	Larsh, Susannah to Vanor, Philip*
Feb 20 1798	Lary, Julian to White, Michael
Jan 2 1796	Laryou, Peter to Poe, Jane*
Jun 3 1783	Lascault, Lewis to Sligh, Mary
Dec 15 1780	Laser, John to Tular, Margaret
Nov 21 1796	Lasher, Ann to Morrin, James*
Dec 31 1782	Lasher, Frederick to Sweeney, Mary*
Feb 1 1794	Lashrow, Margaret to Barnor, Alexander Peter*
Dec 30 1794	Laske, Margaret to Sampson, Joseph*
Aug 7 1789	Lasqu, Mary to Thoucas, Lewis*
Mar 26 1791	Latchaw, Magdeline to Williams, John*
Feb 7 1794	Latil, Joseph to Owens, Anna*
Sep 10 1798	Latimor, Nicholas to Ryan, Margaret
Oct 23 1795	Latour, John to Smith, Grace*
Jul 20 1782	Latreyte, John to Desshiels, Polly
Nov 19 1778	Laudiger, Caterena to Caldwell, John*
Jul 25 1798	Lauhar, Elizabeth to Heide, Henry*
Mar 23 1793	Laurence, William to Shields, Mary*
Oct 25 1798	Lavele, Michael to Bulk, Mary*
Jan 22 1784	Lavely, Andrew to Dentling, Elizabeth*
Nov 9 1780	Lavely, George to Rees, Sarah*
Sep 2 1795	Lavely, Sarah to Milburne, Cotton*
Sep 4 1794	Lavely, Susannah to Herring, Robert*
Jan 12 1790	Laverty, James to Holland, Catherine*
May 28 1788	Laverty, James to Moore, Elizabeth*
Feb 12 1794	Lavigne, Augustine to Andrew, Casandra*
Feb 12 1795	Lavinder, Levin to Beaty, Mary*
Apr 12 1797	Law, Catharine to Barils, Henry*
Jul 7 1795	Law, James to Davis, Elizabeth*
Nov 24 1785	Lawbright, Elizabeth to McCarty, John
Jan 26 1795	Lawder, Margaret to Bailey, Levin*
Dec 23 1782	Lawrance, Rachel to Newton, William, Capt.
Dec 14 1798	Lawrell, James to O'Neale, Ann*
Feb 23 1796	Lawrence, Elizabeth to Mansfield, Thomas*
May 3 1786	Lawrence, Elizabeth to Pearce, John*
Dec 14 1782	Lawrence, Jacob to Roberts, Sarah*
Apr 4 1778	Lawrence, James to Taylor, Elizabeth*
Aug 19 1786	Lawrence, Leaven to Dorsey, Sarah
May 23 1795	Lawrence, Levin to Dorsey, Mary*
Feb 13 1788	Lawrence, Polly to Dorsey, Elias
Oct 26 1789	Lawrence, Rebecca to Winchester, Richard*
Nov 13 1793	Lawrence, Richard to James, Elizabeth
Feb 21 1786	Lawrence, Susannah to Dorsey, Edward*
Feb 12 1796	Lawrence, Susannah to Mills, James*
Aug 29 1797	Lawrence, Thomas to Mitchell, Mary
Feb 28 1797	Lawrence, Wendel to Steele, Ann*
Apr 7 1798	Lawson, Charles to Green, Elizabeth*
Oct 29 1791	Lawson, Richard to Parkinson, Diannah*
Feb 10 1798	Lawson, Robert to McCallister, Elizabeth*
Sep 3 1794	Laybor, James to Annopotis, Belinda*

Sep 25	1795	Laying, Thomas to Dawson, Henne*
Nov 23	1793	Layman, Jacob to Myers, Philapma
Jun 1	1785	Laymon, Philabina to Smith, William*
Mar 6	1794	Laypold, Catharine to Moore, William Stephen*
Aug 28	1778	Laypole, John to Bridenhart, Dorrity*
Dec 23	1794	Le Monnur, Catharine Marie to Groce, John Antoine*
Apr 30	1791	Leach, Ebeneazer to McNeal, Rebecca*
Apr 12	1784	Leach, John to Holton, Sarah*
Aug 8	1797	Leach, Nancy to Soivers, Edward*
Sep 10	1794	Leach, Sarah to Kelly, Emanuel*
Dec 19	1798	Leaf, Anne to Tipton, Micajah*
Aug 28	1779	Leaf, Catharine to Mason, Michael*
Oct 28	1786	Leaf, Elizabeth to Ritter, Thomas
Dec 31	1792	Leage, Thomas to Spencer, Sarah
Jan 1	1798	League, Abraham to Moore, Elizabeth*
May 18	1793	League, Averilla to Melony, James*
Nov 27	1797	League, Chloe to Freir, John*
Dec 21	1795	League, Chloe to Green, William*
Apr 1	1795	League, Elizabeth to Oram, Arnold*
Sep 5	1797	League, Elizabeth to Snares, William*
Oct 5	1781	League, James to Morgan, Elizabeth*
May 5	1790	League, John to Fowler, Sarah*
Oct 24	1798	League, John to Taylor, Elizabeth*
Jul 29	1795	League, Reubin to Segasey, Margaret*
Nov 25	1790	Leahy, John to Duncan, Easter*
May 28	1783	Leakin, Ann to Todd, Nicholas*
Oct 5	1784	Leakin, John to Irwin, Elizabeth H.
Aug 8	1778	Leakins, Mary to Todd, Lancelot*
Oct 21	1795	Leakins, Rachel to Daughady, John*
May 1	1798	Leakins, Thomas to Smith, Sarah*
Aug 27	1796	Leary, Andrew to Dempsey, Mary*
Jul 14	1792	Leary, Catharine Maryann to Corbin, William*
Dec 10	1794	Leary, Catharine to Cunningham, John*
Feb 11	1786	Leary, Catherine to Morres, Mark
Dec 7	1790	Leary, Daniel to McBride, Mary*
Nov 27	1790	Leary, Margaret to Hailey, Peter*
Jun 4	1790	Lease, William to Jones, Elizabeth*
May 21	1791	Leatherburg, Achsah to Burk, Edward*
Sep 7	1779	Leatherwood, Ann to Hewitt, Nichel
Jun 16	1792	Leatherwood, Ruth to Buckingham, Nathan*
Jan 7	1797	Leatherwood, Ruth to Wood, Robert*
Jan 3	1778	Leatherwood, Sarah to Dicas, John*
Jan 31	1784	Leatherwood, Thomas to Porter, Mary*
Jul 2	1796	Leathorn, Margaret to Ashman, Thomas*
Mar 27	1779	Leavely, Catharine to Askew, William*
Jul 27	1784	Lebanus, Ann to Coleman, William*
Oct 26	1795	LeBaren, Leonard to Elkins, Margaret*
Jul 3	1794	Lebat, Peggy to Ermon, Francis*
Nov 25	1796	Lebourdais, Therese C.M.H. to Delaunay, Jacque A.*
Feb 2	1798	Leclaire, Lewis Sebast to De Narbes, Jeaune J.R.
Oct 13	1783	Ledwidge, Ann to McCloude, Hugh*
Oct 13	1789	Lee, Ann to Cole, Joshua*
Jun 22	1796	Lee, Delilah to Randall, Israel*
May 31	1793	Lee, Eleanor to Floyd, Caleb*
Apr 7	1785	Lee, Elizabeth to Allen, John
Aug 1	1794	Lee, Frances to Batery, Charles*

Jul 1 1783	Lee, George to Zimerman, Mary*
Jan 20 1795	Lee, Hall to Stansbury, Keziah*
Mar 28 1792	Lee, James to Riley, Nancy*
Oct 17 1798	Lee, John to Cook, Mary*
Apr 2 1796	Lee, John to Stinchcomb, Ann*
Sep 5 1796	Lee, Joshua to Mathias, Priscilla*
Aug 31 1798	Lee, Keziah to Halton, Aquilla*
Nov 17 1792	Lee, Mary to Brown, Joshua*
May 28 1783	Lee, Priscilla to Presbury, George Gouldth.
Dec 22 1791	Lee, Rachel to Spicer, John*
Apr 10 1794	Lee, Samuel to Jackson, Mary*
Nov 19 1787	Lee, Samuel to Rush, Margaret*
Oct 13 1796	Lee, Thomas to Cromwell, Eleanor*
Aug 12 1797	Lee, William to Connoway, Rebecca*
Aug 11 1792	Lee, William to Roberts, Priscilla
Dec 19 1795	Lee, William to Watts, Milly*
Jan 10 1785	Leech, Benjamin to Gutridge, Sarah*
Dec 11 1795	Leech, John to Howard, Elizabeth*
Feb 4 1786	Leech, Mary to Davis, Daniel
Oct 5 1792	Leech, Sally to Addison, John*
Dec 13 1796	Leecoumpt, Sarah E. to Cohoun, Moses*
Feb 14 1798	Leef, Henry to Tipton, Ann
Nov 19 1781	Leef, John to Campbell, Rachel
Jul 27 1782	Leehorn, Margaret to McDonnell, William*
Jun 5 1794	Leern, Elizabeth to Miller, Frederick*
Jul 29 1790	Leese, Elizabeth to Woodrough, John Williams*
Nov 7 1798	Leesh, Greenbury to Loveall, Casandra*
Nov 9 1793	Leeson, Francis to Mackenerney, Catharine*
May 25 1779	Legard, John to Celestin, Mary
Oct 3 1789	Leger, Alizanna to Warner, William*
Feb 26 1785	Legg, Solomon to O'Bryan, Hetty*
Sep 27 1793	Leggett, Amelia to James, Elie Akeum*
Jun 2 1796	Leggett, Violett to Bowser, Isaac*
Jan 14 1797	Legness, Catharine to Demmitt, Burch*
Jul 17 1790	Lehman, Gebhard to Willert, Martha*
Jul 14 1796	Leister, Priscilla to Dickinson, Gideon*
Mar 15 1779	Leiy, Abigail to Goodwin, Lyde*
Dec 9 1777	Lemmon, Alexis to Jones, Rachel*
Aug 3 1796	Lemmon, Benjamin to Turner, Rebecca*
Jul 8 1791	Lemmon, Catharine to Leonard, James*
Nov 20 1793	Lemmon, Elexis to Stansbury, Mary*
Jun 21 1788	Lemmon, Hannah to Cockran, Thomas*
Dec 22 1795	Lemmon, John to Foster, Millison*
Dec 17 1782	Lemmon, Joshua to Priesstman, Sarah*
Nov 17 1787	Lemmon, Lemuel to Burke, Sarah
Jan 20 1784	Lemmon, Martha to Price, Joshua*
Nov 7 1791	Lemmon, Mary to James, George*
Jan 16 1781	Lemmon, Rebecca to Tipton, Jabeus Murray*
Oct 15 1793	Lemmon, Thomas to Foster, Comfort*
Dec 30 1795	Lemmon, Valentine to Irick, Mary*
Jun 17 1790	Lemmons, Thomas to McBride, Elinor
Jan 21 1794	Lennard, Mary to Mullet, John*
Jan 25 1788	Lent, Catherine to Raborg, Michael*
May 13 1786	Lenton, James to Hendrickson, Sarah*
Jul 8 1791	Leonard, James to Lemmon, Catharine*
Jul 11 1793	Leonard, Philip to Gray, Mary Ann

Oct 13	1794	Lepress, Joseph to Gregler, Elizabeth*
Oct 26	1779	Lere, Margaret to Coher, James*
Jun 24	1786	Lesseuir, Margaret to McGill, Charles*
Aug 8	1797	Lester, William to Johnson, Elizabeth*
Mar 17	1792	Letick, George to Sadler, Sarah*
Mar 2	1797	Lettig, Philip to Bosley, Keziah*
Nov 19	1796	Leuder, Pauline Justine to Gaulisa, John Baptista*
Dec 5	1793	Levering, Jesse to McLaughlin, Ann*
May 22	1798	Levering, Peter to Wilson, Hannah*
Feb 12	1795	Levillain, Michael to Hose, Catharine*
Aug 26	1783	Lewin, Ann to Jones, Amos*
Apr 17	1784	Lewis, Ann to Oram, John*
May 29	1797	Lewis, Biddy to Cox, George*
Nov 16	1797	Lewis, Charles to Barnes, Margaret
Aug 17	1793	Lewis, Charles to White, Keziah*
Jun 11	1794	Lewis, Charlotte to Cross, Robert*
Jul 19	1796	Lewis, Elizabeth to Linthicumb, Henry*
Jun 16	1795	Lewis, Elizabeth to Price, James*
Jan 24	1795	Lewis, James to Christie, Bridget*
Jun 20	1778	Lewis, James to Corter, Hannah*
Apr 10	1797	Lewis, John to Gardner, Elizabeth*
Apr 25	1789	Lewis, John to Kirby, Sarah*
Sep 26	1779	Lewis, John to Mayson, Jane*
Oct 21	1783	Lewis, John to Pamell, Elizabeth*
Aug 6	1784	Lewis, John to Seabrooks, Elizabeth*
Feb 16	1789	Lewis, John to Young, Mary*
Jan 22	1789	Lewis, Mary to White, Thomas*
Apr 12	1796	Lewis, Nathan to Toy, Frances*
Dec 22	1778	Lewis, Rachel to Partridge, Robert*
Nov 21	1793	Lewis, Richard to Myers, Elizabeth*
Sep 4	1783	Lewis, Richard to Warrell, Hannah*
Jan 21	1783	Lewis, Ruth to China, Zephaniah*
May 5	1798	Lewis, Susanna to Hedley, Anthony*
Jan 4	1798	Lewis, William to Jessop, Elizabeth*
Oct 28	1797	Lewis, William to Porter, Catharine*
May 8	1798	Lewis, William Y. to Stewart, Rachel C.*
Jul 7	1797	Lewthwaite, Christian to Carlile, Agnes*
Dec 19	1798	Lewy, Martha to Sandiford, Michael*
Oct 18	1798	Leypold, Frederick to Bridenbaugh, Elizabeth*
Mar 11	1779	Lick, Peter to Herring, Mary
Dec 7	1782	Liddel, Elizabeth to Foster, John*
May 25	1796	Liddle, John to Foy, Catharine*
Feb 9	1793	Lidiard, John to Garty, Mary*
Dec 20	1797	Lidiard, Susannah to Oyton, Benjamin
Jun 24	1784	Lighthold, Andrew to Stigar, Catharine*
Dec 12	1790	Lilley, Jane to McMahon, James*
Jul 19	1790	Limes, Barbara to Taylor, William*
Apr 30	1785	Limes, Barnett to Turvin, Margaret
Feb 4	1797	Limes, Catharine to Warden, William*
Aug 10	1790	Limes, Elizabeth to Rogers, Jacob*
Jan 4	1783	Limes, Harman to Barrett, Ann*
May 1	1792	Limes, Margaret to Aldridge, John*
Mar 27	1798	Limmon, Elinor to Tracey, Warnell*
Nov 14	1795	Linaham, William to Young, Mary*
Nov 9	1797	Linard, John to Cook, Zany*
Feb 8	1783	Linch, Sarah to Richardson, John*

Nov 20	1790	Lindenberger, Charles to Randell, Susannah*
Jan 6	1795	Lindenberger, George to Stevenson, Ann Heniy*
Jun 8	1782	Lindenberger, Susanna to McIhammer, John*
Sep 18	1778	Lindle, Philip to Horton, Elizabeth*
Jun 11	1798	Lindon, Elizabeth to Bennett, Joseph*
Dec 30	1783	Lindsay, Adam to Bennett, Jane
Oct 4	1797	Lindsay, Ann Fox to Taylor, Francis S.*
Apr 2	1795	Lindsay, John to Yengland, Sarah*
Apr 13	1796	Lindsay, Joshua to Barnett, Catharine*
Mar 14	1798	Lindsay, Mary to Shipley, Peter
Dec 16	1794	Lindsay, Michael to Porter, Catherine*
Apr 8	1797	Lindsey, Kassandra to Dorsey, Nicholas*
Nov 7	1798	Lindsey, Sarah to Elder, Deliah*
Apr 12	1797	Ling, Robert to Chapman, Ann*
Dec 31	1791	Linham, John to Baxter, Elizabeth*
Dec 26	1797	Linhart, Sarah to Tundas, Philip*
May 7	1784	Linigan, John to King, Mary*
Feb 9	1782	Link, Stephen to Tenton, Mary
Jan 29	1793	Linkens, Hannah to Hannah, John*
Jun 6	1793	Linkert, Frederick to Ifler, Mary*
Aug 20	1794	Linkwest, John to Roister, Catherine*
Jan 9	1781	Lintenberger, Catherine to Mackinhamer, Peter*
Dec 11	1790	Linthicum, Abner to Jacob, Rachael*
Jan 10	1792	Linthicum, Amasa to Cromwell, Sarah*
May 31	1782	Linthicum, Milkey to Bateman, Henry*
Nov 25	1790	Linthicum, Zachariah to Hewitt, Rachel*
Jul 19	1796	Linthicumb, Henry to Lewis, Elizabeth*
Dec 22	1794	Linton, Charlotte to Coats, Francis*
Nov 10	1779	Linton, Easter to Butterworth, Benjamin
Nov 17	1789	Linton, Mary to McConnel, Alexander
Jul 2	1785	Linton, Sarah to Armitage, John
Jun 15	1791	Linvill, John to McAlister, Martha*
Dec 17	1794	Linwell, Susannah to Abraham, Daniel*
Oct 10	1785	Liscom, Elizabeth to Suffrace, Charles
Mar 2	1781	Liscum, John to Dower, Elizabeth*
Jan 2	1798	Lisst, Henry to Brown, Johanna*
Aug 1	1795	Liston, Ann to Pocock, George Adwell*
Dec 31	1798	Litchfield, Rachel to Jeffrey, Thomas*
Feb 25	1792	Litler, Catherine to Horn, Phillip*
Oct 10	1796	Littig, George to Bosley, Rachel*
Jul 11	1798	Little, Ann to Abbitt, John*
Aug 24	1797	Little, Peter to Hughes, Anna Bella*
Apr 29	1794	Little, Polly to Lanes, Christopher*
Sep 13	1791	Little, Robert to Connolly, Lucy*
Sep 26	1792	Littlejohn, Miles to Paine, Sarah*
Mar 28	1796	Littlejohn, Thomas to McCarty, Sarah*
Jul 17	1782	Littlemire, Mary to White, William
Dec 30	1793	Litzenberger, John to McClintick, Martha*
Aug 4	1778	Litzinger, George to Pulamas, Elizabeth*
Feb 8	1786	Litzinger, Henry to Warner, Dorcus
Jan 31	1788	Litzinger, William to Schreagly, Elizabeth*
Sep 22	1798	Livers, Arnold to Stansbury, Polly*
Apr 17	1795	Livingston, Paul Bartholomew H. to Smith, Letitia*
Jun 8	1778	Lizer, Margaret to Miles, Samuel*
Nov 29	1796	Llighteiser, Elizabeth to Oram, Joshua*
Jun 9	1791	Lloyd, Robert to Shaw, Kitty

```
Aug 22 1796    Loca, Levin to Burk, Winny*
Jun 28 1783    Lock, Jacob to Smith, Sarah
Mar 29 1791    Lock, Nathaniel to Hand, Amelia*
Dec 10 1793    Lock, Thomas to Dunkin, Sarah*
Apr 19 1783    Lockard, Matthew to Cook, Elizabeth
Jun  3 1783    Locker, George Andrew to Alexander, Mary Estus*
Apr 18 1795    Lockerd, Thomas to Ford, Ruth*
Oct  9 1792    Lodue, Laurent to Mifford, Susannah
Dec 31 1791    Loe, George to Peterkin, Rosannah
Jan  8 1782    Logan, Michael to Kailland, Hamutril*
Oct 15 1796    Logan, Neale to White, Mary*
Jun 25 1783    Logan, Sarah to Wright, Thomas*
Sep 22 1790    Logsden, Jeb to Helms, Patience*
Dec  8 1794    Logue, Catherine to Floyd, Joseph*
May 23 1785    Logue, John Smith to Cromwell, Lydia
Jun 12 1779    Logue, Mary to Bulger, Martin
Feb 18 1789    Logue, Richard to Stansbury, Mary
Nov 26 1791    Lohr, Johan Carl to Weston, Catrina Elizabeth*
Jun  9 1794    Lombard, Elizabeth to Jennings, Peter*
Jun 13 1794    Lombord, Elizabeth to Weaver, Lewis*
Sep  9 1786    Londerman, Elizabeth to Fields, William
May  2 1785    Londiman, Catherine to Davis, Edward
Sep  6 1786    Lone, Abagail to Edgar, Mark*
Nov 28 1782    Loney, Amos to Donnellan, Mary
Jan 24 1793    Loney, Amos to Flinn, Alice
Apr 28 1789    Loney, Eleanor to Jones, Salsbury*
Dec 12 1785    Loney, Mary to Connor, Arthur
Apr  9 1791    Long, Elizabeth to Bradey, John*
Nov 17 1790    Long, Elizabeth to Groff, Henry*
Jun 12 1782    Long, Elizabeth to Johnson, Basil
Sep 17 1791    Long, Hannah to Kearns, Charles*
Dec 15 1788    Long, Hugh to Muflin, Margaret*
Dec  8 1789    Long, Janes to Carty, Biddy*
Nov  9 1791    Long, John to Partridge, Elizabeth*
Dec  9 1797    Long, Nathaniel to McCann, Susanna*
Oct 11 1797    Long, Robert Carey to Carmaghan, Sarah*
May  4 1784    Long, Robert to Wilson, Sarah*
Jun 27 1797    Long, Samuel to Cummins, Mary*
Oct 18 1792    Long, Thomas to Inkston, Elizabeth*
Jun 13 1793    Longfield, George to Crawford, Ann*
Aug 11 1794    Longley, Edmund to Cromwell, Sarah*
Jan 11 1797    Longley, John to Cain, Margaret
Jul 27 1797    Longley, Samuel to Rusk, Catharine*
May 16 1778    Longwell, Martha to Rutter, Jonathan*
Aug 23 1792    Lonhart, Mary to Everson, Richard*
Sep  4 1786    Lonkert, Henry to Poucher, Lona*
Oct 18 1798    Loor, Rachel to Trumps, Casper*
Apr 28 1778    Loose, Johann A. to Hugin, Barbara
Oct 31 1778    Lootherwood, Urath to Oliver, John*
Sep 28 1785    Lore, Barbara to Rigor, Henry
Apr 13 1797    Loreny, Margaret to Willis, Cornelius*
Apr  2 1794    Lorman, William to Fulford, Mary*
Oct 31 1796    Lose, Arsella to Otto, Anthony*
Apr  9 1778    Loten, Ann to Dudley, Joseph*
Apr 25 1785    Loubies, Philipe to Adams, Mary
Apr 25 1785    Loubies, Philipe to Helm, Mary
```

```
Sep  6 1790    Louderman, Frederick to Weckman, Mary*
Jun 20 1792    Louderman, George to Jameson, Anne*
Apr 19 1794    Louderman, George to Joyce, Sarah*
Jan 15 1791    Louderman, John Christian to King, Ann
Jun  2 1798    Louderman, Sarah to Weaver, Jacob*
Aug  6 1791    Louderman, Susannah to Pindell, John Larkin*
Jan 29 1798    Loudermer, Mary to Sliop, John
Jul 13 1790    Loughhead, Adam to Connally, Sarah*
Sep 12 1798    Lourey, Samuel to Cooper, Agnes*
Oct 18 1784    Love, Christiana to Snider, George*
Jun  3 1794    Love, Rebecca to Fowler, Samuel*
Nov  7 1798    Loveall, Casandra to Leesh, Greenbury*
Jan 21 1785    Loveall, Hannah to Plowman, Jonathan*
Dec 26 1777    Loveall, Martha to Kelly, William Jr.*
Mar  8 1797    Loveall, Zachariah to Plowman, Ruth
Jun  2 1798    Lovitt, William to Holmes, Sarah*
Jan  9 1796    Low, David to Demmitt, Margaret*
Oct 10 1786    Low, Florah to Gerry, James
Apr  2 1784    Low, James to Shelby, Jane*
Jul 24 1783    Low, Jane to White, Simon
Jul 24 1784    Low, John to Deblegey, Elizabeth*
Aug 19 1778    Low, John to Hewit, Hannah*
Sep  2 1797    Low, John to Jones, Mary*
Sep  2 1790    Low, Rachael to Elson, Henry*
May 11 1793    Lowe, Cornelius to Beavan, Elizabeth*
May 30 1795    Lowe, Ellin to Smith, Nicholas*
Aug  4 1783    Lowe, Jane to Choate, Richard*
Oct 21 1789    Lowei, Elizabeth to Hettinger, Michael
Jun  6 1795    Lower, Samuel to Lammot, Elizabeth*
Dec 30 1782    Lowery, Joseph to Fennell, Sarah
Sep 29 1798    Lowman, Lydia to Davidson, John*
Nov  3 1796    Lowman, Margaret to Westwood, John*
Jul 13 1778    Lown, Cartrout to Miller, Frederick*
Oct 26 1790    Lowndes, Benjamin to Buchanan, Dorathy*
Mar 12 1778    Lownea, Rebecca to Dean, Ezekiah*
Aug 22 1786    Lowry, James to McCaioley, Margaret
Apr 17 1795    Lowry, Jane to Caswell, Thomas*
May  7 1785    Lowry, Mary to Reaugh, John
Mar 19 1788    Lowry, Sarah to Bridges, Daniel*
Aug 12 1782    Loyd, Elizabeth to Spices, Thomas*
Aug 20 1793    Loyd, John to Rear, Catherine*
Mar  6 1798    Loyd, Mary to Ratcliff, Joseph
Oct 17 1791    Loyd, Mary to Shipley, Levin*
Oct 24 1795    Loyd, Peregrine to Evans, Sally*
Nov 13 1793    Loyd, Thomas to Price, Nancy*
Dec  8 1794    Loyd, William to O'Donnell, Catharine*
Apr  4 1785    Lucas, Catherine to Harrison, John
Sep  1 1791    Lucas, Elizabeth to Hogan, Dennis*
May 20 1793    Lucas, Elizabeth to Reed, Matthew*
Apr 18 1795    Lucas, Jane to Shipley, Jesse*
Jan 22 1793    Lucas, John to Divers, Sarah*
Jan 22 1785    Lucas, Lizbeth to Taylor, James*
Feb 28 1785    Lucas, Mary to Clark, Samuel*
Mar  9 1793    Lucas, Mary to Harbest, Frederick*
Oct 13 1798    Lucas, Rebecca to Touman, Valentine*
Apr 19 1788    Lucas, Thomas to Lynch, Sarah*
```

Apr 18 1789	Luce, Elizabeth to Hopkins, Gerrard of R.*
Apr 14 1789	Luce, Mary to Johns, Richard*
Jan 6 1786	Ludwick, Charles to Jennet, Eleanor
Jan 26 1781	Lugar, Jacob to Dear, Elizabeth*
May 22 1784	Luis, Charles to Oram, Hannah*
Mar 7 1794	Luke, Eliza to Vernon, A. Zeagers*
Sep 15 1778	Lummers, John to Spear, Elizabeth*
Jul 3 1797	Lundragan, Mary to Reily, John*
Dec 29 1790	Lunt, Henry to Stewart, Sarah*
Jan 23 1795	Lush, Polly to White, Edward*
May 9 1788	Lushy, Bartholomew to Patterson, Elizabeth*
Aug 19 1784	Luten, King to Baker, Providence
Jan 6 1778	Luton, Isabella to Harrison, Charles*
Jan 16 1798	Luttig, John C. to Pratt, Sally*
Feb 20 1798	Lux, Darby to Nicholson, Mary*
Apr 12 1798	Lux, Rachel Ridgely to McCormick, James Jr.*
Jun 28 1794	Lybrand, John to Speck, Mary*
May 18 1795	Lydia, Mary to Maloney, Daniel*
Jun 18 1792	Lynch, Anthony to Barton, Mary*
Jan 2 1790	Lynch, Eleanor to Murphy, John*
Nov 22 1780	Lynch, Elizabeth to Chaimberlain, John*
Aug 16 1779	Lynch, Elizabeth to Dellero, Thomas*
Aug 4 1797	Lynch, Elizabeth to Fulhart, Philip*
Sep 12 1795	Lynch, James to Garvey, Bridget*
Jun 16 1781	Lynch, Jane to Brown, John*
Apr 13 1797	Lynch, Jemima to Harker, Richard*
Jun 3 1796	Lynch, Jemimah to Otlay, John*
May 1 1798	Lynch, Joshua to Stansbury, Henrietta Maria*
Feb 11 1795	Lynch, Mary to Robinson, James*
Oct 30 1783	Lynch, Patrick to Welsh, Elizabeth*
Nov 28 1783	Lynch, Sarah to Langdon, Joseph*
Apr 19 1788	Lynch, Sarah to Lucas, Thomas*
Nov 16 1795	Lynch, Susannah to Hall, John*
Jun 12 1779	Lynch, William to Regan, Elizabeth
Feb 7 1782	Lynch, William to Ross, Elizabeth*
Feb 10 1781	Lynch, William to Stansbury, Ruth*
Jun 13 1782	Lyndon, John to Beard, Lindy*
Feb 9 1784	Lyne, Mary to Berrage, Edward*
Aug 5 1794	Lynehart, Elizabeth to Beamer, Frederick*
Nov 3 1792	Lynehart, Jacob to Snyder, Mary*
Jul 15 1797	Lyon, James to Spencer, Anna*
Jun 4 1778	Lyon, Mary to Gerrish, Francis*
Mar 7 1789	Lyon, Samuel to Thomas, Hannah*
Jan 24 1797	Lyons, John to Ragoin, Johanna*
Feb 13 1795	Lyons, Mary to Knopwood, John*
Mar 10 1795	Lyons, William to McCoy, Rachel*
Mar 21 1786	Lysby, Sophia to Squires, Daniel*
Nov 11 1790	Lyston, Mary Ann to Garland, John*
Nov 10 1795	Lytle, John to Conway, Rachel*
Sep 5 1795	Lytle, Rachel to Younger, Nehemiah*
Nov 25 1793	L'Engledene, Jean to Guilman, Suzanne*
May 31 1798	Maackubin, Elizabeth to Johnson, Edward*
May 24 1794	MacBride, Mary to Avery, Robert*
Mar 2 1785	Macclefish, Henry to Spiryou, Sarah*
Jun 2 1798	Maccoy, Ann to Rowe, Peter*
May 6 1794	MacCreery, Nathaniel to Corbin, Sayne*

```
Sep 18 1795    MacCubin, Elizabeth to Burke, William*
Nov  3 1798    Mace, Moses to Jones, Chloe*
Mar 18 1794    Machana, Harriott to Hablestin, Barhtolomew*
Mar 20 1795    Mack, John to Brian, Mary Ann*
Sep 19 1792    Mackelfish, Mary to Tevis, Thomas*
Oct  7 1790    Mackelfresh, Elizabeth to Tevis, Thomas*
Jan 18 1783    Mackelfresh, John to Mackelfresh, Sarah*
Dec 17 1790    Mackelfresh, John to Madeira, Margaret
Jan 18 1783    Mackelfresh, Sarah to Mackelfresh, John*
Sep 28 1784    Mackelfresh, Thomas to Phelps, Martha
Nov  9 1793    Mackenerney, Catharine to Leeson, Francis*
Dec 29 1785    Mackenheimer, Nicholas to Alder, Susannah
Apr 30 1778    Macker, Catharine to Jacobs, Samuel*
May  2 1794    Mackew, Jane to Fitzgerald, Garret*
Nov 19 1795    Mackey, Hugh to Henry, Sarah*
Apr 17 1794    Mackie, Alexander to Murray, Margaret*
Jul 30 1786    Mackie, Ebenezer to Ashton, Ann
Feb  1 1783    Mackie, Susannah to Huitt, William*
Jun 10 1784    Mackinhamer, Catherine to Clark, Jesse
Jan  9 1781    Mackinhamer, Peter to Lintenberger, Catherine*
Feb 11 1795    Macklefish, Susannah to Grimes, Rezin*
Aug  8 1795    Macklefish, William to Bedson, Elizabeth*
Nov 19 1787    Macklefresh, Abner to Spurrier, Rebecca*
Oct 27 1790    Macklefresh, Ely to Grimes, Aery*
Feb 21 1786    Mackubbin, Mary to Dorsey, Henry
May 27 1797    MacMackle, Joseph to Masters, Ann
Sep  8 1796    MacNamarah, Johnannah to Hudson, James*
Jan 19 1789    Macunkey, William to Feltner, Rebecca*
Jul 18 1797    Madden, Sarah to Weir, John*
Dec 15 1783    Madden, Thomas to Brown, Margaret*
Jun  9 1792    Maddox, George to Gladman, Cassandra*
Dec 30 1797    Maddox, Richard to Franklin, Hannah*
Mar 22 1797    Maddox, William to Hughes, Ann
Aug 19 1794    Maddox, William to Hughes, Elizabeth*
Dec 17 1790    Madeira, Margaret to Mackelfresh, John
Jan  4 1791    Madiera, Daniel to Stocksdale, Eleanor*
Oct  2 1798    Madran, Francis to Beat, Elizabeth*
Feb 14 1793    Magar, Belinda to Walker, Elijah
Oct 15 1785    Magnus, Mary to Hatton, John
Dec 12 1796    Magrath, Bartholomew to Wilkinson, Mary*
Feb 21 1792    Magrath, Michael to Carrol, Margaret*
Mar 21 1792    Magun, John to Hutchins, Sarah*
Nov 12 1796    Mahall, Thomas to Burnside, Elizabeth*
Feb 14 1784    Mahanah, Daniel to Griffin, Rebecca*
Apr 20 1789    Mahar, Ann to Froft, George*
Feb 27 1797    Mahar, Jane to Sorver, John*
Jan  6 1790    Mahew, William to McKenzie, Eleanor*
Oct 30 1789    Mahon, Elizabeth to Inkster, James*
Sep 26 1795    Mahon, James to Calhoun, Mary*
Jul 31 1798    Mahon, Mary to Smith, James*
Feb 14 1795    Mahoney, Elizabeth to Hayden, Samuel*
Jun 16 1795    Mahoney, Nancy to Martin, William*
Sep 24 1794    Mahony, Charlotte to Hollins, John*
Jun  8 1796    Mahony, Thomas to Cashman, Sarah*
May 20 1779    Mahue, Samuel to Dennis, Margaret*
Jun 14 1797    Maid, Rachel to Williams, James*
```

Nov 25 1784	Maidscou, Barbara to Jones, Francis*
Jun 18 1795	Maidwell, Alexander to Simmerman, Catherine*
Apr 27 1795	Maidwell, Alexander to Winnick, Elizabeth*
Aug 25 1790	Maidwell, Elizabeth to Siffort, Martin*
Feb 23 1797	Maidwell, James to Bennix, Rachel*
May 24 1798	Maidwell, John to Green, Ann*
May 21 1795	Maidwell, Susannah to Smith, John*
Jul 6 1778	Mailing, Godfrey to Millering, Rehina*
Dec 2 1796	Mainster, Jacob to Gardiner, Mary*
Feb 12 1783	Majors, Deborah to Owings, John
Aug 29 1795	Majors, Thomas to Harding, Mary*
Jul 30 1779	Makaney, Margery to Bossen, William*
Oct 13 1788	Malcom, Jennet to Williams, John*
Jan 29 1781	Males, Hannah to Satch, John
Mar 18 1783	Mallender, Eleanor to Summerville, John*
Oct 10 1798	Mallet, M.M.M. to Marchant, Purre E.*
Nov 20 1784	Mallet, William to Randell, Sophia*
Aug 13 1785	Malone, Mary to Clemins, Thomas
Apr 7 1798	Malonee, Alexander to Jennings, Mary*
Feb 13 1795	Malonee, James to Cullison, Delile*
Sep 12 1795	Malonee, Margaret to Griffith, James*
Oct 19 1798	Malonee, Mary to Smith, George*
May 18 1795	Maloney, Daniel to Lydia, Mary*
Dec 6 1798	Maloney, James to Veale, Catharine*
Jun 28 1788	Maloney, John to Bell, Lucy*
Dec 7 1796	Maloney, Margaret to Bray, James*
Oct 3 1785	Maloney, Peter to Aston, Villey
Apr 6 1779	Maloney, William to Smith, Isabella*
Nov 10 1792	Maloy, Patrick to Nickle, Greay*
Jan 2 1782	Mamabay, Eleanor to Richmond, John*
Dec 10 1784	Mangee, Mary to Coulon, John Baptist*
Feb 26 1784	Manin, Tacy to Lane, Elisha*
Feb 10 1782	Manix, Timothy to Sopellia, Bridgit*
May 20 1789	Manley, Margaret to Thompson, Robert*
Aug 12 1785	Mann, Hannah to Wear, John
Sep 3 1796	Mann, Martha to Ives, James*
Apr 5 1796	Manning, Ann to Sermon, Anthony*
Jun 5 1786	Manning, John to McGuIness, Ann
Aug 1 1782	Manning, Lydia to Griffith, Greenberry*
Jul 7 1795	Mannings, Eliza to Dakings, Joseph*
Dec 20 1788	Mannon, Abraham to Williams, Rachael*
Aug 9 1788	Manro, Nathan to Welsh, Catharine*
Jan 26 1791	Mansell, Elizabeth to Frost, Caleb*
Nov 29 1787	Mansfield, Sarah to China, Nathan*
Feb 23 1796	Mansfield, Thomas to Lawrence, Elizabeth*
Aug 12 1797	Manson, Joel M. to Swan, Ann*
Aug 3 1797	Manson, William to Daugherty, Catharine*
Oct 12 1791	Manus, Joseph to Crombrie, Elizabeth Aber*
Dec 2 1793	Mappet, Margaret to Cook, James*
Nov 8 1785	Maratle, Eleanor to Cole, John
Nov 23 1795	March, Andrew to Stock, Rebecca*
Jan 24 1782	March, Nicholas to Delker, Christiana*
Apr 1 1796	Marchant, John to Harrison, Elizabeth*
Oct 10 1798	Marchant, Purre E. to Mallet, M.M.M.*
May 7 1796	Mariner, Joseph to Rappold, Mary*
Oct 28 1783	Mark, John Peterson to Hazleton, Sarah*

Mar 26 1778	Markell, John to Bender, Sarah*
Jun 27 1779	Markins, Elizabeth to Turner, John
Mar 22 1790	Maroil, Mary to Keirl, Michael*
Jul 16 1798	Marr, Catharine to Caslow, Samuel*
Jun 14 1784	Marr, William to Owings, Arrey*
May 22 1781	Marsden, Jonathan to Carr, Margaret*
Mar 21 1797	Marsh, Beal to Corbin, Elinor*
Jan 15 1791	Marsh, David to Bosley, Nancy
Apr 30 1784	Marsh, John to Huett, Catherine*
Dec 9 1783	Marsh, Joshua to Harriman, Temperence*
Feb 28 1782	Marsh, Nathaniel to Miller, Ann*
Oct 27 1791	Marsh, Pamelia to Tracey, James*
Aug 9 1778	Marsh, Sarah to Osmand, Edward*
Jun 7 1788	Marsh, Sophia to Hendon, Benjamin*
Jun 10 1794	Marsh, Susannah to Downes, Thomas*
Jul 1 1778	Marshall, Hannah to Hicks, Nehemiah*
Apr 14 1798	Marshall, Henry to Rothrock, Eve*
Jul 13 1778	Marshall, Isaac to Quarterman, Mary*
Jan 8 1794	Marshall, Joseph to Procter, Elizabeth*
Jan 11 1782	Marshall, Phebe to Stewart, James*
Feb 26 1781	Marshall, Sarah to Brereton, Thomas*
Apr 27 1796	Marshall, Sarah to Campbell, Aaron*
Dec 18 1790	Marshall, William to Brant, Louisa
Apr 26 1779	Marten, William to Crowley, Margaret
Oct 1 1796	Martin, Alexander to Gipson, Mary*
Oct 1 1798	Martin, Charles to Porter, Philis*
Feb 18 1783	Martin, Elizabeth to Butler, Elisha*
May 30 1795	Martin, George to Jackson, Ann*
May 28 1785	Martin, Henry to Moore, Mary
Aug 26 1785	Martin, Isaac to Dudley, Sarah
Sep 8 1794	Martin, James to Rouse, Sarah*
Oct 28 1797	Martin, James to Yoolt, Julia*
Aug 27 1796	Martin, Jemima to Fish, Joseph*
Sep 8 1795	Martin, John to Warren, Elizabeth*
Dec 22 1783	Martin, Joseph to Foy, Elizabeth
Nov 30 1797	Martin, Lucy to Erskin, Edward*
Sep 8 1791	Martin, Mary to Oram, Thomas*
Apr 16 1796	Martin, Nancy to Needles, Stephen*
Feb 1 1783	Martin, Peter to King, Fanny
Apr 15 1796	Martin, Rachel to Dopp, Henry*
Jan 29 1796	Martin, Sino to Cato, Edward*
May 26 1796	Martin, Thomas to Stokes, Mary*
Apr 13 1784	Martin, William to Ingram, Mary
Jun 16 1795	Martin, William to Mahoney, Nancy*
Jan 26 1796	Marton, Elizabeth to Neale, Edward*
Dec 17 1782	Mary to Charles (free negroes)
Jun 11 1792	Marzial, Marie to Boyreau, John Joseph*
Oct 28 1797	Mash, Joseph to Williams, Ann*
Sep 18 1782	Mason, Abraham to Hays, Sarah
Nov 26 1784	Mason, Ann to Freeman, William*
May 2 1781	Mason, Ann to Pindell, Philip*
Dec 8 1797	Mason, Benjamin to Cooper, Sarah*
Aug 14 1784	Mason, Benjamin to Newman, Sarah
Oct 19 1792	Mason, Bingley to Free, Babby*
Oct 22 1792	Mason, Bingley to Free, Babby*
Aug 17 1782	Mason, John Peter to Ennin, Mary*

Mar 4 1797	Mason, John to Reding, Sarah*
Dec 6 1780	Mason, Leah to Young, Jacob*
Jan 12 1788	Mason, Lydia to Lane, James*
Aug 28 1779	Mason, Michael to Leaf, Catharine*
Aug 27 1784	Mason, Rebecca to Porter, Nathaniel
Oct 12 1792	Mason, Richard to Stear, Mary*
May 10 1778	Mason, Sarah to Townsend, William*
Dec 17 1798	Mason, Thomas to Davis, Sarah*
Aug 15 1779	Mass, Abraham to Sollers, Issabellah
May 27 1797	Masters, Ann to MacMackle, Joseph
Oct 5 1796	Masters, Thomas to Ball, Elizabeth*
Jun 7 1783	Masterson, Honor to Dugan, James*
May 11 1789	Mather, John to Neall, Kitty
May 23 1795	Mathew, Catherine to Bradshaw, William*
Aug 26 1796	Mathias, Jane Mary Ann to Miniere, John Jas. Jos.*
Sep 5 1796	Mathias, Priscilla to Lee, Joshua*
Apr 26 1792	Mathman, Rachel to Oliver, John*
May 20 1779	Matison, Catharine to Gill, James
Oct 9 1798	Matson, Elizabeth to Perkins, Joel G.
Jul 22 1793	Matten, Ann to McKenzie, Roger
Jan 1 1782	Matthews, Edward to Tracey, Sarah
Jul 5 1790	Matthews, Elizabeth to Matthews, Patrick*
Dec 10 1796	Matthews, Hannah to Morgan, William*
Aug 30 1796	Matthews, James to Dauphin, Elizabeth*
Jan 12 1795	Matthews, Jane to Batton, Rene Guillaume*
Jun 1 1796	Matthews, John to Kelly, Susannah*
Nov 23 1782	Matthews, Mary to Rutledge, Thomas
Jul 24 1795	Matthews, Mary to Ryland, Joseph*
Jul 5 1790	Matthews, Patrick to Matthews, Elizabeth*
Jun 19 1798	Matthews, Sarah to Toury, Jeremiah*
Feb 2 1795	Matthews, Thomas to Gill, Ann*
Oct 2 1794	Matthews, William P. to Sterrett, Eliza*
May 20 1779	Mattison, Catharine to Gib, James*
Jun 15 1795	Mattox, Mary to Brown, William*
Mar 23 1782	Mattox, Rachael to Foreman, Ludwig
May 10 1786	Matts, Christina to Bombarger, William*
Aug 6 1792	Matzen, Henry to Lamecole, Hannah*
Jul 30 1789	Maund, John James to Carter, Harriet Lucy*
Apr 6 1792	Maxfield, Hezekiah to Downing, Mary*
Oct 7 1790	Maxwell, Agnes to Swann, Joseph*
Dec 12 1782	Maxwell, James to Grant, Ann*
Dec 2 1794	Maxwell, John to Rowles, Rachel*
Jan 28 1792	Maxwell, John to Stinchcomb, Sarah*
Sep 14 1790	Maxwell, Margaret to Maxwell, William*
Oct 1 1783	Maxwell, Margaret to Stanley, John*
May 17 1788	Maxwell, Marion to Campbell, John*
Jan 11 1796	Maxwell, Mary to Pemberton, William*
Dec 16 1790	Maxwell, Sarah to Barton, Seth*
Sep 14 1790	Maxwell, William to Maxwell, Margaret*
Dec 22 1781	May, Benjamin to Councilman, Margaret
Mar 25 1797	May, Elizabeth to Brays, Joseph*
Nov 10 1784	May, Margaret to Denton, John*
Oct 27 1783	Maybury, Francis to Smith, Catharine*
Apr 28 1783	Maydwell, Hannah to Clark, John*
Jul 11 1785	Maydwell, Mary to Gittelman, John
Oct 31 1795	Mayhew, Elisha Horton to West, Elizabeth*

May 19 1796	Maynard, Foster to Mortemore, Elizabeth*
May 23 1782	Mayo, Sarah to Solman, Johnze
Jun 14 1794	Mayor, Elizabeth to McGoukin, Daniel*
Jun 21 1798	Mayra, Ann to Hanna, Andrew*
Sep 26 1779	Mayson, Jane to Lewis, John*
Sep 1 1795	McAdue, Samuel to Spencer, Ann*
Jun 15 1791	McAlister, Martha to Linvill, John*
Oct 20 1786	McAllister, Charles to Sampson, Ann
Apr 9 1794	McAllister, Elizabeth to Philips, John*
Dec 15 1796	McBraherty, Margaret to Philt, Matthew*
Jun 17 1790	McBride, Elinor to Lemmons, Thomas
Dec 7 1790	McBride, Mary to Leary, Daniel*
Feb 11 1793	McBride, Roger to Phile, Mary
Sep 7 1782	McBride, Rosannah to Turner, John*
Jan 31 1782	McBroom, John to Ellitt, Karenhappah
Feb 22 1796	McCabe, Catharine to Guishard, Mark*
Aug 14 1779	McCabe, Pheby to Hutchenson, Robert*
Jan 27 1797	McCabe, Rebecca to Tripley, John*
Oct 18 1796	McCabe, Thomas to Neiss, Mary*
Dec 24 1793	McCaine, James to Davis, Presilla*
Aug 22 1786	McCaioley, Margaret to Lowry, James
Aug 6 1781	McCall, Elizabeth to Onion, Thomas*
Jan 21 1796	McCallister, Charles to Trainet, Elizabeth*
Feb 10 1798	McCallister, Elizabeth to Lawson, Robert*
Dec 22 1797	McCallister, John to Fields, Anne*
Nov 16 1798	McCallister, Mary to Fawzer, Jonathan*
Mar 7 1789	McCallister, Mary to Hasen, Jessey*
Jan 4 1790	McCan, John to Johnson, Ann*
Dec 2 1794	McCandley, Neale to King, Margaret*
Feb 27 1796	McCann, Ann to Dunwoody, Robert*
Dec 9 1797	McCann, Susanna to Long, Nathaniel*
Mar 14 1796	McCarman, Margaret to Scott, Joseph*
May 20 1779	McCartney, James to Johnson, Esther
Sep 27 1792	McCarty, Cornelius to Pitcher, Sarah*
Jun 11 1791	McCarty, Fanriy to Pratt, Frederick*
Nov 24 1785	McCarty, John to Lawbright, Elizabeth
Apr 9 1796	McCarty, Michael to O'Brien, Ellen*
Mar 28 1796	McCarty, Sarah to Littlejohn, Thomas*
Dec 1 1790	McCarty, William to Peasely, Margaret*
Aug 26 1797	McCaskey, Ann to Kearney, Richard*
Mar 29 1792	McCaskey, Hetty to Coulter, Alexander*
Feb 2 1788	McCasky, Mary to Coulter, John*
Sep 15 1779	McCaslin, Barbary to Heritt, John*
Dec 9 1780	McCauley, John to Welsh, Ann*
Aug 29 1797	McCausland, Susannah to Sharar, Eli*
Dec 2 1784	McCauslind, Marcus to Presstman, Polly*
Mar 16 1786	McChesie, Elizabeth to Read, Thomas*
Oct 31 1785	McClain, Alexander to Haslett, Kesiah
Sep 15 1785	McClain, James to Cowan, Elizabeth*
Nov 25 1795	McClain, Roddy to Connally, Eleanor*
Jul 1 1790	McClan, Robert to Grove, Hannah*
Jul 19 1779	McClane, Adam to Boyer, Hannah
May 16 1795	McClane, Hugh Charles to French, Mary*
Nov 19 1795	McClaskey, James to Meads, Elizabeth*
May 6 1797	McClaskey, John to Wheeler, Mary*
Sep 11 1788	McClaskey, Joseph to Jewell, Aloe*

Oct 20 1790	McCleery, Agnes to Rowland, Robert*
Apr 29 1797	McClellan, Elizabeth to Cooper, John*
Apr 21 1792	McClery, Thomas to Neilson, Susanah*
Mar 6 1786	McCliesh, Alexander to Harris, Nancy
Dec 30 1793	McClintick, Martha to Litzenberger, John*
Aug 1 1791	McCloud, Sarah to Miller, John
Oct 13 1783	McCloude, Hugh to Ledwidge, Ann*
May 15 1792	McClown, Ann to Davis, Benjamin*
Jul 3 1778	McClughan, James to Kelly, Margaret*
Mar 24 1789	McClung, Elizabeth to Jones, William*
Oct 7 1783	McClung, Joseph to Ryston, Cloe
May 25 1798	McClung, Letitia to Clinefitter, John*
Oct 25 1782	McClung, Mary to Givin, John*
Oct 3 1791	McClung, Mary to Gorsuch, John*
Dec 15 1787	McClung, Rachael to Gorsuch, Thomas*
May 3 1784	McClung, Rebecca to Bermingham, James*
Dec 18 1784	McClung, Ruth to Royston, John*
Sep 15 1785	McCocery, James to Neilson, Letitia
Jul 18 1789	McColin, Dennis to Dunkin, Ann*
May 21 1794	McCollom, Ann to Edwards, William*
Jul 1 1797	McCollum, Duncan to Stokes, Temperance*
May 1 1788	McComas, Elizabeth to Anderson, Abraham*
May 31 1779	McComas, Sarah to Anderson, Benjamin
Oct 26 1782	McComes, Pricilla to Slade, William*
Jan 6 1790	McComeskey, Moses to Bosley, Mary*
Jun 8 1782	McComus, Cordelia to Anderson, William*
Dec 12 1795	McConkey, James to Nichol, Agnus*
Jun 27 1789	McConnal, John to Karr, Christiana
Nov 17 1789	McConnel, Alexander to Linton, Mary
Oct 9 1791	McConnell, Alexander to Davis, Sarah*
Nov 25 1783	McConnell, Elizabeth to Hammond, John*
Jan 26 1797	McCoon, Jane to Coulter, Alexander*
Sep 25 1782	McCoon, Sarah to Cole, John*
Oct 22 1796	McCoone, Sarah to Ellis, John*
Jun 30 1783	McCord, John to Steward, Sabella*
Apr 12 1798	McCormick, James Jr. to Lux, Rachel Ridgely
Oct 31 1798	McCormick, Jane to Barktie, Thomas*
Aug 12 1798	McCormick, John to Graydy, Jane*
Sep 29 1784	McCormick, Margaret to Dougherty, John*
Dec 26 1791	McCoy, Catherine to Hague, Hugh*
Jul 1 1790	McCoy, Charles to Cox, Catharine*
Apr 15 1797	McCoy, Charlotte to Tear, Daniel*
May 12 1793	McCoy, George to Read, Elinor*
May 23 1794	McCoy, John to Alley, Elizabeth*
Jul 21 1790	McCoy, John to Wade, Sarah*
Mar 10 1795	McCoy, Rachel to Lyons, William*
Jul 18 1796	McCoy, Richard to Hogan, Catharine*
Feb 26 1782	McCoy, Robert to Pile, Hannah
Feb 28 1785	McCoy, Sarah to Crow, William
May 30 1793	McCoy, William to Joyce, Rachel*
Oct 13 1779	McCracken, Elizabeth to Hamilton, James*
Apr 11 1794	McCrackin, Elizabeth to Stevenson, George*
Jan 22 1782	McCrackin, John to Northemond, Anne*
Jun 8 1781	McCubbin, Deborah to Dorsey, Edward*
Dec 24 1791	McCubbin, John to Tudor, Polly*
Oct 25 1785	McCubbin, Martha Ridgely to Wood, William

Jan 20 1778	McCubbin, Zachariah to Ottey, Ann*
Oct 6 1792	McCubbins, Susannah to Tudor, Joshua*
Jan 19 1782	McCullister, Sarah to Beame, George*
Aug 12 1793	McCuming, Sarah to Dagon, Peter
Nov 29 1793	McCuminon, Joseph to Burk, Sarah*
Jun 17 1794	McCurdy, Hugh to Allison, Grace*
Nov 30 1797	McCurtz, George to Cooper, Mary*
Feb 3 1795	McDade, Milly to Stacey, William*
Apr 6 1790	McDaniel, Ann to McDaniel, Samuel*
Sep 19 1778	McDaniel, Cornelius to Corbin, Unity*
Dec 16 1783	McDaniel, John to Berry, Mary*
Jun 5 1794	McDaniel, Nancy to Doyle, Nicholas*
Apr 6 1790	McDaniel, Samuel to McDaniel, Ann*
Sep 18 1797	McDarmott, John to Joyce, Catharine*
Jan 23 1796	McDermot, Elizabeth to Dempsey, Patrick*
Dec 4 1797	McDermot, Henry to Jordan, Esmy*
Oct 21 1793	McDoe, William to Riddle, Elizabeth*
Jul 23 1790	McDonah, Elizabeth to Pogue, James*
Jun 19 1797	McDonald, Alexander to Davis, Polly*
Jul 6 1785	McDonald, Andrew to Seabrook, Ruth
Sep 16 1784	McDonald, Biddey to Boshockney, Thomas*
Aug 28 1797	McDonald, Dennis to Wilton, Jace*
Nov 30 1777	McDonald, Elizabeth to Cowan, James*
Apr 24 1786	McDonald, Elizabeth to Wicks, Ezekiel
May 29 1792	McDonald, Mary Ann Dorsey to Burn, John*
Feb 1 1793	McDonald, Mary to Anderson, William*
Mar 22 1786	McDonald, Mary to Gilson, Morris
Apr 20 1784	McDonald, Michael to Soloman, Dinah*
May 25 1778	McDonaldson, Thomas to Ross, Margaret*
Jun 12 1782	McDonel, Margaret to McIntosh, George
Jan 25 1794	McDonnell, John to Baum, Barbara*
May 18 1798	McDonnell, John to Hood, Mary*
Jul 27 1782	McDonnell, William to Leehorn, Margaret*
Jun 19 1778	McDonnild, Hugh to McDonnild, Rebecca*
Jun 19 1778	McDonnild, Rebecca to McDonnild, Hugh*
Jan 30 1796	McDonogh, Jane to Young, Jesse*
Feb 4 1797	McDonogh, Mary to Cole, John*
May 12 1797	McDonogh, Sarah to Conden, John*
May 16 1785	McDonough, Jane to McMullin, Patrick*
Jan 7 1782	McDonough, Margaret to Hagan, Hugh*
Oct 4 1796	McDoose, Joseph to Shaw, Rossanna*
Feb 24 1798	McDowell, Thomas to Chesu, Catharine*
Feb 20 1794	McElroy, Nancy to Shruggo, Alexander*
Feb 26 1794	McElroy, William to Hagerty, Elizabeth*
May 23 1783	McFaddin, James to Sligh, Rebecca*
Dec 20 1798	McFadon, John to Wilson, Precilla*
Sep 29 1795	McFadon, Mary to Williams, George*
Aug 4 1792	McFadon, William to Ellick, Ann*
Mar 15 1796	McFall, John to Hays, Margaret*
Dec 18 1783	McFarlen, Edward to Tull, Ann*
Jul 17 1778	McFarlin, Catharine to O'Callahan, James*
Dec 26 1787	McFarlin, Michael to Brand, Peggy*
Feb 23 1788	McFarren, Mary to Murray, Archibald*
Apr 21 1778	McFee, Elizabeth to Collins, Timothy*
Aug 24 1793	McFee, Mary to Brady, John*
Dec 4 1794	McFeel, Mary to Weary, John*

Sep 30 1785	McFerson, William to Weaver, Margaret
May 25 1785	McGackey, Mary to Ensloe, Joseph
Nov 8 1798	McGale, Margaret S. to Dunington, Handley*
Jun 20 1793	McGee, Elizabeth to Wallington, Demas*
May 24 1783	McGee, Joseph to Farrel, Rebecca*
May 11 1783	McGill, Ann to Cockran, William*
Jun 24 1786	McGill, Charles to Lesseuir, Margaret*
Apr 21 1798	McGill, Zachariah to Cooper, Margaret*
Aug 25 1785	McGlachan, William to Primrose, Isabel
Apr 14 1778	McGloughlin, Catharine to Green, James*
Nov 21 1798	McGoiff, Sarah to Hoit, Israel*
Sep 28 1797	McGoivan, Eleanor to Jennings, James*
Oct 9 1797	McGonagall, Rowland to De Breelin, Aramintha
Jun 14 1794	McGoukin, Daniel to Mayor, Elizabeth*
Dec 1 1790	McGowing, Nancy to Mowbray, James*
Sep 11 1786	McGrah, Thomas to Kirby, Catey*
Jan 15 1798	McGrath, James to Comen, Catharine*
Oct 5 1795	McGray, John to Ellis, Mary*
Dec 24 1794	McGreggin, Patrick to Owings, Charlotte*
Oct 30 1792	McGreggory, Rebecca to Hall, James*
Sep 27 1790	McGregory, Ann to Brown, Thomas
Apr 8 1781	McGrevey, James to White, Hannah
Jun 5 1786	McGuiness, Ann to Manning, John
Apr 1 1779	McGuire, Anthony to Murphey, Mary*
Jan 8 1793	McGuire, Hugh to McMacken, Nancy*
Jul 25 1778	McGuire, Martin to Taylor, Ann*
Jul 9 1788	McGuire, Mary to Dunn, Michael*
Oct 21 1795	McGuire, Roger to Casey, Eleanor*
Apr 13 1779	McGuire, Thomas to Stevenson, Mary
Feb 27 1797	McGwinn, William to Ransford, Elizabeth*
Dec 13 1794	McHaffe, Robina Kennedy to Hilton, Thomas*
Oct 7 1794	McHenry, Dennis to Young, Mary*
Jun 8 1782	McIhammer, John to Lindenberger, Susanna*
Mar 15 1778	McIlvain, Andrew to Cloud, Elizabeth*
Jul 29 1779	McInburmer, Cabrena to Miller, Nicholas*
Jun 28 1781	McInhamer, Mary to Storey, Ezekiel*
Sep 28 1785	McIntosh, Catharine to Burton, Richard
Jun 12 1782	McIntosh, George to McDonel, Margaret
Sep 7 1784	McKean, Ann to Swan, Matthew*
Mar 7 1798	McKean, Peggy to Cramer, Philip*
Aug 8 1797	McKeay, William to Haley, Peggy*
Sep 10 1798	McKeen, James to Wells, Elizabeth*
Apr 4 1795	McKeen, John to Helm, Ann*
Sep 7 1790	McKenny, Roddey to Higginbothom, Elizabeth*
Dec 26 1794	McKenzie, Barbara to Stockett, Henry*
May 15 1794	McKenzie, Eleanor to Donnavan, Valentine*
Jan 6 1790	McKenzie, Eleanor to Mahew, William*
Feb 15 1783	McKenzie, Orpha to Young, Johua*
Jul 22 1793	McKenzie, Roger to Matten, Ann
Jul 20 1785	McKim, Alexander to Davey, Catherine Sarah
Jul 14 1792	McKinley, Robert to McLaughlin, Elizabeth*
Jul 26 1784	McKinnan, Susannah to Parkhouse, William*
May 4 1779	McKinsay, Charlotte to Riddle, William*
Mar 11 1789	McKinsey, Aaron to Harp, Rachael*
Apr 21 1785	McKinsey, Eleanor to Harp, Joshua
Dec 4 1797	McKinsey, Mary to Wilson, James

Nov 6 1790	McKinsley, Alice to Green, John*
Jan 26 1786	McKinze, Mary to Jones, William*
May 24 1798	McKinzie, Archibald to Doyle, Elizabeth*
May 2 1793	McKinzie, Elizabeth to Reeves, Anthony*
Nov 23 1798	McKinzie, George to Jackson, Mary*
Jan 10 1792	McKinzie, John to Strawble, Ann*
Aug 4 1795	McKinzie, John to Warner, Elizabeth*
Jan 5 1796	McKinzie, Mary to Arnold, Joseph*
Apr 2 1798	McKinzie, Mary to Donnelly, James*
Apr 7 1798	McKinzie, Mary to Young, Dinton*
Nov 19 1789	McKirdy, Elizabeth to Hughes, William*
Dec 4 1787	McKlevane, Ann to Clarke, John*
Dec 28 1790	McKoy, Abraham to Mumford, Elizabeth*
Feb 4 1794	McKoy, Charlotte to Ogleby, Francis*
Feb 4 1795	McKubbin, James to Collins, Lydia*
Nov 11 1797	McKubbin, Samuel to Williams, Frances*
Nov 11 1797	McKubbin, Sarah to Quay, William*
Jun 21 1793	McKubbins, Nancy to Seadley, Isaac
Jul 19 1796	McKuven, Owen to Christman, Elizabeth*
Aug 20 1789	McLain, Kezia to Sinklair, James*
Oct 10 1793	McLane, Robert to Wheeler, Elizabeth*
Aug 25 1792	McLarnan, John to Taylor, Ann*
Dec 5 1793	McLaughlin, Ann to Levering, Jesse*
Apr 11 1794	McLaughlin, Catharine to Cantler, Barnett*
Jun 23 1790	McLaughlin, Catherine to Gray, Lynch*
Jul 14 1792	McLaughlin, Elizabeth to McKinley, Robert*
Apr 18 1793	McLaughlin, Mary to Chambers, William*
Apr 10 1794	McLaughlin, Sarah to Lake, Michael*
Dec 2 1796	McLaughlin, William to Cannon, Mary*
Sep 4 1783	McLellan, John to Hargan, Mary
Feb 28 1797	McLinsy, Michael to Hackey, Mary*
Apr 14 1795	McLure, Elizabeth to Adams, Alexander*
Jan 20 1792	McLure, Elizabeth to Ross, Robert Lockart*
Mar 13 1779	McLure, John to Douglass, Rebecca*
Nov 7 1797	McLure, Rebecca to Hannah, Edward*
Jan 8 1793	McMacken, Nancy to McGuire, Hugh*
Nov 30 1793	McMahan, Judith to Flinn, John*
Dec 12 1790	McMahon, James to Lilley, Jane*
Dec 11 1794	McMahon, Mary to Davis, William*
Sep 12 1792	McMann, Patrick to Brown, Nancy
Nov 11 1779	McMasters, Ann to Waters, Isaac
Oct 13 1790	McMasters, Martha to Rullston, William*
May 20 1789	McMcKen, Rosannah to McMcKen, Thomas*
May 20 1789	McMcKen, Thomas to McMcKen, Rosannah*
Mar 9 1796	McMechen, Barnard to Miller, Anne*
Aug 5 1795	McMechen, Hugh to Hewitt, Emelia*
Sep 24 1789	McMechen, Rebecca to Cox, Matthew*
Jan 30 1793	McMeckin, Mary to Coleman, Joseph*
Apr 30 1794	McMicken, Sarah to Wilkinson, David*
May 16 1785	McMullin, Patrick to McDonough, Jane*
Jan 15 1794	McMyer, John to Pitt, Elizabeth*
Mar 28 1796	McNamar, John to Clarke, Judith*
Mar 14 1795	McNamara, Hugh to Williams, Ann*
Jun 15 1793	McNamarak, Matthew to Glaply, Nancy*
May 3 1788	McNamee, John to Justice, Elizabeth*
Jun 10 1782	McNeal, Kitty to Waters, William*

Apr 30 1791	McNeal, Rebecca to Leach, Ebeneazer*
Dec 18 1778	McNeall, Mary to Flemman, David*
Mar 22 1782	McNeil, Mary to Riddle, Robert
Jul 26 1798	McNeir, John B. to Pumphrey, Mary*
Dec 24 1796	McNeire, William to Warner, Rachel*
Oct 10 1786	McNight, Mary to Ingram, Samuel
Nov 5 1795	McNutty, Thomas to Freeman, Elizabeth*
Oct 29 1795	McPellon, Mary to Gamble, Thomas*
Oct 22 1796	McPherson, Isaac to Ellicott, Tacey*
Jun 21 1794	McQueen, Gracy to Nash, Charles*
Jul 11 1788	McQuina, William to Shoemaker, Jane*
Sep 19 1795	McSherry, Elizabeth to Deliquit, _____*
Apr 10 1790	McSherry, Patrick to Clemments, Elizabeth*
Mar 29 1786	McShroyan, Ann to Ritter, John
Dec 6 1798	McSure, John to Thornbury, Mary Ann*
Apr 12 1797	Meads, Benjamin to Jessop, Mary*
Nov 19 1795	Meads, Elizabeth to McClaskey, James*
Jan 21 1786	Meah, James to Taylor, Providence*
Aug 4 1785	Meak, William to Gold, Mary
Sep 20 1784	Meake, Catharine to Grafft, William*
Apr 13 1784	Mealey, Margaret to Besse, Clodius
Jan 30 1797	Mealy, Peggy to Mendall, Samuel*
Aug 10 1782	Mear, Michael to Woods, Susannah*
Feb 21 1789	Mecaroly, Catharine to Morrow, Thomas*
Dec 13 1781	Mechannah, Elizabeth to Hilton, William*
Oct 1 1798	Medley, John to Buckley, Rachel*
Sep 24 1796	Medlicoat, Samuel to Carter, Anne*
Nov 17 1796	Meek, Margaret to Godin, Francis
Aug 25 1795	Meem, John Jr. to Moore, Martha*
Nov 10 1779	Megregger, Mary to Smith, Joseph
Oct 28 1797	Mekin, Judy to Foharty, Edward*
May 15 1784	Melanson, Elizabeth to Tiellen, John
Dec 12 1787	Meldrum, James to Cooke, Hannah
May 18 1793	Melony, James to League, Averilla*
Apr 24 1792	Mencer, George to Creamer, Elizabeth*
Aug 16 1794	Menchins, Jain to Vinsy, Mary*
Jan 30 1797	Mendall, Samuel to Mealy, Peggy*
Jun 15 1795	Menson, Gabriel to Deiter, Margaret*
May 4 1779	Mentin, Catarina to Ritter, Henry*
May 17 1790	Mercer, Benjamin I. to Strophel, Anna*
Feb 17 1786	Mercer, Peregrine to Dorsey, Rebecca
Oct 21 1779	Mercer, Rebecca to Salmon, George
May 1 1779	Mercer, Richard to Tevis, Cassander*
Jan 1 1789	Meredith, Agness to Foster, Absalom*
Jun 17 1782	Meredith, Ariminta to Walker, Joseph*
Aug 7 1782	Meredith, Keziah to Sample, John*
Apr 14 1796	Meredith, Mary to Conner, William*
Apr 5 1794	Merrick, Agness to Worrel, Jesse*
Feb 18 1784	Merrick, Ann to Crocket, Henry*
Aug 7 1794	Merrick, Catharine to White, James*
Oct 20 1790	Merrick, Patrick to Hamilton, Ann*
Sep 4 1790	Merrick, William to Dearmona, Catharine*
Oct 29 1778	Merriett, Sarah to Ham, Thomas
Jun 28 1786	Merrikin, John to Jacob, Sarah*
May 9 1778	Merrikin, Sarah to Allen, John
Nov 3 1798	Merritt, Martha to Foose, William*

Dec 20 1785	Merritt, Mary to Conchlin, John
Oct 5 1781	Merritt, Sarah to Harrison, John
Apr 29 1786	Merryman, Benjamin of William to Doyle, Cynthia*
Jan 2 1781	Merryman, Caleb to Wells, Ann
Nov 18 1793	Merryman, Catharine to Buck, John*
Nov 14 1785	Merryman, Elijah to Cromwell, Elizabeth
Apr 12 1792	Merryman, Elizabeth to Bowen, Benjamin*
Jun 20 1786	Merryman, Jemima to Bowen, Solomon*
Aug 4 1791	Merryman, Job to Neale, Ann*
Nov 24 1796	Merryman, John to Bryan, Elinor*
Dec 11 1790	Merryman, John to Johnson, Sarah
Dec 8 1777	Merryman, John to Smith, Sarah
Mar 12 1785	Merryman, John to Trequil, Nancy
Apr 25 1793	Merryman, Joseph to Gorsuch, Eleanor*
Jan 29 1794	Merryman, Luke to Gorsuch, Elizabeth*
Sep 4 1793	Merryman, Mary to Baxley, George*
Oct 17 1795	Merryman, Mary to Welsh, Laban*
May 13 1778	Merryman, Nackey to Stinchcomb, McLain*
Jun 22 1798	Merryman, Nicholas to Anderson, Sarah
Feb 16 1792	Merryman, Nicholas to Comley, Mary*
Feb 5 1778	Merryman, Nicholas to Ensor, Deborah*
Apr 14 1781	Merryman, Nicholas to Ogg, Mary
Oct 10 1781	Merryman, Nicholas to Sater, Ruth
Feb 15 1798	Merryman, Rachel to Chapman, James*
Oct 17 1778	Merryman, Rachel to Stewart, Charles*
Dec 9 1783	Merryman, Rebecca to Dimmitt, Richard*
Dec 8 1787	Merryman, Sarah to Scott, William*
Sep 9 1783	Merson, Mary to Nicholson, Benjamin
Dec 31 1796	Meshaw, Achsah to Meshaw, David*
Dec 31 1796	Meshaw, David to Meshaw, Achsah*
Aug 30 1794	Messersmith, Catharine to Jones, Daniel*
Jun 19 1783	Messersmith, Elizabeth to Diffenderffer, Samuel*
Jan 9 1794	Messersmith, William to Cromwell, Frances*
Aug 1 1781	Messonier, Henry to Weisenthal, Elizabeth*
Sep 9 1785	Metzler, Nicholas to Frolick, Jacobina*
Jun 10 1782	Mewshaw, Elizabeth to Hubbert, John
Nov 17 1778	Mewshaw, Sarah to Forrest, Vincent*
Dec 31 1794	Michael, John to Cannesseke, Mary*
Dec 24 1795	Mickle, Robert to Etling, Eliza
Aug 28 1793	Middleton, John to Cowan, Mary*
Dec 7 1796	Middleton, Mary S. to Edwards, Jonathan*
Aug 2 1792	Miercken, David to Hicks, Louisa*
Oct 9 1792	Mifford, Susannah to Lodue, Laurent
Jul 8 1790	Miflin, James to Potter, Catherine*
Feb 27 1798	Migarnty, Thomas to Gray, Elizabeth*
Jun 5 1793	Mijors, John to Reeves, Sarah*
Sep 2 1795	Milburne, Cotton to Lavely, Sarah*
Dec 29 1781	Mildews, Mary to Hughes, Frs.*
Aug 7 1784	Mildews, Mary to Parks, William
Apr 28 1785	Mildews, Prisila to Rummage, Nicholas
Mar 5 1791	Miles, Abigall to Row, Edward
Oct 20 1788	Miles, Daniel to Gorman, Mary*
Nov 7 1797	Miles, Fanny to Burch, John
Sep 6 1784	Miles, Fealey to Haycock, William*
Feb 5 1785	Miles, Joshua to Glen, Jean*
Jun 8 1778	Miles, Samuel to Lizer, Margaret*

```
Nov  6 1778    Miles, Thomas to Cromwell, Sarah*
Jun 18 1793    Miles, Zachariah to Bell, Rebecca*
Oct  7 1797    Milford, James to Stom, Mary Ann*
Apr 12 1779    Millard, Kingsby to Johns, Anne
Oct 24 1797    Miller, Adam to Henry, Sophia*
Sep 30 1786    Miller, Ann to Hall, Jonathan
Feb 28 1782    Miller, Ann to Marsh, Nathaniel*
Mar  9 1796    Miller, Anne to McMechen, Barnard*
Sep 16 1788    Miller, Caroline to Darley, Michael*
Oct 25 1797    Miller, Catharine to Carmaghan, James*
May 14 1796    Miller, Catharine to Smith, Joshua*
May 21 1785    Miller, Charles to Jones, Mary
Sep 19 1794    Miller, Christian to Cromley, Mary*
May 23 1796    Miller, Daniel to Collentine, Rebecca*
Sep 16 1795    Miller, Elijah to Stinchcomb, Hannah*
Jan  9 1782    Miller, Elizabeth to Banks, David*
May 17 1778    Miller, Elizabeth to Davidson, Job*
Jan 13 1797    Miller, Elizabeth to Emench, Philip*
Jun  5 1794    Miller, Frederick to Leern, Elizabeth*
Jul 13 1778    Miller, Frederick to Lown, Cartrout*
Oct 11 1794    Miller, George to Frazier, Peggy*
Sep 27 1786    Miller, George to Oyston, Sarah
Dec  5 1794    Miller, Hannah to Back, John*
May  9 1797    Miller, Henry to Bradis, Caroline*
Jun  7 1794    Miller, Henry to Fields, Ann*
Apr  5 1795    Miller, Isabella to Groom, William*
Jan 23 1796    Miller, Jacob to Walter, Mary*
Mar 29 1788    Miller, John to Hunt, Mary
Dec 18 1790    Miller, John to Jones, Hannah*
Aug  1 1791    Miller, John to McCloud, Sarah
Sep 16 1796    Miller, John to Reed, Peggy*
Oct 22 1778    Miller, John to Royston, Belinda*
Oct 16 1782    Miller, John to Sollors, Mary
Feb 12 1781    Miller, John to Stambleton, Rebecca*
Mar 24 1784    Miller, Joshua to Hicks, Hannah*
Jul 27 1796    Miller, Juliet to Hay, Alexander*
Nov 19 1791    Miller, Ludwick to Young, Aryminta
May  6 1794    Miller, Margaret to Freeberger, Henry*
Mar  7 1792    Miller, Margaret to Nagle, Edward*
Sep 17 1792    Miller, Margaret to Reeves, George
Nov 24 1797    Miller, Mary to Brian, Michael*
Aug 19 1782    Miller, Mary to Chambers, Martin*
Jun 23 1781    Miller, Mary to Ellison, Matthew
Aug 10 1793    Miller, Mary to Griffin, Abraham*
Jun 22 1792    Miller, Mary to Hammer, Henry*
Jul 30 1795    Miller, Mary to Pain, John*
Aug 15 1778    Miller, Mary to Shults, Andrews*
Jun  4 1795    Miller, Matthew to Hanken, Elizabeth*
Jan 12 1784    Miller, Matthias to Warne, Barbara*
Sep  2 1797    Miller, Nicholas to Criswell, Ann*
Jul 29 1779    Miller, Nicholas to McInburmer, Cabrena*
Oct  6 1792    Miller, Rachel to Rardin, William
Nov  7 1782    Miller, Rebecca to Tumbler, George*
May 17 1788    Miller, Rebecca to Watkins, James*
Sep  7 1796    Miller, Richard to Fields, Eleanor*
Jan 11 1786    Miller, Ruth to Jean, William
```

Aug 2 1783	Miller, Samuel to Burke, Mary
Feb 7 1798	Miller, Sophia to Rubbett, James
Jan 19 1785	Miller, Susannah to Heter, Jacob*
Apr 30 1778	Millering, Ann to Book, John*
Jul 6 1778	Millering, Rehina to Mailing, Godfrey*
May 7 1795	Millerman, George to Coleman, Pese Ann*
Apr 17 1783	Millesh, Cosin Constinate to Granger, Mary Ann
Oct 28 1797	Millhall, Patrick to Scall, Barbara*
Dec 24 1785	Milligan, Margaret to Wooden, John
Dec 20 1791	Milliken, Susannah to Barton, Asael*
Dec 23 1797	Millin, Charles to Stewart, Anne*
Aug 13 1796	Milliron, Mary to Lane, John*
Dec 25 1777	Mills, Elizabeth to Todd, Thomas*
Feb 12 1796	Mills, James to Lawrence, Susannah*
Mar 2 1797	Mills, Jane to Kirivan, Bryan
Jul 27 1798	Mills, John to Bruse, Sarah*
May 18 1797	Mills, Joseph to Cochran, Polly*
Sep 3 1797	Mills, Theodore to Sellers, Catharine*
Aug 23 1798	Millward, Mary to Parker, Robert*
Jul 26 1779	Milone, Mark to Nesbitt, Elinor
May 11 1797	Miltenberger, Mariah to Thompson, William*
Jul 10 1795	Milward, Latitia to Payne, James*
Dec 16 1791	Minchen, William to Kaney, Elizabeth*
Jan 6 1796	Mincher, Sally to Rode, John*
Dec 21 1793	Minci, Detestemona to Renous, Trope*
Mar 16 1793	Mincoy, Anna Mana to Donnalls, Anthony*
Aug 4 1794	Mine, Michael to Stopps, Catharine*
Aug 26 1796	Miniere, John Jas. Jos. to Mathias, Jane Mary Ann*
May 3 1792	Minksey, Susannah to Wattkins, William*
Aug 25 1783	Minnaham, Elizabeth to Sherman, Jiman
Jan 17 1797	Minsky, Catharine to Young, William*
Sep 9 1792	Mintz, Absalom to Jones, Mary*
Apr 10 1797	Mintz, Rebecca to Hover, Sebastian*
Nov 20 1779	Minutan, Charles to Fitzgerald, Ann*
Jan 31 1798	Mirceall, John to Shammo, Mary*
Mar 8 1779	Mirclay, Ortha to Morris, Joseph*
May 6 1794	Missee, Mary to Hawkins, Robert*
Dec 20 1798	Misser, Hyland to Murphy, Susanna*
Dec 31 1794	Mitchell, Arler to Cannon, Elizabeth*
Nov 17 1791	Mitchell, Edward to Valentine, Sharlot*
Jan 24 1798	Mitchell, Elizabeth to Fossey, John*
Apr 12 1790	Mitchell, Elizabeth to Pluch, Andrew*
Apr 19 1788	Mitchell, Gideon to Frigele, Margaret
Nov 1 1794	Mitchell, Jane to Cabrera, John*
May 14 1782	Mitchell, John to Daffin, Mary*
Nov 30 1793	Mitchell, John to Denning, Peggy*
May 13 1797	Mitchell, John to Murphey, Jane*
Apr 24 1779	Mitchell, Joshua to Abbott, Ann
Nov 15 1794	Mitchell, Lazarns to Roberts, Adalaide*
Mar 29 1786	Mitchell, Martha to Lannum, Lewis*
Aug 27 1796	Mitchell, Mary to Davis, Barny*
Mar 14 1795	Mitchell, Mary to Haile, Robert*
May 19 1798	Mitchell, Mary to Jiami, Benjamin*
Aug 29 1797	Mitchell, Mary to Lawrence, Thomas
Oct 6 1784	Mitchell, Mary to Scott, William
Jun 22 1786	Mitchell, Michael to Botts, Mary*

Jan 12 1792	Mitchell, Sarah to Clark, Patrick*
Sep 14 1793	Mitchell, Sarah to Stansbury, Daniel*
Dec 30 1784	Mitchell, William to Hanley, Susannah
Jan 20 1781	Mitchenner, Margaret to Sneesby, Richard*
Sep 20 1788	Mitcheson, Henry to Kingdon, Mary
Nov 18 1794	Mitcheson, Mary to Courtenay, James*
Mar 5 1796	Moak, John to Wooden, Eleanor*
Mar 13 1794	Moale, Elizabeth to Curson, Richard*
Jan 22 1788	Moale, Frances Halton to Harris, David*
Oct 5 1790	Moale, John to Morton, Lucy*
Apr 15 1797	Moale, Richard H. to Armistead, Judith Carter*
Mar 21 1793	Moale, Thomas to Owings, Eleanor*
Aug 23 1791	Moales, Nicholas to Price, Elizabeth*
Feb 9 1798	Mobberly, John to Barbon, Delila*
Jan 5 1796	Mobbly, Mary to Nicholson, John*
Nov 16 1787	Moberry, Milkey to Waggoner, Andrew*
Jan 18 1791	Mockbee, John to Howard, Nancy*
Apr 21 1790	Mockbee, William to Groven, Jemima*
Feb 24 1795	Moffett, Jane to Ruarke, Holsworth*
Jan 13 1784	Moffett, John to Ford, Ollive*
Sep 17 1783	Moher, Thomas Jr. to Philpott, Mary*
Jul 18 1782	Moire, Catherine to Renner, Leonard*
Aug 9 1792	Moloney, Ann to Pierce, James Logan*
Apr 14 1789	Mombley, Mordecai to Brown, Elizabeth*
Apr 17 1783	Momillan, Madaline to Garar, Peter*
Oct 29 1790	Mondgomery, Letty to Gore, Richard*
Jan 9 1793	Mongean, Margaret to Duckeman, Francis*
Jan 13 1795	Monro, Jonathan to Conner, Sarah*
Jun 26 1795	Montalebor, Josephine Grissure to Changeur, Leon*
Dec 13 1778	Montgomery, Alexander to Zimmerman, Elizabeth*
Oct 4 1794	Montonroy, Louis to de Rabar de Bomale, Marie Claire*
Sep 25 1788	Moody, Fanny to Watson, Joseph*
Jan 6 1790	Moody, Frances to Campbell, James*
Nov 24 1797	Moody, William to Brackett, Mary*
Aug 27 1785	Moon, Sarah to Wharton, Arthur*
Oct 12 1797	Mooney, Eleanor to Boyes, Hugh*
Jun 28 1798	Mooney, William to Haymaker, Mary*
Nov 21 1794	Moonshot, Sarah to Collings, James*
Apr 20 1790	Moor, Robert to Reynolds, Lear*
Oct 10 1788	Moore, Abarilla to Stevenson, William*
Mar 20 1786	Moore, Ann to Kelly, Stephen*
Oct 30 1783	Moore, Ann to Nowland, Thomas*
Jan 19 1781	Moore, Easther to Mortimore, Thomas
Nov 18 1797	Moore, Eleanor to Belt, James*
Jan 28 1795	Moore, Eleanor to Harris, James*
Sep 22 1797	Moore, Elizabeth to Barbarin, Louis*
Apr 20 1795	Moore, Elizabeth to Fowler, James*
May 28 1788	Moore, Elizabeth to Laverty, James*
Jan 1 1798	Moore, Elizabeth to League, Abraham*
Dec 24 1790	Moore, George to Winchester, Lydia*
Dec 30 1788	Moore, Jacob to Fromiller, Kitty*
Mar 29 1797	Moore, James Augustus to Roohe, Elizabeth*
Apr 19 1794	Moore, James to Plankett, Elizabeth*
Jun 9 1796	Moore, Jane to Jacobs, George*
Aug 3 1786	Moore, John Gay to Allender, Averilla
Feb 12 1784	Moore, John to Curry, Ann*

Jul 2 1791	Moore, Joseph to Waters, Susannah*
May 5 1798	Moore, Judy to Carey, Dennis*
Nov 26 1798	Moore, Margaret to Dowdd, Charles*
Aug 25 1795	Moore, Martha to Meem, John Jr.*
May 28 1785	Moore, Mary to Martin, Henry
Jul 24 1793	Moore, Mary to Richardson, Robert*
Dec 20 1782	Moore, Mary to Stevenson, Nicholas
Jul 21 1779	Moore, Nicholas Ruston to Orrick, Elizabeth*
Dec 25 1793	Moore, Nicholas Ruxton to Kelsoe, Sarah*
Aug 9 1797	Moore, Peggy to Cohen, Isaac*
Dec 4 1794	Moore, Philip to Giles, Susannah*
Oct 21 1790	Moore, Polly to Alder, Frederick*
Jul 20 1782	Moore, Robert to Chapman, Ruth*
May 13 1793	Moore, Robert to Galloway, Jane*
Nov 19 1791	Moore, Robert to Holmes, Elizabeth*
Feb 16 1784	Moore, Ruth to Skerrett, Clemment*
Feb 17 1794	Moore, Susannah Aisquith to Bayzana, William*
Aug 9 1788	Moore, Susannah to Toole, James*
Jan 19 1797	Moore, Thomas to Richardson, Ruth*
Mar 6 1794	Moore, William Stephen to Laypold, Catharine*
Nov 9 1791	Moore, William to Allender, Sarah*
Mar 31 1794	Moorehead, Susannah to Newel, William*
May 28 1798	Moorehead, Thomas to Broadburn, Eleanor*
Jan 30 1797	Moorly, Henry to Walker, Elizabeth*
Dec 5 1795	Mooshaw, David to Appleby, Urath*
Dec 15 1785	Morchead, Jane to Burroughs, Thomas
Dec 24 1795	Morean, Jonas to Gardner, Mary*
May 6 1796	Morel, Mane Margt. Adelaide to Pascal, Paul Frs. V.*
Feb 15 1786	Morfoot, John to Kelly, Nancy
Nov 7 1794	Morford, John to Chamberlain, Susannah*
Jan 29 1783	Morford, Thomas to Presbury, Hannah*
Jan 24 1793	Morgan, Eliza to Slade, Richard*
Oct 5 1781	Morgan, Elizabeth to League, James*
Sep 15 1798	Morgan, Elizabeth to Pugh, Jacob*
Aug 1 1783	Morgan, Elizabeth to Wilks, William*
Nov 21 1782	Morgan, James to Traverse, Nancy*
Aug 19 1795	Morgan, Jesse to Scott, Sarah*
Nov 17 1797	Morgan, Joel to Norris, Elizabeth*
Apr 2 1778	Morgan, John to Prentice, Jane*
Jan 5 1778	Morgan, Mary to Bailey, Philip*
Oct 9 1798	Morgan, Roie to O'Neale, Tilie*
Feb 1 1788	Morgan, Sarah to Higham, Abraham L.*
Mar 19 1794	Morgan, Thomas to Mullin, Sarah*
Jan 17 1793	Morgan, William to Anderson, Mary*
Nov 16 1796	Morgan, William to Baker, Keturah*
Dec 10 1796	Morgan, William to Matthews, Hannah*
Feb 20 1797	Morgan, William to Scanlan, Catharine*
Nov 18 1789	Morgolle, John Baptiste to Owin, Ann Marie*
Sep 26 1798	Morie, Benedictus to Fessen, Elizabeth*
Oct 12 1793	Morie, Joseph to Serote, Josephoria*
Nov 3 1798	Morin, Nancy to Breidenbaugh, John*
Jan 29 1794	Morine, Susannah to Lafen, Barnard*
Aug 11 1785	Morman, Nancy to Richardson, John*
Dec 21 1796	Morossa, John Joseph to Payne, Mary*
May 31 1784	Morren, Mary to Nelson, John*
Feb 11 1786	Morres, Mark to Leary, Catherine

Nov 21 1796	Morrin, James to Lasher, Ann*
Nov 11 1797	Morrin, Paul to Priestman, Priscilla*
Jan 24 1797	Morris, Augustus to Keirn, Christina*
Aug 17 1795	Morris, Augustus to Owings, Charlotte*
Mar 20 1794	Morris, Elizabeth to Bond, Peter*
Oct 17 1798	Morris, Elizabeth to Brown, John*
Nov 27 1782	Morris, Elizabeth to Clements, Edward*
May 29 1778	Morris, James to Burk, Jane*
Mar 23 1785	Morris, John to Hammond, Rachel
Jun 29 1784	Morris, John to Myers, Barbara
Jul 27 1792	Morris, John to White, Margaret*
Mar 8 1779	Morris, Joseph to Mirclay, Ortha*
Jun 12 1781	Morris, Mary to Croxall, Charles*
Apr 28 1781	Morris, Samuel to Roe, Rebecca*
Aug 12 1797	Morrison, James to Ilessen, Elizabeth*
Sep 6 1788	Morrison, Jane to Williams, John*
Jun 26 1795	Morrison, John to Hamilton, Margaret*
Nov 19 1782	Morrison, John to Rolph, Mary*
Dec 29 1792	Morrison, Margery to Morrison, Robert*
Oct 2 1790	Morrison, Mary to Grimes, John*
Jul 12 1796	Morrison, Patrick to Constable, Priscilla*
Dec 29 1792	Morrison, Robert to Morrison, Margery*
Apr 1 1783	Morriss, Edward to Scott, Sarah*
May 29 1794	Morriss, Rachel to Wise, William*
Jun 4 1784	Morriss, William to Cannon, Neomi
Mar 17 1785	Morrisson, Ann to Weeks, John
May 26 1795	Morrow, Jane to Crook, George*
Jul 20 1795	Morrow, Kennedy to Wilson, Mary*
Feb 21 1789	Morrow, Thomas to Mecaroly, Catharine*
Jul 29 1779	Mortan, Iszabellah to Rogers, Thomas*
May 19 1796	Mortemore, Elizabeth to Maynard, Foster*
Apr 5 1798	Mortimer, Thomas to Burk, Rebecca*
Jan 19 1781	Mortimore, Thomas to Moore, Easther
May 15 1794	Morton, Adalin to De Margueret, Tourneroche*
Jan 26 1795	Morton, John Andrew to Granget, Mary*
Oct 5 1790	Morton, Lucy to Moale, John*
Sep 3 1779	Morton, Mary to Murray, Edward*
Aug 15 1779	Mose, Philip to Sculd, Sarah*
Nov 24 1796	Moseh, Mary to Green, Josias*
Sep 11 1793	Mosher, Philip to Robinson, Jehannah*
Dec 29 1787	Mosier, James to Ridgely, Nancy*
Nov 17 1797	Moss, David to Welsh, Hannah*
Nov 27 1782	Moss, Elizabeth to Riff, John
Jul 27 1784	Moss, Frederick to Wheeler, Nancy
Jun 19 1779	Mosser, Kid to Clayton, Tabitha*
Jun 30 1795	Moutre, James to Jones, Pheby*
Dec 1 1790	Mowbray, James to McGowing, Nancy*
Nov 25 1783	Mowlon, John to Plackroot, Catharine*
Apr 17 1790	Moxley, Aseneth to Young, William*
Dec 20 1785	Moxley, William to Holland, Elizabeth
Jun 27 1778	Mucava, Martin to Calep, Susannah*
Nov 3 1796	Muckleroy, Margaret to Coulter, John*
Jun 28 1791	Mucklevain, Alexander to Pontenay, Sarah*
Oct 26 1778	Mucmen, Nathaniel to Golligen, Mary*
Dec 15 1788	Muflin, Margaret to Long, Hugh*
Jul 29 1797	Mulhern, Bernard to Randall, Susanna

Jan 5 1790	Mulholand, Charles to Riddle, Elizabeth*
Jun 19 1794	Mull, Mary to Donnallin, Nehemiah*
Dec 28 1790	Mulla, Thomas to Preschoe, Nancy
Dec 10 1798	Mullen, Catharine to Tygart, John
Dec 21 1782	Mullen, Patrick to Askew, Sarah
Jan 21 1794	Mullet, John to Lennard, Mary*
Dec 14 1795	Mullet, Juliet to Williamson, David*
Aug 27 1782	Mulligan, Catherine to Owings, Edward*
Oct 6 1798	Mulligan, Henrietta to Isaac, Isaac*
Mar 19 1794	Mullin, Sarah to Morgan, Thomas*
Oct 25 1797	Mully, Sarah to Peale, John*
Sep 6 1783	Mumford, Catherine to Steward, Henry*
Dec 28 1790	Mumford, Elizabeth to McKoy, Abraham*
Mar 8 1779	Mumma, Ann to Shunk, John*
May 5 1781	Mumma, Christian to Watts, Catherine
Jul 8 1783	Mumma, David to Hickman, Barbara
Jun 7 1797	Mumma, Kitty to O'Laughlin, Bryan*
Jul 13 1797	Mummey, Thomas to Fishburn, Catharine*
Feb 6 1786	Munday, William to Simpson, Leah
Feb 20 1798	Munge, Elizabeth to Lamosne, Peter
Mar 19 1794	Munnings, Maria Adelaide to Thompson, James*
Jan 17 1795	Murehert, John to Eastburn, Hetty*
Dec 2 1797	Mureno, Catharine E. to Danfary, Barthazan Maurice*
Oct 26 1778	Murfort, Elizabeth to Jordan, Henry*
Nov 13 1792	Murphey, Amon to Ward, Mary*
Dec 21 1795	Murphey, Bazel to Cross, Jemima*
Jun 19 1779	Murphey, Edward to Seal, Mary
Jul 21 1788	Murphey, Elinor to Sladen, James
Mar 1 1788	Murphey, Elizabeth to Burke, David
Sep 8 1797	Murphey, Frances to Jones, James*
Aug 31 1782	Murphey, Jane to Farnworth, James*
May 13 1797	Murphey, Jane to Mitchell, John*
Dec 14 1777	Murphey, Mary to Cannon, Clement*
Apr 1 1779	Murphey, Mary to McGuire, Anthony*
Aug 30 1794	Murphey, Peter to Collard, Sarah*
Jun 1 1784	Murphey, Susannah to Cooper, George
Sep 23 1779	Murphey, William to Warner, Mary*
Dec 31 1789	Murphy, Ann to Cannon, William*
Feb 20 1798	Murphy, Daniel to Weaver, Letitia*
Dec 7 1793	Murphy, Eleanor to Cahil, George*
Jan 2 1790	Murphy, John to Lynch, Eleanor*
Nov 7 1793	Murphy, John to Warmingham, Anne*
Mar 9 1797	Murphy, Margaret to Norton, Dennis*
May 20 1779	Murphy, Mary to Perry, John
Jun 20 1790	Murphy, Patrick to Kearns, Susannah
Sep 11 1790	Murphy, Rachael to Pross, Jacob
Jul 11 1793	Murphy, Sarah to Walker, Robert*
Dec 20 1798	Murphy, Susanna to Misser, Hyland*
Jul 30 1778	Murphy, Thomas to Forkner, Sidney*
Jun 11 1793	Murphy, William to Willmon, Ann*
Feb 23 1788	Murray, Archibald to McFarren, Mary*
Sep 3 1779	Murray, Edward to Morton, Mary*
Dec 18 1788	Murray, Elan to Hickens, Ann
Jan 23 1796	Murray, Elizabeth to Danososte, Guilliaume*
Jul 29 1790	Murray, Elizabeth to Kerby, Joshua*
Jul 7 1797	Murray, Elizabeth to Nace, William*

Nov 20 1793	Murray, Elizabeth to Wheaton, John A.*
Mar 18 1788	Murray, Ephraim to Doyle, Margaret
Sep 15 1795	Murray, Francis to Hutton, Jane*
Mar 10 1796	Murray, George William to Higginbothom, Elizabeth*
Nov 27 1785	Murray, James to Reyney, Margaret
Nov 28 1792	Murray, Jamima to Gill, Benjamin*
Apr 9 1792	Murray, John to Heirs, Elizabeth*
Nov 13 1779	Murray, John to Turner, Sarah*
Apr 15 1782	Murray, Joseph to Chilcoat, Ann
Apr 17 1794	Murray, Margaret to Mackie, Alexander*
Oct 13 1792	Murray, Margaret to Taylor, James*
Sep 28 1793	Murray, Martha to Perry, Andrew*
May 3 1794	Murray, Nicholas to Barneth, Susannah*
Jan 14 1783	Murray, Polly to Richards, Samuel*
Oct 15 1794	Murray, Rachel to Cole, Mordecai*
Sep 2 1793	Murray, Ruth to Church, Rossway
Dec 14 1795	Murray, Thomas to Rollins, Keziah*
Jan 7 1782	Murray, Winney to Penrice, Joseph*
May 27 1789	Murry, Elizabeth to Wilkerson, John*
Dec 3 1796	Musgrove, Samuel to Davis, Elizabeth*
May 10 1798	Mushaw, David to Stewart, Rachel*
Nov 13 1778	Mushaw, Elizabeth to Dicas, James*
May 28 1788	Musson, John to Turner, Susannah*
Dec 18 1784	Mutchener, Rachel to Slade, Thomas*
Dec 6 1788	Mutchner, Ann to Slade, Abraham*
Jul 2 1791	Myer, Casper Wilen to Sumvalt, Margaret*
Feb 3 1785	Myer, Christian to Baum, Catharine*
Oct 29 1791	Myer, Margaret to Cronmiller, Philip*
Dec 5 1789	Myer, Mary to Sholl, Philip*
May 23 1797	Myer, Patty to Blot, Francis*
Apr 21 1783	Myers, Ann to Bonhorn, Blathwaite*
Jun 29 1784	Myers, Barbara to Morris, John
Aug 28 1794	Myers, Benjamin to Kelly, Susannah*
Aug 23 1798	Myers, Catharine to Aldridge, Thomas H.*
Aug 26 1782	Myers, Catherine to Buchanan, William*
Jun 25 1783	Myers, Catherine to Thomas, Philip*
Jun 10 1785	Myers, Christian to Koh, Elizabeth*
Dec 22 1781	Myers, Elizabeth to Batter, William
Feb 2 1782	Myers, Elizabeth to Foster, George*
Nov 21 1793	Myers, Elizabeth to Lewis, Richard*
Aug 2 1794	Myers, Eve to Sholly, John
Nov 15 1784	Myers, Henry to Gardinner, Cathrine
Mar 22 1783	Myers, Henry to Stroven, Sarah*
Dec 21 1797	Myers, Jacob to Hankin, Ann*
Nov 7 1795	Myers, Jacob to Spicer, Loveasa*
Apr 20 1786	Myers, Jacob to Welsh, Mary*
May 18 1796	Myers, Joseph to Shuck, Mary*
Jul 14 1796	Myers, Joseph to Small, Catharine*
Jul 21 1782	Myers, Joshua to Young, Mary*
Jul 1 1785	Myers, Magdaline to Weaver, Peter
Mar 3 1794	Myers, Margaret to Fitzgerald, Garrett*
Jan 6 1798	Myers, Margaret to Kent, Robert*
Jul 25 1781	Myers, Margaret to Kilsomor, Frs.*
Sep 29 1798	Myers, Margaret to Rosensteel, John*
Aug 19 1794	Myers, Mary to Doyne, John*
Aug 27 1778	Myers, Mary to Yates, Thomas*

```
Nov 18 1795    Myers, Nicholas to Daley, Mary*
Mar 18 1797    Myers, Patrick to Ensor, Honor
Jul 15 1794    Myers, Patrick to Haley, Ann*
Dec 10 1798    Myers, Peter Nelson to Sapstone, Betsy*
Nov 23 1793    Myers, Philapma to Layman, Jacob
Mar 15 1786    Myers, Philip to Catherina, Maria
Nov  5 1798    Myers, Philip to Henley, Hannah*
Sep 14 1796    Myers, Polly to Doah, James*
Aug 11 1784    Myers, Polly to Keerl, Henry*
Feb 12 1795    Myers, Robert to James, Mary*
Feb 10 1795    Myers, Sophia to Gordon, John*
Mar 25 1796    Mynch, Joseph to Reese, Lilly*
Dec 30 1797    Myran, Mary to Walker, John*
Aug 26 1778    Nabbs, Thomas to Goodinn, Margaret*
Oct  1 1790    Nabours, Margaret to Rudricks, Anthony
Jul  7 1797    Nace, William to Murray, Elizabeth*
Mar  7 1792    Nagle, Edward to Miller, Margaret*
Jul 23 1796    Nailor, Hannah to Green, Samuel*
Jul 14 1785    Napear, Elizabeth to Scott, George
Jun 21 1794    Nash, Charles to McQueen, Gracy*
Aug  1 1795    Nash, Elsbeth to Everson, Nathaniel*
Jul  3 1783    Nash, John to Couch, Ann*
Feb  4 1797    Nash, Sarah to Smith, Jacob*
Mar 22 1796    Nau, John to Roco, July*
Jan 14 1795    Naylor, Samuel to Perrigoe, Rebecca*
May 20 1779    Naylor, William to Abercromby, Clementine
Jul 24 1783    Neace, Mary to Ukler, Erasmus
May 16 1795    Neal, Thomas to Rie, Mary*
Aug  4 1791    Neale, Ann to Merryman, Job*
Jan 26 1796    Neale, Edward to Marton, Elizabeth*
Mar 21 1793    Neale, Jane to Pennington, Henry*
May 11 1789    Neall, Kitty to Mather, John
Jul 31 1784    Neary, Peter to Shamino, Polly
Oct 19 1778    Neat, Barbara to Clarke, Ambrose*
Apr 16 1796    Needles, Stephen to Martin, Nancy*
Apr  6 1779    Neff, Caterena to Drumbo, Conrad*
Dec 24 1793    Neighbours, Henry to Knott, Ann
Mar 19 1798    Neighbours, Sarah Edmondson to Haile, Thomas*
Sep 28 1784    Neil, James to Elliot, Susannah
Aug 17 1797    Neill, Catharine to Pepper, Frederick*
Nov 10 1792    Neill, Mary to Burland, John
Sep 15 1785    Neilson, Letitia to McCocery, James
Oct  6 1792    Neilson, Mary to Dowlen, James
Apr 21 1792    Neilson, Susanah to McClery, Thomas*
Oct 18 1796    Neiss, Mary to McCabe, Thomas*
Mar 11 1786    Nelson, Burgess to Ridgely, Sarah
Jan 24 1781    Nelson, Elizabeth to Penal, John*
Aug  7 1794    Nelson, Isabella to Grant, Daniel*
Sep 16 1778    Nelson, James to Brown, Mary*
Aug  1 1786    Nelson, James to Summers, Anne
May 31 1784    Nelson, John to Morren, Mary*
Sep 25 1783    Nelson, Mary to Robinson, James*
Dec 19 1785    Nelson, Priscilla to Drew, Anthony*
Feb 12 1786    Nelson, Rebecca to Wilson, Stephen
Nov 25 1791    Nelson, Sarah to Stewart, Archibald*
May  9 1793    Nelson, Thomas to Johnson, Metilida*
```

```
Jan 18 1791    Nennanis, Nathan to Ridgely, Elizabeth
May 19 1781    Nerovil, Peter to Blossom, Rose*
Jul 26 1779    Nesbitt, Elinor to Milone, Mark
Dec  4 1790    Nevis, Hezekiah to Clarke, Ann*
Jan 28 1797    Newbay, Godfrey to Blood, Rachel*
Dec  9 1794    Newcomb, Mary to Smith, Robert*
Mar 31 1794    Newel, William to Moorehead, Susannah*
Nov 22 1796    Newlin, David to Carroll, Jane*
Oct 27 1792    Newman, Elizabeth to Ruckle, Paul*
Jan  2 1796    Newman, Harriet to Dillihunt, John*
Apr 28 1791    Newman, Henry to James, Sarah*
Oct 19 1795    Newman, Jacob to Reed, Mary*
Sep 28 1795    Newman, Mary to Killion, Jacob*
Aug 14 1784    Newman, Sarah to Mason, Benjamin
Aug 23 1794    Newshaw, Nathan to Holloway, Ann*
Dec 23 1782    Newton, William, Capt. to Lawrance, Rachel
Nov 22 1779    Nice, Christina to Rutter, Henry*
Mar 26 1785    Nice, Cornelius to Webster, Elizabeth
Oct  7 1789    Nice, David to Peck, Catherine*
May 31 1783    Nice, Dorothy to Barton, John
Jun 11 1796    Nice, Elizabeth to Hubbert, William*
Jul 26 1790    Nice, Mary to Alder, Robert*
Nov 14 1787    Nice, Susanna to Kraner, Michael*
Mar 12 1796    Nice, Susannah to Perkins, Benjamin*
Dec 12 1795    Nichol, Agnus to McConkey, James*
Sep  9 1783    Nicholson, Benjamin to Merson, Mary
Nov 10 1798    Nicholson, David to Sank, Nancy*
Aug 11 1795    Nicholson, Elizabeth to Weaver, Jacob*
Sep  1 1786    Nicholson, James to Aires, Hannah*
Jan  5 1796    Nicholson, John to Mobbly, Mary*
Mar 24 1794    Nicholson, John to Smith, Matilda*
Feb 20 1798    Nicholson, Mary to Lux, Darby*
Aug 29 1789    Nicholson, Nancy to Welsh, Edward*
Jul  6 1796    Nicholson, Rachel to Smith, Larkin*
Aug 25 1784    Nicholson, Thomas to Brady, Nancy*
Nov 10 1792    Nickle, Greay to Maloy, Patrick*
Feb 13 1798    Nicodemus, Elizabeth to Geisenderfer, Jacob*
Mar 14 1794    Nicodemus, Esther to Haynes, Michael*
Jun 25 1797    Nicole, David to Allen, Darcas*
Jan 25 1797    Nicoll, Christina to Carter, Thomas
Feb 24 1796    Nicoll, Jane to Jackson, Collin*
Jul  7 1798    Nicoll, Precilla to Ray, Benjamin
Dec  5 1798    Nicolls, Sarah to Hunt, William*
Dec  4 1793    Nicols, Henry to Smith, Rebecca
Nov 30 1793    Night, David to Harwood, Blanckey*
Jan  2 1791    Night, Joseph to Keens, Susannah
Dec 20 1783    Night, Shedrick to Bark, Capus*
Feb 24 1797    Ninde, James to Blyth, Catharine*
Feb 27 1797    Nisser, Martha to Garland, George
May 13 1796    Nixon, Hetty to Pike, Daniel*
Feb  2 1798    Nobs, Mary to Norbaurch, John*
Jun  6 1793    Noel, James to Noel, Sophia
Apr 28 1791    Noel, Margaret to Tomlinson, Joseph*
Jun  6 1793    Noel, Sophia to Noel, James
Mar 16 1782    Noex, John to Stiles, Ann*
Apr 19 1795    Nolan, William to Silzel, Barbara*
```

```
Oct  5 1798    Noland, Peregrine to Combesh, Elizabeth*
May 13 1797    Noles, Joseph to Ryan, Biddy*
Aug 23 1794    Nondenbory, Rachel to Goetz, John*
Feb 12 1782    Noody, Sarah to Turner, Charles*
Aug 28 1790    Noon, Mary to Evans, Evan*
May  8 1797    Noonan, Edward to Fitzpatrick, Mary*
Feb  2 1798    Norbaurch, John to Nobs, Mary*
Sep 22 1798    Norbury, George to Burges, Martha*
Jun  5 1782    Norman, Henry to Cockran, Mary*
Sep  7 1781    Norman, Henry to Nut, Elizabeth*
Jul 24 1798    Norman, John to Randall, Hannah*
Apr 17 1797    Norman, Levy to Godfrey, Mary*
Jul 15 1795    Norquay, Magness to Trotman, Jane*
Feb  6 1797    Norquey, Magnus to Gette, Marie Charlotte*
Jan 22 1783    Norris, Abraham to Cross, Rebecca*
Apr  3 1795    Norris, Alice to Barber, Daniel*
Apr 30 1796    Norris, Belinda to Hughes, Abraham*
Dec 11 1788    Norris, Benjamin to Butler, Margaret
Mar 11 1789    Norris, Delia to Parrish, Edward*
Nov 17 1797    Norris, Elizabeth to Morgan, Joel*
Mar  4 1795    Norris, Hannah to Scott, Joseph Jr.*
May 31 1798    Norris, James to Willoughby, Mary*
May 10 1798    Norris, John to Daughaday, Mary*
May  5 1798    Norris, Mary to Shock, Peter*
Oct 27 1791    Norris, Rebecca to Bull, Josias Slade*
Dec  5 1783    Norris, Sarah to Thomas, Daniel*
Oct 22 1784    Norris, William to Bosley, Mary*
Jun  2 1779    Norsod, Philip Odle to Tasker, Ann Harden
Jun 26 1795    North, Rebecca to Burk, Thomas*
Sep  2 1795    North, Sophia to Clarke, Oliver*
Jan 22 1782    Northemond, Anne to McCrackin, John*
Mar  8 1790    Northon, Benjamin to Panier, Mary*
Mar  9 1797    Norton, Dennis to Murphy, Margaret*
Oct 29 1796    Norton, Mary to Dell John*
Mar 10 1796    Norwood, Edward to Howard, Jemimah*
Apr 23 1785    Norwood, Edward to Odle, Sarah
Nov  9 1793    Norwood, Hannah to Hobbs, Caleb*
Jun 17 1782    Norwood, John to Haile, Mary*
Nov 19 1791    Norwood, Mary to Hobbs, Denton
Dec 14 1785    Norwood, Pleasance to Brand, George
Nov 26 1787    Norwood, Samuel to Brown, Rebecca
Apr 15 1788    Norwood, Samuel to Dorsey, Mary*
Jan 12 1791    Norwood, Samuel to Howard, Patience*
Aug  6 1783    Nouls, James to Sawer, Ann
Oct 30 1783    Nowland, Thomas to Moore, Ann*
Mar  2 1785    Noyle, Henry to Warnar, Catharine*
Feb 17 1784    Null, Francis to Rynehart, Elizabeth*
Dec 20 1798    Nussen, Elizabeth to Hayden, James*
Sep  7 1781    Nut, Elizabeth to Norman, Henry*
Mar  5 1795    Nuval, Susannah to Whitney, Thomas*
Apr  2 1785    Oadle, Sarah to Baker, Samuel
Sep 18 1784    Oatmer, Elizabeth to Giles, Robert*
Jul  7 1796    Ober, Elizabeth to Gordon, George*
Nov 18 1795    Ober, John to Woodward, Elizabeth*
Dec  7 1784    Odel, Rachel to Dorsey, Bazel*
Jan 17 1795    Odell, John to Cooper, Anney*
```

Jun 28 1785	Odenbaugh, Charles to Dean, Martha*
Dec 6 1788	Odle, Elizabeth to Ebert, John*
Jul 16 1779	Odle, Mary to Johnson, Thomas
Apr 23 1785	Odle, Sarah to Norwood, Edward
Mar 9 1796	Odle, Sarah to Pemberton, William*
Feb 7 1797	Odle, William to Walter, Rachel*
Dec 11 1784	Offert, Charles to Richards, Rosa*
Mar 6 1795	Ogden, Ann to Watson, Thomas*
Jan 4 1798	Ogeir, John to Reese, Margaret*
Dec 10 1789	Ogg, Benjamin to Hooker, Mary*
Oct 26 1779	Ogg, Catharine to Griffith, Nathan*
Dec 8 1783	Ogg, George to Headington, Mary*
Mar 25 1791	Ogg, James to Baseman, Sarah*
Apr 14 1781	Ogg, Mary to Merryman, Nicholas
Jun 27 1781	Ogg, Mary to Sater, Charles*
Nov 25 1784	Ogle, George to Flanagan, Alazane*
Dec 11 1798	Ogle, George to Smothers, Mary*
Feb 4 1794	Ogleby, Francis to McKoy, Charlotte*
Mar 6 1793	Ogston, Henry to Deveney, Darcus*
Feb 1 1785	Ogston, Henry to Puntaney, Margaret*
Jul 23 1788	Ogston, Lawrence to Perrigoe, Rebecca*
May 2 1797	Oldfield, Jane to Guyer, Dennis*
Nov 20 1784	Oldham, Edward to Ensor, Mary*
Apr 11 1795	Oldham, John to Allbright, Nancy*
Aug 26 1782	Oldis, Ann to Shriver, John
Aug 7 1781	Oley, Sebastian to Rodwell, Jeminah*
Oct 7 1796	Oliver, Catharine to Harryman, Nathaniel*
Jan 2 1790	Oliver, John to Hughes, Catherine*
Oct 31 1778	Oliver, John to Lootherwood, Urath*
Apr 26 1792	Oliver, John to Mathman, Rachel*
Oct 31 1781	Oliver, John to Thralls, Sophiah
Oct 12 1793	Ollives, John B. to Epiron, Louisa*
Oct 28 1778	Onbahand, Eve Barbary to Spick, William*
May 16 1788	Onion, Patty to Gough, Harry*
Jun 20 1783	Onion, Stephen to Crone, Kitty*
Aug 6 1781	Onion, Thomas to McCall, Elizabeth*
Apr 1 1795	Oram, Arnold to League, Elizabeth*
Aug 25 1790	Oram, Benjamin to Runnels, Sarah*
Mar 17 1794	Oram, Elizabeth to Johnson, Elijah*
May 22 1784	Oram, Hannah to Luis, Charles*
Jun 11 1779	Oram, Henry to Johnson, Sarah
Jan 2 1778	Oram, Henry to Ridgely, Ann*
Apr 17 1784	Oram, John to Lewis, Ann*
Nov 29 1796	Oram, Joshua to Lighteiser, Elizabeth*
Aug 17 1790	Oram, Mary to Harryman, Nathaniel
Dec 23 1793	Oram, Nancy to Jarvis, Edward*
May 3 1783	Oram, Rachel to Forester, George*
Oct 2 1782	Oram, Ruth to Forrest, Nicholas
Sep 8 1791	Oram, Thomas to Martin, Mary*
Apr 24 1786	Orban, Henry to Hook, Catharine*
Feb 9 1791	Ore, Margaret to Reeves, Richard*
Jul 2 1795	Orndorff, Peter to Allen, Margaret*
Mar 18 1795	Orrick, Anna to Harris, Asact*
Jul 21 1779	Orrick, Elizabeth to Moore, Nicholas Ruston*
Dec 24 1794	Orrick, John to Gervey, Mary*
Dec 26 1781	Orrick, Margaret to Smith, Job*

Aug 23 1785	Orrick, Sarah to Jourdan, Thomas
Apr 28 1792	Orrick, Sarah to Shepherd, Samuel* (free blacks)
Jan 7 1784	Orrick, Susannah to Butler, Absalom
Oct 14 1789	Orrick, Susannah to Roberts, John*
Feb 5 1778	Orsler, Charles to Candley, Martha M.*
Jan 14 1778	Orsler, William to Parker, Mary*
Dec 27 1787	Osborn, Ann to Taylor, George*
May 13 1786	Osborn, Cary to Towson, James
Oct 12 1784	Osborn, Cordelia to Langston, Nehemiah
Feb 27 1796	Osborn, Daniel to Busby, Melinda*
Apr 8 1786	Osborn, James to Haley, Eleanor*
May 17 1785	Osborn, Jonas to Warnell, Elizabeth
Aug 14 1794	Osborn, Joseph to Burke, Elizabeth*
Jan 23 1793	Osborn, Ruth to Armacoste, Michael*
Dec 24 1788	Osborn, Sophia to Cole, Joseph*
May 7 1785	Osborne, John Jr. to Armagost, Mary*
Dec 25 1777	Osborne, Mary to Simpson, Samuel*
Feb 15 1791	Osborne, Sarah to Cole, Giles*
Jun 2 1798	Osburn, Michael to Christopher, Susanna*
Mar 18 1790	Osburn, Samuel to Aiels, Susannah*
Aug 9 1778	Osmand, Edward to Marsh, Sarah*
Aug 17 1791	Otherson, Rebecca to Wright, John*
Jun 3 1796	Otlay, John to Lynch, Jemimah*
Jan 20 1778	Ottey, Ann to McCubbin, Zachariah*
Oct 31 1796	Otto, Anthony to Lose, Arsella*
Sep 5 1798	Oursler, Elizabeth to Jacob, Benjamin*
Apr 27 1782	Ousler, John to Baker, Sarah
Sep 30 1795	Outter, Catharine to Righter, Abraham*
Nov 29 1794	Oval, Catharine to Johnson, James*
Jul 23 1793	Overton, John to Weaver, Mary*
Apr 22 1779	Overy, Mary to Judah, Jacob
Nov 22 1791	Overy, Rheanna to Stull, Andrew*
Feb 7 1794	Owens, Anna to Latil, Jacob*
Nov 18 1789	Owin, Ann Marie to Morgolle, John Baptiste*
Nov 11 1794	Owings, Achsah to Stevens, John*
Jun 14 1784	Owings, Arrey to Marr, William*
Feb 18 1790	Owings, Beale to Dorsey, Ruth*
Dec 8 1792	Owings, Benjamin to Zimerman, Catherine*
Mar 14 1786	Owings, Betsy to Wells, Joseph
Jul 17 1790	Owings, Casandra D. to Van Pradellis, Benedict F.*
Mar 27 1779	Owings, Catherine to Watkins, William*
Dec 24 1794	Owings, Charlotte to McGreggin, Patrick*
Aug 17 1795	Owings, Charlotte to Morris, Augustus*
Aug 27 1782	Owings, Edward to Mulligan, Catherine*
Mar 21 1793	Owings, Eleanor to Moale, Thomas*
Sep 26 1795	Owings, Elizabeth to Cockey, Thomas*
Nov 3 1796	Owings, Esther to Wilkins, Henry Dr.*
Mar 26 1781	Owings, George to Wells, Ann*
Oct 30 1779	Owings, George to Wells, Ann*
Jan 28 1798	Owings, Hellen to Wells, Absalom*
Mar 13 1794	Owings, Isaac to Dorsey, Achsah*
Feb 12 1783	Owings, John to Majors, Deborah
Oct 22 1790	Owings, Joshua to Frost, Ruth*
May 24 1796	Owings, Kitty to Hynson, Nathaniel*
May 6 1796	Owings, Letty to Peck, John*
Jan 4 1790	Owings, Mary to Barnett, Peter*

Dec	6	1780	Owings, Mary to Beanman, John*
Apr	5	1786	Owings, Massella to Worthington, Thomas*
Oct	23	1790	Owings, Micha to Brown, Charles*
Dec	31	1794	Owings, Nancy to Wooden, Charles*
Jan	21	1786	Owings, Nicholas to Risteau, Frances
Mar	6	1782	Owings, Pamelia to Galloway, Moses*
Oct	16	1781	Owings, Rachel to Crooks, John
Jun	30	1796	Owings, Ruth to Davis, William*
Apr	11	1778	Owings, Ruth to Stinchcomb, Thomas*
Mar	22	1791	Owings, Samuel to Cockey, Ruth*
May	15	1788	Owings, Samuel to Dorsey, Arianna*
Apr	8	1797	Owings, Samuel to Gevane, Mary*
Oct	28	1796	Owings, Sarah to Reynolds, John*
Dec	10	1793	Owings, Sarah to Winchester, James*
Jun	13	1781	Owings, Stephen Jr. to Jones, Lucy
Dec	5	1798	Owings, Susanna to Daughady, Johnsey*
Mar	25	1796	Owings, Thomas to Squires, Sarah*
Dec	6	1787	Owings, Urath to Cromwell, John*
May	3	1784	Oyston, Elizabeth to Smith, Caleb*
Sep	27	1786	Oyston, Sarah to Miller, George
Sep	16	1795	Oyston, Tabatha to Young, John*
Dec	20	1797	Oyton, Benjamin to Lidiard, Susannah
Nov	4	1796	Ozard, Robert to Johnson, Ann*
Sep	4	1783	O'Brian, Ann to Herron, Timothy*
Apr	9	1788	O'Brian, Biddy to Hoofman, Daniel
Feb	4	1792	O'Brian, Charles to Coskery, Patty*
Jun	30	1795	O'Brian, Daniel to Askew, Mary*
Sep	28	1778	O'Brian, Daniel to Fin, Mary Ann*
May	14	1796	O'Brian, Joseph D. to Flattery, Mary*
Mar	21	1796	O'Brian, Margaret to O'Brian, Michael*
Mar	21	1796	O'Brian, Margaret to O'Neill, Bernard*
Sep	17	1796	O'Brian, Mary to Gormley, Cornelius*
Mar	19	1794	O'Brian, Mary to Jackson, Thomas*
Dec	1	1791	O'Brian, Michael to Hook, Margaret*
Mar	21	1796	O'Brian, Michael to O'Brian, Margaret*
Jan	21	1786	O'Brian, Nancy to Clark, Joseph*
Aug	15	1793	O'Brian, Patrick to Johnson, Penia*
Jul	31	1782	O'Brian, Patrick to Steward, Elizabeth*
Apr	9	1796	O'Brien, Ellen to McCarty, Michael*
Feb	26	1785	O'Bryan, Hetty to Legg, Solomon*
Jul	16	1781	O'Bryan, James to Beech, Margaret*
Jul	17	1778	O'Callahan, James to McFarlin, Catharine*
Jul	4	1798	O'Cay, Elizabeth to Davidson, James*
Dec	20	1797	O'Conner, Margaret to Holland, Thomas
Feb	17	1798	O'Conner, Michael to Welsh, Catharine*
Aug	9	1796	O'Conners, Sybel to Tyson, Henry Sanders*
Sep	17	1796	O'Donnell, Biddy to Campbell, John*
Dec	8	1794	O'Donnell, Catharine to Loyd, William*
Oct	15	1794	O'Donnell, Elizabeth to Shock, Jacob*
Oct	12	1785	O'Donnell, John to Elliott, Tarah Chew
Apr	13	1797	O'Haben, David to Gregory, Rebecca*
Jun	14	1794	O'Hagan, Mary to Dunn, Edward*
Oct	19	1795	O'Han, Samuel to Rolves, Juliana*
Jun	7	1797	O'Laughlin, Bryan to Mumma, Kitty*
Nov	3	1792	O'Leary, Julia to Castaignet, Paul*
May	6	1797	O'Mara, Patrick to Rattig, Mary*

```
Dec 14 1798    O'Neale, Ann to Lawrell, James*
Aug  5 1797    O'Neale, Nancy to Sindall, Solomon*
Oct  9 1798    O'Neale, Tilie to Morgan, Roie*
Mar 21 1796    O'Neill, Bernard to O'Brian, Margaret*
Dec  1 1791    O'Neill, Catharine to Bennett, Stephen*
May  5 1785    Pack, Rosannah to Hannen, George
Aug  9 1783    Packett, Elizabeth to Rawlings, Adam
Sep 30 1781    Padwell, Simon to Strauhon, Margaret*
Jun 17 1797    Page, Daniel to Hughes, Polly*
Feb  3 1781    Page, Elizabeth to Knox, William*
Apr 17 1798    Pagely, Samuel to Parrott, Harriot
Jun 11 1795    Pagges, John to Botton, Mary*
Jul 30 1795    Pain, John to Miller, Mary*
Dec 31 1796    Paine, John to Foreman, Christina*
Sep 26 1792    Paine, Sarah to Littlejohn, Miles*
Oct 27 1792    Painter, Ann to Green, James*
Oct 13 1792    Painter, Elizabeth to Fouble, Peter
Sep  4 1788    Palmer, Edward to Knowland, Mary*
Apr 18 1795    Palmer, Horace to Bedry, Elizabeth*
Mar 11 1784    Palmer, Philip to Webb, Jane*
May  8 1779    Palmer, Thomas to English, Margaret*
Sep 29 1796    Palmer, William to Jarvis, Averilla*
Oct 21 1783    Pamell, Elizabeth to Lewis, John*
Sep 30 1790    Pamphelon, Thomas to Weary, Rebecca*
Mar 21 1792    Pampillion, Mary to Parker, James*
Sep  5 1795    Pancess, Hetty to Sincklair, Robert*
Feb 24 1778    Pangle, Elizabeth to Holler, Francis*
Mar  8 1790    Panier, Mary to Northon, Benjamin*
Dec 21 1795    Pannell, John to Smull, Margaret*
Feb 12 1795    Panterr, Antoine to Daplan, Marie Caterine*
Dec 29 1787    Paradise, Sophia to Fisher, Basil*
Apr  4 1794    Parce, Anna Savon to Bourgeois, A. Chapol*
Oct  4 1782    Parish, Ann to Gill, Edward*
Jun  6 1789    Parish, Aquila to Tipton, Rebecca*
Feb 18 1792    Parish, Benjamin to Hunter, Nancy*
Jan 15 1795    Parish, Elizabeth to Semans, John*
Jun 13 1783    Parish, Mary to Hooker, Jacob*
Oct 20 1798    Park, Elizabeth to Dunns, Daniel*
Feb 21 1794    Parker, Ann to Crawford, Samuel*
Sep 15 1796    Parker, Ann to Snider, John*
Oct 11 1794    Parker, Barbara to Harrywood, Robert*
Aug 13 1778    Parker, Edward to Stewart, Ann*
Mar 21 1792    Parker, James to Pampillion, Mary*
Jul 11 1795    Parker, John to Lamb, Rebecca*
Jan 14 1778    Parker, Mary to Orsler, William*
Aug 23 1798    Parker, Robert to Millward, Mary*
Oct 12 1782    Parker, Sarah to Squire, William
Mar  8 1788    Parker, William to Gosnel, Rachel
Jul 26 1784    Parkhouse, William to McKinnan, Susannah*
Sep 30 1790    Parkin, Rachael Lyde to Hollingsworth, Jesse*
Nov 27 1793    Parkins, Catherine to Brown, John*
Oct 29 1791    Parkinson, Diannah to Lawson, Richard*
Jul 16 1785    Parkinson, Edward to James, Dinah*
Oct 19 1796    Parkinson, Edward to Ward, Mary*
Sep 27 1797    Parks, Abraham to Wallen, Eleanor*
Feb 23 1793    Parks, Ann to Isor, Nicholas*
```

```
Aug 26 1789    Parks, Archibald to Bosley, Ann*
Sep 27 1783    Parks, Benjamin to Jones, Eleanor*
May 12 1784    Parks, Charlotte to Fivcash, Peter*
Apr  7 1794    Parks, David to Towson, Elizabeth*
Jun 16 1798    Parks, Delia to Hatton, Aquilla*
Sep 23 1796    Parks, Dorothy to Downey, William*
Mar  2 1785    Parks, Elisha to Brannon, Rachel*
Dec  1 1787    Parks, Frederick to Parks, Rachel*
Sep  1 1788    Parks, John to Hendrickson, Ruth*
Apr 30 1796    Parks, John to Stewert, Mary*
Apr 10 1784    Parks, Mary to Whiteby, James*
Jun 25 1796    Parks, Mayberry to Collins, Mary*
Nov 18 1796    Parks, Nathan to Griffith, Rachel*
Sep 11 1790    Parks, Peter to Jones, Precilla*
Nov  1 1783    Parks, Priscilla to Bell, Henry*
Nov  2 1791    Parks, Rachael to Dixon, Raphael*
Dec  1 1787    Parks, Rachel to Parks, Frederick*
Apr  7 1785    Parks, Rebeccah to Richards, Nicholas
Jun 20 1778    Parks, Sarah to Waller, Basal*
May 12 1785    Parks, Thomas to Philips, Lucy*
Oct  3 1798    Parks, William to Corbin, Eleanor*
Mar 30 1782    Parks, William to Greene, Cloe*
Aug  7 1784    Parks, William to Mildews, Mary
Feb 17 1784    Parlet, Rachael to German, Benjamin*
Mar 27 1784    Parlett, David to German, Hosannah*
Mar  8 1785    Parlett, Joshua to Price, Catharine*
Sep 27 1788    Parlett, Martin to Barns, Sarah
Feb 24 1778    Parlett, William to Garman, Elizabeth*
May  7 1795    Parlett, William to Woolrick, Elizabeth*
Jan 12 1781    Parnel, Eleanor to Shipley, John*
May  2 1798    Parnett, Hannah to Wight, Charles*
Oct  7 1785    Parrin, Ann Helen to White, Samuel*
Oct 10 1795    Parrish, Benjamin to Porter, Mary*
Feb  5 1794    Parrish, Carey to Garner, Flinn*
Mar 11 1789    Parrish, Edward to Norris, Delia*
Aug 19 1793    Parrish, Elizabeth to Williams, Robert*
Aug 13 1794    Parrish, Honour to Porter, Alexis*
Dec  5 1793    Parrish, James to Gardner, Catherine
Apr  7 1796    Parrish, John to Yaun, Elizabeth*
Mar 23 1796    Parrish, Mary to Swann, Leonard*
Dec  8 1792    Parrish, Nicholas to Johnson, Elizabeth*
Sep 20 1786    Parrot, Mary Ann to Hooper, John Ashcom*
Apr 17 1798    Parrott, Harriot to Pagely, Samuel
Nov 15 1789    Parsons, Ann to Brown, William*
Sep 27 1783    Parsons, John to House, Susanna*
Aug 25 1783    Parsons, Rebecca to Lancaster, Nathan
Jul 25 1796    Parsons, Sarah to Brown, John*
Aug  2 1791    Parsons, Sarah to Williams, Nathan
Jun 21 1784    Partle, Peggy to Kentlemyer, John Mike*
Nov  9 1791    Partridge, Elizabeth to Long, John*
Dec 22 1778    Partridge, Robert to Lewis, Rachel*
May  3 1798    Partridge, Sarah to Sollers, Elisha*
Jul 26 1779    Partridge, Sarah to Wert, Caspar*
Jan  8 1795    Partridge, William to Wells, Ann*
Nov 24 1780    Pary, Judy to Charles, Abram*
May  6 1796    Pascal, Paul Frs. V. to Morel, Mane Margt. Adelaide*
```

Jun 24 1796	Pasely, David to Wright, Sarah*
Dec 6 1798	Pate, Eliza to Whipple, William*
Aug 21 1794	Paterson, Margaret to Bizourd, Joseph*
Oct 24 1778	Patience - negro to Joice, Peter Anthony *
Apr 21 1797	Patrick, Elizabeth to Harvey, Joshua*
Nov 24 1797	Patrick, Mary to Brook, Basil*
Feb 25 1792	Patrick, Nancy to Wilkinson, Joshua*
Apr 29 1794	Patridge, Ann to Wilson, David*
Mar 2 1785	Patridge, Danberry Buckler to Porter, Elizabeth*
Jan 8 1784	Patridge, Robert to Randall, Catherine*
May 7 1779	Pattan, Thomas to Harn, Mary*
May 9 1788	Patterson, Elizabeth to Lushy, Bartholomew*
May 12 1789	Patterson, James to Keath, Jane*
Oct 29 1796	Patterson, John to Bradshaw, Nancy*
Jun 25 1790	Patterson, Kitty to Anderson, William
Jul 17 1784	Patterson, Lawrence to Septon, Nancy*
Aug 8 1797	Patterson, Martha to Clark, Raphael
Jul 8 1782	Patterson, Mary to Rust, John*
Mar 4 1789	Patterson, Rachel to Guishard, David*
Jun 15 1796	Patterson, Samuel to Fugate, Alice*
Jul 2 1795	Patterson, William to Craig, Nancy*
May 15 1779	Patterson, William to Spear, Dorcas
Dec 22 1797	Pattingall, Jonathan to Steward, Elizabeth*
May 29 1794	Pattison, Elizabeth to Pattison, John*
Jan 4 1786	Pattison, John to Fugate, Elizabeth
May 29 1794	Pattison, John to Pattison, Elizabeth*
Jun 25 1784	Patton, Gaskwell to Bows, Anne*
Oct 8 1791	Paul, Elizabeth to Tustin, Septimus*
Jan 9 1790	Paul, Nancy to Stuback, Christian*
Jul 7 1781	Pauling, Mary to Todd, Nicholas
Jun 13 1795	Pawson, Margaret to Roberts, Owen*
Jul 10 1795	Payne, James to Milward, Latitia*
Dec 21 1796	Payne, Mary to Morossa, John Joseph*
Feb 21 1797	Payne, Zachariah to Taylor, Ann*
Mar 25 1797	Payson, Nancy to Steele, John*
Sep 18 1790	Peach, John Battis to Chamean, Peggy*
Dec 1 1789	Peach, William to Woods, Elizabeth*
Jun 30 1781	Peacock, John to Smith, Elizabeth*
Aug 30 1796	Peacock, Mary to Reed, John*
Jul 16 1796	Peacock, William to Baker, Nancy*
Apr 20 1797	Peake, Eleanor to Kennedy, William*
Oct 25 1797	Peale, John to Mully, Sarah*
Oct 20 1796	Peale, William to Berry, Elizabeth*
Dec 24 1793	Peale, William to Berry, Polly*
Sep 13 1779	Pearce, Balasha to Gorsuch, Nathan*
Dec 3 1796	Pearce, Betsey to Williams, Basel
Sep 2 1793	Pearce, Charles to Stansbury, Drusilla*
Nov 28 1781	Pearce, Daniel to Anckers, Ann
Nov 22 1781	Pearce, Elizabeth to Sillers, Thomas*
May 3 1786	Pearce, John to Lawrence, Elizabeth*
May 13 1797	Pearce, John to Warrick, Elizabeth*
Aug 21 1781	Pearce, Joseph to Wyle, Comfort
Apr 9 1796	Pearce, Josiah to Stevens, Elizabeth*
Jun 24 1785	Pearce, Mary to Barton, Thomas*
Nov 25 1797	Pearce, Mary to Baxley, Nicholas
Dec 29 1780	Pearce, Mary to Hendrickson, Joseph*

Jan 29 1796	Pearce, Philip to Wilson, Sarah*
Jan 23 1796	Pearce, Samuel to Skillhamer, Margaret*
Apr 16 1795	Pearce, Thomas to Cummins, Elizabeth*
May 31 1796	Pearson, Andrew to Smith, Patty*
Jan 30 1798	Pearson, David to Kimbs, Mary Ann*
Apr 7 1796	Pearson, Elizabeth to Griffen, Walter*
Oct 19 1795	Pearson, Henry to Childs, Mary*
Nov 23 1789	Pearson, Lucy to Gibson, John*
Nov 25 1797	Pearson, Mary to Scanlan, James*
Aug 15 1795	Pease, Dennis to Edwards, Margaret*
Jun 6 1784	Pease, Elisha to Rohrback, Clara*
Dec 1 1790	Peasely, Margaret to McCarty, William*
Jan 22 1781	Peasly, Mary to Scarf, George*
Aug 24 1782	Peat, Claude to Hurley, Mary*
Jul 4 1795	Peathers, Elizabeth to Stevenson, Samuel*
Oct 7 1789	Peck, Catherine to Nice, David*
Jun 9 1795	Peck, Elizabeth to Huston, John*
Nov 18 1788	Peck, John to Brown, Sharlotte*
May 6 1796	Peck, John to Owings, Letty*
Mar 3 1791	Peck, John to Piper, Eleanor*
Jan 12 1791	Peck, Nicholas to Flud, Deborah*
Feb 18 1795	Pecker, Joseph to Deale, Mary*
Oct 31 1795	Pecker, Mary to Wright, James*
Oct 8 1785	Peddicoart, Jasper to Hobbs, Amelia
Nov 5 1788	Peddicoart, William to Hobbs, Elizabeth*
Feb 26 1793	Peddicoat, Morris to Bond, Keturah*
Feb 24 1783	Peddicord, Adam to Zimmerman, Elizabeth*
Sep 6 1786	Peddicord, Elizabeth to Inloes, Henry
Sep 3 1782	Peddicord, Sopiah to Greenwood, Thomas*
Sep 4 1797	Peduze, Peter to Shaw, Sally*
Jul 6 1778	Peirce, Rebecca to Whips, Benjamin*
Sep 27 1794	Peirpoint, Thomas to Wells, Margaret*
Aug 13 1796	Pelts, Jacob to Barkman, Elizabeth*
Jan 11 1796	Pemberton, William to Maxwell, Mary*
Mar 9 1796	Pemberton, William to Odle, Sarah*
Jan 24 1781	Penal, John to Nelson, Elizabeth*
Aug 7 1784	Pendon, Katharine to Knap, Jacob
Aug 28 1798	Peniston, Samuel to Renaud, Ariana*
Aug 29 1795	Penman, Martha Fredericka C. to Follmar, Martin*
May 23 1795	Penn, Catharine to Glenn, Hanson William*
Nov 9 1796	Penn, Mary to Williams, Benjamin*
Feb 24 1783	Penn, Ruth to Barnes, Philemon*
Aug 13 1778	Penn, Sarah to Robinson, Richard*
May 15 1779	Penn, Shaderick to Chaney, Ann
Aug 23 1790	Penn, Shadrack to Holland, Margaret*
Sep 25 1794	Penn, William to Connoway, Deborah*
Apr 8 1788	Penn, William to Ijams, Mary*
Mar 21 1793	Pennington, Henry to Neale, Jane*
May 24 1796	Pennington, Mary to Rutter, Josias*
Sep 19 1794	Pennington, Nathan to Clerage, Elizabeth*
Apr 25 1797	Pennington, Sarah to Sollers, Thomas*
Oct 12 1797	Pennington, Susannah to Baker, Allen*
Jan 14 1791	Penny, Alexander to Ford, Susannah*
Mar 23 1790	Penny, Lucreta Christiana to Allen, John*
Jul 7 1796	Penny, Prudence to Waters, Stephen*
Jan 7 1782	Penrice, Joseph to Murray, Winney*

Nov 5 1795	Penrice, Thomas to Webb, Mary*
Sep 14 1798	Peoins, Drucilla to Clarke, Thomas
Dec 25 1795	Peola, Mary to Cunningham, John*
Mar 11 1793	Peot, Peter to Avelin, Louisa*
Aug 17 1797	Pepper, Frederick to Neill, Catharine*
Jan 13 1795	Pepper, Pamelia to Tanner, Pearce Lacey*
Nov 5 1783	Perdue, Prudence to Walker, Daniel*
Aug 16 1779	Perdue, Rachael to Sparks, Thomas*
Jun 12 1790	Perdue, Walter to Bosley, Elizabeth
Aug 4 1784	Perdue, Walter to Corbin, Mary*
May 9 1783	Perego, Joseph to Woodward, Jemima*
Oct 31 1794	Perenne, Magdalen to Hattier, Henry
Jun 28 1795	Perigo, Deborah to Curtis, Benjamin*
Feb 1 1792	Perigo, Sarah to Baxter, Nicholas*
Nov 30 1798	Perine, Margaret to Perine, Peter*
Oct 22 1793	Perine, Maulden to Brown, Hepkabah*
Nov 17 1797	Perine, Peter to Howard, Mary*
Nov 30 1798	Perine, Peter to Perine, Margaret*
Apr 3 1795	Perine, Simon to Porter, Margaret*
Aug 1 1798	Pering, Abraham to Tracy, Elizabeth*
Mar 12 1796	Perkins, Benjamin to Nice, Susannah*
Oct 9 1798	Perkins, Joel G. to Matson, Elizabeth
Feb 27 1797	Perling, Peter to Field, Mary*
Dec 16 1785	Peron, Caterina to Riter, Christian*
Apr 30 1796	Perrigo, Edith to Read, Larkin*
May 8 1797	Perrigo, Elinor to Boss, Hays*
Aug 1 1798	Perrigo, Rebecca to Weary, Joseph*
Jun 7 1786	Perrigoe, Elizabeth to Jones, Jacob*
Mar 12 1785	Perrigoe, Floria to Watts, Josias
Jun 30 1781	Perrigoe, Jemimah to Sindell, David
Jul 23 1788	Perrigoe, Rebbecca to Ogston, Lawrence*
Jan 14 1795	Perrigoe, Rebecca to Naylor, Samuel*
Jun 15 1785	Perrigoy, Charles to Gorsuch, Ruth
Jun 14 1786	Perrigoy, Elisha to Hall, Welthy*
Jul 4 1786	Perrigoy, Hellena to Price, Nehemiah*
Aug 11 1795	Perrigoy, James to Gorsuch, Ruth*
Apr 27 1785	Perrigoy, Joseph to Gorsuch, Mary
Oct 13 1786	Perrigoy, Joseph to Green, Susannah*
Nov 14 1797	Perrigoy, Rebecca to Stansbury, Daniel
Jun 17 1795	Perrigoy, Sarah to Weary, Thomas*
Sep 28 1793	Perry, Andrew to Murray, Martha*
Mar 27 1798	Perry, Ann to Cavill, John*
Jul 11 1779	Perry, Ann to Kannady, John
Nov 3 1798	Perry, Anne to Hunby, John*
Nov 4 1783	Perry, John to Hoffman, Barbara*
May 20 1779	Perry, John to Murphy, Mary
Aug 30 1797	Perry, Martha to Skeeman, Henry*
Dec 27 1797	Perry, Peter to Henderson, Phebe*
Oct 6 1789	Perry, Richard to Thomas, Sophia*
Jun 9 1798	Perry, Samuel to Langwall, Mary*
Apr 1 1790	Perry, Sarah to Quay, John
Sep 19 1797	Perton, Catharine to Toner, Jacob*
Oct 12 1784	Peshaw, Joseph to Grainger, Ann*
Mar 27 1789	Pest, Daniel to Barkley, Isabella*
Dec 31 1791	Peterkin, Rosannah to Loe, George
May 2 1785	Peterkin, Sarah to Ennis, Joshua

Nov	7	1794	Peters, Conrod to Haile, Lydia*
Nov	3	1779	Peters, Daniel to Seaboreng, Margaret
May	16	1781	Peters, Daniel to Shriver, Elizabeth*
Sep	22	1798	Peters, Dorothy to Weston, Guy*
Dec	16	1780	Peters, Frances to Cowden, John*
Mar	25	1796	Peters, George to Tremble, Polly*
Sep	4	1783	Peters, Henry to Castle, Mary*
Apr	28	1796	Peters, John to Healds, Phebe*
Jan	27	1791	Peters, John to Steitz, Mary*
Nov	28	1795	Peters, Samuel to Stevenson, Mary*
Oct	29	1783	Peters, Thomas to Johnson, Rebecca
Jun	30	1794	Peterson, Ann to Hoffer, John*
Aug	27	1795	Peterson, Eve to Button, George*
Oct	13	1798	Peterson, Lawrence to Cousins, Mary*
Aug	9	1783	Petteric, James to Walker, Jane
Apr	23	1793	Petticoat, James to Bell, Mary*
Dec	31	1793	Petticoat, Pleasant to Elder, Michael*
Jan	2	1786	Petty, John to Fauster, Margery*
Mar	25	1794	Pewley, Paul to Ross, Mary*
Jan	7	1790	Phalan, Jepe to Dean, Lydia*
Jul	21	1781	Phehraat, Geo. Henry to Plock, Elizabeth*
Apr	24	1793	Phell, William to Jackson, Elizabeth*
Sep	28	1784	Phelps, Martha to Mackelfresh, Thomas
Dec	31	1796	Phenie, Margaret to Strike, Nicholas*
Dec	11	1790	Phields, Dorothy to Giles, Samuel*
Jan	7	1784	Phields, Elizabeth to Hodg, Joseph*
Sep	5	1792	Phile, Charles to Hershberger, Catherine
Feb	11	1793	Phile, Mary to McBride, Roger
Jun	17	1784	Philips, Henrietta to Talbott, John*
Apr	1	1797	Philips, James to Barnes, Elizabeth
Apr	9	1794	Philips, John to McAllister, Elizabeth*
May	12	1785	Philips, Lucy to Parks, Thomas*
Sep	19	1795	Philips, Nancy to Ponoiby, Thomas*
Apr	17	1795	Philips, Nathan to Clarke, Elizabeth*
Dec	31	1789	Philips, Parker to Jacob, Anna*
Apr	2	1789	Philips, Patience to Wages, Luke*
Apr	8	1797	Philips, Priscilla to Donaldson, John*
Sep	3	1796	Philips, Samuel to Jones, Mary*
Oct	9	1778	Philips, Samuel to Steel, Mary*
Dec	5	1789	Philips, Thomas to Welsh, Margaret*
Nov	14	1797	Philips, Vachel to Younger, Elizabeth*
Oct	28	1795	Philips, William to Younger, Nancy*
May	16	1794	Philling, Mary M. to Keifle, Nicholas*
May	5	1796	Phillipe, Joseph to Boulay, Sophia*
Jan	22	1791	Phillips, James to Frizzel, Catherine*
Jan	5	1782	Phillips, Mary to Bennett, George*
Feb	3	1792	Phillips, Patsy to Cole, Elijah
Jul	27	1793	Phillips, Samuel to Harris, Roseanah*
Nov	16	1796	Philpot, Bryan to Johnson, Elizabeth*
Sep	17	1783	Philpott, Mary to Moher, Thomas Jr.*
Mar	26	1783	Philpott, Mary to Usher, Thomas Jr.
Dec	15	1796	Philt, Matthew to McBraherty, Margaret*
Mar	1	1798	Phipps, Austin to Stansbury, Elizabeth*
Sep	22	1785	Pian, Catharine to Bower, Conrad
Aug	8	1792	Pichaven, Jonathan to Sarter, Ellinor
Dec	26	1796	Pickard, William to Jackson, Mary*

Nov 24 1787	Pickerin, Peter to Hook, Elizabeth
Oct 2 1795	Pickersgill, John to Young, Mariah*
May 20 1779	Picket, Mary to Allen, Robert
Feb 2 1788	Picket, Rebecca to Barney, Joseph Bosley*
Oct 15 1783	Pickett, Blanche to Brotherton, Thomas
Oct 14 1783	Pickett, Blanche to Brotherton, Thomas*
Jul 23 1779	Pickett, Elizabeth to Simpson, Walter*
Mar 29 1783	Pickett, Mary to Waten, David
Aug 30 1784	Pickett, Susannah to Cullison, Jesse Stansbury
Dec 13 1777	Pickett, William to Deaver, Jemima*
Mar 23 1790	Pidden, Thomas to Brown, Priscilla*
Jan 7 1794	Pierce, Ann to Poole, John Whipps*
Oct 7 1779	Pierce, Charles to Smith, Deborah*
Oct 6 1790	Pierce, Deborah to Deaver, Richard*
Aug 6 1789	Pierce, Humphrey to Williamson, Ann*
Jun 11 1794	Pierce, Israel to Barton, Lettisha*
Aug 9 1792	Pierce, James Logan to Moloney, Ann*
Dec 27 1798	Pierce, Joseph to Cabler, Mary
Oct 22 1792	Pierpoint, Benedict to Griffith, Milky*
Sep 24 1783	Pierpoint, Henry to Randall, Sissin*
Oct 20 1779	Pierpoint, John to Hush, Mary
May 26 1783	Pierson, Bridget to Kennedy, John*
Jan 9 1788	Pigman, Joseph Waters to Hood, Ruth
May 13 1796	Pike, Daniel to Nixon, Hetty*
Jan 9 1794	Pike, James to Butler, Alice*
Feb 26 1782	Pile, Hannah to McCoy, Robert
May 9 1795	Pilkington, Mary to Purse, Thomas*
Dec 24 1796	Pillerin, Marie Rose to Rossinot, Michael*
May 24 1785	Pilling, Jonathan to Keys, Margaret*
Oct 1 1792	Pinbarton, Ruth to Gosnell, Greenberry*
Feb 3 1778	Pindell, Catharina to Bond, Edward*
Aug 29 1785	Pindell, Eleanor to Covenhoon, William*
Aug 6 1791	Pindell, John Larkin to Louderman, Susannah*
May 2 1781	Pindell, Philip to Mason, Ann*
Dec 13 1787	Pindell, Sarah to Bond, Christopher*
Jun 30 1790	Pindell, Thomas to Gorsuch, Margaret*
Oct 23 1781	Pindle, Philip to Ashman, Mary*
Oct 11 1797	Pine, Thomas to Cremore, Susannah*
May 21 1795	Pineau, Anne to Ducatel, Edna*
May 20 1784	Pines, William to Carback, Temperance*
Dec 7 1797	Pinfield, Ann to Rhodes, Andrew*
Dec 26 1785	Pingle, Sarah to Smith, Frederick
Oct 21 1779	Pinlater, Alexander to Smith, Mary*
Jan 10 1792	Pinnell, John to Saunders, Ann*
Jan 5 1793	Pinson, Mary to Drinan, Thomas*
Mar 8 1794	Pintes, James to Burgess, Comfort*
Mar 3 1791	Piper, Eleanor to Peck, John*
Mar 8 1797	Piper, Grace to Johnson, William*
Sep 18 1798	Pipperman, Anthony to Clayton, Mary*
Jul 18 1795	Pitch, James to Butler, Elizabeth*
Jul 27 1793	Pitcher, Hannah to Church, Samuel*
Dec 3 1796	Pitcher, Mary to Treakle, James*
Sep 27 1792	Pitcher, Sarah to McCarty, Cornelius*
Mar 29 1785	Pithington, Thomas to Workman, Mary
Jan 15 1794	Pitt, Elizabeth to McMyer, John*
Oct 8 1783	Pitt, George to Punteney, Rosanna

Nov 30 1797	Pittengill, James to Green, Rebecca
Feb 11 1795	Pitts, Henrietta to Price, William*
Jun 2 1789	Pitts, Lewis to Cole, Sarah*
Nov 7 1778	Pitts, Sarah to All, Benjamin*
Sep 26 1794	Place, John to Herbert, Mary*
Sep 19 1797	Placide, Paul to Duvernous, Louise*
Nov 25 1783	Plackroot, Catharine to Mowlon, John*
Apr 19 1794	Plankett, Elizabeth to Moore, James*
Aug 7 1790	Pleasants, James to Brooke, Deborah*
Sep 11 1795	Plishow, Nicholas to Hawkins, Rebecca*
Jul 21 1781	Plock, Elizabeth to Phehraat, Geo. Henry*
Mar 31 1791	Plowman, Ann to Johnson, Edward*
Dec 12 1781	Plowman, Edward to Fresh, Catherine*
Oct 27 1797	Plowman, Jonathan to Fesset, Jemima*
Jan 21 1785	Plowman, Jonathan to Loveall, Hannah*
Dec 31 1788	Plowman, Richard to Kelly, Ruth*
Mar 8 1797	Plowman, Ruth to Loveall, Zachariah
Apr 12 1790	Pluch, Andrew to Mitchell, Elizabeth*
Sep 9 1798	Plueburn, Mary to Dunning, James*
Sep 19 1795	Plumb, Elizabeth to Butcher, Bartholomew*
Jan 13 1796	Plumber, Charles to Hendricks, Jane*
Jan 7 1783	Pocock, Ann to Pocock, James*
Apr 18 1788	Pocock, Elizabeth to Gordon, William
Aug 1 1795	Pocock, George Adwell to Liston, Ann*
Feb 4 1782	Pocock, James to Fugate, Ann
Jan 7 1783	Pocock, James to Pocock, Ann*
Nov 5 1788	Pocock, John to Isgrig, Temperance*
Nov 18 1784	Pocock, Kasenhappuck to Biddison, Mashack
May 22 1783	Pocock, Mary to Fugate, Martin*
May 4 1785	Pocok, James to Biddison, Rebecca
May 28 1784	Poddewang, Peggy to Ford, Romman*
Jan 2 1796	Poe, Jane to Laryou, Peter*
Jan 24 1786	Poe, Jane to Thompson, Alexander*
Mar 12 1791	Poe, Mary to Thompson, William*
Jul 23 1790	Pogue, James to McDonah, Elizabeth*
Feb 24 1789	Pogue, Jane to Slappy, Jacob*
Nov 9 1796	Polk, David to Cooper, Margaret*
Feb 7 1793	Pollock, Sarah to Heathrington, Thomas*
Mar 24 1798	Pollock, Susannah to Jordon, Hugh*
Jul 25 1789	Pomp, Catherine to Hilderbrant, Jacob
Sep 19 1795	Ponoiby, Thomas to Philips, Nancy*
Dec 31 1791	Pontany, Elizabeth to Whiffing, Thomas*
Dec 31 1788	Pontenay, Ann to Rea, William
Oct 18 1798	Pontenay, James to Wood, Achsah*
Jun 28 1791	Pontenay, Sarah to Mucklevain, Alexander*
Jul 30 1779	Ponteniey, Sarah to Forrester, Alexander*
Jan 10 1789	Poole, Barbara to Wages, James
Sep 30 1795	Poole, Benjamin to Goslin, Mary*
May 20 1782	Poole, Hannah to Wilson, Joseph
Jan 19 1778	Poole, Henrietta to Whips, Samuel*
Jan 7 1794	Poole, John Whipps to Pierce, Ann*
Mar 16 1781	Poole, Minah to Eaden, Robert
Mar 11 1779	Poole, Sarah to Thomas, William
Aug 15 1785	Pope, John to Reterine, Catharine*
Aug 3 1782	Porce, Frs. to Celiston, Martha
Feb 19 1785	Poreura, Mara Rose to Delislle, Hillaire*

Nov 13 1779	Porine, Jane to Griffith, Kinsey*
May 16 1786	Porter, Airey to Shook, John*
Aug 13 1794	Porter, Alexis to Parrish, Honour*
Jan 9 1790	Porter, Amana to Kirby, John*
Mar 30 1779	Porter, Amaner to Gladman, Michael*
Mar 23 1796	Porter, Ann to Evans, Francis*
Aug 19 1795	Porter, Archibald to Baughman, Susannah*
Jan 30 1794	Porter, Caleb to Hudson, Priscilla*
Mar 8 1778	Porter, Caroline to Gibson, Thomas*
Oct 28 1797	Porter, Catharine to Lewis, William*
Dec 16 1794	Porter, Catherine to Lindsay, Michael*
Feb 24 1778	Porter, Delila to Babbs, James*
Jan 19 1798	Porter, Elijah to Spear, Nancy*
Nov 24 1790	Porter, Elizabeth to Clark, Elisha
Mar 2 1785	Porter, Elizabeth to Patridge, Danberry Buckler*
Dec 20 1793	Porter, Greenbury to Stocksdale, Amelia*
May 2 1782	Porter, James to Barns, Ann*
Feb 2 1798	Porter, John to Sexton, Philis
Aug 5 1797	Porter, Kettuel to Hall, Henry*
Jan 16 1795	Porter, Lewis to Brown, Catharine*
Apr 3 1795	Porter, Margaret to Perine, Simon*
Dec 10 1793	Porter, Mary to Askew, Jonathan*
Feb 18 1794	Porter, Mary to Dorsey, David*
Jan 31 1784	Porter, Mary to Leatherwood, Thomas*
Oct 10 1795	Porter, Mary to Parrish, Benjamin*
Aug 27 1784	Porter, Nathaniel to Mason, Rebecca
May 1 1798	Porter, Peregrine to Raven, Mary*
Oct 1 1798	Porter, Philis to Martin, Charles*
Oct 29 1791	Porter, Providence to Hudson, Edward*
Dec 19 1782	Porter, Rachel to Frizzel, Absalom*
Nov 20 1798	Porter, Rebecca to Brown, Dennis*
Dec 8 1798	Porter, Rebecca to Stone, Henry*
Dec 16 1793	Porter, Robert to Buck, Susanna*
Jan 31 1798	Porter, Shadrack to Banks, Prudence*
Feb 14 1795	Porter, Susannah to Randall, Brice*
Nov 7 1788	Porter, Tabitha to Gardiner, William*
Aug 28 1783	Post, Elizabeth to Heninger, John*
Jan 6 1782	Potter, Andrew to Kain, Mariah*
Jul 8 1790	Potter, Catherine to Miflin, James*
Jul 4 1798	Potter, Charlotte to Forney, Nicholas*
Dec 3 1795	Potter, John to Snider, Kitty*
Dec 24 1792	Potter, Margaret to Davis, Kiddwallader*
Sep 4 1786	Poucher, Lona to Lonkert, Henry*
Oct 7 1794	Powel, Peter to Foster, Elizabeth*
Nov 3 1783	Powell, Richard to Deffin, Delila*
Nov 14 1781	Powell, Susanna to Evans, William
Dec 11 1790	Powell, Thomas to Doyle, Margaret*
Nov 24 1794	Powers, Barnet to Bennet, Rachel*
Oct 1 1796	Powers, Rachel to Dresser, Alfred*
Jun 11 1791	Pratt, Frederick to McCarty, Fanriy*
Jan 12 1791	Pratt, James to Shaw, Sarah*
Jan 16 1798	Pratt, Sally to Luttig, John C.*
Apr 18 1798	Pratt, Sarah to Gilberthorp, Francis*
Apr 2 1778	Prentice, Jane to Morgan, John*
Mar 8 1784	Presbury, Frances to Presbury, Joseph*
Jul 27 1786	Presbury, George Gould to Furgason, Elizabeth

May 28 1783	Presbury, George Gouldth. to Lee, Priscilla
Jan 29 1783	Presbury, Hannah to Morford, Thomas*
Mar 8 1784	Presbury, Joseph to Presbury, Frances*
Mar 24 1781	Presbury, Martha Goldsmith to Anderson, George*
Nov 11 1787	Presbury, Mary to Day, Edward
Aug 29 1797	Presbury, Walter to Galloway, Mary
Dec 28 1790	Preschoe, Nancy to Mulla, Thomas
Dec 2 1784	Presstman, Polly to McCauslind, Marcus*
Sep 13 1784	Presston, John Diamond to Atherton, Rebecca*
Mar 9 1797	Prestman, Thomas to Kelly, Phebe*
Jan 23 1795	Preston, Clementine to Dorsey, Samuel*
Mar 8 1785	Price, Catharine to Parlett, Joshua*
Jun 30 1797	Price, Elizabeth to Buck, William*
Mar 9 1797	Price, Elizabeth to Buldger, Henry*
Oct 22 1791	Price, Elizabeth to Gorsuch, John*
Aug 23 1791	Price, Elizabeth to Moales, Nicholas*
Sep 5 1795	Price, Ellin to Buster, John*
May 4 1778	Price, Hatridge to Cole, Mordecai*
Apr 27 1796	Price, Hezekiah to Bond, Leah*
Mar 8 1793	Price, Honor to Brown, Richard
Sep 10 1779	Price, James to Fling, Margaret*
Jun 16 1795	Price, James to Lewis, Elizabeth*
Apr 1 1797	Price, John to Sanderson, Sarah*
Jun 8 1797	Price, Joseph to Fisher, Hannah*
Jan 20 1784	Price, Joshua to Lemmon, Martha*
Jan 8 1793	Price, Mary to Ross, William Thomas*
Nov 13 1793	Price, Nancy to Loyd, Thomas*
Feb 16 1785	Price, Nathan to Thomas, Ruth*
Jul 4 1786	Price, Nehemiah to Perrigoy, Hellena*
Apr 22 1783	Price, Peter to Harget, Mary*
Apr 18 1789	Price, Rachel to Scott, Amos*
Sep 16 1795	Price, Richard to Evans, Mary*
Aug 12 1778	Price, Sarah to Wicks, Epenet*
Dec 26 1782	Price, Stephen to Rolls, Susannah*
Jul 27 1785	Price, Susannah to Bosley, John
Sep 11 1788	Price, William to Brown, Elizabeth*
Dec 8 1784	Price, William to Butler, Mary*
Feb 11 1795	Price, William to Pitts, Henrietta*
Oct 22 1783	Price, Zachariah to Richardson, Sarah*
Dec 17 1782	Priesstman, Sarah to Lemmon, Joshua*
Nov 11 1797	Priestman, Priscilla to Morrin, Paul*
Nov 30 1797	Primrose, Asbury to Summer, Mary
Aug 25 1785	Primrose, Isabel to McGlachan, William
Nov 28 1795	Primrose, Robert to Clement, Sidney*
Nov 13 1794	Prince, John to Towrell, Elizabeth*
Nov 9 1785	Pringle, James to Forsythe, Sarah
Jun 11 1794	Pringle, Mark to Russell, Frances*
Jul 6 1797	Pringle, Mark to Stith, Lucy*
Oct 9 1783	Prister, Valentine to Ream, Mary*
May 5 1785	Pritchard, Jane to Bennurman, John*
Oct 21 1795	Pritchard, William to Flinn, Eliza*
Jan 8 1794	Procter, Elizabeth to Marshall, Joseph*
Feb 19 1778	Proctor, Catherine to Allen, Richard*
Dec 2 1796	Proctor, Hugh to Grooen, Priscilla*
Jul 14 1798	Proctor, Isaiah to Chaney, Margaret*
Dec 7 1796	Proctor, Mary to Stansbury, John E.*

Sep 11 1790	Pross, Jacob to Murphy, Rachael
Oct 26 1782	Prosser, Charles to Colegate, Elizabeth*
Oct 16 1784	Prout, Richard to Hannah (negroes)
Mar 13 1793	Prout, William to Slater, Sarah*
Aug 13 1793	Prudheimme, John Baptiste to Gledine, Mary*
Aug 13 1782	Pruet, Sylvester to Dicks, Ann*
Sep 8 1784	Prust, Mary to Robinson, Elihu*
May 29 1784	Ptoxall, Emey to Downey, John*
Nov 26 1794	Pue, Ann to West, Stephen*
Sep 15 1798	Pugh, Jacob to Morgan, Elizabeth*
Aug 4 1778	Pulamas, Elizabeth, to Litzinger, George*
Aug 2 1783	Pumesho, Joseph to Landre, Mary*
Jul 1 1795	Pumphrey, Achsah to Walker, William*
Jun 1 1791	Pumphrey, Ann to Steward, David*
Nov 20 1787	Pumphrey, Catherine to Hawkins, Samuel*
Oct 8 1796	Pumphrey, Cockey to Cromwell, Margaret*
Oct 1 1795	Pumphrey, Frederick to Smick, Polly*
Oct 22 1793	Pumphrey, Joseph to Steward, Sarah*
Mar 26 1785	Pumphrey, Joshua to Stewart, Dinah
Mar 21 1782	Pumphrey, Margaret to Cromwell, Oliver*
Jul 26 1798	Pumphrey, Mary to McNeir, John B.*
Apr 25 1778	Pumphrey, Rachel to Stansbury, Emanuel*
Dec 24 1798	Pumphrey, Warfield to Williams, Elizabeth*
Sep 18 1782	Pumphrey, William to Cromwell, Mary
Feb 1 1785	Puntaney, Margaret to Ogston, Henry*
Dec 7 1790	Puntany, Mary to Jeffery, William*
May 6 1778	Puntenay, Susannah to Swann, Samuel*
Oct 8 1783	Punteney, Rosanna to Pitt, George
Dec 4 1778	Puntney, Elinor to Hush, Conrod*
Jun 30 1784	Puntney, Rachel to Armor, William*
Oct 21 1778	Puntoney, Edward to Read, Elizabeth*
Sep 10 1798	Purce, Levy to Williamson, Elizabeth*
Jan 7 1797	Purdin, Michael to Kinsly, Alice*
Aug 22 1795	Purdon, William to Esseck, Susannah*
Feb 11 1796	Purle, Mary to Calwell, John*
May 9 1795	Purse, Thomas to Pilkington, Mary*
Oct 13 1798	Pursile, Mary to Ryan, James*
Aug 4 1796	Purtel, Robert to Sitler, Catharine*
Feb 19 1781	Pye, James to Bangham, Urith*
Jan 9 1778	Pyeday, Thomas to Roberts, Eleanor*
May 28 1783	Pyne, John to Brown, Mary*
Dec 31 1792	Quail, Robert to Rainkin, Agness*
Jul 13 1778	Quarterman, Mary to Marshall, Isaac*
Apr 1 1790	Quay, John to Perry, Sarah
Apr 7 1794	Quay, Sarah to Stubbs, John*
Apr 25 1778	Quay, Susannah to Fenn, William*
Nov 7 1795	Quay, William to Burk, Nancy*
Nov 11 1797	Quay, William to McKubbin, Sarah*
Apr 14 1798	Quesany, John to Wipple, Eliza*
Oct 27 1798	Quidane, Nancy to Ellirt, James*
Jun 12 1781	Quilland, Milly to Barker, Joseph*
Oct 19 1796	Quinlan, Mary to Turner, John*
Jan 30 1790	Quinland, Edmund to Cox, Jane*
Nov 26 1787	Quinley, William to Casey, Mary*
Nov 30 1785	Raborg, Andrew to York, Sarah
Jan 25 1788	Raborg, Michael to Lent, Catherine*

Aug 7 1798	Raboy, Rachel R. to Wagmer, Jacob*
Sep 15 1779	Raby, Richard to Denton, Elizabeth*
Oct 8 1794	Racine, Daniel to Gentille, Hamot Perry*
Nov 27 1798	Rackle, Thomas to Chambers, Mary*
Nov 5 1784	Radley, Peggy to Shaffer, Jacob
Nov 22 1779	Rady, Ann to Huety, Vachel
Jun 14 1790	Rady, Joshua to Hughes, Elizabeth
Jan 24 1797	Ragoin, Johanna to Lyons, Joohn*
Sep 16 1783	Rainer, Mary to Coleman, John
Apr 25 1793	Rainer, William to Stigors, Elizabeth*
Dec 31 1792	Rainkin, Agness to Quail, Robert*
Mar 1 1779	Randall, Aquilla to Cord, Rebecca*
Feb 14 1795	Randall, Brice to Porter, Susannah*
Jan 8 1784	Randall, Catherine to Patridge, Robert*
Jan 22 1785	Randall, Delilah to Davis, Ichabod*
Jul 5 1791	Randall, Eleanor to Chord, Henry
Sep 30 1793	Randall, Ellin to Belt, Joseph*
Jul 24 1798	Randall, Hannah to Norman, John*
Jun 22 1796	Randall, Israel to Lee, Delilah*
Sep 20 1796	Randall, John to Willess, Ann*
Jun 17 1795	Randall, Margaret to Dilworth, Amos*
Nov 1 1793	Randall, Mary to Rowles, Jacob*
Nov 1 1793	Randall, Mary to Tipton, Solomon*
Oct 16 1790	Randall, Nathan to Davis, Ruth*
Dec 8 1787	Randall, Rebecca to Hayworth, Jonathan*
Oct 14 1786	Randall, Ruth to Cramblet, Michael*
Dec 13 1794	Randall, Sarah to Belt, Merryman*
Sep 24 1783	Randall, Sissin to Pierpoint, Henry*
Jul 29 1797	Randall, Susanna to Mulhern, Bernard*
Feb 9 1785	Randell, Cassandra to Gassaway, Nicholas*
Nov 25 1795	Randell, Milcah to Barlow, John*
Aug 27 1785	Randell, Nancy to Hobbs, Joseph
Jul 29 1786	Randell, Rebecca to Culverwell, Richard
Jul 5 1788	Randell, Roger to Burgess, Elizabeth*
Nov 20 1784	Randell, Sophia to Mallet, William*
Nov 20 1790	Randell, Susannah to Lindenberger, Charles*
Nov 29 1792	Randell, William to James, Sarah*
Jul 31 1790	Raner, Samuel to Watts, Rachael*
Aug 10 1779	Ranford, Sarah to Sanders, Edward*
Nov 2 1797	Rankin, Hugh to Hughes, Margaret*
Feb 27 1797	Ransford, Elizabeth to McGwinn, William*
Sep 18 1793	Ranty, Catharine to Campbell, Robert*
Jun 29 1798	Rapp, Ann Catharine to Bitton, Thomas S.*
Aug 8 1796	Rapp, Dederick to Tiche, Lend*
Jul 19 1798	Rapp, Juliet Francisia to West, Joel*
May 7 1796	Rappold, Mary to Mariner, Joseph*
Oct 6 1792	Rardin, William to Miller, Rachel
May 9 1796	Rareton, Margaret to Holliday, John*
Nov 5 1790	Ratcliff, Catherine to Dean, Barney
Nov 19 1783	Ratcliff, Elizabeth to Davis, Gilbert
Mar 6 1798	Ratcliff, Joseph to Loyd, Mary
Mar 20 1782	Ratcliff, Susannah to Davis, Robert
Oct 21 1794	Ratlief, Thomas to Cannon, Elizabeth*
May 6 1797	Rattig, Mary to O'Mara, Patrick*
Sep 5 1778	Ravelling, Ann to Hall, Thomas*
Jan 1 1795	Raven, Elizabeth to Joyce, Elisha*

May 1 1798	Raven, Mary to Porter, Peregrine*
Aug 9 1783	Rawlings, Adam to Packett, Elizabeth
Jan 2 1781	Rawlings, Elizabeth to Brown, Hugh*
May 30 1798	Rawlings, Isaac to Warrington, Ann*
Aug 25 1797	Rawlings, Jane to Carback, John*
Nov 4 1778	Rawlings, Mary to Williams, Charles*
Nov 4 1783	Rawlins, Elizabeth to Biddison, Daniel*
Aug 29 1793	Rawlins, John to Smith, Margaret*
Feb 9 1792	Rawlins, Sarah to Sellman, Johnzee
May 10 1779	Rawson, William to Jewell, Barbara*
Jul 7 1798	Ray, Benjamin to Nicoll, Precilla
Sep 24 1789	Ray, Jane to Dunwick, Isaac*
Apr 6 1798	Raynaud, Francis R.B. to Dulany, Mary*
Sep 26 1778	Rayner, Benjamin to Hodges, Ann*
Oct 30 1783	Raynor, John to Watts, Rachael
Oct 9 1793	Rea, Sarah to King, Samuel*
Nov 5 1792	Rea, William to Gardiner, Mary*
Dec 31 1788	Rea, William to Pontenay, Ann
Mar 3 1791	Read, Ann to Stryer, George*
May 12 1793	Read, Elinor to McCoy, George*
Oct 21 1778	Read, Elizabeth to Puntoney, Edward*
Nov 6 1790	Read, George to Lane, Deriah*
Oct 20 1789	Read, Jacob to Russell, Elizabeth
Nov 18 1779	Read, John to Rolam, Martha*
Feb 24 1789	Read, Joseph to Smith, Agness
Apr 30 1796	Read, Larkin to Perrigo, Edith*
Mar 16 1786	Read, Thomas to McChesie, Elizabeth*
Dec 23 1794	Reader, Catharine to Smith, Henry John*
Aug 27 1798	Reading, Margaret to Clashe, Patrick*
Mar 9 1797	Ready, Samuel to Aldridge, Mary*
Sep 23 1790	Reafew, Mary to Steinbeck, John George*
Oct 9 1783	Ream, Mary to Prister, Valentine*
Nov 18 1797	Reams, Elizabeth to Taylor, James*
Jul 10 1797	Reaner, Uli to Spencer, Stephen*
Aug 20 1793	Rear, Catherine to Loyd, John*
Oct 9 1779	Reardon, Mary to Stevens, John*
May 7 1785	Reaugh, John to Lowry, Mary
Jun 11 1778	Reddick, James to Chapline, Elizabeth*
Mar 4 1797	Reding, Sarah to Mason, John*
Jun 21 1793	Redstone, Ann to Barneyfish, Gilbert
Oct 22 1782	Reece, Sarah to Brown, Richard*
Mar 15 1794	Reed, Eleanor to Wells, Luke*
Apr 16 1795	Reed, Elizabeth to Volmar, John*
May 28 1778	Reed, Hannah to Cassidy, Patrick*
Nov 28 1792	Reed, Hugh to Elfry, Mary*
Dec 14 1791	Reed, James to Burnham, Ann*
Aug 28 1779	Reed, John to Johnson, Mary*
Aug 30 1796	Reed, John to Peacock, Mary*
Jan 3 1794	Reed, Lydia to Carpenter, Isaac*
Oct 19 1795	Reed, Mary to Newman, Jacob*
May 20 1793	Reed, Matthew to Lucas, Elizabeth*
Sep 16 1796	Reed, Peggy to Miller, John*
Jul 23 1796	Reed, Peter to Caton, Jane*
Nov 6 1797	Reed, Sally to Conley, Philip*
Mar 31 1796	Reemey, Tacy to Baker, Ephraim*
Nov 9 1780	Rees, Sarah to Lavely, George*

Mar 7 1778	Reese, Ann to Reese, George*
Jul 10 1790	Reese, Catharine to Ward, Thomas*
Jul 28 1790	Reese, Daniel to Bond, Elizabeth*
Feb 20 1784	Reese, George to Eaglestone, Elizabeth*
Mar 22 1791	Reese, George to Frazier, Lilly*
Mar 7 1778	Reese, George to Reese, Ann*
May 19 1791	Reese, Henry to Burtell, Mary*
Oct 18 1783	Reese, John to Kelly, Elinor*
Sep 26 1789	Reese, John to Sheens, Mary*
Jul 27 1798	Reese, Joseph to Jervis, Elizabeth*
Mar 25 1796	Reese, Lilly to Mynch, Joseph*
Jan 4 1798	Reese, Margaret to Ogeir, John*
Nov 11 1784	Reese, Margaret to Tanner, Isaac
Apr 15 1786	Reese, Mary to Clarke, William*
Nov 26 1794	Reese, Mary to Fowler, Samuel*
Nov 17 1783	Reese, William to Hively, Elizabeth*
May 2 1793	Reeves, Anthony to McKinzie, Elizabeth*
Sep 17 1792	Reeves, George to Miller, Margaret
Jul 6 1795	Reeves, Margaret to Holmes, Anthony*
Feb 9 1791	Reeves, Richard to Ore, Margaret*
Jun 5 1793	Reeves, Sarah to Mijors, John*
Apr 22 1795	Reeves, William to Grate, Abigail*
Jun 12 1779	Regan, Elizabeth to Lynch, William
Nov 4 1796	Regan, Lydia to Blaking, John*
Aug 29 1783	Reid, Emmanuel to Elliott, Precilla*
Apr 12 1790	Reid, James to Unich, Eleanor*
Oct 11 1786	Reid, John G. to Allen, Mary
Jun 8 1790	Reid, Nelson to Stiger, Nancy*
Apr 14 1781	Reighnor, Sarah to Joyce, Zachariah
Nov 11 1797	Reiley, Mary to Wolf, Michael*
Sep 8 1797	Reily, Elizabeth to Jackson, Thomas*
Jul 3 1797	Reily, John to Lundragan, Mary*
Jun 27 1796	Reily, John to Scanllon, Lucy*
Dec 25 1794	Reily, William to Foose, Mary*
May 1 1793	Reinhart, Philip to Richardson, Susannah*
Jan 7 1790	Reinicker, Conrad to Fete, Eve*
Mar 10 1791	Reinicker, Nancy to Fite, Jacob*
Apr 13 1790	Reith, Margaret to Hamilton, John*
Jun 12 1794	Remage, Nicholas to Divirce, Ann
Jan 6 1798	Remage, Rachel to Sylvester, George*
Aug 28 1798	Renaud, Ariana to Peniston, Samuel*
Aug 25 1796	Renaud, John to Finagan, Ariana*
Nov 11 1785	Rennals, Monacha to Abraham, John
Apr 29 1786	Rennehan, Ann to Taylor, Hymmers Henry*
Jul 18 1782	Renner, Leonard to Moire, Catherine*
Sep 5 1782	Reno, Mary to Brigs, John*
Dec 21 1793	Renous, Trope to Minci, Detestemona*
Oct 8 1795	Renshaw, Deborah to Davis, Samuel*
Jan 23 1796	Renshaw, James to Cole, Eleanor
Nov 11 1788	Renshaw, Martin to Jones, Magdaline*
Oct 3 1795	Renshaw, Martin to Sark, Jane*
Mar 21 1784	Renshaw, Philip to German, Ruth*
Jun 2 1794	Renuleau, Marie Martha to Calman, Joseph*
Jun 23 1797	Reo, Peter to De Boydene, Marie*
Nov 30 1797	Resensteel, George Jr. to White, Barbara*
Aug 15 1785	Reterine, Catharine to Pope, John*

May 16 1778	Rettig, Christian to Thomas, Mary*
Nov 3 1796	Revena, Lidia to Wilmer, James*
Apr 2 1784	Reves, Richard to West, Margaret*
Jul 14 1794	Rew, James to Ashmore, Nancy*
Mar 26 1796	Rey, Charles to Beaufire, Elizabeth*
Nov 27 1785	Reyney, Magaret to Murray, James
Apr 13 1785	Reynolds, Benedict to Harmon, Mary*
Nov 5 1794	Reynolds, Elsey to Sadler, Joseph*
Jun 22 1791	Reynolds, Hetty to Forrester, William*
May 17 1793	Reynolds, James to Johnson, Sarah*
Oct 28 1796	Reynolds, John to Owings, Sarah*
Apr 20 1790	Reynolds, Lear to Moor, Robert*
Jun 28 1794	Reynolds, Rebecca to Harman, Andrew*
Jun 1 1778	Reynolds, Robert to Corty, Mary*
Jul 20 1791	Reynolds, Robert to Floyd, Elizabeth*
Jul 27 1785	Reynolds, Tobias to Griffith, Sarah*
Jan 13 1783	Rhea, Joseph to Conn, Elizabeth*
Oct 26 1779	Rheabottom, Thomas to Conden, Mary*
Feb 9 1796	Rhearns, Ann to Bailey, Amos*
Mar 28 1798	Rheem, William to Shartle, Susannah*
Oct 21 1778	Rheme, John to Smith, Elizabeth
Feb 9 1793	Rhode, George to Gorsuch, Mary*
Dec 7 1797	Rhodes, Andrew to Pinfield, Ann*
Mar 23 1793	Rhodes, Sarah to Coale, Charles C.*
Feb 1 1794	Rice, Bridget to Dunkin, William*
Oct 26 1794	Rice, James to Davenport, Elizabeth*
Feb 16 1788	Rice, Joseph to Gray, Ann
May 7 1791	Rice, Sarah to Bigger, Gilbert
Aug 15 1779	Richards, Isaac to Scar, Margaret*
Nov 13 1779	Richards, John to Gist, Sarah*
Jun 2 1797	Richards, Joseph to Barbine, Margaret*
Oct 25 1791	Richards, Joseph to Burgen, Ann*
Oct 5 1790	Richards, Margaret to Crisall, Peter*
Nov 30 1797	Richards, Nancy to Henwood, Robert*
Apr 7 1785	Richards, Nicholas to Parks, Rebeccah
Dec 19 1781	Richards, Richard to Brown, Ann*
Dec 11 1784	Richards, Rosa to Offert, Charles*
Jan 14 1783	Richards, Samuel to Murray, Polly*
Mar 15 1785	Richards, Sarah to Brown, Edwards
Nov 19 1778	Richards, William to Kirk, Mary*
Mar 21 1791	Richardson, Cloe to Key, David*
Dec 27 1794	Richardson, Elizabeth to De Carnass, Jasper*
Feb 18 1794	Richardson, Elizabeth to Johnson, Charles*
Aug 6 1794	Richardson, Elizabeth to Webster, William*
Nov 27 1789	Richardson, Francis to White, Elizabeth*
Jul 13 1778	Richardson, George to Burns, Bridget*
Aug 16 1796	Richardson, Hannah to Williams, James Pettingill*
Dec 31 1790	Richardson, James to Drane, Rachael*
Nov 11 1797	Richardson, James to Sullivan, Eleanor*
Jun 18 1794	Richardson, John to Hays, Mary*
Feb 8 1783	Richardson, John to Linch, Sarah*
Aug 11 1785	Richardson, John to Morman, Nancy*
Mar 26 1796	Richardson, Robert R. to Ridgely, Eliza
Jul 24 1793	Richardson, Robert to Moore, Mary*
Jan 19 1797	Richardson, Ruth to Moore, Thomas*
Oct 22 1783	Richardson, Sarah to Price, Zacchariah*

Sep 29 1784	Richardson, Sarah to Willks, Joseph*
May 1 1793	Richardson, Susannah to Reinhart, Philip*
Jul 30 1785	Richardson, Thomas to Botts, Elizabeth
Feb 12 1782	Richardson, Thomas to Standiford, Mary*
Oct 8 1795	Richardson, Vincent to Standiford, Pernelloper*
Jul 5 1783	Richardson, William to Tracey, Ann*
Jan 2 1782	Richmond, John to Mamabay, Eleanor*
Jul 1 1795	Ricker, Nicholas Augustine to Joffray, Mary Theresa*
Sep 1 1791	Ricketts, Benjamin to Forrester, Cassandra*
Nov 3 1784	Ricketts, Edward to Green, Millison*
Apr 21 1794	Ricketts, Hugh to Carr, Mary*
May 19 1783	Ricks, Barbary to Twooshears, George*
Jul 17 1797	Riddan, Mary Ann to Small, James*
Mar 10 1794	Riddell, James to Adams, Jane*
Mar 11 1786	Riddell, Robert to Hawksworth, Mary
Jul 1 1793	Ridden, George to Thompson, Eleanor*
Mar 28 1798	Riddle, Ann to Barton, William*
Jan 16 1796	Riddle, Eleanor to Wilson, William*
Oct 21 1793	Riddle, Elizabeth to McDoe, William*
Jan 5 1790	Riddle, Elizabeth to Mulholand, Charles*
Oct 6 1792	Riddle, John to Taylor, Ann
Apr 17 1797	Riddle, Patty to Rosenhazard, Casper*
Mar 22 1782	Riddle, Robert to McNeil, Mary
Feb 21 1795	Riddle, Sarah to Dicus, Jacob*
May 4 1779	Riddle, William to McKinsay, Charlotte*
Jul 4 1781	Riddy, Margaret to Elivil, Samuel*
Sep 27 1794	Ridenduer, Mary to Wilson, James*
Dec 9 1788	Ridenhour, Margaret to Rutter, Solomon*
Aug 9 1792	Rider, Benjamin to Burke, Charlotte*
Feb 11 1795	Rider, Elizabeth to Barker, John*
Aug 23 1794	Rider, Eve to Hainsworth, Aaron*
Dec 16 1794	Rider, Mary to Beach, William*
Oct 16 1786	Rider, Sarah to _____
Feb 26 1798	Ridgely, Ann to Hawley, Thomas
Jan 2 1778	Ridgely, Ann to Oram, Henry*
Nov 16 1797	Ridgely, Ann to Wilmon, William*
May 24 1783	Ridgely, Basil to Gaither, Actions*
Jan 21 1793	Ridgely, Beale to Dills, Sarah
Feb 17 1778	Ridgely, Belinda to Hancock, Stephen*
Jun 13 1798	Ridgely, Clarisa to Slugounene, Alexis*
Oct 30 1790	Ridgely, Deborah to Willson, William*
May 13 1782	Ridgely, Delilah to Robinson, O'Neill*
Feb 9 1793	Ridgely, Edward to Worthington, Martha
Jan 13 1784	Ridgely, Eleanor to Laming, Benjamin*
Mar 26 1796	Ridgely, Eliza to Richardson, Robert R.
Sep 29 1795	Ridgely, Elizabeth to Chadders, Robert*
Mar 5 1778	Ridgely, Elizabeth to Griffen, John*
Jan 18 1791	Ridgely, Elizabeth to Nennanis, Nathan
Sep 11 1794	Ridgely, Elizabeth to Young, Joseph*
Apr 7 1785	Ridgely, Harriot to Fish, Benjamin
Jan 15 1791	Ridgely, John to Emmitt, Mary
Jan 9 1796	Ridgely, Mary to Young, William*
Nov 4 1795	Ridgely, Mordecai to Johnson, Patience*
Dec 13 1798	Ridgely, Mordecai to Willmore, Mary*
Dec 29 1787	Ridgely, Nancy to Mosier, James*
Dec 1 1791	Ridgely, Rachel to Dorsey, George*

```
Jun 28 1783    Ridgely, Sarah to Gaither, Razin*
Mar 11 1786    Ridgely, Sarah to Nelson, Burgess
Jul  3 1790    Ridgely, Thomas to Bryan, Polton Sarah*
Feb 24 1783    Ridgely, William to Izzard, Elizabeth*
Mar  1 1779    Ridges, Jonathan to Elder, Elinor*
May 16 1795    Rie, Mary to Neal, Thomas*
Nov 27 1782    Riff, John to Moss, Elizabeth
Mar  8 1788    Riffett, Rachel to Barnaby, Elias
Jun  9 1796    Rigby, Robert to Robinson, Elizabeth*
Mar 11 1797    Riggen, Edmond to Coleman, Elizabeth*
Jul 23 1781    Riggs, Carline to Holland, Jacob*
Aug 12 1786    Right, Ann to Rosson, William*
Oct  9 1784    Right, Ruth to Stallings, John*
Sep 30 1795    Righter, Abraham to Outter, Catharine*
Sep 28 1785    Rigor, Henry to Lore, Barbara
Dec 15 1784    Rihn, Elizabeth to Brill, Frederick*
Sep 19 1797    Riland, Arthur to Gott, Elizabeth*
Nov  7 1795    Riley, Alice to Kilman, John*
Oct  7 1784    Riley, Benjamin to Dukehart, Sarah*
Nov 29 1797    Riley, Mary to Gorsuch, John*
Mar 28 1792    Riley, Nancy to Lee, James*
Jan  2 1783    Riley, Stephen to Hook, Mary*
Sep 28 1791    Riley, William to Hodghin, Barbara
Nov 14 1793    Rinaudet, Pierre Abraham to Gauterot, Anne*
May  1 1797    Rindley, John to Armstrong, Rachel*
Dec 15 1796    Riner, Sebastian to Witherholt, Euliana*
Oct 18 1794    Riney, John to Dunnaway, Nancy*
Feb  9 1795    Ringold, Thomas to Gittings, Mary*
Sep  6 1790    Ringrow, Aaron to Jones, Ann*
Dec 21 1798    Risley, Elizabeth to Shaw, John*
Mar 25 1793    Ristean, Ann to Cockey, Thomas Deye
Jan 21 1786    Risteau, Frances to Owings, Nicholas
Jan 22 1785    Risteau, John Talbott to Denny, Elizabeth*
May 19 1795    Risteau, Rebecca to Wells, Bazabel*
Oct 10 1783    Rister, Mary to Beckley, John*
Jul 23 1779    Rister, Sarah to Wyley, William
Oct 20 1790    Riston, Abraham to Hughes, Susannah*
Apr 17 1790    Riston, Margaret to Thomas, Benjamin*
Feb 21 1785    Ristun, Ann to Wheeler, Solomon*
Apr  8 1789    Ritcherson, Elizabeth to Chinnuth, William*
Dec  7 1785    Ritchie, William to Hooper, Patty
Dec 16 1785    Riter, Christian to Peron, Caterina*
Feb 21 1784    Ritler, John to Burk, Eleanor*
Apr 12 1782    Ritter, Caterena to Ebbert, John
Jan 14 1778    Ritter, Catharine to Hook, Rudolph*
Apr 10 1798    Ritter, Catharine to Sanford, Nicholas*
May  4 1779    Ritter, Henry to Mentin, Catarina*
Mar 29 1786    Ritter, John to McShroyan, Ann
Dec 10 1798    Ritter, Rebecca to Burton, Joseph
Apr 22 1791    Ritter, Richard to Key, Mary*
Oct 28 1786    Ritter, Thomas to Leaf, Elizabeth
Sep 28 1796    Rix, Elizabeth to Woolen, James*
Feb 10 1785    Rix, Robert to Hanley, Mary
Nov 17 1784    Roach, Mary to Burk, John*
Jan  3 1783    Roach, Michael to Bryan, Tabitha
Oct  1 1782    Roach, Thomas to Hendrickson, Mary*
```

Mar 1 1794	Road, Mary to Weller, Andrew*
Nov 27 1788	Roads, Andrew to Jones, Susanna*
Aug 2 1798	Roaker, Samuel to Jervis, Mary
Nov 23 1798	Roan, John to Robinson, Jane*
Dec 23 1791	Robb, John to Dunkin, Susannah*
Apr 14 1791	Robb, William to Garts, Elizabeth*
Jul 29 1795	Robberds, Susannah to Wells, Colin C.*
Sep 3 1779	Robbert, Mary to Tea, Michael
Oct 2 1793	Robbins, Roger to Freeland, Rebeccah*
Sep 24 1794	Roberson, George to Graves, Mary*
Nov 15 1794	Roberts, Adalaide to Mitchell, Lazarns*
Dec 17 1785	Roberts, Benjamin to Stansbury, Terry*
Sep 23 1779	Roberts, Clovander to Dixen, John*
Jan 9 1778	Roberts, Eleanor to Pyeday, Thomas*
Jan 11 1790	Roberts, Elizabeth to Bremner, George*
Apr 6 1779	Roberts, Elizabeth to Glynn, James*
Jul 25 1798	Roberts, George to Foster, Ann*
Oct 14 1789	Roberts, John to Orrick, Susannah*
Jul 9 1778	Roberts, Levy to Flood, Elizabeth*
Feb 28 1797	Roberts, Mary to Jones, John*
Jun 13 1795	Roberts, Owen to Pawson, Margaret*
Aug 11 1792	Roberts, Priscilla to Lee, William
Oct 23 1789	Roberts, Rachel to Garrettson, Thomas*
Apr 28 1794	Roberts, Richard to Johnson, Daphne*
Dec 14 1782	Roberts, Sarah to Lawrence, Jacob*
Feb 16 1792	Roberts, Thomas to Toole, Elizabeth*
Mar 19 1795	Robertson, Ann to Dawson, William*
Jun 29 1798	Robertson, John to Askew, Margaret*
Dec 16 1793	Robertson, John to Wilson, Mariah*
Aug 12 1794	Robertson, Joseph to Gray, Nancy*
Jul 23 1781	Robertson, Mary to Welsh, John*
Aug 16 1790	Robeson, Thomas to Denny, Hanny
Jan 26 1793	Robinson, Anne to Wilson, John*
Jan 28 1796	Robinson, Catharine to Jeffords, George*
Jun 22 1798	Robinson, Charlotte to Butler, John*
Sep 8 1784	Robinson, Elihu to Prust, Mary*
Feb 24 1778	Robinson, Elijah to Walker, Mary*
Oct 3 1783	Robinson, Elizabeth to Davis, Andrew*
May 9 1788	Robinson, Elizabeth to Hall, George
Jun 9 1796	Robinson, Elizabeth to Rigby, Robert*
Oct 9 1795	Robinson, Elizabeth to Yearly, Nathaniel*
Jan 23 1794	Robinson, Hannah to Turnbull, Andrew*
Apr 19 1778	Robinson, Harriott to Culbertson, William*
Feb 11 1795	Robinson, James to Lynch, Mary*
Sep 25 1783	Robinson, James to Nelson, Mary*
Oct 3 1792	Robinson, Jane to Cornmiller, Jacob*
Nov 23 1798	Robinson, Jane to Roan, John*
Sep 11 1793	Robinson, Jehannah to Mosher, Philip*
Oct 28 1790	Robinson, John to Greenfield, Joanna*
May 6 1797	Robinson, John to Holmes, Elizabeth*
May 20 1797	Robinson, John to Jordan, Mary*
Jun 22 1797	Robinson, John to Rothrock, Catharine*
Jun 28 1778	Robinson, Liba to Graham, William*
Nov 9 1797	Robinson, Lydia to Williams, John*
Dec 21 1782	Robinson, Margaret to Bowen, James*
Sep 23 1782	Robinson, Mary Ann to Brice, John*

```
Dec 24 1796    Robinson, Mary to Russort, Martin*
May 13 1782    Robinson, O'Neill to Ridgely, Delilah*
May 31 1783    Robinson, Richard to Hands, Lydia
Aug 13 1778    Robinson, Richard to Penn, Sarah*
Jul 28 1798    Robinson, Robert to Fonder, Abigail*
Jul 31 1789    Robinson, Samuel to Holmes, Ann*
Jan 24 1798    Robinson, Thomas to Steward, Sarah*
Dec 12 1788    Robinson, William to Gladman, Rachel
Sep  4 1782    Rochafied, Hannah to Rohrbuck, Adam*
Nov 27 1795    Roches, Catharine to Brittingham, Joseph*
Dec 16 1784    Rock, Barbary to Clarke, James*
Jun 23 1783    Rockholt, Ann to Goddard, William
Mar 22 1796    Roco, July to Nau, John*
May 15 1782    Roddy, Ann to Frances, Renick*
Jan  6 1796    Rode, John to Mincher, Sally*
Nov  1 1796    Rodenheiser, Catharine to Sheller, Jacob*
Aug  7 1781    Rodwell, Jeminah to Oley, Sebastian*
Apr  4 1795    Roe, Barbara to Honser, John*
Jan 11 1781    Roe, James to Daizell, Elizabeth*
Apr 29 1797    Roe, Mary Ann to Turner, Elisha*
Apr 28 1781    Roe, Rebecca to Morris, Samuel*
Apr 11 1792    Rogers, Allen to Evans, Rebecca*
Jan 17 1786    Rogers, Eleanor Addison to Boyce, John
Sep 12 1795    Rogers, Elizabeth to Elvans, William*
Nov  9 1795    Rogers, Elizabeth to Hunt, James*
Apr 21 1795    Rogers, Elizabeth to Hunter, Peter*
Jun 18 1796    Rogers, Hannah to Wilson, John*
Aug 10 1790    Rogers, Jacob to Limes, Elizabeth*
Oct  2 1793    Rogers, John to Barbini, Mary*
Sep 15 1783    Rogers, Joseph to Halbert, Sarah
Apr 13 1796    Rogers, Joseph to Shepherd, Sarah*
Jun 10 1783    Rogers, Nicholas to Buchanan, Elinor
Nov  7 1789    Rogers, Sarah to Carroll, Henry Hill*
Jul 29 1779    Rogers, Thomas to Mortan, Iszabellah*
Aug 18 1798    Rogin, Henry to Chiver, Mary*
Jun  6 1784    Rohrback, Clara to Pease, Elisha*
Mar 11 1790    Rohrback, George to Smith, Hannah*
Aig 10 1793    Rohrback, Mary Magdalin to Whatson, David*
Sep  4 1782    Rohrbuck, Adam to Rochafied, Hannah*
Aug 20 1794    Roister, Catherine to Linkwest, John*
Sep 22 1786    Roiston, Joshua to Hooker, Mary*
Jan 27 1781    Roiston, Mary to Sampson, Emanuel*
Nov 18 1779    Rolam, Martha to Read, John*
Aug  8 1778    Roland, Samuel to Holland, Elizabeth*
Oct 28 1781    Roles, Ara to Hanum, Christian
Jul 18 1785    Roles, John to Jacob, Elizabeth
Dec  7 1778    Roles, Susannah to Hawkins, Aaron*
Jul  6 1793    Rolles, Rebecca to Ammett, William*
Mar 28 1793    Rollins, Ann to Edwards, Philip*
Dec 14 1795    Rollins, Keziah to Murray, Thomas*
Dec 26 1782    Rolls, Susannah to Price, Stephen*
Nov 19 1782    Rolph, Mary to Morrison, John*
Oct 19 1795    Rolves, Juliana to O'Han, Samuel*
Aug 16 1782    Rondet, Francis to Celiston, Margaret*
Jul 12 1794    Rondlet, Francis to Wright, Margaret*
May 29 1782    Rone, Ann to Glen, Samuel*
```

```
Dec 15 1785    Roney, Judah to Welsh, John
Mar 29 1797    Roohe, Elizabeth to Moore, James Augustus*
May 23 1794    Rook, Sarah to Alcock, Joseph*
May 25 1779    Ropkins, Samuel to Deawannah, Sealer
Oct  7 1794    Rose, Rachell to Kelly, James*
Jul  6 1778    Rose, William to Welsh, Mary*
Jun 18 1795    Rosell, Charles to Holston, Margaret*
Apr 17 1797    Rosenhazard, Casper to Riddle, Patty*
Sep 29 1798    Rosensteel, John to Myers, Margaret*
Nov 23 1798    Rosenstell, Mary to Brown, John*
Nov  2 1795    Roser, Margaret Amy to Yarida, John Peter*
Nov 11 1784    Ross, Ann to Botten, Robert
Jul 16 1781    Ross, Charles to Smith, Barbary*
Apr 24 1794    Ross, Charles to Smith, Mary*
May 25 1785    Ross, Daniel to West, Mary*
May 11 1793    Ross, Elizabeth to Hettlestem, Thomas
Jan  7 1796    Ross, Elizabeth to James, Henry*
Feb  7 1782    Ross, Elizabeth to Lynch, William*
Feb 11 1786    Ross, Frances to Delat, Augustine
Oct  9 1792    Ross, Ham to Stocks, Mary*
Apr 22 1788    Ross, Hams to Copeland, Rachael*
Nov 17 1788    Ross, John to Smith, Hannah*
Oct 26 1790    Ross, John to Smith, Mary*
Jul 23 1795    Ross, Macarit to Carroll, Patrick*
May 25 1778    Ross, Margaret to McDonaldson, Thomas*
Dec 31 1795    Ross, Martha to Shanern, John*
Mar 25 1794    Ross, Mary to Pewley, Paul*
Nov  4 1789    Ross, Richard to Brereton, Sarah*
Jan 20 1792    Ross, Robert Lockart to McLure, Elizabeth*
Jan  8 1793    Ross, William Thomas to Price, Mary*
Dec 24 1796    Rossinot, Michael to Pillerin, Marie Rose*
Aug 12 1786    Rosson, William to Right, Ann*
Jul 30 1790    Rotch, George to Green, Catherine*
Feb 27 1797    Rothnick, Jacob to Baxley, Catharine*
Jun 22 1797    Rothrock, Catharine to Robinson, John*
Jun 16 1783    Rothrock, Elizabeth to Cafues, Abraham*
Apr 14 1798    Rothrock, Eve to Marshall, Henry*
Feb  5 1784    Roulison, Moses to Collins, Sarah*
Aug 30 1794    Round, Charlotte to Crosillant, Joackim*
Feb  3 1784    Round, John to Gibbons, Margaret*
Dec 21 1798    Rous, Elizabeth to Chapman, Christopher*
Sep  8 1794    Rouse, Sarah to Martin, James*
Sep 20 1797    Rousseau, Charles to Debraudon, Theresa*
Mar  5 1791    Row, Edward to Miles, Abigall
Nov 23 1791    Rowan, John to Howard, Elizabeth*
Jun  2 1798    Rowe, Peter to Maccoy, Ann*
May 19 1795    Rowes, Thomas to Adams, Martha*
May 24 1793    Rowlana, Rosend to Clouse, Stephen
Oct 25 1783    Rowland, Elizabeth to England, Joseph*
Feb 24 1796    Rowland, Elizabeth to Smith, William*
Mar 18 1796    Rowland, Nancy to Truiet, George*
Oct 20 1790    Rowland, Robert to McCleery, Agnes*
Oct  7 1795    Rowland, Thomas to Hale, Delila*
Nov 17 1796    Rowles, Alice to Croney, James*
Sep  7 1795    Rowles, Ann to Shipley, Richard*
Aug 27 1784    Rowles, Catharine to Davis, Joseph*
```

Aug	1	1781	Rowles, David to Davis, Sarah*
Dec	7	1787	Rowles, Elizabeth to Jarvis, Aquila
Sep	12	1793	Rowles, Elizabeth (widow) to Cromwell, John*
Sep	27	1788	Rowles, Ely to Cord, Sarah*
Jul	28	1797	Rowles, Henrietta to Shipley, Ezekiel*
Jul	16	1794	Rowles, Jacob to Dungan, Elizabeth*
Nov	1	1793	Rowles, Jacob to Randall, Mary*
Dec	21	1782	Rowles, Leah to Cunningham, Michael
Sep	30	1784	Rowles, Rachael to Shaw, William*
Dec	2	1794	Rowles, Rachel to Maxwell, John*
Mar	21	1789	Rowleson, Sarah to Smith, Thomas*
Jul	25	1798	Rowson, Ann to Barrenea, Richard*
Mar	15	1792	Royal, John to Shiels, Mary*
Oct	22	1778	Royston, Belinda to Miller, John*
Dec	18	1784	Royston, John to McClung, Ruth*
Mar	18	1784	Royston, Samuel to Jacobs, Rachel*
May	7	1791	Royston, Sophia to Spindler, John*
Feb	24	1795	Ruarke, Holsworth to Moffett, Jane*
Feb	7	1798	Rubbett, James to Miller, Sophia
Nov	14	1798	Ruckle, John to Dorsey, Ellin*
Oct	27	1792	Ruckle, Paul to Newman, Elizabeth*
May	22	1788	Ruddy, John to Brown, Deborah
Oct	1	1790	Rudricks, Anthony to Nabours, Margaret
Sep	5	1786	Ruff, Hanna to Rutledge, Shadrack*
Aug	8	1778	Ruff, William to Barry, Mary*
Oct	3	1798	Ruil, William A. to Hughes, Eleanor*
Mar	26	1785	Rule, Peter to Bordley, Sarah
Dec	31	1777	Ruliff, Gilbert to Curran, Mary*
Oct	13	1790	Rullston, William to McMasters, Martha*
Nov	4	1797	Rumag, Nicholas to Slater, Mary*
Apr	28	1785	Rummage, Nicholas to Mildews, Prisila
Nov	10	1788	Rumsey, Hannah to Rumsey, Henry*
Nov	10	1788	Rumsey, Henry to Rumsey, Hannah*
Aug	25	1790	Runnels, Sarah to Oram, Benjamin*
May	27	1784	Rush, Agness to Kerr, William
Apr	17	1782	Rush, Elizabeth to Hunt, Thomas*
Sep	25	1779	Rush, George to Harris, Ann*
Nov	19	1787	Rush, Margaret to Lee, Samuel*
Sep	18	1779	Rush, Mary to Hariy, David
May	31	1788	Rush, Stephen to Sinclair, Sarah*
Aug	22	1797	Rusk, Anne to Dungan, Benjamin*
Nov	23	1784	Rusk, Catharine to Hillen, John*
Jul	27	1797	Rusk, Catharine to Longley, Samuel*
Jan	10	1793	Rusk, Mary to Bevans, James*
Sep	4	1794	Rusk, Robert to Balspack, Barbary*
Oct	17	1778	Russel, Richard to Tumbletind, Margaret*
Oct	1	1795	Russell, Eliza to Johnson, Thomas*
Nov	29	1783	Russell, Elizabeth to Cahill, William*
Oct	20	1789	Russell, Elizabeth to Read, Jacob
Feb	24	1786	Russell, Emsey to Gill, Hugh
Jun	11	1794	Russell, Frances to Pringle, Mark*
Jul	30	1798	Russell, Robert to Hobbs, Elizabeth*
Feb	13	1798	Russell, Samuel to German, Sally*
Dec	14	1795	Russell, William to Dagan, Elizabeth*
Jan	21	1795	Russell, William to Williamson, Elizabeth
Dec	24	1796	Russort, Martin to Robinson, Mary*

Jan	5	1785	Rust, Charles to Sharmellor, Mary*
Mar	30	1796	Rust, Hannah to Davis, Samuel*
Jul	8	1782	Rust, John to Patterson, Mary*
Dec	26	1792	Rust, Mary to Clery, Michael*
Jun	1	1795	Ruth, John to Barton, Charlotte*
Jan	14	1795	Rutledge, Elizabeth to Talbott, Thomas*
Jun	23	1779	Rutledge, Jane to Wilson, Gitting*
Nov	10	1792	Rutledge, Joshua to Biddel, Augustine*
Apr	22	1789	Rutledge, Penelope to Kelso, Thomas*
Sep	5	1786	Rutledge, Shadrack to Ruff, Hanna*
Nov	23	1782	Rutledge, Thomas to Matthews, Mary
Oct	28	1780	Rutledge, Zack to Sinclair, Isabella*
Mar	30	1790	Rutler, Moses to Hubbort, Elizabeth*
Jan	7	1789	Rutler, Sally to Cockey, Caleb*
Jan	20	1795	Rutler, Sophia to Iser, Nicholas*
Nov	17	1787	Rutler, Thomas Jr. to Graybill, Mary
Jan	17	1792	Rutter, Ann to Burneston, Isaac*
May	7	1779	Rutter, Easter to Spisor, Voluntine
Sep	30	1786	Rutter, Eleanor to Snyder, John
Nov	22	1779	Rutter, Henry to Nice, Christina*
Feb	16	1786	Rutter, John to Askew, Elizabeth*
May	16	1778	Rutter, Jonathan to Longwell, Martha*
May	24	1796	Rutter, Josias to Pennington, Mary*
Jan	12	1781	Rutter, Richard to Brooks, Tasey
Jul	2	1783	Rutter, Sarah to Gray, Lynch*
Dec	9	1788	Rutter, Solomon to Ridenhour, Margaret*
dec	6	1798	Ryal, Martha to Joice, Nathan*
Nov	18	1778	Ryan, Ann to Hist, Gideon*
May	13	1797	Ryan, Biddy to Noles, Joseph*
Oct	13	1798	Ryan, James to Pursile, Mary*
Sep	10	1798	Ryan, Margaret to Latimor, Nicholas
Jun	13	1798	Ryan, Mary to Lanahan, Timothy*
Sep	19	1798	Ryan, Philip to Dickson, Sarah*
Jan	13	1796	Ryan, Sarah to Crawford, Alexander*
Sep	12	1797	Rye, John to Barbary, Mary*
Apr	15	1797	Ryland, John Burk to Jones, Sarah*
Jul	24	1795	Ryland, Joseph to Matthews, Mary*
Feb	17	1778	Ryleyson, Ula to Bower, John*
Feb	17	1784	Rynehart, Elizabeth to Null, Francis*
Oct	7	1783	Ryston, Cloe to McClung, Joseph
Oct	11	1781	Sacklow, Aaron to Barnes, Tabitha
Dec	16	1797	Sadler, Ann to Gardner, John*
Jan	27	1783	Sadler, Catherine to Daniley, Michael*
May	11	1796	Sadler, Elizabeth to Browner, Peter*
Nov	5	1794	Sadler, Joseph to Reynolds, Elsey*
Dec	17	1793	Sadler, Mary to Connaway, America*
Dec	10	1796	Sadler, Nancy to Sheron, Thomas*
Jun	20	1796	Sadler, Sarah to Hutton, Henry*
Mar	17	1792	Sadler, Sarah to Letick, George*
Nov	6	1793	Sadler, Thomas to Howard, Eliza G.*
Sep	5	1792	Safington, Rebecca to Turner, William
Dec	10	1796	Saglekin, John to Heshogan, Catharine*
Dec	23	1797	Sailors, Hannah to Shillman, Robert*
Aug	17	1793	Saker, Elizabeth to Scott, John*
Jul	31	1793	Saker, William to Scott, Catherine*
Oct	17	1781	Salmon, Benjamin to Ennis, Mary

Oct 21 1779	Salmon, George to Mercer, Rebecca
Aug 1 1779	Salocen, Margaret to Scarborough, Thomas
Jul 22 1797	Salter, Thomas to Clebe, Charlotte*
Dec 26 1795	Salvan, Joseph Lewis to Deshayes, Lucy Jane*
Aug 7 1782	Sample, John to Meredith, Keziah*
Mar 30 1795	Sample, Sarah to Cooper, William*
Oct 20 1786	Sampson, Ann to McAllister, Charles
Jan 27 1781	Sampson, Emanuel to Roiston, Mary*
Jul 18 1794	Sampson, George to Dysort, Catharine*
Dec 30 1794	Sampson, Joseph to Laske, Margaret*
Jan 14 1797	Sampson, Rachel to Sanders, George*
Jul 17 1789	Sanback, Francis to Sellman, Lydia*
Aug 10 1779	Sanders, Edward to Ranford, Sarah*
Jan 14 1797	Sanders, George to Sampson, Rachel*
Oct 1 1796	Sanders, Humphrey to Simpson, Urith*
Oct 3 1792	Sanders, Jasie to Allen, Darcus*
Apr 22 1794	Sanders, John to Harker, Mary*
Apr 27 1785	Sanders, Martha to Wheeler, John
Jun 7 1778	Sanderson, Peggy to Hughes, Christopher
Apr 1 1797	Sanderson, Sarah to Price, John*
Dec 19 1798	Sandiford, Michael to Lewy, Martha*
Nov 7 1794	Sandillend, Allay to Gore, Richard*
Apr 12 1788	Sands, Alexander to Burke, Delili
May 5 1798	Sands, Mary to Jones, Joshua*
Apr 10 1798	Sanford, Nicholas to Ritter, Catharine*
Aug 7 1794	Sanger, Seth to Elkins, Catharine*
Apr 4 1795	Sank, Achsah to Frizzle, John*
Mar 30 1796	Sank, John to Stewart, Rachel*
Nov 10 1798	Sank, Nancy to Nicholson, David*
Dec 10 1794	Sank, Samuel to Gray, Sarah*
Jul 25 1792	Sanks, Mary to Allen, James*
Mar 6 1797	Sap, George to Stops, Polly
Jun 3 1786	Sapen, Magdeline to Fleury, Sebastien
Oct 18 1793	Sapet, John Francis to Kettler, Mary*
Oct 15 1790	Sappington, Jacob to Brown, Elizabeth*
Jun 23 1781	Sappinton, John to Ducker, Elizabeth
Dec 10 1798	Sapstone, Betsy to Myers, Peter Nelson*
Nov 12 1798	Sarah, Susannah to Dickson, Isaac
Mar 28 1796	Sargent, Samuel to Silvey, Mary*
Oct 3 1795	Sark, Jane to Renshaw, Martin*
Aug 8 1792	Sarter, Ellinor to Pichaven, Jonathan
Aug 24 1793	Satch, Hannah to Ball, Stephen*
Jan 29 1781	Satch, John to Males, Hannah
Jun 17 1789	Sater, Charles to Beasman, Ruth
Jun 27 1781	Sater, Charles to Ogg, Mary*
Apr 16 1791	Sater, Darcus to Stansbury, John*
Oct 10 1781	Sater, Ruth to Merryman, Nicholas
Aug 14 1798	Saul, Christian to Dava, Sarah*
Jan 10 1792	Saunders, Ann to Pinnell, John*
Jul 31 1792	Saunders, Levin to Woodland, Amelia*
Jul 5 1794	Savage, Frances to Gordon, Michael*
Oct 20 1784	Savage, Margaret to Stokes, John*
May 26 1796	Savage, Patrick to Corrie, Elizabeth*
Aug 6 1783	Sawer, Ann to Nouls, James
Dec 14 1797	Sayborne, John to Smith, Elizabeth*
Oct 28 1797	Scall, Barbara to Millhall, Patrick*

Mar 27 1783	Scampen, Antony to Hubbard, Mary*
Feb 20 1797	Scanlan, Catharine to Morgan, William*
Nov 25 1797	Scanlan, James to Pearson, Mary*
Jun 27 1796	Scanllon, Lucy to Reily, John*
Aug 15 1779	Scar, Margaret to Richards, Isaac*
Dec 1 1784	Scarborough, Hannah to Carter, John
Aug 1 1779	Scarborough, Thomas to Salocen, Margaret
Dec 20 1783	Scarf, Elizabeth to Shrap, John*
Jan 22 1781	Scarf, George to Peasly, Mary*
Dec 21 1781	Scarf, Rachel to Chew, Richard*
Dec 30 1794	Scarfe, William to Taylor, Hannah*
Oct 6 1797	Schlieper, Hannah to Errickson, Barnet*
Jun 27 1795	Schlocman, Johanna Franciocus to Gath, John Henry*
Nov 2 1784	Scholl, Mary Elizabeth to Swarts, John*
May 29 1794	Schott, Christina Margaret to Toole, John*
Jan 31 1788	Schreagly, Elizabeth to Litzinger, William*
Jan 28 1796	Schriver, Julianna to Hill, Christian*
Feb 23 1795	Scoarce, John A. to Summers, Elizabeth*
Feb 20 1798	Scocofer, Catharine to Cobben, Joseph*
Nov 24 1781	Scoice, Hannah to Wilson, Samuel
Dec 11 1787	Scotland, Anthony to Campbell, Ann*
Apr 18 1789	Scott, Amos to Price, Rachel*
Jul 13 1786	Scott, Andrew to Calvin, Priscilla
Feb 21 1786	Scott, Andrew to Watson, Rosannah
May 31 1794	Scott, Ann to Wise, Levin*
Nov 3 1788	Scott, Burrage to Davis, Ann*
Jul 31 1793	Scott, Catherine to Saker, William*
Sep 28 1797	Scott, David to Kilbreath, Elizabeth*
Dec 3 1795	Scott, Delila to Irons, Thomas*
Nov 30 1792	Scott, Esther to Hunter, Peter*
Dec 23 1781	Scott, George to Bateman, Elinor
Jul 14 1785	Scott, George to Napear, Elizabeth
May 15 1788	Scott, John Jr. to Dorsey, Elizabeth Goodwin*
Dec 23 1790	Scott, John to Baise, Ann*
Aug 17 1793	Scott, John to Saker, Elizabeth*
May 12 1798	Scott, John to Wood, Ann*
Mar 4 1795	Scott, Joseph Jr. to Norris, Hannah*
Mar 14 1796	Scott, Joseph to McCarman, Margaret*
Nov 29 1783	Scott, Mary to Corrigan, Edward*
Mar 15 1796	Scott, Nancy to Caswell, Josiah*
Aug 24 1793	Scott, Samuel to Duncan, Nancy*
Jun 3 1788	Scott, Sarah to Dempsey, Luke*
Aug 19 1795	Scott, Sarah to Morgan, Jesse*
Apr 1 1783	Scott, Sarah to Morriss, Edward*
Sep 4 1786	Scott, Temperance to Deavour, Jonas
Jan 25 1788	Scott, Walter to York, Blanch*
Dec 8 1787	Scott, William to Merryman, Sarah*
Oct 6 1784	Scott, William to Mitchell, Mary
Sep 25 1783	Scovey, Elizabeth to Spicer, James*
Aug 15 1779	Sculd, Sarah to Mose, Philip*
Nov 3 1779	Seaboreng, Margaret to Peters, Daniel
Jul 6 1785	Seabrook, Ruth to McDonald, Andrew
Aug 6 1784	Seabrooks, Elizabeth to Lewis, John*
Mar 31 1778	Seabrooks, Lippy to Goslin, Mordecai*
Jun 21 1793	Seadley, Isaac to McKubbins, Nancy
Nov 19 1796	Seal, Hillen to Wasson, John*

Jun 19 1779	Seal, Mary to Murphey, Edward
Feb 21 1789	Seargant, Priscila to Cranford, John*
May 26 1785	Sears, Hannah to Caulk, Thomas Ward*
Mar 31 1798	Seaver, Elizabeth to Grant, John*
Dec 24 1796	Segan, Elizabeth to Feit, Henry*
Jul 29 1795	Segasey, Margaret to League, Reubin*
Mar 26 1798	Seigfried, Charles Lewis to Frazer, Charlotte*
Jun 23 1795	Selbrue, Louis to Dailey, Margaret*
Jan 23 1794	Selby, Eli to Shipley, Ruth*
Nov 10 1785	Selby, Hannah to Shipley, Elijah
Apr 15 1797	Selby, Loyd to Evans, Elizabeth
Sep 3 1797	Sellers, Catharine to Mills, Theodore*
Dec 17 1785	Sellers, William to Shepperd, Margaret
Sep 3 1778	Sellers, William to Wells, Susannah*
Dec 24 1783	Sellman, Ann to Holmes, Joshua*
Feb 9 1792	Sellman, Johnzee to Rawlins, Sarah
Jul 17 1789	Sellman, Lydia to Sanback, Francis*
Apr 5 1782	Sellman, Mordecai to Franklin, Lydia*
Nov 30 1784	Sellman, Pamelia to Dorsey, Benjamin
Aug 8 1793	Sellman, Vachel to Gill, Eleanor*
Feb 5 1782	Selman, Henrietta to Trumbo, Adam*
Jun 16 1781	Selman, Jonathan to Dawson, Elizabeth
Mar 3 1778	Selman, Mary to Geoghegan, Ambross*
Jun 18 1783	Selmon, Ann to Dorsey, John Lawrence*
Jan 30 1798	Selvers, John to Densel, Elizabeth*
Jan 15 1795	Semans, John to Parish, Elizabeth*
Jul 17 1784	Septon, Nancy to Patterson, Lawrence*
Mar 29 1786	Serber, Charles to Smelser, Catherine*
Apr 5 1796	Sermon, Anthony to Manning, Ann*
Oct 12 1793	Serote, Josephoria to Morie, Joseph*
Nov 20 1783	Settlemyer, Christopher to Smith, Eve*
May 10 1779	Sewell, Barbara to Rawson, William*
May 23 1797	Sewell, Cornelia to Sotheren, John*
Oct 15 1785	Sewell, James to Watts, Ann*
Mar 6 1778	Sewell, John to Young, Elizabeth
Feb 11 1786	Sewell, Mary to Kerwan, John
Mar 24 1794	Seweth, Sarah to Sthall, Charles*
Aug 8 1789	Sexsmith, Simoin to Groves, Mary*
Feb 2 1798	Sexton, Philis to Porter, John
Jul 2 1796	Sexton, Philis to Smith, William*
Oct 5 1792	Shadders, Elizabeth to Calvert, James*
Aug 3 1796	Shadders, Ruth to Appleby, William
Jun 20 1783	Shafer, George to Wamler, Elizabeth
Mar 16 1791	Shaffer, Apeloni to Cooper, John
Nov 11 1795	Shaffer, Elizabeth to Evans, John*
Nov 5 1784	Shaffer, Jacob to Radley, Peggy
Oct 29 1798	Shaffer, Lewis to Valentine, Rosanna*
Dec 4 1777	Shaffner, Barbara to Boughon, Stephen*
Mar 16 1791	Shak, Margaret to Ellis, Stephen*
Jan 27 1781	Shakespear, Samuel to Brown, Martha*
Oct 16 1779	Shall, Barbara to Isor, Richard
Jul 12 1794	Shally, Elizabeth to Hay, Jacob*
Jul 31 1784	Shamino, Polly to Neary, Peter
Jan 31 1798	Shammo, Mary to Mirceall, John*
Sep 5 1795	Shane, Joseph to Curtfield, Mary*
Dec 31 1795	Shanern, John to Ross, Martha*

Apr 20 1795	Shaney, John to Chester, Elizabeth*
Jun 27 1797	Shaney, Polly to Watkins, Joseph*
Dec 29 1785	Shannon, Michael to Strawbridge, Elizabeth
Aug 29 1797	Sharar, Eli to McCausland, Susannah*
Jan 5 1785	Sharmellor, Mary to Rust, Charles*
Dec 1 1784	Sharmiller, Catharine to Baxley, Samuel
May 19 1798	Sharp, Andrew to Glodin, Juliana*
Oct 11 1781	Sharp, Benjamin to Wright, Elizabeth
Dec 15 1781	Sharp, George to Wyley, Martha
Mar 26 1783	Sharp, Peter to Dickinson, Ann*
Mar 23 1786	Sharp, Providence to Sparks, Matthew*
Jan 4 1786	Sharp, Shratio to Elliott, Betsy Ann
Mar 10 1796	Sharp, William to Cowan, Susannah*
Jul 7 1794	Sharpe, Jacob to Forney, Mary*
Sep 13 1782	Sharpe, William to James, Elizabeth*
Jul 22 1783	Sharper, Enoch to Beard, Mary
Dec 30 1795	Shartel, Jacob to Simmon, Elizabeth*
Apr 6 1786	Shartel, Margaret to Graner, Daniel*
Nov 18 1785	Shartle, Mary to Weidner, Henry
Mar 28 1798	Shartle, Susannah to Rheem, William*
Feb 24 1781	Shaver, Balser to Larsh, Elenor*
Apr 21 1789	Shaw, Eleanor to Stevinson, Moses
Dec 23 1780	Shaw, Elinor to Cockran, George*
Jun 13 1796	Shaw, Eve to Thompson, John*
Feb 28 1784	Shaw, Jane to Hendricks, Eldert*
Apr 30 1778	Shaw, John to Hawkins, Mary*
Dec 21 1798	Shaw, John to Risley, Elizabeth*
Nov 12 1785	Shaw, Joshua to Hutchings, Alice
Jun 9 1791	Shaw, Kitty to Lloyd, Robert
Oct 4 1796	Shaw, Rossanna to McDoose, Joseph*
Sep 4 1797	Shaw, Sally to Peduze, Peter*
Jan 12 1791	Shaw, Sarah to Pratt, James*
Dec 31 1777	Shaw, Thomas N. to Stansbury, Sarah*
May 19 1778	Shaw, Thomas to Horton, Ann*
May 24 1778	Shaw, Thomas to Horton, Ann*
May 27 1797	Shaw, William to Anderson, Elizabeth*
Mar 15 1797	Shaw, William to Davis, Rebeccah*
Sep 30 1784	Shaw, William to Rowles, Rachael*
Jan 20 1796	Shaw, William to Wood, Sophia*
Jun 28 1794	Shay, James to Green, Mary*
Apr 22 1786	Shea, Daniel to Jurdan, Elizabeth
Oct 30 1783	Shead, John to Boyd, Mary
Dec 21 1785	Shean, David to Kenocken, Matte*
Jul 31 1786	Shean, Dennis to Kidd, Bridget
Feb 18 1797	Shearly, Thomas to Harris, Sarah*
Dec 6 1783	Shearman, Benjamin to Spencer, Rebecca*
Sep 25 1783	Shears, Richard to Evans, Sarah*
Apr 20 1797	Sheck, Henry to Spicer, Hannah*
Sep 8 1794	Sheekan, Cornelius to Thompson, Catharine*
Sep 26 1789	Sheens, Mary to Reese, John*
Apr 7 1783	Sheers, Elizabeth to Fuller, Samuel
Sep 2 1785	Sheilds, Frances to Bryan, Daniel*
Apr 2 1784	Shelby, Jane to Low, James*
Dec 10 1793	Sheldecker, Joseph to Brown, Barbara
Jul 24 1783	Sheldron, Martha to Turner, William*
Nov 1 1796	Sheller, Jacob to Rodenheiser, Catharine*

May 21 1782	Shelock, William to Bennett, Mary
Apr 1 1796	Shepburn, Thomas to Woolhouse, Mary*
May 7 1784	Shepherd, Ann to Davis, Luke
Feb 17 1783	Shepherd, Edward to Shorn, Catherine*
Feb 22 1781	Shepherd, John to Galloway, Mary Ann*
Aug 21 1797	Shepherd, Josias to Jones, Elizabeth*
Aug 8 1782	Shepherd, Margaret to Hamilton, John Agnu*
May 25 1786	Shepherd, Mary to Adamson, John*
Mar 9 1786	Shepherd, Nathaniel to Barney, Hannah
Apr 28 1792	Shepherd, Samuel to Orrick, Sarah* (free blacks)
Apr 13 1796	Shepherd, Sarah to Rogers, Joseph*
May 16 1778	Sheppard, Mary to Bannan, Thomas*
Oct 31 1795	Sheppard, Thomas to Amos, Nancy*
Dec 17 1785	Shepperd, Margaret to Sellers, William
May 3 1797	Shepperd, Thomas to Weary, Ann*
Apr 17 1793	Sheppherd, Ann to Curtis, William
Oct 3 1781	Sheriff, Martha to Bashier, Benedict*
Oct 25 1798	Sherlock, John to Gilmore, Eliza*
Aug 25 1783	Sherman, Jiman to Minnaham, Elizabeth
Dec 10 1796	Sheron, Thomas to Sadler, Nancy*
Jun 17 1795	Sherrud, Elizabeth to Johnson, Lake*
Mar 31 1798	Shertain, Maria D. to Brentinger, John C.*
Apr 7 1796	Sherwood, Elizabeth to Butner, John*
Jun 30 1798	Shield, Zachariah to Bailey, Ann*
Nov 7 1793	Shields, Jane to Johnson, Caleb, Revd.*
Apr 19 1779	Shields, Mary to Bozemin, Edward
Nov 11 1793	Shields, Mary to Cavarre, Francois*
Dec 6 1782	Shields, Mary to Herd, John
Mar 23 1793	Shields, Mary to Laurence, William*
Apr 11 1786	Shields, Rebecca to Joyce, Thomas
Mar 15 1792	Shiels, Mary to Royal, John*
Aug 4 1783	Shilling, Elizabeth to Stansbury, Caleb*
Feb 17 1778	Shilling, Michael to Weister, Catharine*
Dec 29 1792	Shillingsburgh, Mary to French, Dominick
Mar 9 1779	Shillirn, William to Harper, Elephel*
Mar 17 1779	Shillirn, William to Harper, Eliphel*
Dec 23 1797	Shillman, Robert to Sailors, Hannah*
May 25 1784	Shinaman, Abraham to Shultz, Ulianna*
Dec 24 1794	Shipey, David to Toy, Ann*
Aug 24 1792	Shipley, Absalom to Shipley, Providence*
Apr 27 1784	Shipley, Adam to Frost, Rachel*
Apr 12 1783	Shipley, Agness to Harrison, George*
Aug 13 1791	Shipley, Benjamin to Hobb, Amelia*
Jan 4 1792	Shipley, Brice to Beaseman, Elizabeth*
Aug 2 1798	Shipley, Catharine to Henry, John*
Oct 19 1782	Shipley, Charle to Grimes, Jenny*
Sep 21 1791	Shipley, Duncan to Chew, Cassandra
Feb 14 1795	Shipley, Edward to Everson, Elizabeth*
Sep 10 1790	Shipley, Elijah to Dean, Milcah*
Nov 10 1785	Shipley, Elijah to Selby, Hannah
Jul 28 1797	Shipley, Ezekiel to Rowles, Henrietta*
Dec 23 1790	Shipley, George Ogg to Barnes, Hannah*
Mar 2 1784	Shipley, George to Frost, Susannah*
Feb 17 1795	Shipley, Groves to Frizzle, Elizabeth*
Sep 11 1782	Shipley, Henry to Howard, Ruth*
Apr 18 1795	Shipley, Jesse to Lucas, Jane*

Dec 8 1797	Shipley, John to Gilliss, Arraminta*
Dec 17 1791	Shipley, John to Kindell, Sarah
Jan 12 1781	Shipley, John to Parnel, Eleanor*
Aug 10 1784	Shipley, Katharine to Barns, Elijah
Oct 17 1791	Shipley, Levin to Loyd, Mary*
Jan 4 1783	Shipley, Lloyd to Frost, Margaret*
Sep 6 1797	Shipley, Margaret to Hipsley, Caleb*
Aug 19 1791	Shipley, Mary Ogg to Frost, William*
Jan 22 1791	Shipley, Mary to Hobbs, Hanson*
Jan 21 1791	Shipley, Nancy to Gosnell, Peter*
Mar 14 1798	Shipley, Peter to Lindsay, Mary
Aug 24 1792	Shipley, Providence to Shipley, Absalom*
Apr 2 1796	Shipley, Rachel to Kendal, Vachel*
Apr 3 1790	Shipley, Rezin to Brooks, Eleanor*
May 21 1795	Shipley, Richard to Jones, Elizabeth*
Sep 7 1795	Shipley, Richard to Rowles, Ann*
Feb 27 1789	Shipley, Robert to Elder, Providence*
Jan 23 1794	Shipley, Ruth to Selby, Eli*
Oct 21 1784	Shipley, Samuel to Sutton, Kitty*
Jun 25 1783	Shipley, Sarah Hood to Hipsley, Caleb*
Dec 22 1785	Shipley, Sarah to Grimes, William*
Jun 25 1789	Shipley, Susannah to Cushion, Robert*
Jul 23 1792	Shipley, Susannah to Gilliss, John*
Nov 3 1792	Shipley, Susannah to Whips, George*
Jun 17 1778	Shipley, Talbott to Burgiss, Ruth*
Jul 16 1779	Shipley, Talbott to Chice, Rachel
Jun 5 1782	Shipley, Vachel to Garner, Ann*
Jun 22 1778	Shipton, Henry to Broderick, Mary*
Oct 15 1795	Shipway, Elizabeth to Wilson, Nathaniel*
Jul 10 1792	Shirk, Peter to Chaney, Margaret*
Nov 30 1780	Shirock, John to Iser, Elizabeth
Oct 28 1783	Shock, Catharine to Bomer, Peter*
Oct 15 1794	Shock, Jacob to O'Donnell, Elizabeth*
Dec 10 1796	Shock, Julianna to Bryan, Isaac*
Jul 16 1794	Shock, Mary to Wilkinson, Joseph*
May 5 1798	Shock, Peter to Norris, Mary*
Mar 23 1790	Shockny, Margaret to Galloway, Francis*
Jan 16 1790	Shoemaker, Adam to Switzer, Elizabeth*
Feb 12 1795	Shoemaker, Ignatius to Cherves, Louisa*
Jul 11 1788	Shoemaker, Jane to McQuina, William*
Apr 14 1796	Shoeman, Catharine to Fous, Theobald*
Oct 27 1798	Sholl, Catharine to Frederick, Michael*
Apr 25 1795	Sholl, Mary to Barnes, Leaven*
Dec 5 1789	Sholl, Philip to Myer, Mary*
Aug 2 1794	Sholly, John to Myers, Eve
May 16 1786	Shook, John to Porter, Airey*
Dec 13 1785	Shope, William to Barnaby, Elizabeth
Feb 17 1783	Shorn, Catherine to Shepherd, Edward*
Sep 14 1797	Short, Richard to Cheney, Susannah*
Jul 15 1796	Showers, Adam to Troxall, Elizabeth*
Apr 7 1798	Shraden, James to Johnson, Jemima*
Dec 20 1783	Shrap, John to Scarf, Elizabeth*
Apr 20 1796	Shreader, Jacob to Johnson, Mary*
Oct 15 1796	Shrebeck, William to Kline, Margaret*
Sep 7 1796	Shreen, Joseph to Green, Asenath*
May 16 1781	Shriver, Elizabeth to Peters, Daniel*

```
Aug 26 1782    Shriver, John to Oldis, Ann
Jan  2 1791    Shriver, Mary to Himmelbright, Samuel*
Jan 12 1790    Shroad, John to Ward, Mary*
Nov 19 1794    Shroeder, Anna Doratha to Heiecke, Frederick*
Aug 13 1796    Shrote, Barbara to Welsh, Henry*
Jan 28 1793    Shrote, Mary to Hoofman, Daniel*
Feb 20 1794    Shruggo, Alexander to McElroy, Nancy*
Apr 16 1798    Shrurick, Elizabeth to Devin, Cain*
May 11 1793    Shryar, Lewis to Kepp, Sarah
Sep 26 1793    Shryock, Jacob to Duln, Elizabeth*
Dec  5 1793    Shryock, Rachel to Jennings, John
May 18 1796    Shuck, Mary to Myers, Joseph*
Jul 16 1794    Shuett, Phebe to Brunner, Andrew*
Aug 15 1778    Shults, Andrew to Miller, Mary*
Jul 20 1794    Shultz, Christiana to Krems, Joseph*
Oct  7 1784    Shultz, Polly to Devilbiss, Frederick*
May 25 1784    Shultz, Ulianna to Shinaman, Abraham*
Mar  8 1779    Shunk, John to Mumma, Ann*
Jun 23 1795    Shurred, Matthew to Hale, Elizabeth*
Aug  2 1788    Shut, Jacob to Snider, Peggy*
Oct 15 1795    Shute, Henry to Hislet, Mary*
Feb  3 1778    Shutom, Barbara to Burns, Stephen*
Mar 30 1785    Shyor, Ann to Wood, John
Jan  3 1784    Siberuy, William to Taylor, Rebecca*
Aug 13 1782    Sicamore, Lydia to Hilton, John*
Nov 28 1798    Sidden, Mary to Burton, John*
Mar  8 1791    Sidden, William to Biddison, Mary*
Jun 13 1797    Sies, Mary to Wineland, Frank*
Aug 25 1790    Siffort, Martin, Maidwell, Elizabeth*
Jul 12 1779    Sighsurger, Rosannah to Hoofman, William
Dec  3 1788    Sigler, John to Keys, Ann*
Aug 12 1796    Silk, Mary to Boner, Hugh*
Nov 22 1781    Sillers, Thomas to Pearce, Elizabeth*
Jul 22 1781    Sillet, Sarah to Hand, William*
Mar 31 1779    Silverwoods, Hannah to Fields, John*
Mar 28 1796    Silvey, Mary to Sargent, Samuel*
Apr 19 1795    Silzel, Barbara to Nolan, William*
Jun 18 1795    Simmerman, Catherine to Maidwell, Alexander*
Dec 30 1795    Simmon, Elizabeth to Shartel, Jacob*
Jul 23 1798    Simmon, Joseph to Browr, Jemima Margaret*
Mar 10 1784    Simmons, Elizabeth to White, Luke*
Oct 10 1797    Simmons, James to Coe, Elizabeth
Nov  2 1784    Simmons, John to Bouden, Jane*
Aug  9 1796    Simmons, William to Darton, Sarah*
Oct 16 1779    Simon, Andrew to Belhisle, Anastize*
Jan 20 1798    Simon, Jacob to Waggoner, Catharine*
Feb 27 1786    Simpson, Achsah to China, James
Aug 19 1783    Simpson, Amos to Strong, Rebecca*
Dec 17 1798    Simpson, Elizabeth to Fee, John*
Apr  2 1784    Simpson, James to Hicks, Dalsey*
Oct 27 1794    Simpson, James to Yale, Ann*
Feb  6 1786    Simpson, Leah to Munday, William
Jan 18 1794    Simpson, Lucy to Welsh, John*
Feb 14 1794    Simpson, Lydia to Landres, Peter*
Jun 13 1778    Simpson, Mary to Cook, Thomas*
Aug  9 1785    Simpson, Mary to Waters, Thomas
```

Feb	1	1786	Simpson, Reagen to Burgess, Jane*
Apr	5	1790	Simpson, Rebecca to Butler, John*
Dec	25	1777	Simpson, Samuel to Osborne, Mary*
Nov	6	1781	Simpson, Sarah to Frost, James
Apr	9	1791	Simpson, Sarah to Tucker, Edward
Oct	1	1796	Simpson, Urith to Sanders, Humphrey*
Jul	23	1779	Simpson, Walter to Pickett, Elizabeth*
Jan	9	1784	Simpson, Walter to Stewart, Jane*
Nov	3	1785	Sin, Edward to Condreu, Ann
Dec	28	1782	Sincklair, Moses to Jemmison, Mary
Sep	5	1795	Sincklair, Robert to Pancess, Hetty*
May	19	1785	Sinclair, Elizabeth to Edwards, Ephraim*
Oct	28	1780	Sinclair, Isabella to Rutledge, Zack*
Dec	11	1784	Sinclair, Martha to Street, John*
Mar	30	1797	Sinclair, Sarah to Campbell, Thomas J.*
May	31	1788	Sinclair, Sarah to Rush, Stephen*
Aug	5	1797	Sindall, Solomon to O'Neale, Nancy*
May	12	1795	Sindall, Urath to Weatherby, William*
Oct	23	1781	Sindall, William to Alder, Hannah
Nov	30	1791	Sindell, David to Cook, Urith*
Jun	30	1781	Sindell, David to Perrigoe, Jemimah
Jun	4	1781	Sindoll, Elizabeth to Carter, Sol.*
Nov	23	1797	Singary, Anne to Foster, Elijah*
Mar	20	1793	Singleton, William to Slater, Elizabeth*
Oct	29	1796	Sinklair, Elizabeth to Hamilton, Charles*
Aug	20	1789	Sinklair, James to McLain, Kezia*
Dec	24	1795	Sinners, Elijah R. to Jones, Elizabeth*
May	5	1795	Sinwal, Elinor to Corbin, Thomas*
Aug	10	1786	Sire, James to Hart, Ann*
Oct	30	1798	Sisannick, Rose to Hains, Benjamin*
Jan	19	1797	Sisler, Philip to Burk, Polly*
May	13	1781	Sither, Catherine to Varle, Bartelemy*
May	19	1796	Sitler, Ann S. to Smith, Samuel A.*
Aug	4	1796	Sitler, Catharine to Purtel, Robert*
Jun	3	1778	Sitler, Mary to Stroman, John*
Jul	8	1783	Sittlemire, Christian to Butler, Margaret
Mar	6	1798	Sivan, James to Wright, Sophia*
Nov	26	1791	Skeel, William to Staple, Ann*
Aug	30	1797	Skeeman, Henry to Perry, Martha*
May	10	1794	Skerret, John to Kenedy, Ann*
Feb	16	1784	Skerrett, Clemment to Moore, Ruth*
May	9	1795	Skeuse, Ann to Carpenter, Allen*
Jan	23	1796	Skillhamer, Margaret to Pearce, Samuel*
Aug	1	1778	Skinner, Jane to Gordon, James*
Oct	3	1786	Skinner, Thomas to Crockett, Elizabeth
Apr	21	1778	Skinner, Thomas to Warner, Darcus*
Apr	25	1791	Skipper, Rachael to Hanson, James*
Nov	3	1791	Skipper, Thomas to Barry, Abigail*
Aug	19	1795	Sklipp, William to Zimmer, Elizabeth*
Sep	4	1783	Slack, Hannah to Barns, Eliven*
Dec	6	1788	Slade, Abraham to Mutchner, Ann*
Jan	12	1785	Slade, Ann to Bull, Jacob*
Jan	28	1783	Slade, Ezekiel to Hodgkin, Mary*
Nov	7	1797	Slade, Mary to Talbott, John*
Dec	22	1794	Slade, Penelope to Johns, Hosea*
Jan	24	1793	Slade, Richard to Morgan, Eliza*

Dec 18 1784	Slade, Thomas to Mutchener, Rachel*
Oct 26 1782	Slade, William to McComes, Pricilla*
Jul 21 1788	Sladen, James to Murphey, Elinor
Apr 19 1794	Sladsmon, Michael to Harp, Mary*
Mar 4 1784	Slagel, Christiana to Bahn, Jacob*
Feb 24 1789	Slappy, Jacob to Pogue, Jane*
Mar 20 1793	Slater, Elizabeth to Singleton, William*
May 3 1792	Slater, Elizabeth to Watts, Benjamin*
Sep 14 1793	Slater, Joseph to Smith, Sarah
Aug 13 1794	Slater, Julia to Fitzpatrick, Hugh*
Nov 24 1785	Slater, Margaret to Burnsides, James
Nov 4 1797	Slater, Mary to Rumag, Nicholas*
Mar 13 1793	Slater, Sarah to Prout, William*
Mar 22 1797	Slaughter, Elizabeth to Keppard, Louis*
Jun 4 1798	Slebe, Thomas to Doyle, Elizabeth*
Dec 10 1796	Slemmer, Christian to Vaughan, Elizabeth*
Aug 11 1786	Slider, Sarah to Borein, John*
Jan 17 1785	Sligh, John to Elizabeth, Mariah*
Jun 3 1783	Sligh, Mary to Lascault, Lewis
May 23 1783	Sligh, Rebecca to McFaddin, James*
May 2 1783	Slingsby to Griffith, Mary*
Jan 29 1798	Sliop, John to Loudermer, Mary
Nov 30 1789	Sloan, John to Jeffery, Sarah*
May 3 1791	Slomaker, James to Zuile, Clarinda*
Jun 13 1798	Slugounene, Alexis to Ridgely, Clarisa*
Jan 3 1786	Sly, John to Botram, Catharine
Jul 14 1796	Small, Catharine to Myers, Joseph*
Dec 11 1794	Small, Jacob to Fleetwood, Nancy*
Mar 25 1794	Small, Jacob to Hopkins, Eliza*
May 29 1789	Small, James to Gressman, Agnes*
Jul 17 1797	Small, James to Riddan, Mary Ann*
Aug 25 1796	Smallwood, Robert to Keilholtz, Margaret*
Mar 29 1786	Smelser, Catherine to Serber, Charles*
Jan 6 1795	Smich, Elizabeth to Toole, Daniel*
Oct 1 1795	Smick, Polly to Pumphrey, Frederick*
Dec 12 1778	Smith, Adam to Hoffstetter, Cartrout*
Feb 24 1789	Smith, Agness to Read, Joseph
Dec 6 1784	Smith, Ann to Chamillon, Joseph*
Dec 4 1788	Smith, Ann to Forbes, James*
Jun 24 1795	Smith, Ann to Gorsuch, Joshua*
Apr 13 1784	Smith, Ann to Hanson, Peter*
Jun 5 1798	Smith, Anna to Sutton, Matthias*
Sep 5 1785	Smith, Aquila to Connaway, Catharine
Jan 28 1794	Smith, Arthur to Anderson, Mary*
Sep 29 1783	Smith, Barbara to Swartz, Henry*
Jul 16 1781	Smith, Barbary to Ross, Charles*
Oct 19 1798	Smith, Barnet to Glovers, Charlotte*
Jan 23 1790	Smith, Bazel Lowman to Frazier, Ann*
Apr 12 1796	Smith, Bazel to Cole, Elizabeth*
Nov 12 1778	Smith, Bazil to Davis, Avis*
May 30 1786	Smith, Biddy to Smith, Ephraim*
Aug 22 1782	Smith, Biddy to Thomas, John
May 3 1784	Smith, Caleb to Oyston, Elizabeth*
Oct 17 1793	Smith, Catharine to Benson, Richard*
Nov 10 1791	Smith, Catharine to Campbell, Robert*
May 30 1795	Smith, Catharine to Cushion, Thomas*

```
Jun  1 1797    Smith, Catharine to Davis, Elias*
May 29 1782    Smith, Catharine to Hiland, George*
Jan 14 1796    Smith, Catharine to Johnston, Barney*
Oct 27 1783    Smith, Catharine to Maybury, Francis*
Jan 27 1791    Smith, Catherine to Bailey, Thomas*
Mar 12 1783    Smith, Catherine to Wells, William
Apr 29 1795    Smith, Christian to Bolehouse, Magdalina*
Sep 28 1792    Smith, Daniel to Gallop, Hannah*
Jun  5 1794    Smith, Daniel to Yates, Elizabeth*
Oct  7 1779    Smith, Deborah to Pierce, Charles*
Jun 15 1796    Smith, Doman to Jaffray, Frances*
Nov 10 1781    Smith, Easther to Wilcoxson, William
Dec 24 1795    Smith, Edward to Coughlin, Frances*
Dec 16 1797    Smith, Eleanor to Ensor, John*
Sep  7 1790    Smith, Eleanor to Hobbs, Beall*
Aug 16 1794    Smith, Elizabeth to Bodmim, John*
Dec 13 1797    Smith, Elizabeth to Buckingham, Benjamin*
Mar 20 1797    Smith, Elizabeth to Dodd, Abraham*
Apr 24 1794    Smith, Elizabeth to Key, James E.*
Jun 30 1781    Smith, Elizabeth to Peacock, John*
Oct 21 1778    Smith, Elizabeth to Rheme, John
Dec 14 1797    Smith, Elizabeth to Sayborne, John*
Sep 14 1779    Smith, Elizabeth to Spear, John*
May 30 1786    Smith, Ephraim to Smith, Biddy*
Apr  9 1798    Smith, Eve to Hahn, Peter
Nov 20 1783    Smith, Eve to Settlemyer, Christopher*
Dec  7 1791    Smith, Frances to Bell, Thomas Clarke*
Oct 23 1792    Smith, Frances to Walker, Samuel*
Sep 16 1778    Smith, Francis to Hagerty, Catharine*
Nov 22 1779    Smith, Francis to Thorrington, Elizabeth*
Dec 26 1785    Smith, Frederick to Pingle, Sarah
Aug 23 1794    Smith, Gasper to Weaver, Mary*
Jan 15 1795    Smith, George to Bates, Elizabeth*
Dec  5 1792    Smith, George to Frick, Mary*
Feb 18 1797    Smith, George to Grant, Nancy*
Oct 19 1798    Smith, George to Maloney, Mary*
Oct 23 1795    Smith, Grace to Latour, John*
Oct  5 1778    Smith, Hannah to Hayes, Arche*
Nov 17 1788    Smith, Hannah to Ross, John*
Mar 11 1790    Smith, Hannnah to Rohrback, George*
Dec 23 1794    Smith, Henry John to Reader, Catharine*
Sep  4 1778    Smith, Henry to Conaway, Sarah*
Jan 11 1783    Smith, Henry to Stout, Elizabeth
Feb  3 1791    Smith, Hetty to Stevenson, George P.*
Apr  6 1779    Smith, Isabella to Maloney, William*
Nov  8 1785    Smith, Jacob to Gardiner, Sarah
Feb  4 1797    Smith, Jacob to Nash, Sarah*
Aug 17 1784    Smith, James to Davis, Mary*
Jul 31 1798    Smith, James to Mahon, Mary*
May 24 1794    Smith, James to Tucker, Elizabeth*
Jan 11 1796    Smith, Jane to Gilmore, John*
Dec 30 1785    Smith, Jane to Hollins, John*
Dec 21 1793    Smith, Jane to Wily, George*
Oct 21 1784    Smith, Jeremiah to Atherton, Rebecca*
May  2 1791    Smith, Jeremiah to Henly, Letitia*
Dec 27 1798    Smith, Job to Bussey, Martha*
```

Dec 26 1781	Smith, Job to Orrick, Margaret*
Jun 28 1784	Smith, Job to Smith, Margaret
Feb 9 1789	Smith, John Jacob to Hillen, Jane Paron*
Oct 13 1778	Smith, John to Amos, Susannah*
Sep 28 1789	Smith, John to Arnold, Sarah*
Oct 9 1797	Smith, John to Cheddick, Sarah*
May 30 1795	Smith, John to Connor, Jane*
Jun 4 1779	Smith, John to Delay, Catharine
Sep 25 1793	Smith, John to Eagleston, Delinah*
Oct 8 1789	Smith, John to Eden, Elizabeth*
Aug 29 1792	Smith, John to Jackson, Ann*
Dec 9 1797	Smith, John to Jackson, Rosannah*
May 21 1795	Smith, John to Maidwell, Susannah*
Jul 2 1778	Smith, Joseph to Gist, Sarah*
Sep 15 1779	Smith, Joseph to Gregory, Margaret*
Dec 13 1783	Smith, Joseph to Ketcham, Sarah
Nov 10 1779	Smith, Joseph to Megregger, Mary
Feb 8 1783	Smith, Joshua to Howard, Elizabeth*
May 14 1796	Smith, Joshua to Miller, Catharine*
Sep 16 1796	Smith, Joshua to Wells, Susannah
Nov 3 1792	Smith, Lambert to Gittings, Elizabeth*
Jul 6 1796	Smith, Larkin to Nicholson, Rachel*
Apr 28 1795	Smith, Leakin to Dunn, Ann*
Apr 17 1795	Smith, Letitia to Livingston, Paul Bartholomew H.*
Apr 2 1779	Smith, Margaret to Batson, Henry
Aug 31 1790	Smith, Margaret to Bolton, William*
Jan 1 1791	Smith, Margaret to Branson, William
Jan 29 1785	Smith, Margaret to Cary, Nicholas Wilson*
Aug 29 1793	Smith, Margaret to Rawlins, John*
Jun 28 1784	Smith, Margaret to Smith, Job
Dec 7 1790	Smith, Margaret to Smith, Robert*
Sep 19 1798	Smith, Margaret to Smuoalt, John*
Dec 6 1784	Smith, Margaret to Wilson, Hugh*
Apr 28 1783	Smith, Mary to Harvey, Patrick*
Oct 21 1779	Smith, Mary to Pinlater, Alexander*
Apr 24 1794	Smith, Mary to Ross, Charles*
Oct 26 1790	Smith, Mary to Ross, John*
Oct 20 1790	Smith, Mary to Taylor, Matthew*
Nov 7 1789	Smith, Mary to Thompson, Ingree*
Apr 10 1783	Smith, Mary to Watts, Isaac*
Dec 18 1794	Smith, Mary to Weist, Jacob*
Oct 18 1785	Smith, Mary to Williams, Otho Holland*
Mar 24 1794	Smith, Matilda to Nicholson, John*
Apr 17 1794	Smith, Michael to Houk, Catherine*
Oct 6 1797	Smith, Nancy to Burke, Edward
Feb 6 1796	Smith, Nathaniel to Wood, Sarah*
Oct 25 1783	Smith, Nicholas to Hissey, Rebecca
May 30 1795	Smith, Nicholas to Lowe, Ellin*
Jan 3 1794	Smith, Patrick to Bishop, Nancy*
May 31 1796	Smith, Patty to Pearson, Andrew*
Oct 31 1795	Smith, Philip to Storey, Mary*
May 20 1785	Smith, Providence to Hammond, Charles*
Dec 23 1797	Smith, Rachel to Barton, James*
Nov 13 1794	Smith, Rachell to Williams, Frederick*
Jun 30 1795	Smith, Rebecca to Barnet, George*
Dec 4 1793	Smith, Rebecca to Nicols, Henry

Sep 24 1791	Smith, Richard to Bevan, Mary*
Nov 2 1798	Smith, Richard to Freeman, Sinney*
Feb 21 1797	Smith, Richard to Smith, Sarah*
Dec 9 1794	Smith, Robert to Newcomb, Mary*
Dec 7 1790	Smith, Robert to Smith, Margaret*
Apr 17 1798	Smith, Sabritt to Hawkins, Mary
Aug 27 1795	Smith, Sally to Cantwell, Thomas
May 19 1796	Smith, Samuel A. to Sitler, Ann S.*
Jun 9 1783	Smith, Samuel to Wheeler, Tabitha*
Dec 9 1795	Smith, Sarah to Ensor, George*
Dec 9 1780	Smith, Sarah to Hyson, Josiah*
Oct 8 1794	Smith, Sarah to Jackson, William*
Aug 23 1792	Smith, Sarah to Jardon, James*
May 1 1798	Smith, Sarah to Leakins, Thomas*
Jun 28 1783	Smith, Sarah to Lock, Jacob
Dec 8 1777	Smith, Sarah to Merryman, John
Sep 14 1793	Smith, Sarah to Slater, Joseph*
Feb 21 1797	Smith, Sarah to Smith, Richard*
Aug 24 1786	Smith, Sarah to Wheeler, Joseph
Sep 24 1790	Smith, Solomon to Vershon, Letitia*
Jun 20 1789	Smith, Stephen to Burns, Juliet*
Aug 18 1796	Smith, Susannah to Johnson, John*
Feb 8 1791	Smith, Thomas to Brooks, Sarah*
Mar 21 1789	Smith, Thomas to Rowleson, Sarah*
Jul 11 1794	Smith, William Baxter to Steele, Frances*
Oct 2 1798	Smith, William R. to Dugan, Margaret*
Aug 29 1785	Smith, William to Bateman, Sarah*
Apr 29 1797	Smith, William to Bishop, Mary*
Jan 28 1795	Smith, William to Bosman, Rosanna*
May 24 1794	Smith, William to Bryan, Mary*
Jul 22 1779	Smith, William to Flood, Catharine*
Dec 5 1785	Smith, William to Kelly, Eleanor
Jun 1 1785	Smith, William to Laymon, Philabina*
Feb 24 1796	Smith, William to Rowland, Elizabeth*
Jul 2 1796	Smith, William to Sexton, Philis*
Feb 2 1792	Smith, Zachariah to Harrowod, Elizabeth Ann*
Apr 10 1784	Smithers, Ann to Bethune, Louis*
Dec 10 1782	Smithson, Daniel to Anderson, Margaret*
Nov 14 1778	Smitson, Sarah to Alderson, Thomas*
Nov 27 1794	Smoot, Eleanor to Beech, Ebenezer*
Dec 11 1798	Smothers, Mary to Ogle, George*
Dec 21 1795	Smull, Margaret to Pannell, John*
Oct 15 1791	Smythe, Samuel to Wignell, Elizabeth*
Sep 5 1797	Snares, William to League, Elizabeth*
Nov 10 1796	Snead, Edward to Webb, Jane*
Jan 20 1781	Sneesby, Richard to Mitchenner, Margaret*
Apr 19 1794	Snider, Andrew to Trauzbaugh, Christinia*
Oct 18 1784	Snider, George to Love, Christiana*
Sep 15 1796	Snider, John to Parker, Ann*
Dec 3 1795	Snider, Kitty to Potter, John*
Aug 2 1788	Snider, Peggy to Shut, Jacob*
Aug 5 1786	Snider, Sarah to Bradford, William*
Sep 18 1792	Snidorff, Mary to Edwards, Paul*
Jun 2 1779	Snoden, Susannah to Dorsey, Elias*
Apr 25 1797	Snowden, Mary to Brown, Moses*
Dec 9 1797	Snuggrass, William to Hart, Catharine*

Sep 30 1786	Snyder, John to Rutter, Eleanor
Nov 3 1792	Snyder, Mary to Lynehart, Jacob*
Aug 8 1797	Soivers, Edward to Leach, Nancy*
Jan 17 1786	Soles, Eleanor to Houlton, John
Feb 17 1783	Sollers, Anexa to Brown, Henry*
Nov 19 1788	Sollers, Ann to Allender, William*
Jan 24 1782	Sollers, Ann to Haines, Daniel*
May 8 1793	Sollers, Ann to Johnson, Houkman*
Apr 2 1785	Sollers, Ara to Walters, Jacob
Dec 8 1784	Sollers, Barbara to Drain, John*
May 3 1798	Sollers, Elisha to Partridge, Sarah*
Aug 15 1779	Sollers, Issabellah to Mass, Abraham
Sep 17 1783	Sollers, John to Allender, Sarah*
Nov 22 1796	Sollers, Rebecca to Hicks, Joshua*
Mar 5 1793	Sollers, Sarah to Trotten, John*
Apr 25 1797	Sollers, Thomas to Pennington, Sarah*
Feb 4 1797	Sollers, William to Barry, Elinor*
Oct 16 1782	Sollors, Mary to Miller, John
May 23 1782	Solman, Johnze to Mayo, Sarah
Apr 20 1784	Soloman, Dinah to McDonald, Michael*
Jan 3 1793	Solomon, Elkin to Hasolton, Abigail*
Jun 15 1793	Somclin, Fanny to Floyd, Samuel*
Nov 13 1795	Somerville, Mary to Davidson, Andrew*
Jan 7 1784	Somevault, Philip to Krebs, Elizabeth*
Feb 11 1782	Sonders, James to Andrews, Ruth
Feb 10 1782	Sopellia, Bridgit to Manix, Timothy*
Aug 12 1786	Soreah, Sarah to Curry, John
Feb 3 1785	Sorivenor, Mary to Graham, James*
Nov 7 1793	Sorter, Mary to Harman, James*
Feb 27 1797	Sorver, John to Mahar, Jane*
May 23 1797	Sotheren, John to Sewell, Cornelia*
Nov 27 1794	Soulsby, Matthew to Travici, Prudence*
Jul 23 1796	Sowers, Mary to Fisher, Jacob*
Mar 23 1786	Sparks, Matthew to Sharp, Proidence*
Aug 16 1779	Sparks, Thomas to Perdue, Rachael*
Jan 10 1798	Spear, Barbara to Spear, Joseph*
May 15 1779	Spear, Dorcas to Patterson, William
Sep 15 1778	Spear, Elizabeth to Lummers, John*
Nov 20 1790	Spear, Jane to Forman, William, Loe*
Sep 14 1779	Spear, John to Smith, Elizabeth*
Jan 10 1798	Spear, Joseph to Spear, Barbara*
Jan 19 1798	Spear, Nancy to Porter, Elijah*
Nov 20 1781	Speass, Thomas to Boil, Amey
Nov 4 1779	Speck, Henry to Kerns, Mary
Jun 28 1794	Speck, Mary to Lybrand, John*
Sep 22 1797	Spellard, Matthias to Gleeson, Winiford*
Aug 6 1791	Spence, John to Jaffray, Mary
Sep 1 1795	Spencer, Ann to McAdue, Samuel*
Jul 15 1797	Spencer, Anna to Lyon, James*
Dec 6 1783	Spencer, Rebecca to Shearman, Benjamin*
Nov 19 1794	Spencer, Sarah to Johnston, James*
Dec 31 1792	Spencer, Sarah to Leage, Thomas
Jul 10 1797	Spencer, Stephen to Reaner, Uli*
Jan 13 1791	Spicer, Abraham to Sulivan, Sarah*
Jun 11 1782	Spicer, Edward to Wheeler, Isabella*
Jan 8 1785	Spicer, Eleanor to Taylor, Richard

Apr 20 1797	Spicer, Hannah to Sheck, Henry*
Sep 25 1783	Spicer, James to Scovey, Elizabeth*
Jul 17 1781	Spicer, Jean to Conroy, Barneby
Dec 22 1791	Spicer, John to Lee, Rachel*
Nov 7 1795	Spicer, Loveasa to Myers, Jacob*
Feb 16 1797	Spicer, Temperance to Jones, Charles*
Apr 4 1791	Spicer, Valentine to Bowers, Sarah*
Aug 12 1782	Spices, Thomas to Loyd, Elizabeth*
Oct 28 1778	Spick, William to Onbahand, Eve Barbary*
Aug 9 1792	Spiller, Timothy to Collins, Mary
May 7 1791	Spindler, John to Royston, Sophia*
Mar 2 1785	Spiryou, Sarah to Macclefish, Henry*
May 7 1779	Spisor, Voluntine to Rutter, Easter
Jul 31 1788	Spray, John to Summers, Mary*
Nov 4 1797	Sprigg, Delilah to Herston, Charles
Jul 26 1783	Sprigg, Mary to Ham, John
May 20 1786	Springer, Gamaliel to Walker, Araminta*
Dec 5 1787	Springfield, Leah to Coleman, John*
Jan 7 1797	Sprucebunk, Abraham to Kelso, Ann*
Aug 22 1785	Spurrier, John to Cole, Ann
Dec 24 1787	Spurrier, Pamelia to Stringer, Richard
Jun 7 1796	Spurrier, Priscilla to Young, Nathaniel*
Nov 19 1787	Spurrier, Rebecca to Macklefresh, Abner*
Dec 21 1789	Spurrier, Sarah to Griffith, Ely Ridgely*
May 11 1797	Spurrier, Thomas to Hawkins, Sarah*
Feb 7 1789	Spurrier, William to Thackrell, Sophia*
Oct 12 1782	Squire, William to Parker, Sarah
Mar 21 1786	Squires, Daniel to Lysby, Sophia*
Jun 7 1778	Squires, Elinor to Burdan, John*
May 20 1778	Squires, Peter to Clun, Mary M.*
Mar 25 1796	Squires, Sarah to Owings, Thomas*
Jan 3 1795	St Clair, George to Connally, Ceile Ann*
Oct 23 1795	Stacey, Rebecca to Ford, Nathaniel*
May 18 1778	Stacey, Robert to Carter, Rebecca*
Feb 3 1795	Stacey, William to McDade, Milly*
Oct 19 1790	Stack, Samuel to Ladler, Susannah
Dec 16 1783	Stacker, Mary to Bacon, Lemuel*
Aug 8 1782	Stafford, Elizabeth to Byal, William*
Apr 16 1779	Stafford, Hannah to High, James*
Jul 15 1796	Stafford, Nicholas to Breidner, Eliza*
Dec 8 1798	Stagle, Catharine to Stagle, John*
Dec 8 1798	Stagle, John to Stagle, Catharine*
Aug 14 1798	Stagons, Catharine to Trench, Peter
Mar 29 1798	Stains, William to Hughes, Susannah*
Oct 9 1784	Stallings, John to Right, Ruth*
Feb 12 1781	Stambleton, Rebecca to Miller, John*
Mar 22 1794	Stammer, Ulerick Barnhart to Bombarger, Mary*
Apr 2 1784	Standfast, William to Wilson, Elizabeth*
Aug 1 1793	Standiford, Elizabeth to Kelso, James*
Nov 22 1783	Standiford, Elizabeth to Talbott, Edward*
Feb 12 1782	Standiford, Mary to Richardson, Thomas*
Oct 8 1795	Standiford, Pernelloper to Richardson, Vincent*
Feb 10 1786	Standiford, Rachel to Hunt, William
Oct 1 1783	Stanley, John to Maxwell, Margaret*
Oct 10 1793	Stansbury, Ann to Dodge, Samuel*
May 3 1796	Stansbury, Ann to Gunby, Stephen*

Aug 22 1791	Stansbury,	Ann to Wheeler, Stephen*
Oct 31 1778	Stansbury,	Caleb to Cook, Rebecca*
Aug 4 1783	Stansbury,	Caleb to Shilling, Elizabeth*
Dec 23 1783	Stansbury,	Cassandra to Benfield, John*
Mar 25 1789	Stansbury,	Catharine to Green, Joseph*
Feb 17 1798	Stansbury,	Catharine to Welsh, William
Dec 3 1796	Stansbury,	Charles to Thompson, Mary Ann*
Sep 14 1793	Stansbury,	Daniel to Mitchell, Sarah*
Nov 14 1797	Stansbury,	Daniel to Perrigoy, Rebecca
May 1 1788	Stansbury,	Daniel to Stansbury, Elizabeth*
Apr 11 1786	Stansbury,	David to Fowler, Henrietta Marion*
Sep 2 1793	Stansbury,	Drusilla to Pearce, Charles*
Nov 15 1783	Stansbury,	Elijah to Gorsuch, Elizabeth*
Dec 18 1782	Stansbury,	Elizabeth to Brown, James*
Mar 2 1786	Stansbury,	Elizabeth to Clopper, John*
Jul 23 1796	Stansbury,	Elizabeth to Dew, Robert
Dec 22 1792	Stansbury,	Elizabeth to Dutro, George
Mar 1 1798	Stansbury,	Elizabeth to Phipps, Austin*
May 1 1788	Stansbury,	Elizabeth to Stansbury, Daniel*
Apr 25 1778	Stansbury,	Emanuel to Pumphrey, Rachel*
May 10 1794	Stansbury,	Hannah to Davis, Eloha*
May 21 1794	Stansbury,	Hannah to Henderson, William*
May 1 1789	Stansbury,	Henrietta Maria to Lynch, Joshua*
Feb 7 1789	Stansbury,	James to Gorsuch, Jemima*
Jul 19 1790	Stansbury,	Jane to Brotherson, Charles Moore*
Mar 13 1795	Stansbury,	Jemimah to Barry, Lavallin*
Dec ?? 1794	Stansbury,	John Dixon to Johnson, Elizabeth*
Dec 7 1796	Stansbury,	John E. to Proctor, Mary*
Apr 16 1791	Stansbury,	John to Sater, Darcus*
Apr 28 1794	Stansbury,	Joseph of John to Gough, Frances Philips*
May 8 1788	Stansbury,	Joseph to Chineth, Ruth*
Dec 10 1780	Stansbury,	Keziah to Cromwell, Joseph*
Aug 30 1796	Stansbury,	Keziah to Greenwood, Thomas*
Jan 20 1795	Stansbury,	Keziah to Lee, Hall*
Dec 11 1790	Stansbury,	Lucreatia to Caldwell, John*
Oct 7 1791	Stansbury,	Mary to Hughes, James
Nov 20 1793	Stansbury,	Mary to Lemmon, Elexis*
Feb 18 1789	Stansbury,	Mary to Logue, Richard
May 2 1793	Stansbury,	Mary to Taylor, John*
Sep 22 1798	Stansbury,	Polly to Livers, Arnold*
May 18 1797	Stansbury,	Prudence to Bowen, Josias*
Nov 24 1792	Stansbury,	Rebecca to Bowen, Edward*
Dec 23 1789	Stansbury,	Rebecca to Watts, Nathaniel*
Jan 27 1785	Stansbury,	Richard to French, Elinor*
Apr 13 1791	Stansbury,	Richardson to Bavin, Sarah*
Aug 24 1784	Stansbury,	Ruth to Carnowles, Charles
Feb 10 1781	Stansbury,	Ruth to Lynch, William*
Dec 23 1791	Stansbury,	Sarah to Bowen, Josias Jr.*
Dec 31 1777	Stansbury,	Sarah to Shaw, Thomas N.*
Jan 3 1798	Stansbury,	Susan to Cassat, Peter*
Nov 7 1792	Stansbury,	Susannah to Wails, William Wilkinson*
Dec 17 1785	Stansbury,	Terry to Roberts, Benjamin*
Oct 18 1798	Stansbury,	Thomas to Hatton, Mary*
May 1 1784	Stansbury,	Tobias to Buffington, Mary*
Jan 26 1782	Stansbury,	William to Welsh, Ruth
Nov 26 1791	Staple,	Ann to Skeel, William*

Jun 2 1795	Stapleton, Mary to Bonsal, Jesse*
Aug 1 1798	Stark, Catharine to Bordely, John
Jan 18 1797	Starkins, Thomas to Cosset, Catharine*
Aug 6 1795	Starr, Obediah to Boyd, Ruth*
Aug 7 1794	Stauvern, Maria to Bell, Russell*
Oct 12 1792	Stear, Mary to Mason, Richard*
Jan 10 1795	Stearns, William to Astermon, Catharine*
Aug 6 1783	Steed, Sarah to Hall, William*
Nov 5 1783	Steel, Elizabeth to Walsh, Robert*
Apr 9 1789	Steel, John to Hayes, Mary*
Oct 9 1778	Steel, Mary to Philips, Samuel*
Feb 28 1797	Steele, Ann to Lawrence, Wendel*
Jun 6 1786	Steele, Ann to Stiles, George
Jul 11 1794	Steele, Frances to Smith, William Baxter*
Mar 25 1797	Steele, John to Payson, Nancy*
Jan 6 1797	Steele, Sarah to Conway, John*
May 12 1790	Steffee, Harman to Griffith, Rebecca*
Oct 7 1794	Steigar, John to Kiplinger, Catherine
Oct 29 1793	Stein, Rebecca to Herach, Jacob*
Sep 23 1790	Steinbeck, John George to Reafew, Mary*
Jul 30 1798	Steinmetz, Michael to Williams, Mary Ann*
Mar 3 1791	Steitz, Ann to Daugherty, Hugh*
May 12 1791	Steitz, Ann to Hay, William*
Jan 27 1791	Steitz, Mary to Peters, John*
Apr 22 1793	Sterett, Harriott to Gittings, James*
Nov 20 1788	Sterett, Mary to Gittings, Richard*
May 19 1782	Sterling, James to Gibson, Elizabeth
Oct 2 1794	Sterret, Eliza to Matthews, William P.*
Jan 23 1778	Sterrett, Mary to Gist, Mordecai*
Dec 13 1783	Stevens, Alice to Finch, Thomas*
Oct 29 1791	Stevens, Dolly to Kilman, Edward*
May 18 1779	Stevens, Elizabeth to Coale, John
Apr 9 1796	Stevens, Elizabeth to Pearce, Josiah*
Jun 6 1795	Stevens, James to Boyer, Elizabeth*
Nov 11 1794	Stevens, John to Owings, Achsah*
Oct 9 1779	Stevens, John to Reardon, Mary*
Jul 21 1797	Stevens, Joseph to Ingram, Nancy*
Jun 15 1795	Stevens, Lydia to Truelock, Daniel*
Dec 22 1795	Stevens, Messer to Jacobs, Ruth*
Feb 7 1783	Stevens, Nathaniel to Hatton, Sarah
Aug 28 1786	Stevens, Rachel to Boyer, Nicholas
Dec 23 1783	Stevens, Richard to Keistord, Jane*
Dec 12 1782	Stevens, Sarah to Stinchcomb, Charles*
Aug 6 1793	Stevens, Sophia to Kandley, Joseph*
Jan 5 1795	Stevenson, Ann Henly to Lindenberger, George*
Oct 5 1782	Stevenson, Edward to Chamberlain, Mary
Jun 14 1791	Stevenson, Edward to Stevenson, Mary
Nov 21 1795	Stevenson, Elizabeth to Bryson, John*
Feb 3 1791	Stevenson, George P. to Smith, Hetty*
May 1 1794	Stevenson, George to Cromwell, Margaret*
Dec 10 1798	Stevenson, George to Hains, Rose*
Apr 11 1794	Stevenson, George to McCrackin, Elizabeth*
Oct 8 1794	Stevenson, Henry, Dr. to Caulk, Ann
Dec 29 1783	Stevenson, John to Cowan, Elizabeth*
Jun 23 1778	Stevenson, John to Gott, Sarah*
Feb 28 1795	Stevenson, Josias to Stevenson, Urath*

Jul 16 1793	Stevenson, Mary to Baxley, John Jr.*
Aug 29 1789	Stevenson, Mary to Bond, Nicodemus*
Oct 28 1791	Stevenson, Mary to Chamberlain, Hoops*
Apr 13 1779	Stevenson, Mary to McGuire, Thomas
Nov 28 1795	Stevenson, Mary to Peters, Samuel*
Jun 14 1791	Stevenson, Mary to Stevenson, Edward
Mar 8 1791	Stevenson, Mary to Woodrow, Andrew*
Apr 19 1794	Stevenson, Meshach to Jones, Ester*
Aug 10 1778	Stevenson, Mordecai to Bowen, Sarah*
Dec 20 1782	Stevenson, Nicholas to Moore, Mary
Sep 17 1778	Stevenson, Patty to Henry, Robert Jenkins
Aug 1 1782	Stevenson, Rachel to Bond, Richard
Oct 25 1788	Stevenson, Samuel to Dorsey, Lucy*
Jul 4 1795	Stevenson, Samuel to Peathers, Elizabeth*
May 31 1798	Stevenson, Sarah to Glanvile, Stephen*
Dec 23 1783	Stevenson, Sater to Cromwell, Ann*
Feb 28 1795	Stevenson, Urath to Stevenson, Josias*
Feb 14 1784	Stevenson, William to Boon, Mary*
Apr 19 1784	Stevenson, William to Brant, Elizabeth*
Oct 10 1788	Stevenson, William to Moore, Abarilla*
Dec 23 1780	Stevins, William to Carter, Susannah*
Apr 21 1789	Stevinson, Moses to Shaw, Eleanor
Jun 1 1791	Steward, David to Pumphrey, Ann*
Jul 31 1782	Steward, Elizabeth to O'Brian, Patrick*
Dec 22 1797	Steward, Elizabeth to Pattingall, Jonathan*
Feb 13 1784	Steward, Ezekiel to Boon, Mary*
Sep 6 1783	Steward, Henry to Mumford, Catherine*
Jan 25 1783	Steward, Rachael to Jacobs, Joseph*
Dec 8 1798	Steward, Rebecca to Williams, Thomas*
Jun 30 1783	Steward, Sabella to McCord, John*
Oct 22 1793	Steward, Sarah to Pumphrey, Joseph*
Jan 24 1798	Steward, Sarah to Robinson, Thomas*
May 24 1788	Steward, William to Guyton, Elizabeth*
Aug 13 1778	Stewart, Ann to Parker, Edward*
Dec 23 1797	Stewart, Anne to Millin, Charles*
Nov 25 1791	Stewart, Archibald to Nelson, Sarah*
Nov 17 1787	Stewart, Catherine to Cowan, William*
Oct 17 1778	Stewart, Charles to Merryman, Rachel*
Sep 27 1793	Stewart, Charles to Stewart, Elizabeth*
Mar 26 1785	Stewart, Dinah to Pumphrey, Joshua
Jan 20 1793	Stewart, Elinor to Bugan, John
Jul 13 1798	Stewart, Elizabeth to Colegate, John*
Sep 27 1793	Stewart, Elizabeth to Stewart, Charles*
Apr 11 1795	Stewart, Hannah to Conway, William*
Feb 24 1795	Stewart, Hugh to Wooden, Margaret*
Aug 10 1793	Stewart, James to Britt, Margaret*
Jun 25 1791	Stewart, James to Deigers, Rachel*
Dec 23 1785	Stewart, James to Ewing, Eleanor
Jan 11 1782	Stewart, James to Marshall, Phebe*
Jan 9 1784	Stewart, Jane to Simpson, Walter*
Dec 28 1790	Stewart, John Cowden to Barrett, Mary*
Jun 10 1795	Stewart, John to Bowny, Mary*
Nov 24 1798	Stewart, John to Clarke, Sarah*
Dec 27 1798	Stewart, John to Treakle, Elizabeth*
Oct 18 1797	Stewart, Mark to Killman, Priscila*
Aug 11 1781	Stewart, Mary to Caple, Abraham*

```
Jul 24 1798    Stewart, Patty to Adams, William*
May  8 1798    Stewart, Rachel C. to Lewis, William Y.*
Feb  2 1798    Stewart, Rachel to Gardner, William*
May 10 1798    Stewart, Rachel to Mushaw, David*
Mar 30 1796    Stewart, Rachel to Sank, John*
Dec 29 1790    Stewart, Sarah to Lunt, Henry*
Apr 30 1796    Stewert, Mary to Parks, John*
Mar 24 1794    Sthall, Charles to Seweth, Sarah*
Dec 12 1783    Sthall, Elizabeth to Hyner, Joseph*
Dec 24 1783    Sticker, Elizabeth to Beckem, John*
Jun 24 1784    Stigar, Catharine to Lighthold, Andrew*
Jul 31 1788    Stigar, Jacob to Atkinson, Margaret*
Oct 12 1793    Stigar, Matthias to Crissman, Mary*
Jun  8 1790    Stiger, Nancy to Reid, Nelson*
Apr 25 1793    Stigors, Elizabeth to Rainer, William*
Mar 16 1782    Stiles, Ann to Noex, John*
Aug  3 1784    Stiles, Chanty to Barney, John*
Jun  6 1786    Stiles, George to Steele, Ann
Nov 26 1783    Stiles, Hannah to Deal, Christian*
Dec 24 1783    Stiles, Lawrence to Hammond, Mary*
Dec 15 1781    Still, Lydia to Jones, Solomon*
Feb 27 1797    Stillinger, Jacob to Labough, Christina*
Jul  6 1789    Stillwell, John to Allender, Deborah*
Nov 17 1792    Stinchcomb, Achsah to Green, William*
Apr  2 1796    Stinchcomb, Ann to Lee, John*
Dec 29 1785    Stinchcomb, Catharine to Brown, Zachariah*
Dec 12 1782    Stinchcomb, Charles to Stevens, Sarah*
Oct 16 1793    Stinchcomb, Christopher to Zimmerman, Magdaline*
Nov 28 1797    Stinchcomb, Elizabeth to Zimmerman, George*
Mar  5 1792    Stinchcomb, Enoch to Howard, Sarah*
Jun 21 1783    Stinchcomb, George to Andrews, Aberilla
Sep 16 1795    Stinchcomb, Hannah to Miller, Elijah*
Oct 30 1794    Stinchcomb, Hannah to Wood, Womal*
Jan  9 1793    Stinchcomb, John to Deaver, Mary*
Nov 23 1792    Stinchcomb, Larkin to Stocksdale, Rachel*
May 13 1778    Stinchcomb, McLain to Merryman, Nackey*
Oct  6 1791    Stinchcomb, Nathaniel to Cannon, Airy
Apr 19 1794    Stinchcomb, Rebecca to Jarviss, Robert*
Oct 28 1794    Stinchcomb, Rebecca to Zimmerman, George*
Jan 28 1792    Stinchcomb, Sarah to Maxwell, John*
Apr 11 1778    Stinchcomb, Thomas to Owings, Ruth*
Feb 27 1790    Stinchcomb, Victory to Cord, Ann*
Sep 12 1795    Stine, Mariah Rosannah to Hammitt, Thomas*
Nov  8 1798    Stiner, Nancy to Barton, Thomas*
Apr 20 1798    Stitford, Mary to Keith, William*
Jul  6 1797    Stith, Lucy to Pringle, Mark*
Jun 28 1794    Stoare, John to Fifer, Rachel*
Nov 23 1795    Stock, Rebecca to March, Andrew*
Dec 26 1794    Stockett, Henry to McKenzie, Barbara*
Oct  7 1791    Stockett, Mary to Hayes, William Jr.*
Oct  9 1792    Stocks, Mary to Ross, Ham*
Sep 28 1791    Stocksdale, Airy to Dorsey, John*
Dec 20 1793    Stocksdale, Amelia to Porter, Greenbury*
Nov 21 1789    Stocksdale, Edmund H. to Evans, Naomi*
Feb  6 1778    Stocksdale, Edward to Bennett, Elinor*
Mar 31 1795    Stocksdale, Edward to Stocksdale, Hellen*
```

Jan 4 1791	Stocksdale, Eleanor to Madiera, Daniel*
Mar 28 1781	Stocksdale, Hannah to Hook, William
Mar 31 1795	Stocksdale, Hellen to Stocksdale, Edward*
Nov 23 1792	Stocksdale, Rachel to Stinchcomb, Larkin*
Jul 16 1779	Stokes, Ann to Davisen, Andrew
Oct 20 1784	Stokes, John to Savage, Margaret*
May 26 1796	Stokes, Mary to Martin, Thomas*
Jul 1 1797	Stokes, Temperance to McCollum, Duncan*
Jan 14 1784	Stoller, Catharine to Bibby, John*
Oct 7 1797	Stom, Mary Ann to Milford, James*
Mar 12 1796	Stonall, William to Ensor, Mary*
Dec 16 1785	Stone, Ann to Forrest, Josiah
Jan 25 1796	Stone, Edward to Chattle, Nancy*
Dec 8 1798	Stone, Henry to Porter, Rebecca*
Jan 28 1796	Stone, Thomas to Jenkins, Henrietta*
Apr 18 1778	Stone, William to Cockey, Hannah*
Dec 15 1794	Stoner, Catharine to Bender, Jacob*
Aug 4 1794	Stopps, Catharine to Mine, Michael*
Mar 6 1797	Stops, Polly to Sap, George
Jun 28 1781	Storey, Ezekiel to McInhamer, Mary*
Jul 18 1796	Storey, John to Geoghegan, Mary*
Oct 31 1795	Storey, Mary to Smith, Philip*
Jul 24 1784	Storm, George to Armagost, Margaret*
Aug 3 1795	Story, George L. to Dashiell, Christy*
Jan 11 1783	Stout, Elizabeth to Smith, Henry
Jun 22 1796	Stover, Mary to Yoner, Samuel*
Oct 3 1782	Stover, Susannah to Whiton, Henry
Dec 19 1798	Stoxdale, Polly to Brown, Nicholas
May 10 1798	Stoxdale, Rachel to Deddep, John*
Feb 17 1784	Strabble, Mary to Bowles, John*
Sep 29 1790	Stran, John to Johnson, Rebecca*
Oct 17 1798	Stran, Rebecca to Jaqut, John P.*
Feb 20 1797	Stratton, William to Howard, Mary*
Sep 30 1781	Strauhon, Margaret to Padwell, Simon*
Jan 10 1792	Strawble, Ann to McKinzie, John*
Feb 29 1788	Strawble, Rebecca to Branch, John*
Dec 29 1785	Strawbridge, Elizabeth to Shannon, Michael
Feb 17 1796	Strawbridge, Theophelus to Edger, Abigail*
Apr 11 1786	Strayer, Mary to Betz, Conrad
May 17 1783	Strebeck, Christiana to Keener, Michael*
Sep 12 1785	Streeback, Rachel to Jones, Jacob*
Dec 6 1782	Street, Benjamin to Cambridge, Martha
Mar 11 1784	Street, Daniel to Amoss, Elizabeth*
Dec 11 1784	Street, John to Sinclair, Martha*
Nov 19 1779	Street, Samuel to Halmoney, Elizabeth
May 16 1788	Streney, Nicholas to Green, Mary*
Nov 12 1798	Stricker, Louisa to Carson, Henry*
Dec 31 1793	Strike, Nicholas to Flinn, Eleanor*
Dec 31 1796	Strike, Nicholas to Phenie, Margaret*
Jul 22 1783	Stringer, Elizabeth to Everton, Daniel
Mar 17 1786	Stringer, Mary to Hoofnagle, George Jr.*
Dec 24 1787	Stringer, Richard to Spurrier, Pamelia
Oct 11 1783	Strobe, Jacob to Hughes, Sarah*
Jun 3 1778	Stroman, John to Sitler, Mary*
Nov 1 1789	Strong, Joseph to Hale, Rachael*
Oct 28 1785	Strong, Ludwick to Hill, Mary

```
Aug 19 1783    Strong, Rebecca to Simpson, Amos*
May 17 1790    Strophel, Anna to Mercer, Benjamin I.*
May  3 1793    Strophel, Mary to Buckingham, Thomas*
Mar 22 1783    Stroven, Sarah to Myers, Henry*
Mar  3 1791    Stryer, George to Read, Ann*
Jan  9 1790    Stuback, Christian to Paul, Nancy*
Apr  7 1794    Stubbs, John to Quay, Sarah*
May  8 1795    Stubbs, Sarah to Davis, William L.*
Nov 22 1791    Stull, Andrew to Overy, Rheanna*
Feb 12 1784    Stull, Margaret to Donning, John*
Oct 17 1779    Stump, John to Wilson, Cassandra
Jul 25 1798    Stupery, Pierce to Duharty, Susanna Catharine*
Feb 24 1781    Sturgiss, Thomas to Thompson, Marian*
Oct 10 1785    Suffrace, Charles to Liscom, Elizabeth
Jun  8 1778    Sulivan, Daniel to Henderson, Mary*
Nov  2 1780    Sulivan, Hannah to House, Thomas*
Jun 22 1778    Sulivan, Mary to Anderson, William*
Jan 13 1791    Sulivan, Sarah to Spicer, Abraham*
Apr  4 1778    Sullers, Elizabeth to Couling, James*
Oct  6 1792    Sullivan, Allender to Benson, Benjamin*
Mar 24 1798    Sullivan, Andrew Moon to Burnham, Araminta*
Mar 11 1797    Sullivan, Biddy to Foche, Anthony*
Oct 14 1784    Sullivan, Daniel to Gray, Mary*
Nov 11 1797    Sullivan, Eleanor to Richardson, James*
Jul 15 1783    Sullivan, Hannah to Lanahan, Lewis
Jun  2 1783    Sullivan, Jeremiah to Hoy, Ann
Aug 31 1790    Sullivan, Margaret to Harris, Edward*
Apr 13 1791    Sullivan, Thomas to Heir, Jemima*
Sep 23 1794    Sumblin, William to Davis, Harriot*
Nov 30 1797    Summer, Mary to Primrose, Asbury
Jul 19 1795    Summers, Andrew to Harp, Catharine*
Aug  1 1786    Summers, Anne to Nelson, James
Feb 23 1795    Summers, Elizabeth to  Scoarce, John A.*
Jun 28 1798    Summers, Jane to Thompson, William*
Feb 11 1795    Summers, John to Workman, Ann*
Jul  5 1781    Summers, Margaret to Cooper, Thomas*
Nov  9 1797    Summers, Margaret to Device, John Darch Livel*
Apr 17 1784    Summers, Martin to Knoutten, Elizabeth*
Dec 17 1780    Summers, Mary to Fellon, John*
Jul 31 1788    Summersby, Mary to Spray, John*
Sep  8 1778    Summersby, Sarah to Harnett, James*
Mar 18 1783    Summerville, John to Mallender, Eleanor*
Sep 19 1798    Sumoalt, John to Smith, Margaret*
Jul  2 1791    Sumvalt, Margaret to Myer, Casper, Wilen*
Nov 18 1797    Sumvalt, Mary to Kregs, John*
Oct 16 1784    Sumwald, George to Wort, Mary
Nov 14 1796    Sunderlun, Mary to Gilberthorp, Francis*
Dec 15 1777    Sutton, Alice to Farran, Joseph*
Jul 29 1779    Sutton, Ann to Keephost, Michael*
Nov  1 1780    Sutton, Isaac to Grimes, Ann*
Oct 21 1784    Sutton, Kitty to Shipley, Samuel*
Jan 13 1784    Sutton, Mary to All, Edward*
Jun  5 1798    Sutton, Matthias to Smith, Anna*
May 20 1779    Sutton, Thomas to Corginton, Mary
Jan 19 1785    Sutton, Thomas to Gotset, Anne*
Jun 22 1796    Suyman, Catharine to Forsyth, John*
```

```
Jul 21 1785    Swain, Jeremiah to Herbert, Rebecca
Aug 12 1797    Swan, Ann to Manson, Joel M.*
Aug  1 1779    Swan, Mary to Hull, Richard*
Sep  7 1784    Swan, Matthew to McKean, Ann*
Oct  2 1788    Swan, Susannah to Armur, Samuel*
Oct  7 1790    Swann, Joseph to Maxwell, Agnes*
Dec 26 1795    Swann, Joshua to Helm, Nancy*
Mar 23 1796    Swann, Leonard to Parrish, Mary*
Mar 15 1782    Swann, Rachel to Anderson, Nathan*
May  6 1778    Swann, Samuel to Puntenay, Susannah*
Nov  2 1784    Swarts, John to Scholl, Mary Elizabeth*
Mar 16 1786    Swartz, George to Kimmell, Mary*
Sep 29 1783    Swartz, Henry to Smith, Barbara*
Dec 31 1782    Sweeney, Mary to Lasher, Frederick*
Jul 14 1797    Sweeny, Biddy to Hawkins, Daniel*
Oct  1 1796    Sweeny, Edward to Blackford, Elizabeth*
Jul 18 1789    Sweeny, Hugh to Hook, Priscilla*
Jul 14 1795    Sweeting, Charlotte to Hiser, David*
Mar 28 1793    Sweeting, John to Heiser, Susannah*
Jul 25 1784    Sweeting, Mary to Davis, Christian
Apr  6 1786    Swindall, Peter to Hisdale, Catharine*
Apr  1 1793    Swingle, George to Householder, Mary*
Oct 23 1784    Swingle, Magdelana to Teice, Jacob*
Feb 24 1784    Swingler, Barbara to Hoffman, Jacob*
Jan 16 1790    Switzer, Elizabeth to Shoemaker, Adam*
Oct 17 1798    Switzer, John to Kimble, Patty*
Dec 13 1777    Swoope, Benedict Jr. to Keener, Margaret*
May  4 1784    Swope, Mary to Brevitt, John*
Jan  6 1798    Sylvester, George to Remage, Rachel*
Aug  2 1784    S____ley, Ruth to Barns, Adam*
Oct  6 1783    Tador, William to Griffith, Martha*
Oct 11 1790    Tagert, John to Williamson, Mary*
Aug  5 1794    Tagler, Mary to Capoot, Jeremiah*
Jul 13 1793    Tague, Thomas to Henley, Rebecca
Jun  9 1778    Talbot, Benjamin R. to Deaver, Martha*
Dec 16 1795    Talbot, James to Darbin, Polly*
Sep  4 1790    Talbot, Martha to Duncan, William*
Oct 29 1792    Talbot, Richard to Todd, Rachel*
Dec 20 1791    Talbott, Ann to Bond, Thomas*
May 29 1798    Talbott, Catharine to Talbott, Joshua
Nov 22 1783    Talbott, Edward to Standiford, Elizabeth*
Apr  9 1794    Talbott, Henry to Davis, Susannah*
Jan 26 1782    Talbott, Jeremiah to Grover, Elizabeth
Jun 17 1784    Talbott, John to Philips, Henrietta*
Nov  7 1797    Talbott, John to Slade, Mary*
Oct 19 1796    Talbott, John to Taylor, Sarah*
May 29 1798    Talbott, Joshua to Talbott, Catharine
Nov 30 1797    Talbott, Mary to Dorsey, Derias*
Dec  8 1798    Talbott, Mary to Dorsey, Hezekiah*
Mar 24 1794    Talbott, Mary to Gorsuch, Dickinson
Oct  5 1782    Talbott, Providence to Wells, Nicholas
Sep  6 1785    Talbott, Rebecca to Watson, Archabald*
Nov  4 1788    Talbott, Richard Colegate to Grover, Drusilla*
Aug 15 1778    Talbott, Richard to Wells, Aehsa*
Mar 25 1782    Talbott, Temperence to Brittain, Richard
Jan 14 1795    Talbott, Thomas to Rutledge, Elizabeth*
```

Jul	1	1784	Taler, Frances to Greenfield, Thomas Truman*
Apr	1	1793	Tally, Martha to Howard, Thomas Gassaway*
Feb	13	1794	Tane, Jane to Garnes, William*
Nov	11	1784	Tanner, Isaac to Reese, Margaret
Mar	19	1796	Tanner, Nancy to Grigley, William*
Jan	13	1795	Tanner, Pearce Lacey to Pepper, Pamelia*
Aug	15	1783	Tarmer, Elizabeth to Hams, Jacob*
Jul	14	1797	Taron, William to Cook, Susanna*
Dec	31	1794	Tarr, Levin to Tuplessa, Rosella*
Jun	28	1797	Tassey, Elizabeth to Hebert, John Baptiste*
Jul	30	1785	Tate, Elizabeth to Bleany, Nathaniel
Jan	29	1782	Tate, James to Corilter, Elizabeth*
Dec	1	1789	Tate, Jane to Thornell, Robert*
Oct	6	1778	Taumble, John to Carnes, Catharine*
Feb	4	1789	Taylor, Acquila to Holland, Sarah*
Jul	25	1778	Taylor, Ann to McGuire, Martin*
Aug	25	1792	Taylor, Ann to McLarnan, John*
Feb	21	1797	Taylor, Ann to Payne, Zachariah*
Oct	6	1792	Taylor, Ann to Riddle, John
Jul	24	1779	Taylor, Ann to Walter, John
Jan	20	1798	Taylor, Averilla to Craff, Jacob
Jan	20	1792	Taylor, Edward to Brown, Ann
Mar	8	1793	Taylor, Eleanor to Everitt, John*
Apr	10	1784	Taylor, Elizabeth to Carson, William*
Apr	21	1796	Taylor, Elizabeth to Landers, William*
Apr	4	1778	Taylor, Elizabeth to Lawrence, James*
Oct	24	1798	Taylor, Elizabeth to League, John*
Oct	4	1797	Taylor, Francis S. to Lindsay, Ann Fox*
Nov	19	1792	Taylor, George to Gouldsmith, Martha*
Dec	27	1787	Taylor, George to Osborn, Ann*
Dec	30	1794	Taylor, Grace to Kelly, Edward*
Dec	30	1794	Taylor, Hannah to Scarfe, William*
May	24	1794	Taylor, Henry to Willson, Margaret*
Jul	6	1796	Taylor, Hetty to Adams, Isaac*
Sep	12	1786	Taylor, Hugh to Currey, Elizabeth
Apr	29	1786	Taylor, Hymmers Henry to Rennehan, Ann*
Nov	4	1796	Taylor, James to Coward, Jemina*
Jun	15	1784	Taylor, James to Jones, Mary*
Jan	22	1785	Taylor, James to Lucas, Lizabeth*
Oct	13	1792	Taylor, James to Murray, Margaret*
Nov	18	1797	Taylor, James to Reams, Elizabeth*
Oct	5	1784	Taylor, John to Dean, Sarah
Oct	10	1790	Taylor, John to Hooper, Elinor
May	2	1793	Taylor, John to Stansbury, Mary*
Feb	18	1792	Taylor, Joseph to Campbell, Nancy*
Sep	22	1789	Taylor, Joseph to Dunkin, Hester*
Mar	22	1785	Taylor, Levin to Hoppen, Ruth
Aug	15	1782	Taylor, Margaret to Williams, John*
Jun	11	1784	Taylor, Mary to Baker, Thomas*
Oct	3	1778	Taylor, Mary to Benson, James*
Apr	19	1786	Taylor, Mary to Hart, Charles*
Mar	24	1794	Taylor, Mary to Laman, James*
Nov	26	1798	Taylor, Matthew to Fossham, Mary*
Oct	20	1790	Taylor, Matthew to Smith, Mary*
Jan	21	1786	Taylor, Providence to Meah, James*
Jan	3	1784	Taylor, Rebecca to Siberuy, William*

```
Jan  8 1785    Taylor, Richard to Spicer, Eleanor
Mar  8 1793    Taylor, Robert to Etling, Frances*
Feb 26 1794    Taylor, Ruth to Gash, Benjamin*
Feb 26 1795    Taylor, Sarah to Bradburn, Alexander*
Jun  8 1790    Taylor, Sarah to Daughaday, Joseph*
Oct 19 1796    Taylor, Sarah to Talbott, John*
Dec  2 1778    Taylor, Thomas to Evans, Elizabeth*
May 21 1795    Taylor, Thomas to Hook, Barbara*
Mar 19 1778    Taylor, William to Connough, Mary*
Jan 28 1786    Taylor, William to Cooper, Keziah*
Jan  9 1783    Taylor, William to Judah, Hannah*
Jul 19 1790    Taylor, William to Limes, Barbara*
Jul 27 1797    Taylor, William to Thomas, Mary*
Sep  3 1779    Tea, Michael to Robbert, Mary
Sep 16 1793    Tea, Sarah to Jaffris, John*
Jun 15 1796    Teague, Laban to Kilbourn, Elizabeth*
Jun  4 1778    Tear, Ann to Yedlie, Moses*
Apr 15 1797    Tear, Daniel to McCoy, Charlotte*
Dec 11 1778    Tear, Ignatius to Hudless, Ann*
Aug 20 1791    Tearson, Bridget to Aleach, William*
Jul  6 1791    Tedford, Sarah to Turnbull, William*
Oct 17 1790    Teer, Owen to Greenfield, Patty
Oct 23 1784    Teice, Jacob to Swingle, Magdelana*
Sep 10 1779    Teisel, Ann to Blake, Francis*
Aug 15 1795    Telour, Nancy to Amay, Francis*
Nov  8 1796    Tenant, Thomas to Waters, Mary*
Feb 27 1788    Tener, Hester to Buckingham, George*
Nov 14 1797    Tenis, Sarah to Kitely, Abraham*
Oct 13 1785    Tennant, Phebe to Hardesty, Levy
Sep 26 1797    Tennis, Jacob to Williams, Sarah*
Feb  9 1782    Tenton, Mary to Link, Stephen
Nov  1 1791    Teret, Valentine to Eara, Elizabeth*
Sep  2 1797    Tesh, Peter to Bankards, Polly*
Dec  1 1785    Test, Deborah to Thompson, John
Nov 22 1785    Tevis, Agness to Cadle, Griffith
May  1 1779    Tevis, Cassander to Mercer, Richard*
Jan 26 1792    Tevis, Daniel to Woolery, Elizabeth*
May 30 1789    Tevis, Rachael to Crow, James*
Apr 23 1778    Tevis, Ruth to Boyd, Francis*
Sep 19 1792    Tevis, Thomas to Mackelfish, Mary*
Oct  7 1790    Tevis, Thomas to Mackelfresh, Elizabeth*
Feb  7 1789    Thackrell, Sophia to Spurrier, William*
Feb  3 1785    Thatcher, Henry to Warrell, Catherine*
Nov 13 1790    Thomas, Ann to Jones, William
Apr 17 1790    Thomas, Benjamin to Riston, Margaret*
Dec 29 1796    Thomas, Bethia to Craig, Thomas*
Apr 28 1791    Thomas, Catherine to Koniche, Nicholas*
Dec  5 1783    Thomas, Daniel to Norris, Sarah*
Apr  1 1796    Thomas, Edward to Bishop, Mary*
Jan 16 1796    Thomas, Eliza to Hannan, James*
Oct  9 1793    Thomas, Elizabeth to Impford, Titus*
Feb 26 1781    Thomas, Evin to Arnold, Ruth
Mar  7 1789    Thomas, Hannah to Lyon, Samuel*
Apr  8 1778    Thomas, James to Crowe, Margaret*
Apr  6 1778    Thomas, James to Crowe, Margaret*
Jun 18 1778    Thomas, John to Henderson, Marthen*
```

Aug 22 1782	Thomas, John to Smith, Biddy
May 16 1778	Thomas, Mary to Rettig, Christian*
Jul 27 1797	Thomas, Mary to Taylor, William*
Nov 16 1795	Thomas, Milcha to Kessuck, Roger*
Jun 25 1783	Thomas, Philip to Myers, Catherine*
Feb 11 1797	Thomas, Rebecca to Field, Thomas*
Feb 16 1785	Thomas, Ruth to Price, Nathan*
Jan 7 1778	Thomas, Sarah to Allen, Bartholomew*
Oct 6 1798	Thomas, Sarah to Hambleton, Benjamin*
Oct 6 1789	Thomas, Sophia to Perry, Richard*
Mar 22 1794	Thomas, Susannah to Griffith, Nathan*
Oct 15 1783	Thomas, William to Baxter, Margaret
Feb 15 1798	Thomas, William to Bradshaw, Catharine*
Jan 29 1794	Thomas, William to Faure, Jariet Ann*
Mar 11 1779	Thomas, William to Poole, Sarah
May 25 1786	Thombury, Robert to Berbine, Magdaline*
May 26 1789	Thompson, Agnes to Adams, Samuel*
Nov 20 1798	Thompson, Alexander to Arnest, Margaret*
Jan 24 1786	Thompson, Alexander to Poe, Jane*
Jul 12 1793	Thompson, Amos to Hayes, Elizabeth*
Feb 23 1778	Thompson, Aquila to Wallingsford, Elizabeth*
Oct 24 1796	Thompson, Catharine to Badger, Bela*
May 22 1794	Thompson, Catharine to Hilton, Abraham*
Sep 8 1794	Thompson, Catharine to Sheekan, Cornelius*
Dec 25 1794	Thompson, David to Egleston, Sarah*
Oct 19 1793	Thompson, Edward to Dunn, Mary*
Nov 19 1778	Thompson, Edward to Fitzgerald, Mary*
Jul 1 1793	Thompson, Eleanor to Ridden, George*
Jan 22 1788	Thompson, Hester to Israel, Joseph*
Sep 5 1786	Thompson, Hugh to Black, Jane
Nov 7 1789	Thompson, Ingree to Smith, Mary*
May 21 1794	Thompson, James to Cleaves, Elizabeth*
Apr 18 1782	Thompson, James to Hickey, Johannah*
Mar 19 1794	Thompson, James to Munnings, Maria Adelaide*
Jun 25 1797	Thompson, James to Turner, Sophia*
Jun 13 1796	Thompson, John to Shaw, Eve*
Dec 1 1785	Thompson, John to Test, Deborah
Aug 15 1797	Thompson, Jonathan to Dells, Elizabeth*
Nov 19 1795	Thompson, Josias to Forsyth, Jane*
Feb 24 1781	Thompson, Marian to Sturgiss, Thomas*
Dec 3 1796	Thompson, Mary Ann to Stansbury, Charles*
Nov 30 1793	Thompson, Mary to Bernett, Jacob*
Dec 13 1796	Thompson, Mary to Farien, John*
May 25 1791	Thompson, Mary to Fenning, Thomas*
Dec 2 1796	Thompson, Mary to Harvey, Joseph*
Oct 11 1788	Thompson, Nancy to Barry, Standish*
Sep 12 1795	Thompson, Nathan Sylvester to Henwood, Elizabeth*
Jul 28 1792	Thompson, Nathaniel G. to Jackson, Elizabeth*
May 11 1791	Thompson, Prudence to Hammersley, Thomas
Dec 20 1794	Thompson, Robert to Askew, Catharine*
May 20 1789	Thompson, Robert to Manley, Margaret*
Dec 25 1780	Thompson, Thomas to Adams, Elizabeth*
Aug 10 1797	Thompson, William to Anderson, Elizabeth*
May 11 1797	Thompson, William to Miltenberger, Mariah*
Mar 12 1791	Thompson, William to Poe, Mary*
Jun 28 1798	Thompson, William to Summers, Jane*

Nov 14 1793	Thornburgh, Robert to Kettleman, Elizabeth*
Dec 6 1798	Thornbury, Mary Ann to McSure, John*
Dec 1 1789	Thornell, Robert to Tate, Jane*
Dec 31 1787	Thornton, Hannah to Harvey, Thomas*
Mar 27 1798	Thornton, Henry to Bowly, Ann Lux*
Apr 25 1795	Thornton, Rachel to Alexander, William*
Aug 28 1782	Thorpe, Benjamin to Deverex, Sarah*
Nov 22 1779	Thorrington, Elizabeth to Smith, Francis*
Aug 7 1789	Thoucas, Lewis to Lasqu, Mary*
Jul 16 1785	Thralls, Samuel to Collins, Ann*
Oct 31 1781	Thralls, Sophiah to Oliver, John
Dec 21 1785	Thrap, William to _____, Frances
Jul 2 1783	Tibbet, Walter to Green, Delilah*
Aug 8 1796	Tiche, Lend to Rapp, Dederick*
Jan 3 1791	Tidy, Sarah to Whiting, Elisha*
May 15 1784	Tiellen, John to Melanson, Elizabeth
Jun 25 1797	Tillon, Thomas to Joyce, Elizabeth*
Dec 14 1795	Tilly, Marie Claire LG. to Desbordes, Antoine G.L.*
Feb 23 1795	Timbull, Sarah to Bryan, Richard*
Apr 27 1795	Tinges, Henry Walker to Ilker, Sarah*
Oct 19 1791	Tinges, Mary to Ecle, Philip*
Jan 11 1778	Tinker, William to Wilperd, Mary*
Dec 8 1782	Tippet, Margaret to Davis, Thomas
Feb 14 1798	Tipton, Ann to Leef, Henry
Nov 29 1783	Tipton, Ann to Wheeler, Samuel*
May 6 1778	Tipton, Aquila to Bell, Rebecca*
Dec 19 1796	Tipton, Brian to Deaver, Ann*
Jan 9 1783	Tipton, Caroline to Gorsuch, William*
Sep 30 1779	Tipton, Cassanna to Cox, Abraham*
Aug 1 1795	Tipton, Elizabeth to Boreing, Joshua*
Dec 4 1795	Tipton, Elizabeth to Whiteford, John*
Jan 16 1781	Tipton, Jabeus Murray to Lemmon, Rebecca*
May 20 1779	Tipton, Jemimah to Acton, Richard*
Dec 19 1798	Tipton, Micajah to Leaf, Anne*
Nov 14 1787	Tipton, Penelope to Gorsuch, William*
Feb 2 1798	Tipton, Rebecca to Cox, William*
Jun 6 1789	Tipton, Rebecca to Parish, Aquila*
Sep 23 1786	Tipton, Richard to Wilson, Susannah*
Dec 15 1778	Tipton, Samuel to Bowen, Ruth*
Nov 1 1793	Tipton, Solomon to Randall, Mary*
Apr 20 1782	Titmon, Christopher to Vellers, Barbara*
Mar 15 1782	Tobit, James to English, Margaret
Jan 5 1795	Toby, Eleanor to Andrew, Robert*
Sep 23 1795	Todd, Ann to Floyd, Thomas*
Dec 10 1781	Todd, Benjamin to Ford, Elinor
Mar 15 1791	Todd, Elizabeth to Walker, Matthew*
Jan 18 1783	Todd, Elizabeth to Young, Nathan
Aug 8 1778	Todd, Lancelot to Leakins, Mary*
Jun 23 1788	Todd, Mary to Hall, Elisha*
Jun 3 1789	Todd, Mary to Watts, Josias*
Jun 15 1795	Todd, Nancy to Aithenson, Francis*
May 28 1783	Todd, Nicholas to Leakin, Ann*
Jul 7 1781	Todd, Nicholas to Pauling, Mary
Oct 22 1795	Todd, Philip to Goulding, Elizabeth*
May 14 1796	Todd, Rachel to Hughes, John*
Oct 29 1792	Todd, Rachel to Talbot, Richard*

Date	Marriage
Mar 19 1796	Todd, Rebecca to Green, Clement*
Oct 10 1795	Todd, Thomas to Brown, Mary*
Dec 25 1777	Todd, Thomas to Mills, Elizabeth*
Aug 3 1795	Toley, Joseph to Burnet, Mary*
Aug 17 1784	Tolley, Edward Carvel to Worthington, Elizabeth*
Jan 17 1797	Tolson, Elizabeth to Watson, William*
Mar 21 1796	Tomblinson, Samuel to Fox, Hannah*
Apr 28 1791	Tomlinson, Joseph to Noel, Margaret*
Jul 19 1785	Tompanks, Elizabeth to Clarkson, Thomas
Sep 19 1797	Toner, Jacob to Perton, Catharine*
Mar 26 1788	Tonerey, Peggy to Bidot, John Peter
Jun 30 1781	Tonstell, Henry to Elder, Delilah
Jan 6 1795	Toole, Daniel to Smich, Elizabeth*
Feb 16 1792	Toole, Elizabeth to Roberts, Thomas*
Aug 19 1784	Toole, James to Cruise, Catherine*
Aug 9 1788	Toole, James to Moore, Susannah*
May 29 1794	Toole, John to Schott, Christina Margaret*
Feb 1 1781	Tooly, Abigail Harper to Cornish, Joseph Rouse*
Jun 1 1796	Topham, Matthew to Jacobs, Mary*
Jul 21 1792	Totten, Joseph to Kline, Elizabeth*
Oct 13 1798	Touman, Valentine to Lucas, Rebecca*
Jun 19 1798	Toury, Jeremiah to Matthews, Sarah*
Jun 22 1784	Toury, Polly to Vouchez, John Baptist*
Jan 8 1795	Towers, George to Acken, Mary*
Aug 18 1792	Towers, John to Hannan, Elizabeth*
Jan 3 1795	Towers, Margaret to Hannan, John*
Sep 28 1793	Townsend, Elijah to Coghan, Nancy*
Feb 7 1798	Townsend, Julian to Hall, John*
Jun 29 1797	Townsend, Nancy to Hinder, Thomas*
Jan 17 1794	Townsend, Robert to Freeland, Juliet*
May 10 1778	Townsend, William to Mason, Sarah*
Nov 13 1794	Towrell, Elizabeth to Prince, John*
Feb 11 1794	Towson, Abraham to Gates, Jane*
Dec 30 1785	Towson, Ann to Wallace, John
Jul 15 1784	Towson, Dorcas to Edwards, Heathcoat
Mar 10 1779	Towson, Elizabeth to Hick, Lewis
Apr 7 1794	Towson, Elizabeth to Parks, David*
Apr 19 1788	Towson, Jacob T. to Boyd, Jane*
May 13 1786	Towson, James to Osborn, Cary
Jul 12 1791	Towson, Rachel to Kitten, John*
Apr 27 1790	Towson, Ruth to Daugherty, William*
Mar 15 1793	Towson, Susannah to Worman, George*
Jul 16 1785	Towson, William to Young, Rebecca
Dec 24 1794	Toy, Ann to Shipey, David*
Apr 12 1796	Toy, Frances to Lewis, Nathan*
Jul 5 1783	Tracey, Ann to Richardson, William*
Aug 4 1781	Tracey, Bazel to Cammell, Mary*
Sep 6 1797	Tracey, George to Cox, Sarah*
Oct 27 1791	Tracey, James to Marsh, Pamelia*
Oct 30 1794	Tracey, Joshua to Goodfellow, Mary*
Dec 11 1798	Tracey, Martha to Cole, Thomas
Jan 1 1782	Tracey, Sarah to Matthews, Edward
Mar 27 1798	Tracey, Warnell to Limmon, Elinor*
Aug 1 1798	Tracy, Elizabeth to Pering, Abraham*
Feb 18 1797	Tracy, John to Downey, Margaret*
Dec 14 1798	Tracy, Margaret to Downie, Thomas*

```
Oct 12 1779    Trager, Rebecca to Williams, Francis*
Jan 21 1796    Trainet, Elizabeth to McCallister, Charles*
Aug 30 1796    Traplin, Nancy to Demmitt, William*
Oct  4 1779    Trapnall, William to Wheeler, Honeror
Apr 19 1794    Trauzbaugh, Christinia to Snider, Andrew*
Mar 26 1796    Travelet, Francis to Hines, Betsey*
Sep 18 1784    Travers, Matthew to Biays, Jane
Nov  9 1791    Travers, William Briscoe to Flanteroy, Sarah*
Jul  2 1790    Traverse, Elizabeth to Allmon, David*
Nov 21 1782    Traverse, Nancy to Morgan, James*
May 10 1788    Traverse, Sarah to Trott, Alexander*
Nov 27 1794    Travici, Prudence to Soulsby, Matthew*
Oct  8 1783    Travis, Ann to Amos, Thomas*
Nov 21 1781    Travis, Mary to Fravis, Matthew
Sep 10 1785    Travolet, Sarah to Edwards, Paul*
Jun 26 1782    Treacle, William to Kirby, Amey
Dec 17 1791    Treagle, Mary to Wilson, Ephairm*
Dec 15 1792    Treakle, Christopher to Wilson, Mary*
Dec 27 1798    Treakle, Elizabeth to Stewart, John*
Dec  3 1796    Treakle, James to Pitcher, Mary*
May 30 1778    Treakle, Stephen to Hooper, Orpah*
Nov 23 1798    Treict, Henry to Walker, Margaret*
Mar 25 1796    Tremble, Polly to Peters, George*
Aug 14 1798    Trench, Peter to Stagons, Catharine
Mar 12 1785    Trequil, Nancy to Merryman, John
Jul 27 1785    Trigger, Sarah to Ward, James
May 28 1778    Trimble, Cornelous to Geiter, Elizabeth*
Aug  5 1797    Trimble, John to Brick, Lydia*
Oct 18 1798    Trimble, John to Hugo, Julia*
May 20 1784    Trimble, John to Kirby, Sarah*
May 12 1796    Trimble, Sarah to Biays, James*
Feb  8 1786    Trimble, William to Collins, Hannah*
Nov 13 1783    Trip, Frances to Gist, John Elder*
Dec 20 1783    Tripilet, Polly to Kellen, John
Jan 22 1784    Triplet, Caroline to Zollickhoffer, John Conrod*
Jan 27 1797    Triplet, John to McCabe, Rebecca*
Apr 15 1789    Tripp, Ann to Caulk, Joseph*
May  5 1798    Tripp, Harry to Waters, Jane*
Feb 25 1794    Trippe, Edward to Barney, Elizabeth*
Mar 27 1794    Trisler, George to Breidenbach, Catherine*
Aug 25 1784    Tritely, Freak to Keys, Charlotte
Jul 15 1795    Trotman, Jane to Norquay, Magness*
May 10 1788    Trott, Alexander to Traverse, Sarah*
May  5 1781    Trott, Sarah to Jones, John*
Oct  5 1795    Trotten, George to Wilson, Judah*
Mar  5 1793    Trotten, John to Sollers, Sarah*
May 10 1784    Trotten, Mary to Howell, James*
Oct  8 1798    Trottenberg, Maria to Lambert, Lewis*
Aug  3 1792    Trouin, Andrew to Foucackon, Mary Theresse*
May  2 1794    Troure, Jane Faurline to Cousron, Olivier*
Jul 15 1796    Troxall, Elizabeth to Showers, Adam*
Aug 17 1785    Truck, Esau to Dewley, Catherine
Jun 15 1795    Truelock, Daniel to Stevens, Lydia*
Mar 18 1792    Truiet, George to Rowland, Nancy*
Aug 29 1798    Trulock, John to Walker, Sidney*
Feb  5 1782    Trumbo, Adam to Selman, Henrietta*
```

Jul 16 1795	Trumbs, Elizabeth to Bermanham, William*
Oct 18 1798	Trumps, Casper to Loor, Rachel*
Jun 28 1784	Tucker, Catherine to Williams, John
Apr 9 1791	Tucker, Edward to Simpson, Sarah
May 24 1794	Tucker, Elizabeth to Smith, James*
Feb 13 1798	Tucker, Mary to Zep, Conrad*
Jan 20 1796	Tucksworth, Robert to Cottrel, Ruth*
Feb 23 1798	Tuder, Elizabeth to Adair, Philip*
Mar 15 1790	Tudor, Darcus to Cole, Nathan*
Apr 17 1795	Tudor, John to Fugate, Sarah*
Oct 6 1792	Tudor, Joshua to McCubbins, Susannah*
Dec 24 1791	Tudor, Polly to McCubbin, John*
Nov 19 1791	Tudor, Salathiel to Frigate, Temperance*
May 5 1786	Tuffts, James to Hurley, Mary*
Sep 2 1797	Tuines, Sophia to Coward, William*
Dec 15 1780	Tular, Margaret to Laser, John
Feb 4 1790	Tulheln, Rebecca to Jenny, Ebenezer*
Dec 18 1783	Tull, Ann to McFarlen, Edward*
Dec 20 1782	Tull, Sarah to Foster, Joseph*
Nov 18 1795	Tull, William to Ball, Mary*
Dec 30 1793	Tully, Elizabeth to Dugan, Peter*
Nov 7 1782	Tumbler, George to Miller, Rebecca*
Oct 17 1778	Tumbletind, Margaret to Russel, Richard*
Jan 2 1783	Tumbletown, Henry to Flemmon, Elizabeth
Mar 25 1778	Tumblison, William to Hambleton, Jane*
Dec 26 1797	Tundas, Philip to Linhart, Sarah*
Dec 1 1795	Tune, Darcus to Wilson, John*
Dec 31 1794	Tupless, Rosella to Tarr, Levin*
Feb 8 1794	Turine, Mary to Curtis, William*
Dec 12 1794	Turine, Nancy to Bishs, Nicholas*
Jan 23 1794	Turnbull, Andrew to Robinson, Hannah*
Mar 13 1790	Turnbull, Robert to Buchanan, Sarah*
Jul 6 1791	Turnbull, William to Tedford, Sarah*
Oct 6 1792	Turner, Ann to Wilson, George*
Apr 15 1795	Turner, Barbara to Armstead, Isaac*
Feb 12 1782	Turner, Charles to Noody, Sarah*
Oct 18 1798	Turner, Eleanor to Hinton, Thomas*
Apr 29 1797	Turner, Elisha to Roe, Mary Ann*
Jan 9 1790	Turner, Elizabeth to Fitch, William*
Nov 10 1790	Turner, Francis to Bradley, Ruth*
Nov 15 1780	Turner, Jeremiah to Lansdell, Sarah*
Jun 27 1779	Turner, John to Markins, Elizabeth
Sep 7 1782	Turner, John to McBride, Rosannah*
Oct 19 1796	Turner, John to Quinlan, Mary*
May 16 1793	Turner, Margaret to Furby, John*
Feb 3 1796	Turner, Nathaniel to Fitz, Elizabeth*
Aug 3 1796	Turner, Rebecca to Lemmon, Benjamin*
Jan 5 1793	Turner, Robert to Greenfield, Elizabeth
Jan 1 1788	Turner, Samuel to Brooks, Mary
Jan 2 1781	Turner, Sarah to Kedie, James*
Nov 13 1779	Turner, Sarah to Murray, John*
Jun 25 1797	Turner, Sophia to Thompson, James*
May 28 1788	Turner, Susannah to Musson, John*
Sep 5 1792	Turner, William to Safington, Rebecca
Jul 24 1783	Turner, William to Sheldron, Martha*
May 9 1788	Turnpaugh, Margaret to Decker, Jacob*

```
Jul 25 1778    Turnpaugh, Mary to Councilman, John*
Dec  3 1785    Turnpaugh, William to Hahn, Mariah
Nov 23 1797    Turviance, James to Young, Eliza*
Apr 30 1785    Turvin, Margaret to Limes, Barnett
May 17 1797    Tusay, Nancy to Christopher, Thomas*
Oct  8 1791    Tustin, Septimus to Paul, Elizabeth*
Dec 19 1797    Twine, Daniel to West, Anne*
May 19 1783    Twooshears, George to Ricks, Barbary*
Aug  7 1797    Tydings, Richard to Hatton, Susannah*
Dec 10 1798    Tygart, John to Mullan, Catharine
Aug  9 1796    Tyson, Henry Sanders to O'Conners, Sybel*
Jan 24 1798    Tyson, Nathan to Jackson, Sally*
Sep  1 1792    Tyson, Susannah Maria to Baxley, John of William*
Jul 24 1783    Ukler, Erasmus to Neace, Mary
Nov  8 1796    Ulary, Anst to Dooley, Sarah*
Mar  1 1784    Ulerick, Rosannah to Wolfe, Tobias*
May  5 1792    Undewood, John to Davis, Elizabeth*
Oct  7 1796    Undusst, Nicholas to Hendricks, Mette Loua*
Apr 12 1790    Unich, Eleanor to Reid, James*
Mar 26 1783    Usher, Thomas Jr. to Philpott, Mary*
Feb  9 1795    Valend, Amanda Victoire S. to Bertrand, John Peter*
Aug  4 1796    Valentine, Elizabeth to Hartong, Godfrey*
Oct 29 1798    Valentine, Rosanna to Shaffer, Lewis*
Nov 17 1791    Valentine, Sharlot to Mitchell, Edward*
May 19 1794    Vallerot, Jeanne S.L.A. to De Ladebat, Auguste P.S.*
May 29 1797    Van Noemer, Susannah J.G. to Backer, Tounis Helmig*
Jul 17 1790    Van Pradellis, Benedict F. to Owings, Casandra D.*
Nov 10 1795    Vanbibber, Abraham to Young, Polly
Jan 21 1795    Vanhorn, Elizabeth to Clarke, Bailey E.*
Oct  6 1784    Vanhorn, Elizabeth to Ferguson, Robert
Mar 31 1781    Vanor, Philip to Larsh, Susannah*
May 13 1781    Varle, Bartelemy to Sither, Catherine*
Mar  2 1798    Vashen, Annestica to Johnson, Matthew*
Aug 14 1783    Vaugh, Ruth to Welsh, James*
Jun  6 1793    Vaughan, Aberellah to Gorsuch, William*
Oct  5 1791    Vaughan, Benjamin Gist to Chapman, Rebecca
May 25 1798    Vaughan, Elizabeth to Barny, Michael*
Feb 24 1796    Vaughan, Elizabeth to Hunter, Peter*
Dec 10 1796    Vaughan, Elizabeth to Slemmer, Christian*
Sep 16 1797    Vaughan, James to Carter, Jane*
Jan 12 1792    Vaughan, Rachel to Williams, John*
Dec  1 1784    Vaughan, Sarah to Davis, John
Jun 27 1794    Veal, Elizabeth to Ball, Samuel*
Dec  6 1798    Veale, Catharine to Maloney, James*
Apr 20 1782    Vellers, Barbara to Titmon, Christopher*
Jul 13 1796    Venny, Margaret to Cowan, Thomas*
Apr  2 1779    Verdelett, John Ely to Hook, Sophiah
Dec 14 1795    Verley, John to Amey, Catharine*
Jan 16 1789    Vernet, Elizabeth to Elliert, Harlman*
Mar  7 1794    Vernon, A. Zeagers to Luke, Eliza*
Sep 24 1790    Vershon, Letitia to Smith, Solomon*
Aug  9 1781    Vetz, Jacob to Iser, Margaret*
Jul 12 1784    Vian, John to Creamer, Mary
Apr 16 1796    Vibert, Francis to Belanger, Mary*
Jul 14 1798    Vincent, Lilly to Goodwin, James*
Sep  9 1789    Vincent, Samuel to Hands, Mary*
```

Sep 28 1778	Vine, Patten to Walsh, Elenor*
Jan 20 1798	Vinny, Catharine to Dalton, George*
Aug 16 1794	Vinsy, Mary to Menchins, John*
Aug 5 1794	Viseur, Francis to Childs, Mary*
Aug 15 1797	Vogel, James to Fowble, Mary*
Apr 16 1795	Volmar, John to Reed, Elizabeth*
Jun 22 1784	Vouchez, John Baptist to Toury, Polly*
Jan 13 1795	Waddle, William to Cox, Sally*
Mar 4 1796	Wade, Charlotte to Clements, Edward*
Jul 21 1790	Wade, Sarah to McCoy, John*
Jul 3 1781	Wadley, Elizabeth to Clarke, Peter*
Sep 12 1794	Wager, Thomas to Wooden, Margaret*
Jan 20 1798	Wagers, Elijah to Kelly, Margaret*
Aug 6 1793	Wagers, Hannah to Walker, Henry*
Aug 11 1798	Wagers, Rachel to Jordon, Caleb*
Apr 9 1791	Wages, Elizabeth to Criswell, James*
Jan 10 1789	Wages, James to Poole, Barbara
Apr 2 1789	Wages, Luke to Philips, Patience*
Mar 23 1796	Wages, William to Frizzle, Nancy*
Nov 16 1787	Waggoner, Andrew to Moberry, Milkey*
Jan 20 1798	Waggoner, Catharine to Simon, Jacob*
Mar 23 1785	Waggoner, George to Cooper, Juliet
Dec 26 1794	Waggoner, Valentine to Fisher, Phebe*
Aug 7 1798	Wagmer, Jacob to Raboy, Rachel R.*
Nov 7 1792	Wails, William Wilkinson to Stansbury, Susannah*
Jun 28 1789	Waitman, Elizabeth to Croghan, James
Nov 23 1796	Waldrern, Sarah to Wheeler, Joseph*
May 4 1793	Waley, Mary to Clarke, John*
Mar 21 1793	Walker, Anne to Cromwell, William
May 20 1786	Walker, Araminta to Springer, Gamaliel*
May 2 1793	Walker, Charles to Woodard, Mary
Jun 8 1782	Walker, Christopher to Foster, Patience*
Nov 5 1783	Walker, Daniel to Perdue, Prudence*
Aug 7 1792	Walker, David to Browning, Elizabeth*
Feb 14 1793	Walker, Elijah to Magar, Belinda
Jan 30 1797	Walker, Elizabeth to Moorly, Henry*
Aug 6 1793	Walker, Henry to Wagers, Hannah*
Aug 9 1783	Walker, Jane to Petteric, James
Dec 30 1797	Walker, John to Myran, Mary*
Jul 11 1798	Walker, Joseph to Frazier, Mary*
Jun 17 1782	Walker, Joseph to Meredith, Ariminta*
Nov 23 1798	Walker, Margaret to Treict, Henry*
Oct 18 1784	Walker, Mary to Curtis, Joseph*
Dec 31 1792	Walker, Mary to Kelso, James*
Feb 24 1778	Walker, Mary to Robinson, Elijah*
Mar 15 1791	Walker, Matthew to Todd, Elizabeth*
Jan 3 1789	Walker, Prudence to Welsh, Edward*
Jul 11 1793	Walker, Robert to Murphy, Sarah*
Oct 23 1792	Walker, Samuel to Smith, Frances*
Apr 2 1782	Walker, Sarah to Foster, William*
Aug 29 1798	Walker, Sidney to Trulock, John*
Oct 21 1795	Walker, Thomas to Dell, Esther*
Jul 1 1795	Walker, William to Pumphrey, Achsah*
Mar 8 1794	Wall, George to Wools, Alicey*
Mar 21 1793	Wall, Jacob to Jones, Hannah*
Oct 23 1790	Wall, John to Harvey, Cassandra*

Aug 25 1791	Wall, Kitty to Carter, Solomon*
Sep 29 1794	Wall, Michael to Chenowith, Ruth*
Sep 6 1788	Wallace, Deborah to Hill, John*
Apr 10 1797	Wallace, John to Alexander, Mary*
Sep 3 1795	Wallace, John to Buckingham, Nancy*
Dec 30 1785	Wallace, John to Towson, Ann
Mar 27 1786	Wallace, Margaret to Kelly, William*
Dec 12 1789	Wallace, Robert to Justis, Rebecca*
Feb 3 1791	Wallace, William to Burgess, Ann*
Jul 22 1786	Wallass, Sarah to Fifer, John*
Sep 27 1797	Wallen, Eleanor to Parks, Abraham*
Jun 6 1792	Waller, Ann (nee Taylor) to Galloway, William*
Jun 20 1778	Waller, Basal to Parks, Sarah*
Jun 21 1781	Wallingsford, Benjamin to Butler, Elizabeth
Feb 23 1778	Wallingsford, Elizabeth to Thompson, Aquila*
Jun 20 1793	Wallington, Demas to McGee, Elizabeth*
Aug 26 1779	Wallis, Aron to Filer, Mary*
Apr 1 1793	Wallon, John to Hook, Barbara*
Jul 2 1790	Walmsley, Rachael to Derochbroom, Lewis*
Sep 28 1778	Walsh, Elenor to Vine, Patten*
Jan 12 1797	Walsh, John to James, Ann*
Nov 13 1778	Walsh, Mary to Crook, William
Feb 28 1793	Walsh, Mary to Curren, John*
Nov 5 1783	Walsh, Robert to Steel, Elizabeth*
Nov 30 1798	Walter, Cassandra to Williams, John*
Jun 27 1798	Walter, Elizabeth to Frymiller, John*
Jul 24 1779	Walter, John to Taylor, Ann
Jan 23 1796	Walter, Mary to Miller, Jacob*
Feb 7 1797	Walter, Rachel to Odle, William*
Jan 14 1794	Walters, Elizabeth to Green, Henry*
Apr 2 1785	Walters, Jacob to Sollers, Ara
Jun 20 1783	Wamler, Elizabeth to Shafer, George
Dec 12 1795	Wamsley, Nancy to Cann, Benjamin*
Jan 16 1793	Wamsley, Sarah to Weedon, James*
May 16 1782	Wandiford, Rebecca to Costin, James
Dec 5 1798	Wann, Ruth to Bosen, Thomas*
Nov 21 1778	Wannell, Henry to Hodge, Jane
Jul 26 1796	Wante, Chas. Stephen Peter to Dubread, Maria Rose*
Oct 16 1779	Ward, Albigail to Woddoms, William*
Jan 8 1794	Ward, Charles to Delahay, Sophia*
Aug 26 1779	Ward, Francis to Goodman, Sarah*
Jul 27 1785	Ward, James to Trigger, Sarah
Aug 30 1784	Ward, Mary to Hatton, Thomas*
Nov 13 1792	Ward, Mary to Murphey, Amon*
Oct 19 1796	Ward, Mary to Parkinson, Edward*
Jan 12 1790	Ward, Mary to Shroad, John*
Jul 10 1790	Ward, Thomas to Reese, Catharine*
Jun 3 1791	Warden, John to Fisher, Ann*
Feb 4 1797	Warden, William to Limes, Catharine*
Feb 27 1783	Ware, Charles to Kenney, Alice
Jan 19 1778	Ware, John to Gosnell, Margaret*
Mar 14 1797	Warfield, Alexander to Dorsey, Jemima*
Jan 18 1792	Warfield, Amelia to Higgins, Joseph*
Mar 12 1788	Warfield, Califf to White, Clara*
Dec 22 1792	Warfield, Edmund to Warfield, Mary Ann*
Feb 2 1793	Warfield, Elizabeth to Dewall, Jeremiah*

Nov 20 1794	Warfield, Elizabeth to Johnson, Horatio*
Feb 17 1792	Warfield, Ely to Chapman, Frances*
Mar 1 1794	Warfield, Ephraim to Watkins, Airianah*
Oct 30 1795	Warfield, George F. to Brown, Rebecca*
Feb 15 1797	Warfield, James to Gassaway, Anne*
Dec 3 1788	Warfield, John to Hobbs, Aserieth*
Jul 13 1798	Warfield, Margaret to Whitterfield, William*
Dec 22 1792	Warfield, Mary Ann to Warfield, Edmund*
Jan 13 1791	Warfield, Mary to Bennett, Elisha*
Jan 30 1778	Warfield, Silvanus to Kirby, Patience*
Nov 7 1793	Warmingham, Anne to Murphy, John*
Mar 2 1785	Warnar, Catharine to Noyle, Henry*
Jan 12 1784	Warne, Barbara to Miller, Matthias*
May 17 1785	Warnell, Elizabeth to Osborn, Jonas
Apr 21 1778	Warner, Darcus to Skinner, Thomas*
Feb 8 1786	Warner, Dorcas to Litzinger, Henry
Aug 4 1795	Warner, Elizabeth to McKinzie, John*
Sep 23 1779	Warner, Mary to Murphey, William*
Dec 24 1796	Warner, Rachel to McNeire, William*
Oct 3 1789	Warner, William to Leger, Alizanna*
Sep 16 1790	Warrell, Abarilla to Wheeler, Nathaniel
Feb 3 1785	Warrell, Catherine to Thatcher, Henry*
Sep 4 1783	Warrell, Hannah to Lewis, Richard*
Mar 5 1782	Warrell, John to Gorsuch, Aberilla*
Sep 8 1795	Warren, Elizabeth to Martin, John*
Apr 2 1784	Warren, Thomas to Corn, Mary*
Nov 20 1779	Warren, Thomas to Fitzgerald, Margaret
Feb 4 1795	Warren, William to Howard, Bethia*
May 13 1797	Warrick, Elizabeth to Pearce, John*
Sep 19 1793	Warrier, William to Hooks, Jane*
May 30 1798	Warrington, Ann to Rawlings, Isaac*
Jul 14 1798	Warrington, Catharine to Callahan, John
Nov 8 1784	Waskey, Christian to Burkect, Ann
Nov 19 1796	Wasson, John to Seal, Hillen*
Mar 11 1779	Watblett, Peter to Wilkins, Sarah*
Mar 29 1783	Waten, David to Pickett, Mary
May 24 1784	Waters, Ann to Cromwell, Thomas
Jun 23 1784	Waters, Ann to Hennen, James*
Oct 20 1781	Waters, Ann to Waters, Benjamin
Dec 23 1797	Waters, Aquila to Hancock, Mary*
Oct 20 1781	Waters, Benjamin to Waters, Ann
Jun 26 1783	Waters, Charles to Horner, Mary*
Dec 11 1781	Waters, Elinor to Bosman, Risdon
Dec 4 1797	Waters, Elizabeth to Bukhead, Thomas*
Jul 14 1798	Waters, Elizabeth to Hancock, William*
Nov 12 1788	Waters, Ellennor to French, Othea*
Jul 9 1791	Waters, George to Williams, Abigail*
Nov 11 1779	Waters, Isaac to McMasters, Ann
May 5 1798	Waters, Jane to Tripp, Harry*
Dec 27 1784	Waters, Judah to Collins, William
Nov 8 1796	Waters, Mary to Tenant, Thomas*
Jun 2 1796	Waters, Philip to Gardner, Sybel
Sep 9 1789	Waters, Philip to Hinchs, Nelly*
Nov 12 1784	Waters, Sarah Arnold to Landsdale, Richard
Jul 7 1796	Waters, Stephen to Penny, Prudence*
Jul 2 1791	Waters, Susannah to Moore, Joseph*

Aug 9 1785	Waters, Thomas to Simpson, Mary
Oct 29 1796	Waters, William to Fallows, Ann*
Jun 10 1782	Waters, William to McNeal, Kitty*
Jul 12 1778	Wates, Elizabeth to Gilling, James*
Mar 1 1794	Watkins, Airianah to Warfield, Ephraim*
Nov 14 1796	Watkins, Elizabeth to Bliss, James
May 17 1788	Watkins, James to Miller, Rebecca*
May 31 1796	Watkins, John to Guyton, Ruth*
Jun 27 1797	Watkins, Joseph to Shaney, Polly*
Mar 17 1792	Watkins, Rebecca to Fowler, William*
Jun 12 1792	Watkins, Rebecca to Gassaway to Croner, Frederick*
Nov 17 1791	Watkins, William to Eccles, Margaret*
Mar 27 1779	Watkins, William to Owings, Catherine*
Sep 2 1786	Watlin, Hannah to Galloway, Marshall*
Jun 2 1797	Watson, Agness to Eden, Garret
Sep 6 1785	Watson, Archabald to Talbott, Rebecca*
Sep 10 1789	Watson, Elizabeth to Fouble, Jasper*
Sep 25 1788	Watson, Joseph to Moody, Fanny*
Feb 21 1786	Watson, Rosannah to Scott, Andrew
Mar 6 1795	Watson, Thomas to Ogden, Ann*
Jan 17 1797	Watson, William to Tolson, Elizabeth*
Mar 6 1782	Watters, Alexander to Hains, Elizabeth*
May 3 1792	Wattkins, William to Minksey, Susannah*
Mar 7 1783	Wattle, Joseph to Jury, Ann
Dec 13 1788	Wattles, Chandler to Goslin, Sarah
Oct 4 1778	Watts, Ann to Barry, Labourn*
Oct 15 1785	Watts, Ann to Sewell, James*
May 3 1792	Watts, Benjamin to Slater, Elizabeth*
May 5 1781	Watts, Catherine to Mumma, Christian
Jan 14 1792	Watts, Edward Allison to Jones, Susannah Watts
Jul 8 1797	Watts, Edward to Aisquith, Elizabeth*
Apr 14 1784	Watts, Frances to Esam, James*
Apr 10 1783	Watts, Isaac to Smith, Mary*
Sep 9 1798	Watts, John G. to Cochran, Sally*
Mar 12 1785	Watts, Josias to Perrigoe, Floria
Jun 3 1789	Watts, Josias to Todd, Mary*
Aug 21 1798	Watts, Josias to Winfield, Tammy
Mar 4 1793	Watts, Margaret to Brown, Thomas*
Dec 19 1795	Watts, Milly to Lee, William*
Dec 23 1789	Watts, Nathaniel to Stansbury, Rebecca*
Jul 31 1790	Watts, Rachael to Raner, Samuel*
Oct 30 1783	Watts, Rachael to Raynor, John
May 27 1785	Watts, Samuel to Donovan, Catherine
Sep 3 1783	Watts, Thomas to Bowen, Lydia
Nov 20 1797	Watts, Thomas to Garns, Elizabeth*
Nov 28 1788	Waupole, Flora to Hornes, Michael*
Jul 23 1781	Way, Michael to Fowle, Mary*
Aug 12 1785	Wear, John to Mann, Hannah
May 3 1797	Weary, Ann to Shepperd, Thomas*
Dec 4 1794	Weary, John to McFeel, Mary*
Aug 1 1798	Weary, Joseph to Perrigo, Rebecca*
Dec 11 1798	Weary, Mary to Wolper, George*
Aug 11 1785	Weary, Peter to Botts, Jemima
Sep 30 1790	Weary, Rebecca to Pamphelon, Thomas*
Jun 17 1795	Weary, Thomas to Perrigoy, Sarah*
Dec 7 1785	Weatherby, Daniel to Gorsuch, Elizabeth

Mar 18 1778	Weatherby, Daniel to Woodard, Sarah*
May 12 1795	Weatherby, William to Sindall, Urath*
Jan 10 1781	Weaver, Casper to Frymiller, Elizabeth*
May 12 1791	Weaver, Casper to Hatton, Ann*
May 5 1795	Weaver, Daniel to Collins, Diannah*
Jun 2 1785	Weaver, Elizabeth to Bowers, George*
Oct 22 1793	Weaver, Elizabeth to Hisson, Cornelius*
Jun 2 1798	Weaver, Jacob to Louderman, Sarah*
Aug 11 1795	Weaver, Jacob to Nicholson, Elizabeth*
Sep 10 1796	Weaver, John to Currough, Sarah*
Apr 29 1789	Weaver, John to Henley, Margaret*
Feb 20 1798	Weaver, Letitia to Murphy, Daniel*
Jun 13 1794	Weaver, Lewis to Lombord, Elizabeth*
Sep 30 1785	Weaver, Margaret to McFerson, William
Jul 23 1793	Weaver, Mary to Overton, John*
Aug 23 1794	Weaver, Mary to Smith, Gasper*
Jul 1 1785	Weaver, Peter to Myers, Magdaline
Sep 16 1798	Webb, Jane to Jenks, Henry*
Mar 11 1784	Webb, Jane to Palmer, Philip*
Nov 10 1796	Webb, Jane to Snead, Edward*
Apr 5 1781	Webb, Joyce to Chilcoat, Robert*
Nov 5 1795	Webb, Mary to Penrice, Thomas*
Mar 26 1785	Webster, Elizabeth to Nice, Cornelius
Aug 6 1794	Webster, William to Richardson, Elizabeth*
Sep 6 1790	Weckman, Mary to Louderman, Frederick*
Nov 23 1798	Wedge, Simon to Herlick, Margaret*
Jan 16 1793	Weedon, James to Wamsley, Sarah*
Mar 17 1785	Weeks, John to Morrisson, Ann
Jun 29 1796	Weelon, Henry to Grover, Jenny*
Jul 9 1795	Wegnemyer, Catharine to Allwine, John*
Nov 18 1785	Weidner, Henry to Shartle, Mary
Jan 24 1798	Weikins, Martha to Whiteside, Bomber
Apr 28 1792	Weir, Eleanor to Gladman, Thomas*
Jul 18 1797	Weir, John to Madden, Sarah*
Aug 1 1781	Weisenthal, Elizabeth to Messonier, Henry*
Dec 10 1796	Weisner, Mary to Johnson, Frederick*
Aug 25 1792	Weiss, Felia to Gross, Barbara
Dec 18 1794	Weist, Jacob to Smith, Mary*
Feb 17 1778	Weister, Catharine to Shilling, Michael*
Mar 1 1785	Welch, Elizabeth to Wells, John*
Nov 4 1797	Welden, Ebenezer to Church, Ruthe*
Dec 15 1791	Weldon, Jane to Hays, Joseph*
Apr 25 1789	Wellar, Margrit to Wilderwan, John*
Mar 1 1794	Weller, Andrew to Road, Mary*
Nov 26 1791	Weller, Catharine to Inloes, Thomas*
Jun 29 1789	Weller, Eve to Calffoos, Lewis*
Jan 28 1798	Wells, Absalom to Owings, Hellen*
Oct 12 1797	Wells, Achsah to Jessop, Abraham*
Aug 15 1778	Wells, Aehsa to Talbott, Richard*
Jun 1 1786	Wells, Ann to Holmes, William James*
Jan 2 1781	Wells, Ann to Merryman, Caleb
Oct 30 1779	Wells, Ann to Owings, George*
Mar 26 1781	Wells, Ann to Owings, George*
Jan 8 1795	Wells, Ann to Partridge, William*
Mar 15 1785	Wells, Ann to Williams, John
May 19 1795	Wells, Bazabel to Risteau, Rebecca*

```
Feb  1 1783    Wells, Charles to Williamson, Mary*
Jul 29 1795    Wells, Colin C. to Robberds, Susannah*
Feb 11 1783    Wells, Cornelius to Creggel, Charlotte
Sep 11 1778    Wells, Cyprian to White, Margaret*
Jun 11 1779    Wells, Elizabeth to Hammond, George
Sep 10 1798    Wells, Elizabeth to McKeen, James*
May 28 1791    Wells, Hannah to Fearson, Jesse*
Mar  1 1785    Wells, John to Welch, Elizabeth*
Mar 14 1786    Wells, Joseph to Owings, Betsy
Mar 15 1794    Wells, Luke to Reed, Eleanor*
Sep 27 1794    Wells, Margaret to Peirpoint, Thomas*
Jan  9 1798    Wells, Martha to Dunbar, William
Oct  5 1782    Wells, Nicholas to Talbott, Providence
Apr  9 1794    Wells, Rachel to Davis, William*
Mar 22 1788    Wells, Richard to Hardesty, Nancy*
Aug 18 1796    Wells, Sarah to Clayton, Joseph*
Feb 19 1781    Wells, Sarah to Johnson, Henry Augustine
Oct 28 1779    Wells, Susannah to Armstrong, James*
Sep  3 1778    Wells, Susannah to Sellers, William*
Sep 16 1796    Wells, Susannah to Smith, Joshua
Feb 15 1796    Wells, Thomas to Devall, Thompsa*
Dec 18 1793    Wells, Thomas to Woodhouse, Mary*
Mar 12 1783    Wells, William to Smith, Catherine
Oct 29 1791    Wellsford, George William to Hill, Eleanor*
Dec  9 1780    Welsh, Ann to McCauley, John*
Aug  9 1788    Welsh, Catharine to Manro, Nathan*
Feb 17 1798    Welsh, Catharine to O'Conner, Michael*
Aug 29 1789    Welsh, Edward to Nicholson, Nancy*
Jan  3 1789    Welsh, Edward to Walker, Prudence*
Jun 29 1785    Welsh, Eleanor to Burgess, John*
Apr 27 1784    Welsh, Elinor to Cohown, Moses*
Jun 16 1798    Welsh, Elizabeth to Christian, Anthony*
May 10 1781    Welsh, Elizabeth to Eichelberger, Martin*
Oct 30 1783    Welsh, Elizabeth to Lynch, Patrick*
Nov 17 1797    Welsh, Hannah to Moss, David*
Jan  5 1796    Welsh, Helene to Welsh, John*
Jul  4 1791    Welsh, Henry to Hamilton, Margaret
Aug 13 1796    Welsh, Henry to Shrote, Barbara*
Aug 14 1783    Welsh, James to Vaugh, Ruth*
Apr 13 1779    Welsh, Jemimah to Wheeler, Greenberry
Sep  3 1783    Welsh, John to Davis, Betsy*
May 10 1798    Welsh, John to Hallock, Anna*
Jul 23 1781    Welsh, John to Robertson, Mary*
Dec 15 1785    Welsh, John to Roney, Judah
Jan 18 1794    Welsh, John to Simpson, Lucy*
Jan  5 1796    Welsh, John to Welsh, Helene*
Oct 17 1795    Welsh, Laban to Merryman, Mary*
Mar 25 1786    Welsh, Leah to Burton, Thomas*
Oct 11 1796    Welsh, Margaret to French, John*
Dec  5 1789    Welsh, Margaret to Philips, Thomas*
Apr 20 1786    Welsh, Mary to Myers, Jacob*
Jul  6 1778    Welsh, Mary to Rose, William*
Feb 20 1786    Welsh, Rachel to Beatle, Henry*
May 17 1786    Welsh, Rachel to Wheeler, Joseph*
Jan 26 1782    Welsh, Ruth to Stansbury, William
Oct 29 1785    Welsh, Thomas to Brooks, Hannah
```

May 7 1781	Welsh, Walter to Burk, Elinor*
Feb 17 1798	Welsh, William to Stansbury, Catharine
Feb 9 1798	Wenberry, Elizabeth to Keaslen, George Dederick*
Jul 26 1779	Wert, Caspar to Partridge, Sarah*
Dec 22 1787	Wescost, John to Johnson, Sarah*
Sep 10 1795	Wessels, Joseph Charles to Yeiser, Mary Feree*
Dec 19 1797	West, Anne to Twine, Daniel*
Oct 13 1794	West, Edward to Johnston, Nancy*
Aug 19 1789	West, Elijah to Harper, Mary*
Oct 31 1795	West, Elizabeth to Mayhew, Elisha Horton*
Jul 19 1798	West, Joel to Rapp, Juliet Francisia*
Dec 1 1784	West, Joseph to Howard, Violetta*
Apr 2 1784	West, Margaret to Reves, Richard*
Aug 19 1789	West, Mary to Cox, William*
May 25 1785	West, Mary to Ross, Daniel*
Apr 17 1797	West, Simeon to Clusby, Polly*
Nov 26 1794	West, Stephen to Pue, Ann*
May 18 1797	West, Sybel to Holland, Francis*
Jun 30 1785	West, William to Cross, Jemimah
Jan 9 1786	West, William to German, Elizabeth*
Nov 26 1791	Weston, Catrina Elizabeth to Lohr, Johan Carl*
Sep 22 1798	Weston, Guy to Peters, Dorothy*
Jan 31 1783	Weston, John to Dey, Rebecca*
Dec 31 1777	Weston, Josephus to Griffin, Rebecca*
Jul 14 1785	Westrum, Andrew to Dresson, Katharine*
Nov 3 1796	Westwood, John to Lowman, Margaret*
Dec 8 1785	Wetherall, James to Day, Sarah
Dec 1 1795	Wetherstrand, Thomas to Dangston, Mary*
Dec 24 1784	Whaland, Elizabeth to Hunt, William*
Jun 11 1798	Whalen, William to Kiteley, Elizabeth*
Aug 27 1785	Wharton, Arthur to Moon, Sarah*
Aug 10 1793	Whatson, David to Rohrback, Mary Magdalin*
Nov 20 1793	Wheaton, John A. to Murray, Elizabeth*
Mar 29 1779	Wheelar, Keziah to Gorsuch, Thomas*
Jun 18 1796	Wheeler, Ann Harret to Gerand, Jam John*
Sep 16 1779	Wheeler, Benjamin to Bosley, Ellen*
Feb 28 1786	Wheeler, Constance to Hall, Elijah
Apr 3 1779	Wheeler, Elizabeth to Cullison, Joshua
Oct 10 1793	Wheeler, Elizabeth to McLane, Robert*
Apr 13 1779	Wheeler, Greenberry to Welsh, Jemimah
Mar 19 1782	Wheeler, Hannah to Wheeler, John*
Jan 1 1788	Wheeler, Hannah to Wilmott, John*
Oct 4 1779	Wheeler, Honeror to Trapnall, William
May 11 1779	Wheeler, Isaac to Young, Pleasant
Jun 11 1782	Wheeler, Isabella to Spicer, Edward*
Feb 2 1786	Wheeler, James to Cole, Honour*
Jan 20 1796	Wheeler, James to Jones, Elizabeth*
Apr 27 1785	Wheeler, John to Sanders, Martha
Mar 19 1782	Wheeler, John to Wheeler, Hannah*
Aug 24 1786	Wheeler, Joseph to Smith, Sarah
Nov 23 1796	Wheeler, Joseph to Waldrern, Sarah*
May 17 1786	Wheeler, Joseph to Welsh, Rachel*
Mar 12 1796	Wheeler, Margaret to Gould, John*
Oct 28 1782	Wheeler, Mary to Finn, Peter*
Jan 9 1778	Wheeler, Mary to Hall, Thomas*
Jul 12 1779	Wheeler, Mary to La Gibson, John

```
May  6 1797    Wheeler, Mary to McClaskey, John*
Nov 21 1787    Wheeler, Nancy to Floyd, Joseph*
Jul 27 1784    Wheeler, Nancy to Moss, Frederick
Sep 16 1790    Wheeler, Nathaniel to Warrell, Abarilla
May 18 1796    Wheeler, Philip to Dines, Mary*
Mar 24 1792    Wheeler, Rachel to Green, John*
Oct 20 1786    Wheeler, Richard to Bosley, Rachel
Jan 23 1782    Wheeler, Ruth to Bradfield, James
Nov 29 1783    Wheeler, Samuel to Tipton, Ann*
Jan 31 1798    Wheeler, Sarah to Childs, John
May 13 1793    Wheeler, Sarah to Wilson, John*
Feb 21 1785    Wheeler, Solomon to Ristun, Ann*
Aug 22 1791    Wheeler, Stephen to Stansbury, Ann*
Jul 30 1793    Wheeler, Susannah to Daughady, Abraham*
Jun  9 1783    Wheeler, Tabitha to Smith, Samuel*
Apr 27 1782    Wheeler, Wayson to Hughes, Martha*
Oct 18 1782    Wheeler, William to Gardiner, Mary*
Dec  8 1780    Wheeler, William to Hall, Actions*
Aug 10 1782    Wheeler, William to James, Temperance*
Feb 25 1795    Wheelin, Thomas to Bowen, Nancy*
Nov 30 1787    Whelan, Lawrence to Williams, Elizabeth*
Jan 10 1792    When, Rachel to Wisebaugh, John*
Dec 31 1791    Whiffing, Thomas to Pontany, Elizabeth*
Jun 12 1779    Whigley, Isaac to Dukes, Elizabeth
Jun  9 1778    Whinrite, Ann to Finley, William*
Apr 14 1798    Whipple, Eliza to Quesany, John*
Dec  6 1798    Whipple, William to Pate, Eliza*
Jul  6 1778    Whips, Benjamin to Peirce, Rebecca*
Nov  9 1796    Whips, Elizabeth to Wooden, Thomas
Nov  3 1792    Whips, George to Shipley, Susannah*
Jan 19 1778    Whips, Samuel to Poole, Henrietta*
Jul 23 1796    Whips, Sarah to Flood, Obediah*
Jan  7 1790    Whitaker, Elizabeth to Winchester, John*
Nov 30 1797    White, Barbara to Resensteel, George Jr.*
Jul  6 1793    White, Benoni to Ankerum, Elizabeth
Aug  3 1796    White, Catharine to Heackley, Sebastian*
Jun  6 1778    White, Charles to Babbs, Elizabeth*
Mar 12 1788    White, Clara to Warfield, Califf*
Jan 23 1795    White, Edward to Lush, Polly*
Feb  4 1790    White, Eleanor to Good, Samuel*
Feb 28 1786    White, Elizabeth to Baker, John Frederick
Sep 23 1795    White, Elizabeth to Brown, Abraham*
Aug  9 1798    White, Elizabeth to Ferley, William*
Nov 27 1789    White, Elizabeth to Richardson, Francis*
Jun  3 1783    White, Elizabeth to Workkman, Hugh
Dec 24 1782    White, Hannah to Ford, Thomas*
Apr  8 1781    White, Hannah to McGrevey, James
Jun 20 1796    White, James to Bostich, Achsah*
Apr 15 1784    White, James to Hart, Mary*
Aug  7 1794    White, James to Merrick, Catharine*
Dec 18 1797    White, John to Wilson, Patty*
Aug 17 1793    White, Keziah to Lewis, Charles*
Mar 10 1784    White, Luke to Simmons, Elizabeth*
Jul 27 1792    White, Margaret to Morris, John*
Sep 11 1778    White, Margaret to Wells, Cyprian*
Mar  9 1784    White, Mary to Arnold, Richard
```

```
Dec  4 1784    White, Mary to Bernard, Charles*
Dec 15 1791    White, Mary to Gould, Pete*
Feb 28 1784    White, Mary to Hynum, Thomas*
Oct 15 1796    White, Mary to Logan, Neale*
Feb 20 1798    White, Michael to Lary, Julian
Jul 11 1795    White, Nancy to Armstrong, Joshua*
Sep 12 1798    White, Polly to Cosh, Joseph*
Oct 28 1797    White, Priscilla to Johnson, Peter*
Dec 16 1797    White, Robert to Annan, Mary*
Sep 17 1782    White, Robert to Woodin, Keziah
Oct  7 1785    White, Samuel to Parrin, Ann Helen*
Oct 16 1784    White, Sarah to Jones, Elisha*
Jul 24 1783    White, Simon to Low, Jane
Jan 22 1789    White, Thomas to Lewis, Mary*
May  5 1784    White, Tomison to Gordon, William*
Jul 17 1782    White, William to Littlemire, Mary
Apr 10 1784    Whiteby, James to Parks, Mary*
Jun 13 1796    Whitefoot, Thomas to Barnes, Betsey*
Oct  8 1793    Whiteford, James to Butler, Margaret*
Dec  4 1795    Whiteford, John to Tipton, Elizabeth*
Oct 15 1798    Whiteford, Margaret to Johnson, Israel*
Jan 24 1798    Whiteside, Bomber to Weikins, Martha
Jan  3 1791    Whiting, Elisha to Tidy, Sarah*
Jan  7 1792    Whitley, John to Burns, Hannah*
Mar  5 1795    Whitney, Thomas to Nuval, Susannah*
Oct  3 1782    Whiton, Henry to Stover, Susannah
Jul 13 1798    Whitterfield, William to Warfield, Margaret*
Dec 20 1783    Whittle, David to Wood, Ann*
Feb  4 1797    Whittle, Elizabeth to Farely, James*
Feb 25 1795    Whittle, Zachariah to Disnee, Elizabeth*
Aug  7 1779    Whood, Mary to Burdsel, Thomas*
Oct 21 1795    Wickley, Ruth to Wooden, John*
Aug 12 1778    Wicks, Epenet to Price, Sarah*
Apr 24 1786    Wicks, Ezekiel to McDonald, Elizabeth
May  2 1798    Wight, Charles to Parnett, Hannah*
Sep  1 1798    Wigley, Ann to Wiloford, George W.*
Sep  2 1783    Wigley, Edward to Eagleston, Mary*
Oct 23 1790    Wigley, Jane to Greogery, James*
Oct 15 1791    Wignell, Elizabeth to Smythe, Samuel*
Oct 11 1797    Wila, Eleanor to Elwood, Thomas*
Oct 28 1789    Wilcocks, James to Gray, Sarah*
Nov 10 1781    Wilcoxson, William to Smith, Easther
Apr 25 1789    Wilderwan, John to Wellar, Margrit*
Dec  5 1783    Wile, Cassandra to Jones, Richard*
Dec 17 1796    Wiley, Catharine to Johnson, Jacob Jr.*
Mar  2 1798    Wiley, Sarah to Cockrill, Thomas*
Jan 21 1795    Wiliamson, Elizabeth to Russell, William
May 27 1789    Wilkerson, John to Murry, Elizabeth*
Jun 16 1796    Wilkerson, Mary to Brown, John*
Apr  1 1779    Wilkerson, Robert to Laboutt, Phebe*
Nov  3 1796    Wilkins, Henry Dr. to Owings, Esther*
Mar 11 1779    Wilkins, Sarah to Watblett, Peter*
Aug  5 1794    Wilkins, William to Goodwin, Achsah*
Apr 30 1794    Wilkinson, David to McMicken, Sarah*
Jul 16 1794    Wilkinson, Joseph to Shock, Mary*
Feb 25 1792    Wilkinson, Joshua to Patrick, Nancy*
```

Dec 12 1796	Wilkinson, Mary to Magrath, Bartholomew*
Dec 10 1795	Wilkinson, Robert to Curnan, Frances Todd*
May 15 1794	Wilkinson, Sarah to Hewitt, Caleb*
Aug 1 1783	Wilks, William to Morgan, Elizabeth*
Sep 12 1778	Wille, Frederick C. to Grasmith, Maydelena*
Jul 17 1790	Willert, Martha to Lehman, Gebhard*
Sep 20 1796	Willess, Ann to Randall, John*
Dec 28 1790	Willey, Harry to Goodridge, Mary
May 5 1796	Willey, Isaac to Hammond, Mary*
Jun 30 1797	Willey, Joseph to Favory, Neomia*
Jan 13 1785	Willey, Sarah to Harryman, Joshua*
Mar 26 1795	Williamea, John Nicholas to Georgia, Mary*
Jul 9 1791	Williams, Abigail to Waters, George*
Aug 16 1797	Williams, Abraham to Barnes, Susanna*
Jun 18 1796	Williams, Ann to Jay, Joseph*
Oct 28 1797	Williams, Ann to Mash, Joseph*
Mar 14 1795	Williams, Ann to McNamara, Hugh*
Dec 3 1796	Williams, Basel to Pearce, Betsey
Jan 20 1789	Williams, Benjamin to Gorsuch, Prudence*
Nov 9 1796	Williams, Benjamin to Penn, Mary*
Feb 24 1778	Williams, Brown to Cromwell, Ruth*
Sep 22 1781	Williams, Catherine to Goodwin, James*
Nov 4 1778	Williams, Charles to Rawlings, Mary*
Jun 14 1791	Williams, Christian to Gray, Mary
Jun 6 1789	Williams, Elizabeth to Gregory, David*
Dec 24 1798	Williams, Elizabeth to Pumphrey, Warfield*
Nov 30 1787	Williams, Elizabeth to Whelan, Lawrence"
Nov 11 1797	Williams, Frances to McKubbin, Samuel*
Oct 12 1779	Williams, Francis to Trager, Rebecca*
Nov 13 1794	Williams, Frederick to Smith, Rachell*
Sep 29 1795	Williams, George to McFadon, Mary*
Feb 2 1798	Williams, Hugh to Dwyer, Mary Ann*
Jun 22 1797	Williams, Jacob to Clower, Polly*
Aug 16 1796	Williams, James Pettingill to Richardson, Hannah*
Jun 14 1797	Williams, James to Maid, Rachel*
Jun 19 1783	Williams, John to Bond, Alisana*
Sep 19 1779	Williams, John to Cazy, Margaret*
Dec 24 1785	Williams, John to Dickson, Eleanor
Nov 26 1791	Williams, John to Gorsuch, Ruth*
Jul 1 1797	Williams, John to Hoggins, Martha*
Mar 26 1791	Williams, John to Latchaw, Magdeline*
Oct 13 1788	Williams, John to Malcom, Jennet*
Sep 6 1788	Williams, John to Morrison, Jane*
Nov 9 1797	Williams, John to Robinson, Lydia*
Aug 15 1782	Williams, John to Taylor, Margaret*
Jun 28 1784	Williams, John to Tucker, Catherine
Jan 12 1792	Williams, John to Vaughan, Rachel*
Nov 30 1798	Williams, John to Walter, Cassandra*
Mar 15 1785	Williams, John to Wells, Ann
Apr 27 1797	Williams, Joseph to Yeiser, Eliza*
Mar 2 1796	Williams, Margaret to Graves, William*
Jul 30 1798	Williams, Mary Ann to Steinmetz, Michael*
Apr 24 1788	Williams, Mary to Brewer, John*
Jan 12 1788	Williams, Mary to Cross, John*
Mar 29 1788	Williams, Mary to Duffey, Owen*
Sep 23 1791	Williams, Mary to Gillingham, Thomas*

Aug 27 1796	Williams, Nancy to Flemming, Joseph*
Feb 2 1791	Williams, Nancy to Israel, Robert*
Jun 3 1795	Williams, Nancy to Jarvis, John*
Dec 10 1793	Williams, Nancy to Joyce, Jacob*
Aug 2 1791	Williams, Nathan to Parsons, Sarah
Oct 18 1785	Williams, Otho Holland to Smith, Mary*
Dec 20 1788	Williams, Rachael to Mannon, Abraham*
Apr 14 1796	Williams, Rachel to Hamilton, George*
Oct 31 1785	Williams, Rachel to Jacob, William
Aug 19 1793	Williams, Robert to Parrish, Elizabeth*
Feb 1 1788	Williams, Ruth to Cromwell, John*
Jan 28 1794	Williams, Sarah to Kelly, Patrick*
Sep 26 1797	Williams, Sarah to Tennis, Jacob*
Nov 27 1795	Williams, Silby to Gordon, Philip*
Jan 20 1797	Williams, Susannah to Dycas, Isaac*
Nov 24 1781	Williams, Thomas to Jourdan, Jane*
Dec 8 1798	Williams, Thomas to Steward, Rebecca*
Aug 6 1789	Williamson, Ann to Pierce, Humphrey*
Dec 14 1795	Williamson, David to Mullet, Juliet*
Sep 22 1784	Williamson, Elizabeth to Askew, Joshua*
Sep 10 1798	Williamson, Elizabeth to Purce, Levy*
Oct 11 1790	Williamson, Mary to Tagert, John*
Feb 1 1783	Williamson, Mary to Wells, Charles*
Nov 21 1778	Williamson, Thomas to Hard, Ruth
Jul 20 1782	Williamson, William to Fouse, Ann
Jul 30 1796	Willima, Nicholas to Cole, Elizabeth*
Aug 18 1795	Willing, William to Gable, Susannah*
Aug 8 1786	Willion, Benjamin to Worthington, Elizabeth
Apr 13 1797	Willis, Cornelius to Loreny, Margaret*
Jan 30 1790	Willis, George to Kelleham, Johannes*
Mar 5 1783	Willis, George to Labat, Sarah*
Mar 16 1792	Willis, Henry to Hollingsworth, Ann*
Jul 2 1783	Willis, John to Hashley, Beatrix
Dec 12 1798	Willis, John to Hill, Nancy*
Sep 29 1784	Willks, Joseph to Richardson, Sarah*
Jun 11 1793	Willmon, Ann to Murphy, William*
Dec 13 1798	Willmore, Mary to Ridgely, Mordecai*
May 31 1798	Willoughby, Mary to Norris, James*
Sep 28 1784	Willoughby, Sarah to Cryer, Jacob
Nov 10 1785	Willson, Eleanor to Bevins, Joshua
Aug 27 1791	Willson, Jane to Bullen, Simon*
May 24 1794	Willson, Margaret to Taylor, Henry*
Aug 26 1790	Willson, Matthew to Conner, Jane*
Feb 18 1788	Willson, Sarah to Brown, Frederick
Oct 30 1790	Willson, William to Ridgely, Deborah*
Nov 3 1796	Wilmer, James to Revena, Lidia*
Nov 16 1797	Wilmon, William to Ridgely, Ann*
Jan 25 1797	Wilmott, John to Gosnell, Sarah*
Jan 1 1788	Wilmott, John to Wheeler, Hannah*
Oct 8 1781	Wilmott, Robert to Dorsey, Prissilla
Jan 26 1784	Wilmott, Ruth to Bowen, Nathan*
Sep 1 1798	Wiloford, George W. to Wigley, Ann*
Jan 11 1778	Wilperd, Mary to Tinker, William*
Oct 17 1779	Wilson, Cassandra to Stump, John
Nov 5 1785	Wilson, Catherine to Bennett, Caleb*
Aug 28 1779	Wilson, Charles to Judy, Elizabeth*

```
Dec  7 1798    Wilson, David to Foller, Mary*
Apr 29 1794    Wilson, David to Patridge, Ann*
Oct 24 1796    Wilson, Drucilla to Chaney, Joseph*
Mar 25 1797    Wilson, Eleanor to Gordon, John*
Aug 13 1792    Wilson, Eleanor to Higginbottom, Arthur*
Sep  1 1792    Wilson, Eleanor to Jenkins, George*
Nov  8 1788    Wilson, Elizabeth to Aylworth, John*
Sep  3 1795    Wilson, Elizabeth to Gray, Joseph*
Apr  2 1784    Wilson, Elizabeth to Standfast, William*
Dec 17 1791    Wilson, Ephairm to Treagle, Mary*
Oct  6 1792    Wilson, George to Turner, Ann*
Jul 26 1798    Wilson, George to Wilson, Hannah*
Jun 23 1779    Wilson, Gitting to Rutledge, Jane*
May 22 1798    Wilson, Hannah to Levering, Peter*
Jul 26 1798    Wilson, Hannah to Wilson, George*
Apr  4 1795    Wilson, Henry to Worthington, Sarah*
Jan 30 1794    Wilson, Hugh to Hill, Hannah*
Dec  6 1784    Wilson, Hugh to Smith, Margaret*
Dec  4 1797    Wilson, James to McKinsey, Mary
Sep 27 1794    Wilson, James to Ridenduer, Mary*
Sep 11 1793    Wilson, James to Wilson, Mary*
Feb  8 1797    Wilson, John to Farguson, Eleanor*
Jan 26 1793    Wilson, John to Robinson, Anne*
Jun 18 1796    Wilson, John to Rogers, Hannah*
Dec  1 1795    Wilson, John to Tune, Darcus*
May 13 1793    Wilson, John to Wheeler, Sarah*
May 20 1782    Wilson, Joseph to Poole, Hannah
Dec  4 1790    Wilson, Joshua to Dorsey, Deborah*
Oct 28 1786    Wilson, Joshua to Grimes, Elizabeth
Oct  5 1795    Wilson, Judah to Trotten, George*
Dec 16 1793    Wilson, Mariah to Robertson, John*
Apr 18 1796    Wilson, Martha to Isabey, Francis*
Aug 11 1784    Wilson, Mary to Bivens, John
Nov 29 1794    Wilson, Mary to Cord, John*
Jul 20 1795    Wilson, Mary to Morrow, Kennedy*
Dec 15 1792    Wilson, Mary to Treakle, Christopher*
Sep 11 1793    Wilson, Mary to Wilson, James*
Oct 15 1795    Wilson, Nathaniel to Shipway, Elizabeth*
Sep 12 1789    Wilson, Nicholas to Frigle, Ruth*
Dec 18 1797    Wilson, Patty to White, John*
Dec 20 1798    Wilson, Precilla to McFadon, John*
Nov  3 1781    Wilson, Rachel to French, Daniel
Sep 24 1796    Wilson, Rebecca to Falls, Moore*
Nov 24 1781    Wilson, Samuel to Scoice, Hannah
Sep 30 1795    Wilson, Sarah to Apple, Christian*
May  4 1784    Wilson, Sarah to Long, Robert*
Jan 29 1796    Wilson, Sarah to Pearce, Philip*
Aug 29 1795    Wilson, Solomon to Judy, Frances*
Feb 12 1786    Wilson, Stephen to Nelson, Rebecca
Sep 23 1786    Wilson, Susannah to Tipton, Richard*
Nov 11 1785    Wilson, Thomas to Brown, Eleanor
Aug 11 1783    Wilson, Thomas to Dorum, Ann*
Apr 12 1797    Wilson, Unity to Hornsby, John*
Jul 28 1792    Wilson, Violet to Cook, Absolam*
Jan 16 1796    Wilson, William to Riddle, Eleanor*
Jul 24 1793    Wilson, Zeperah to Auld, Hugh*
```

Dec 15 1796	Wiltherholt, Euliana to Riner, Sebastian*
Aug 28 1797	Wilton, Jace to McDonald, Dennis*
Dec 21 1793	Wily, George to Smith, Jane*
Feb 24 1794	Wimsel, Charles to Chaney, Ann*
Sep 5 1798	Win, Jane to Frizele, William D.*
Dec 10 1793	Winchester, James to Owings, Sarah*
Jan 7 1790	Winchester, John to Whitaker, Elizabeth*
Dec 24 1790	Winchester, Lydia to Moore, George*
Oct 26 1789	Winchester, Richard to Lawrence, Rebecca*
Jan 4 1798	Windlake, Lawrence to Conley, Margaret*
Jun 13 1797	Wineland, Frank to Sies, Mary*
Aug 21 1798	Winfield, Tammy to Watts, Josias
Jan 2 1783	Wingard, Abraham to Jones, Hannah*
Dec 30 1795	Wingate, Ann to Allen, Reubin*
Oct 22 1795	Winkle, James to Jenkins, Elizabeth*
Apr 27 1795	Winnick, Elizabeth to Maidwell, Alexander*
Jun 25 1783	Winters, John to Jones, Mary
Dec 15 1797	Wise, Ann to Clingan, John*
Dec 17 1795	Wise, Catharine to Grosse, Louis*
May 31 1794	Wise, Levin to Scott, Ann*
Feb 8 1796	Wise, Michael to Young, Catharine*
May 29 1794	Wise, William to Morriss, Rachel*
Dec 9 1796	Wisebaugh, John to Berry, Mary*
Jan 10 1792	Wisebaugh, John to When, Rachel*
Jul 18 1795	Witcomb, _____ to Ingle, John*
Jul 3 1778	Witson, Thomas to Dunbo, Elizabeth*
Jan 7 1784	Wittle, Richard to Burland, Elizabeth
Sep 29 1792	Witzell, Allafar to Downs, Robert
Oct 16 1779	Woddoms, William to Ward, Albigail*
Dec 31 1788	Wolf, Catherine to Beach, John
Nov 11 1797	Wolf, Michael to Reiley, Mary*
Apr 17 1784	Wolfe, Catherine to Fletcher, Philip
Mar 1 1784	Wolfe, Tobias to Ulerick, Rosannah*
Jan 16 1795	Wollen, Anne Margarette to Brower, George Henry*
Dec 11 1798	Wolper, George to Weary, Mary*
Oct 14 1794	Wolslager, Elizabeth to Fisher, Daniel*
Jul 10 1788	Wonder, Elizabeth to Geoghegan, George
Jun 22 1779	Wood, Abraham to Agnew, Jane
Oct 18 1798	Wood, Achsah to Pontenay, James*
May 12 1798	Wood, Ann to Scott, John*
Dec 20 1783	Wood, Ann to Whittle, David*
Jan 23 1793	Wood, Charles to Eagleston, Eleanor*
Nov 12 1796	Wood, Elizabeth to Harman, Martin*
Mar 30 1785	Wood, John to Shyor, Ann
May 2 1785	Wood, Margaret to Englebright, John
Jan 30 1797	Wood, Mary to Wood, Thomas*
May 5 1785	Wood, Nancy to Ford, Thomas*
May 16 1783	Wood, Robert to Dunn, Jane*
Jan 7 1797	Wood, Robert to Leatherwood, Ruth*
Jul 23 1793	Wood, Ruth to Appleby, Charles*
Oct 14 1797	Wood, Sarah to Ford, James*
Feb 6 1796	Wood, Sarah to Smith, Nathaniel*
Jan 20 1796	Wood, Sophia to Shaw, William*
Dec 22 1787	Wood, Thomas to Crook, Margaret*
Jan 30 1797	Wood, Thomas to Wood, Mary*
Oct 25 1785	Wood, William to McCubbin, Martha Ridgely

```
Oct 30 1794   Wood, Womal to Stinchcomb, Hannah*
Jul 28 1792   Woodard, John to Johnson, Rachel*
May  2 1793   Woodard, Mary to Walker, Charles
Mar 18 1778   Woodard, Sarah to Weatherby, Daniel*
Jan 18 1797   Wooden, Benjamin to Kitting, Mary*
Dec 31 1794   Wooden, Charles to Owings, Nancy*
Mar  5 1796   Wooden, Eleanor to Moak, John*
Dec 10 1796   Wooden, John to Caples, Hannah*
Jun 31 1790   Wooden, John to Hooper, Rachel*
Dec 24 1785   Wooden, John to Milligan, Margaret
Oct 21 1795   Wooden, John to Wickley, Ruth*
Oct  2 1797   Wooden, Margaret to Herrick, Thomas*
Feb 24 1795   Wooden, Margaret to Stewart, Hugh*
Sep 12 1794   Wooden, Margaret to Wager, Thomas*
May 13 1796   Wooden, Nancy to Alter, Christian*
May 12 1783   Wooden, Rachel to Gill, William*
Jul 18 1795   Wooden, Rachel to Hensey, Michael*
Apr 13 1796   Wooden, Rebecca to Hagsman, Samuel*
Jun  7 1794   Wooden, Richard to Bond, Leah*
Jan 23 1782   Wooden, Ruth to Johnston, Absolom*
Sep 28 1791   Wooden, Thomas to Hooper, Sarah*
Nov  9 1796   Wooden, Thomas to Whips, Elizabeth
Jul 28 1786   Wooderd, John to Davis, Elizabeth
Dec 25 1777   Woodhouse, George to Keith, Ann*
Dec 18 1793   Woodhouse, Mary to Wells, Thomas*
Sep 17 1782   Woodin, Keziah to White, Robert
Jul 31 1792   Woodland, Amelia to Saunders, Levin*
Nov 26 1790   Woodland, Cassandra Webster to Breuitt, Joseph*
Jan  9 1784   Woodlin, Betsey to Hurst, William*
Jul 29 1790   Woodrough, John Williams to Leese, Elizabeth*
Mar  8 1791   Woodrow, Andrew to Stevenson, Mary*
Dec  1 1789   Woods, Elizabeth to Peach, William*
Jul 27 1796   Woods, Mary to Arnold, Joshua*
Aug 15 1778   Woods, Mary to Burk, Michael*
Dec  1 1789   Woods, Sarah to Chaplin, William*
Aug 10 1782   Woods, Susannah to Mear, Michael*
Nov 14 1798   Woods, William to Hammond, Ann
Nov 18 1795   Woodward, Elizabeth to Ober, John*
May 16 1798   Woodward, Elizabetts Jemima to Coffee, John*
Aug  4 1778   Woodward, James to Bolton, Tamer*
May  9 1783   Woodward, Jemima to Perego, Joseph*
Dec 24 1798   Woodworth, Isaac to Baum, Susanna*
Sep 28 1796   Woolen, James to Rix, Elizabeth*
May 23 1778   Woolen, Margaret to Bates, Rowland*
Aug 19 1783   Woolen, Pamelia to Flosence, Nicholas*
Jun 19 1793   Wooler, Philip to Bedner, Mary*
Feb 23 1791   Woolerick, Mary to Dougherty, John*
Jan 26 1792   Woolery, Elizabeth to Tevis, Daniel*
Aug 23 1778   Woolf, Lovep to Crouder, Ealy*
Dec  5 1789   Woolf, Margaret to Hurley, Dennis*
Apr  1 1796   Woolhouse, Mary to Shepburn, Thomas*
May  7 1795   Woolrick, Elizabeth to Parlett, William*
Mar  8 1794   Wools, Alicey to Wall, George*
Apr 27 1791   Wootton, Maria Sprigg to Heirmance, Jacob I.
Feb 11 1795   Workman, Ann to Summers, John*
Jun  3 1783   Workman, Hugh to White, Elizabeth
```

Aug 10 1784	Workman, Robert to Dunsheaf, Jane
Mar 29 1785	Workmkan, Mary to Pithington, Thomas
Mar 15 1793	Worman, George to Towson, Susannah*
Apr 5 1794	Worrel, Jesse to Merrick, Agness*
May 26 1790	Worrell, Caleb to Gorsuch, Rachel
Jan 6 1795	Worrell, Rachel to Griffith, Benjamin*
May 10 1788	Worrell, Thomas to Conden, Mary*
Nov 8 1785	Worrington, William to Harryman, Nancy
Oct 16 1784	Wort, Mary to Sumwald, George
May 30 1778	Worthington, Cornford to Dorsey, John W.*
Aug 17 1784	Worthington, Elizabeth to Tolley, Edward Carvel*
Aug 8 1786	Worthington, Elizabeth to Willion, Benjamin
Jun 25 1778	Worthington, Henry to Yeister, Mary*
Jan 16 1792	Worthington, James to Griffith, Elizabeth*
Sep 14 1782	Worthington, John to Dorsey, Ann*
Feb 9 1789	Worthington, John Tolley to Worthington, Mary
Nov 25 1784	Worthington, Margaret to Lamar, William*
Feb 9 1793	Worthington, Martha to Ridgely, Edward
Feb 9 1789	Worthington, Mary to Worthington, John Tolley
Jul 25 1778	Worthington, Samuel to Garrison, Martha
Apr 4 1795	Worthington, Sarah to Wilson, Henry*
Apr 5 1786	Worthington, Thomas to Owings, Massella*
Sep 12 1786	Worthington, Walter to Hood, Sarah
Jun 2 1781	Worthington, William to Demsey, Elizabeth*
Mar 31 1795	Wright, Ann to Johnston, Daniel*
Mar 11 1778	Wright, Daniel to Deaver, Susannah*
Apr 13 1796	Wright, Elizabeth to Henry, John*
Oct 11 1781	Wright, Elizabeth to Sharp, Benjamin
Mar 1 1794	Wright, George to Wright, Sophia*
Jan 22 1781	Wright, Hannah to Bond, Thomas*
Oct 31 1795	Wright, James to Pecker, Mary*
Nov 15 1785	Wright, Jane to Carback, William
Jul 16 1792	Wright, John to Brooks, Sarah*
Oct 13 1797	Wright, John to Hatch, Nancy*
Aug 17 1791	Wright, John to Otherson, Rebecca*
Jun 19 1794	Wright, Joshua to Holems, Eleanor*
Jul 12 1794	Wright, Margaret to Rondlet, Francis*
Dec 10 1791	Wright, Mary to Dunkin, Thomas*
Feb 15 1794	Wright, Rachel to Demmitt, Thomas*
Feb 15 1794	Wright, Samuel to Dickinson, Sarah*
Jul 1 1788	Wright, Sarah to Downey, Philip*
Jun 24 1796	Wright, Sarah to Pasely, David*
Mar 6 1798	Wright, Sophia to Sivan, James*
Mar 1 1794	Wright, Sophia to Wright, George*
Jun 25 1783	Wright, Thomas to Logan, Sarah*
Oct 8 1792	Wyant, Elizabeth to Capito, Christian*
Feb 6 1794	Wyeman, Jacob to Bankerd, Easter*
Aug 21 1781	Wyle, Comfort to Pearce, Joseph
Jan 29 1782	Wyley, Elizabeth to Collett, Jacob*
Feb 7 1781	Wyley, John to Hooker, Debora*
Nov 6 1779	Wyley, Joshua to Ford, Elinor*
Dec 15 1781	Wyley, Martha to Sharp, George
Jul 17 1784	Wyley, Mary to Israel, Casper
Aug 25 1781	Wyley, Mary to Wyley, Zachariah*
Jan 14 1783	Wyley, Walter to Cole, Sarah*
Jul 23 1779	Wyley, William to Rister, Sarah

Aug 25 1781	Wyley, Zachariah to Wyley, Mary*
Oct 27 1794	Yale, Ann to Simpson, James*
Nov 2 1795	Yarida, John Peter to Roser, Margaret Amy*
Dec 19 1795	Yarly, Ralph to Burton, Ruth*
Jun 5 1794	Yates, Elizabeth to Smith, Daniel*
Aug 25 1786	Yates, Lucy to FitzPatrick, James
Jan 12 1792	Yates, Sarah to Bond, Thomas*
Aug 27 1778	Yates, Thomas to Myers, Mary*
Apr 7 1796	Yaun, Elizabeth to Parrish, John*
Oct 9 1795	Yearly, Nathaniel to Robinson, Elizabeth*
Mar 11 1797	Yeatman, Henry Lewis to Evans, Molly*
Jun 4 1778	Yedlie, Moses to Tear, Ann*
Apr 27 1797	Yeiser, Eliza to Williams, Joseph*
Sep 10 1795	Yeiser, Mary Feree to Wessels, Joseph Charles*
Jun 25 1778	Yeister, Mary to Worthington, Henry*
Feb 22 1781	Yellott, Jeremiah to Hollingsworth, Mary
Apr 2 1795	Yengland, Sarah to Lindsay, John*
Jun 20 1797	Yepson, Hannah to Hanson, Peter*
Feb 2 1798	Yerrington, Richard to Duvall, Airy*
Jun 22 1796	Yoner, Samuel to Stover, Mary*
Oct 28 1797	Yoolt, Julia to Martin, James*
Jan 25 1788	York, Blanch to Scott, Walter*
Nov 30 1785	York, Sarah to Raborg, Andrew
Jul 31 1783	York, William to Dawbridge, Jane
Feb 27 1792	Young, Agnus to Young, John*
May 6 1794	Young, Arabella to Goulding, Patrick*
Nov 19 1791	Young, Aryminta to Miller, Ludwick
Jul 3 1788	Young, Benjamin to Hodgson, Mary*
Feb 8 1796	Young, Catharine to Wise, Michael*
Oct 11 1794	Young, Clara to Fleury, Mr.*
Mar 13 1790	Young, Delila to Bradhunt, Benjamin*
Apr 7 1798	Young, Dinton to McKinzie, Mary*
Nov 23 1797	Young, Eliza to Turviance, James*
Oct 8 1796	Young, Elizabeth to Bishop, Richard*
Mar 6 1779	Young, Elizabeth to Sewell, John
Jun 7 1790	Young, Gideon to Adams, Elizabeth
Mar 25 1797	Young, Henry to Berry, Sarah*
Dec 6 1780	Young, Jacob to Mason, Leah*
Jun 5 1798	Young, James to Johnson, Martha
Jan 30 1796	Young, Jesse to McDonogh, Jane*
Dec 13 1798	Young, John to All, Martha*
Jun 19 1778	Young, John to Kelly, Mary*
Sep 16 1795	Young, John to Oyston, Tabatha*
Feb 27 1792	Young, John to Young, Agnus*
Feb 15 1783	Young, Johua to McKenzie, Orpha*
Sep 11 1794	Young, Joseph to Ridgely, Elizabeth*
Aug 2 1795	Young, Margaret to Davis, Thomas*
Dec 10 1791	Young, Margaret to Dean, Robert*
Oct 2 1795	Young, Mariah to Pickersgill, John*
Aug 3 1782	Young, Martena to Jones, Samuel*
Mar 1 1791	Young, Mary to Blottenberger, George*
Mar 17 1788	Young, Mary to Davidson, Alexander
Feb 16 1789	Young, Mary to Lewis, John*
Nov 14 1795	Young, Mary to Linaham, William*
Oct 7 1794	Young, Mary to McHenry, Dennis*
Jul 21 1782	Young, Mary to Myers, Joshua*

Feb 6 1798	Young, Michael to Bell, Sarah*
Jan 18 1783	Young, Nathan to Todd, Elizabeth
Jun 7 1796	Young, Nathaniel to Spurrier, Priscilla*
May 11 1779	Young, Pleasant to Wheeler, Isaac
Nov 10 1795	Young, Polly to Vanbibber, Abraham
Jun 1 1797	Young, Rachel to Cole, John*
Aug 5 1786	Young, Rachel to Jones, John
Jul 16 1785	Young, Rebecca to Towson, William
Mar 13 1790	Young, Richard to Hammond, Rebecca*
Nov 24 1787	Young, Susan to Buchanan, James
Apr 16 1785	Young, William Price to Cox, Dinah*
Jan 17 1797	Young, William to Minsky, Catharine*
Apr 17 1790	Young, William to Moxley, Aseneth*
Jan 9 1796	Young, William to Ridgely, Mary*
Nov 14 1797	Younger, Elizabeth to Philips, Vachel*
Oct 28 1795	Younger, Nancy to Philips, William*
Sep 5 1795	Younger, Nehemiah to Lytle, Rachel*
Nov 27 1795	Zeckley, William to Crawley, Eleanor*
Oct 4 1794	Zegland, Catherine to Crouse, Christian*
Mar 28 1797	Zeinsor, Dorothy to Hartzot, George*
Feb 13 1798	Zep, Conrad to Tucker, Mary*
Dec 8 1792	Zimerman, Catherine to Owings, Benjamin*
Jul 1 1783	Zimerman, Mary to Lee, George*
Aug 19 1795	Zimmer, Elizabeth to Sklipp, William*
Dec 13 1778	Zimmerman, Elizabeth to Montgomery, Alexander*
Feb 24 1783	Zimmerman, Elizabeth to Peddicord, Adam*
Nov 28 1797	Zimmerman, George to Stinchcomb, Elizabeth*
Oct 28 1794	Zimmerman, George to Stinchcomb, Rebecca*
Nov 2 1797	Zimmerman, Hannah to Hissey, Charles*
Jun 15 1798	Zimmerman, John to Hissey, Mary*
Oct 16 1793	Zimmerman, Magdaline to Stinchcomb, Christopher*
Mar 14 1798	Zimmerman, Sarah to Emmitt, William*
Jan 22 1784	Zollickhoffer, John Conrod to Triplet, Caroline*
Jan 4 1786	Zoph, John to Carty, Sarah
May 3 1791	Zuile, Clarinda to Slomaker, James*
Apr 29 1786	Zuill, William to Kingslane, Clarinda

www.ingramcontent.com/pod-product-compliance
Lightning Source LLC
Chambersburg PA
CBHW070740160426
43192CB00009B/1512